D1058751

GIL HODGES

GIL HODGES

A HALL OF FAME LIFE

MORT ZACHTER

University of Nebraska Press
Lincoln and London

© 2015 by Mort Zachter

Manufactured in the United States
of America ♾

Library of Congress Control
Number: 2014953036

Set in Lyon Text by Lindsey Auten.
Designed by Rachel Gould.

For another team player,
my wife, Nurit

What you leave behind is not what is engraved in stone monuments, but what is woven into the lives of others.

PERICLES

Gil Hodges was not only a good player and manager; he was a special human being.

SANDY KOUFAX

CONTENTS

ILLUSTRATIONS

PREFACE

> There is a fundamental difficulty in writing about Gil
> Hodges. Voices in the background keep screaming
> for restraint and yet every instinct is to succumb
> to temptation and spill forth the superlatives.
> **ARTHUR DALEY**

I was born in Brooklyn four months, twelve days, and six hours after the Brooklyn Dodgers played their last game at Ebbets Field. I never saw Jackie Robinson steal home or Roy Campanella double down the left-field line or Pee Wee Reese gracefully field a ground ball. But I wish I had.

Gil Hodges, the only Dodgers star player that still called Brooklyn home after the team moved to Los Angeles, lived a few blocks away from where I grew up. Every morning as I walked to my elementary school, PS 197, I crossed Bedford Avenue and looked north in the direction of Hodges's home, proud that he had stayed.

By then Hodges had retired as a player and was managing the New York Mets. In large part due to his leadership, the Mets' annual attendance from 1969 to 1972 exceeded that of the New York Yankees by more than one million each season. That had never happened before, not for one season, let alone for four consecutive seasons, and it hasn't happened since. Yet, however unlikely it may seem today, for a few brief shining seasons nearly half a century ago, the Mets dominated baseball headlines in New York. Paradoxically, during this period of unprecedented popularity, the Mets' manager was—by his own admission—"not colorful, not what you'd call good copy."

In Brooklyn it didn't matter. We knew what we had. Although I never met him, Hodges was a visible figure in the neighborhood. He could be seen walking his dog, a German shepherd named Lady Gina, down Bedford Avenue or stopping by Gil Hodges Field on McDonald Avenue to watch the kids play, or buying Marlboros at Benny's Candy Store on Avenue M.

But Hodges died of a heart attack in 1972 at forty-seven, and with each passing year his name fades from the national consciousness.

For some, memories remain. Well after Hodges's playing career ended, Willie Mays could still recall Hodges's ability to turn the mundane act of tagging a runner on a pickoff attempt into art. "It looked," Mays said, "as if the pitcher's throw hit Hodges' glove and the glove swatted the runner at the same time. The whole thing . . . done in one smooth motion."

Others remain fiercely loyal. Bill "Moose" Skowron, who played for Hodges when he managed the Washington Senators, asked me, "Can you tell me why Gil isn't in Cooperstown?" A good question, since Hodges hit more home runs in his playing career than anyone else that also managed a World Series–winning team. Red Smith, a revered member of the writers' wing of the Baseball Hall of Fame, wrote, "He was a first baseman of rare polish. A hitter with power to swat 42 home runs in a season and a team player who drove in more than 100 runs a year for seven consecutive seasons. If votes are based, as the rule says, on the player's integrity, sportsmanship, and character, Gil Hodges will ride in. Those words were coined for him."

Unfortunately, integrity, sportsmanship, and character are unquantifiable. They are also a challenge for any writer hoping to cut through the legend that surrounds Hodges hoping to find the humanity that lies beneath. Don Demeter, one of Hodges's teammates who later became pastor of Grace Community Baptist Church in Oklahoma City, made this abundantly clear to me. "I don't know anything bad about Gil Hodges," Demeter said, "and you don't either."

Readers will ultimately decide if I've succeeded in finding the man behind the myth. But what I can tell you for certain is this: if you walked into Benny's Candy Store shortly after Hodges had left, you could hear the owner, Ben Chodesh, in a voice so filled with excitement you would have thought the Dodgers had just moved back to Brooklyn, saying over and over again, "Hodges was just here, Hodges was just here, Hodges was just here . . ."

GIL HODGES

1. Shea Stadium, Flushing, New York, October 16, 1969, bottom of the sixth inning of the fifth game of the 1969 World Series: Mets manager Gil Hodges showing umpire Lou DiMuro a shoe-polish-stained baseball as Donn Clendenon looks on. Courtesy of *Sporting News* © 1969. All rights reserved. Reprinted with permission.

PROLOGUE

HIS REPUTATION PRECEDED HIM

No man lives his image.

Gil Hodges stepped out of the Mets' dugout holding a shoe-polish-stained baseball in his right hand.

It was a chilly October afternoon in New York and the Mets manager wore a dark-blue baseball jacket over his uniform. Although the familiar No. 14 that had been stitched onto his jersey ever since his playing days in Ebbets Field wasn't visible to the standing-room-only crowd at Shea Stadium watching the fifth game of the 1969 World Series, it made no difference. If, like Neil Armstrong, who that past July took "one small step for man, one giant leap for mankind," Hodges had been wearing a NASA space suit complete with helmet and darkened visor, the fans would've still recognized him.

He had been, wrote Roger Angell, "perhaps the most popular ballplayer in the major leagues," and although Ebbets Field had crumbled beneath an iron wrecking ball almost a decade before, whenever Hodges stepped onto a baseball field he fortified fading memories of warm summer days when Brooklyn was the best the National League had to offer and no one had yet heard of the New York Metropolitans.

Hodges headed toward home plate slowly in that funny, pigeon-toed walk he had—ramrod-straight like John Wayne in *The Searchers*—but with surprisingly small strides for a man who stood almost six feet two inches tall. His toes touched the ground first, then his instep, and finally the heel of his spikes. A little over a year after surviving his first heart attack, Hodges looked much older than forty-five. Yet, there was still a grace and athleticism in his bearing that exuded a sense of confidence and power.

The Mets were playing in what would turn out to be the final game of the Series. But despite the tension of managing in baseball's ultimate pressure cooker, Hodges appeared no different than usual. "When everyone else got excited . . . Gil remained calm," recalled his best player, Tom Seaver. "The tenser the situation, the more he concentrated. He never wavered, never came within a mile of panic, always observing, always maneuvering, always thinking."

"He had cold water running in his veins," said Mets catcher J. C. Martin.

That morning, Hodges had driven to Shea with his older brother, Bob. Throughout the car ride, Gil never mentioned the game—not once. To Bob, his kid brother seemed so at ease on the ride up the Grand Central it felt as if they were heading out to play eighteen holes of golf. Decades later, their sister, Marjorie, told me it must have been a very long car ride for the outgoing and personable Bob, who would have loved discussing that afternoon's game.

Gil's silence didn't surprise her a bit. The defining experience of his formative years, surviving the savagery of Okinawa during World War II, had only deepened an inborn solemnity. The defining experience of his final years, that afternoon stroll to home plate was the high point of his professional baseball career. Yet, to him, it wasn't life and death, just a ball game. To a deeply religious man like Gil Hodges, there were more important things.

He wore a wedding band on the ring finger of his left hand. And the cross hanging from a thin chain around his neck not only was tiny but—unlike later generations of athletes—was tucked beneath his uniform. On the ring finger of his right hand was a 1955 World Series ring—the only championship the Brooklyn Dodgers ever won. The two rings, and the cross, symbolized the three things that meant the most to Hodges: family, God, and work—in that order. And if ever there was a man who could keep his priorities straight, it was Gil Hodges.

On this particular day, he slowed his pace to give himself time to think about the situation. That was what he did best. From the time he started to play baseball as a boy on Jim Higgins's farm in Petersburg, Indiana, Hodges had shown a knack for determining exactly what had to be done to win. So by the time he reached home plate, his piercing blue eyes locked and loaded, Hodges had the big picture sized up just right.

He considered the Mets' opponent: the Baltimore Orioles, heavy favorites to win the World Series. The Orioles had won 109 games that season—the most in the Majors. Baltimore had won the 1966 Series (and would win another in 1970) with the same core group of players that took the field that afternoon. They had two first-ballot Hall of Fame players in their everyday lineup: outfielder Frank Robinson, who finished his career with 586 home runs, in an era when hitting 500 or more home runs didn't require a visit before Congress to explain that you hadn't used steroids; and clutch-hitting Brooks Robinson, who set the gold standard for fielding for all subsequent generations of third basemen. In addition to the Robinsons, the slugging first baseman Boog Powell, the feisty second baseman Davey Johnson, and the ever-so-smooth center fielder Paul Blair had all been named to the 1969 All-Star team.

Compared to Earl Weaver, the Baltimore manager, Hodges had slim pickings. The Mets' lineup consisted largely of journeymen Hodges had platooned depending on whether they were facing a right- or a left-handed pitcher. That not only maximized his team's limited hitting skills but also kept them fresh for the stretch-run in September.

The Mets' rival for the National League East title that season, the Chicago Cubs, was led by Hodges's first Major League manager, Leo Durocher, a man with the unique ability to irritate his team to a pennant. But he didn't that season. Durocher overworked his starting pitchers and stuck with his everyday players for far too long. Hodges's team blew past the more talented—but tired—Cubs and won the Eastern Division, going on to defeat the Western Division champions, the Atlanta Braves, to win the National League pennant.

The Mets possessed three essential ingredients needed for winning a short series: pitching, defense, and Hodges. As a result, although a 100-to-1 shot to win the World Series when the season started, the "Miracle Mets," as they were then referred to (despite the fact that the Mets players hated it when they were), had won three straight games behind the outstanding pitching of Jerry Koosman, Gary Gentry, Nolan Ryan, and Tom Seaver. Two spectacular catches by center fielder Tommie Agee, and one for the ages by right fielder Ron Swoboda, proved pivotal. Despite losing the opening game of the Series, the Mets never lost confidence.

"The leadership of Hodges created this," wrote Leonard Koppett.

As a result, when Hodges strolled out to the mound with his team holding a three to one lead in the Series, the Mets were only one victory away from becoming champions. For New Yorkers who had come to believe the words *Mets* and *comical* were synonymous, this was nothing short of a revelation. Beginning in their inaugural season (1962), the Mets had set records for ineptitude, finishing last in the National League five times. But in 1968, when Hodges took command, he instilled a seriousness not seen on that side of the East River since the Dodgers left for Los Angeles; and by the summer of 1969, the fans, not just in New York but nationwide, believed that if a man could walk on the moon, the Mets could win the Series.

But the game was in the sixth inning with Baltimore leading, 3–0, and the Mets needed reviving. If they lost, the balance of the Series would be played back in Baltimore. Hodges knew that momentum in the postseason is simply who won the last game; and if the Orioles won, odds were they'd continue winning back in Baltimore. And the Orioles were dominating the game behind some marvelous pitching by their twenty-game winner, Dave McNally. The lefty's curve was breaking sharply and the Mets were struggling to just get a man on base.

Providence provided one. Mets left fielder Cleon Jones was at bat when he was hit in the foot by a curveball in the dirt. But home plate umpire Lou DiMuro didn't think the ball had struck Jones. With their team desperate for base runners, most hitters would have instinctively dropped their bat and head toward first base. Yet, despite a Series batting average less than his weight—and the on-deck hitter, Donn Clendenon, having already hit two homers in the Series—Jones wanted to hit. So it was left to Clendenon to argue with DiMuro, to no avail.

After striking Cleon Jones's shoe, the ball improbably traveled over fifty feet, bouncing into the Mets' dugout. What occurred there, after the ball bounced in but before Hodges stepped out with a shoe-polish-streaked ball in his hand, remains one of New York City's great twentieth-century mysteries. Ron Swoboda didn't see what happened, but decades later he could still recall watching Hodges play cribbage and how only a few seconds would pass from the time Hodges was dealt his cards until he determined which to keep, and which to throw back. Such skills were easily transferable to any and all fast-moving developments in the dugout.

"Whatever happened," Swoboda said, "happened very quickly."

Earl Weaver remembers otherwise. The Baltimore manager told me, "They had time to do anything they wanted with the ball."

Three things are certain. First, immediately after the game, no less an authority than legendary Yankee manager Casey Stengel made it known that ever since the 1957 World Series between the Milwaukee Braves and the Yankees, when a Milwaukee player named Nippy Jones was awarded first after convincing the umpire that the polish on the ball had come from his shoe (which in turn led to a championship for the Braves), Stengel always kept a few shoe-polish-streaked balls close at hand in the dugout for just such occasions.

In addition, before the fifth game of the 1969 World Series, as he did before every game, Nick Torman, the Met clubhouse man, applied shoe polish to all the Mets' game shoes. For this, and for all his hard work during the season, the players would take the unusual step of awarding him a full share of their World Series winnings.

But Hodges's reputation for integrity would prove to be the most crucial certainty that day. Hodges treated umpires with respect. As a player, he held the distinction of never having been thrown out of a game. As a manager, Hodges would argue a call only if he was sure he was right. The umpires, in turn, respected Hodges. Tom Gorman, a National League umpire for a quarter of a century wrote, "Gil Hodges [was] as good a man as you'll find in a long day's march."

Contemporaneous newspaper accounts reported that the ball rolled into the hands of Mets catcher Jerry Grote, who flipped the ball to Hodges as he was stepping out of the dugout. When Hodges reached home plate, he handed the ball to DiMuro and said, "Lou, the ball hit him."

Hodges didn't yell or scream. He didn't have to. It was all measured and calculated—even the modulation in his deep voice. But despite Hodges's quiet demeanor, there was "a certain menace" in his physical prowess that made you wonder "what he would do if he got going," said *New York Times* reporter George Vescey.

Decades later, Vescey, who was at the game, told me, "Hodges had DiMuro hypnotized."

DiMuro looked at the ball. Then he looked at Hodges. Then he reversed his call.

Weaver immediately bounded out of the Orioles' dugout to ask DiMuro if he had kept his eye on the ball the entire time it was in the Mets' dugout. The question implied that shady shoe-polish doings must have occurred there. But Weaver didn't get too excited. The day before, he had become the first manager in thirty-four years to be tossed out of a World Series game, and he didn't want that happening again. Weaver couldn't bring himself to strenuously argue against a call he knew was correct. After the game, Weaver acknowledged that everyone at Shea—except DiMuro—saw the ball hit Jones. But Hodges had done much more than just supply the Mets with a base runner. Five years before, a little-known act of kindness on his part had helped bring the next batter to the Mets.

Donn Alvin Clendenon, a right-handed power-hitting first baseman with a lot of attitude and a big hitch in his swing, stepped up to the plate as Jones took a short lead at first base. At thirty-four, Clendenon was nearing the end of his playing career. In the fall of 1968, after spending his entire career in the Pirates organization, Clendenon had suffered the ignominy of being left unprotected in the expansion draft, and the newly created Montreal Expos had selected him. For a talented black man who had to wait until the age of twenty-seven to become an everyday Major League player due to the unwritten racial quotas of the 1950s, it was a difficult time. To add insult to injury, the Expos then traded him to the Houston Astros. Clendenon wanted no part of Houston, because his former manager from the Pirates, Harry Walker, led them. Rather than play for Walker, whom Clendenon considered "a product of his white southern Alabama environment" and "a big-time racist," Clendenon retired from baseball.

He took a job with Scripto, an Atlanta pen and lighter manufacturer, at a higher annual salary than he ever made as a Major Leaguer in those indentured-servitude-like days before free agency. But extensive pressure was brought upon Clendenon to change his mind; and after being assured his job at Scripto would still be there for him (and supposedly unaware of how a holdout on his part threatened baseball's infamous reserve clause), Clendenon signed a lucrative three-year contract with Montreal.

But Clendenon had little utility to Montreal. The question then became, which team wanted to trade for Clendenon and his new, expensive, long-term contract? And it had to be a team, and more specifically a manager, for whom Clendenon wanted to play. Near midnight on June 15, 1969 (then the Major League trading deadline), that question was answered.

That answer had been percolating since the spring of 1964 when Clendenon, wanting to improve his fielding to keep his job as the Pirates' first baseman, recalled that Jackie Robinson had told him Gil Hodges was both a giving person and an excellent first baseman. So Clendenon—never one to be shy about anything—asked Hodges for help.

In 1964 Hodges had enough to do just managing the lowly Washington Senators and had no obligation to give of his time to instruct a player from another team. But Hodges did. Clendenon couldn't have picked a better tutor than the three-time Gold Glove–winning first baseman, who also happened to be (like Clendenon) right-handed. That spring, whenever the Senators came to Fort Meyers for Grapefruit League games against the Pirates, or when Clendenon was in Pompano Beach (where the Senators trained), the two men met. Clendenon wrote, "Gil would work with me . . . particularly on my fielding and throwing to second . . . for double plays. . . . I became better with his help."

So when Mets general manager John Murphy called Clendenon late in the evening on June 15, he had not forgotten Hodges's kindness. For Clendenon, Hodges was daylight to Harry Walker's perpetual night. Well aware of the Houston debacle, Murphy asked Clendenon if he wanted to play for Hodges, a man who had a reputation for being fair—but very firm—in his ways.

"You're damn right," Clendenon replied.

Before a nation totally unaware of what had transpired to ensure his joining the Mets, Clendenon hit a McNally slider for a home run off the left-field auxiliary scoreboard, cutting the Baltimore lead to 3–2. That was the turning point. The next inning, Al Weis, who had never hit a home run at Shea Stadium in his two seasons with the Mets, hit one to tie the game. As the "all-field, no-hit" second baseman rounded the bases, Clendenon watched the body language of the Baltimore players. Their spirit was broken, but the game was still far from over.

In the eighth inning, doubles by Jones and Swoboda gave the Mets the lead. The Orioles came to bat in the ninth, trailing 5–3. If the Mets' starting pitcher, Jerry Koosman, could shut the Orioles down for one more inning, the Mets would be champions. But that would not be easy. The heart of the Orioles' batting order was due up: Frank Robinson, Boog Powell, and Brooks Robinson.

Koosman walked Robinson. Powell hit into a force play. Brooks Robinson flied out. At 3:17 p.m., with two outs and a man on base, Davey Johnson hit a long fly ball to left field. When Johnson connected, the fans' roar was so loud that Koosman couldn't hear the crack of the bat on the ball—his usual way of determining how well it was hit. Fearing he had given up a game-tying home run, Koosman turned to watch the ball fall back to earth in front of the 371-foot marker and into the glove of Jones, who took a knee to give thanks that the Mets were champions.

After the game, Hodges serenely answered reporters' questions in his office. In the adjoining Mets locker-room, emotions ran wild amid the Moët & Chandon. Swoboda exulted, "It's the first one . . . nothing can ever be [this] sweet again." Cleon Jones, in deference to the Milwaukee Braves' Nippy Jones, said, "Us Jones boys have got to stick together." With his typical dry wit, Hodges would later write to Father Vieck, his priest back home in Petersburg, Indiana, "I think the boys spilled most of the champagne."

A reporter asked Hodges which one of his players deserved to be the Series' Most Valuable Player. Hodges replied that every one of his twenty-five players and all four of his coaches were MVPs, so that would make it twenty-nine, he said.

"And the manager?"

Despite having gotten the better of Durocher and Weaver, both future Hall of Fame managers, Hodges deflected the praise.

"No, no," he said, "not the manager."

The next season, in a game between the Orioles and the Chicago White Sox, Lou DiMuro was umpiring at home plate when Earl Weaver went out to argue a call. As he had in the World Series, Weaver again lost an argument with DiMuro. But before Weaver returned to the dugout, he took a ball out of his back pocket, rubbed it on his shoe, and left it near home plate. DiMuro didn't need to ask who left it. He picked the ball up and threw it at Weaver.

It took four decades for others to appreciate Weaver's feelings. In 2009, during a question-and-answer session held at Citi Field as part of the fortieth anniversary celebration of the Mets' 1969 championship, Jerry Koosman was asked if anyone other than Hodges touched the ball after it bounced into the Mets dugout that October afternoon.

"The ball came to me," Koosman said, "and Gil told me to brush it against my shoe. I did. He came over, took the ball from me, and showed it to DiMuro."

When I had previously discussed the issue with Koosman, he was coy in his response.

"You know how magicians never tell people their tricks. Let's just say, Gil Hodges was quite a magician."

HOME

Princeton and Petersburg (1924–43)

1

COAL MINER'S SON

My dad was not a great man in the sense you would consider a man great. He was just a simple coal miner. He wasn't rich and he wasn't book smart. But he knew everything about two things—baseball and coal mines.

Since 1860, when high concentrations of coal deposits were discovered amid the fertile farm land of rural southwestern Indiana, generation after generation of men have spent their lives eking out a dangerous existence hundreds of feet below the earth's surface in what the locals call "the shafts." One of those men was Charles P. Hodges.

Charlie, as his friends called him, was born in Princeton, Indiana, on January 3, 1901. The largest town in Gibson County, Princeton's focal point was the ornate courthouse and clock tower in its town square. When Charlie was still a teenager, both his parents died, leaving him to earn his keep a few miles outside of town in the Francisco Mine.

Hard-working Charlie married Irene Horstmeyer, a young woman of German-Irish descent from nearby Winslow, Indiana. Their first home was in Princeton, where Gil Hodges was born on April 4, 1924. Irene and Charlie's first child, Bob, had been born fourteen months earlier. A daughter, Marjorie, was born five years after Gil. A fourth child, Kenneth, died of whooping cough as an infant, leaving Bud—as Irene would always call Gil—the middle child.

The year Gil was born, Francisco No. 2 began operating. It was just as dangerous as its predecessor. A combination of exposed gases and coal dust ignited by a miner's open carbide lantern could send an explosive force throughout the mine. Everyone entering the mine wore a brass tag with an identification number, a copy of which was kept in the mine office—just in case.

At 6:30 a.m. on December 9, 1926, as the day and evening shifts were changing—and seventy-one tags hung in the mine office—a gas leak in the mine ignited. The explosion was so powerful it sent men and mules hurtling through the air. Charlie was changing into his work clothes for his day shift when the explosion occurred. But for a matter of only a few minutes, his tag was not in the office.

The blast shot flames up the elevator shaft while men were suspended there. With the mine's only lift destroyed, rescue workers had to carry the injured out on their backs using a narrow airshaft staircase. The injured were in so much pain a nurse had to be sent down to inject them with morphine first so they could be carried out. A triage station in the barn-like shower room slowly filled with injured miners. All wore a black mask of coal dust that had literally been burned onto their faces. The stench of burnt flesh was unforgettable. Thirty-seven miners died.

Charlie saw it all. He vowed that neither of his sons would ever work down in the shafts. And despite his struggles to keep his family fed during the Great Depression (a time when lard sandwiches were standard lunchbox fare in southern Indiana), they never did. But in doing so Charlie sacrificed himself for the sake of his family. First, he lost his right eye to a flying chip of steel. That was only the down payment for knowing "everything" about coal mining. Three of Charlie's toes were cut off when a motor grazed his foot; his back broke when a load of slate fell on him; and after decades of breathing in coal dust, he developed emphysema. When he walked in town his cough was so deep you could hear him coming from blocks away. But Charlie never complained, maintaining a positive disposition. If things didn't go well, he would say, "Not to worry, we'll do it next year!" With fondness, his fellow miners referred to the talkative Charlie as "windy."

Charlie dreamed of his sons avoiding the mines by becoming professional baseball players like Paul and Lloyd Waner, two brothers who were the stars of Charlie's favorite team, the Pittsburgh Pirates. Before he lost his eye, Charlie, a tall, slim man, had been quite "a competitor" when he played first base on several local amateur teams. But even if he could no longer compete, Charlie still loved the game, and whenever he wasn't working and his sons weren't attending elementary school at St. Joseph's Parochial School in Princeton, you could find him instructing a group of neighborhood kids. Charlie had Bob, a left-hander, pitch, and Gil, a righty, catch. As children, Bob was not just a better player than Gil, but had great confidence in his abilities. "Bob knew he was good," said childhood friend Wayne Malotte, "and wasn't afraid to say so."

In contrast, Gil Hodges was already imbued with the reserved, self-effacing demeanor that would be his trademark as an adult. With a tendency that started on the playing fields of Princeton and continued throughout his life, if someone else wanted the spotlight, that was fine with him. In this regard Gil's temperament derived more from Irene, the "stabilizing influence" in the Hodges household, than from Charlie.

Three years younger than Charlie, Irene ruled the roost with an immovable fairness. When Marjorie was in high school, her boyfriend gave her an expensive gift for Christmas. But she didn't have the money to reciprocate in a comparable way, and Irene told her to return it. Gil was then living away from home playing for the Dodgers and sent his sister the money she needed to reciprocate. But in order to keep this a secret from Irene, Gil mailed the cash home to Marjorie using a fictitious name and return address. The story may be quaint, but it shows Irene's rigid moral compass (perhaps fixed in place upon the death of her infant son), and that even as a young man Gil Hodges was not beyond using subterfuge to produce a result he felt was justified. In his letters home, he referred to Charlie as Dad, but Irene was always Mother.

Yet Irene had a soft side. The Hodges family dog was a stray, "a scrawny, filthy, mutt" that Irene had found, took home, fed and bathed, and named Amber. As was typical of a housewife's duties in that era, Irene did all the house cleaning, laundry, and cooking. When he was a child, Gil's favorite food was Irene's navy bean soup. Like many working-class people struggling to survive in the 1930s, Irene brought her politics home, hanging a framed photo of President Franklin D. Roosevelt in the hallway. More significantly, the Hodgeses were devout Catholics, and every Sunday morning the entire family attended church.

In 1932 Charlie went to work in another mine and moved his family from Princeton to Petersburg (population 3,500, or about half that of Princeton), twenty miles northeast in Pike County. Petersburg's hub was its wide Main Street lined with shops like Adams Pharmacy and Howard's Café. Charlie soon changed jobs again and started working at the Ditney Hill Mine, which was closer to Princeton than Petersburg. But rather than uproot his family again, Charlie made the longer commute.

After school, to make spending money, Gil worked as a delivery boy for the Petersburg Home Grocery, earning ten cents an hour. Legend has it that only after furiously pedaling the delivery bicycle and completing all his deliveries did he head over to Higgins Field to play baseball. Yet, up until Gil began to play competitively in high school, he was also described—in comparison to Bob—as "laid-back" when it came to baseball. But when he reached his high school years, he once challenged the kids playing on Higgins Field to throw a baseball to him as hard as they could, promising to catch anything they threw, bare-handed. Wayne Malotte participated and was surprised that Gil caught them all. In retrospect, that wasn't the surprise (Gil's hands were already huge), but rather that Gil was forward enough to want the challenge, indicating, perhaps, that he was ready to play baseball in a more organized setting.

But Petersburg High School didn't have a baseball team. Instead, each spring, the Southern Indiana Invitational Track and Field Meet was held at Petersburg High on a track made of coal cinders that was considered the best in the region. The town took great pride when Gil, who could broad jump over twenty feet, took first place in several local meets and, after breaking the Petersburg High shot put record, qualified for the state finals in Indianapolis. Gil also played halfback on the school's six-man football team. In his senior year, Petersburg lost only one game, to Mt. Vernon, the county champions, by the slimmest of margins, 20–18.

Gil starred in track and played football, but the sport he loved was basketball. In the 1930s, high school basketball in Indiana was already serious business, and Gil had the physical skills to excel, especially at rebounding and ball handling. The summer after his sophomore year, he sprouted to a height of six feet, weighed a solid 175 pounds, and had hands large enough to palm a basketball or hold seven pool balls in one hand. In the low-scoring games of that era, basketball smarts were highly valued; and no matter what game—basketball, baseball, even ping-pong—from early on, Gil possessed an ability to make a quick study of his opponents and figure out how to beat them. In one sectional game in 1940 against a team from the nearby town of

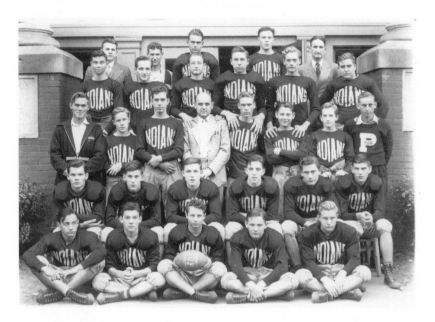

2. Petersburg High School football team, 1940: Gil Hodges, second row from the top, third from the right. Bob Hodges, second row from the bottom, fourth from the right. Courtesy of Sandy McBeth.

Ireland, Petersburg scored twice late in the game on steals by Gil and came from behind to win, 20–19. Bob King, a fellow Petersburg student who attended that game, later recalled, "It was his knowledge of the game that made him great. He was a thinker who could exploit an opponent's weakness. It wasn't quickness, it was just smarts, and it put us into the finals against Huntingburg."

Petersburg lost to Huntingburg. But the next season, in their senior year, Gil and Bob (who was in the same grade as Gil because he had missed a year of elementary school due to illness) led Petersburg to a 13-6 regular season record and first place in the county tournament. Morris Klipsch, a junior on that team, said, "He was always congenial and likeable and he seldom showed any anger." But in an early indication that nice guy Gil Hodges was no pushover, Klipsch added, "If opponents did get under his skin, he could sure move bodies around under the basket."

The basketball team from the nearby town of Washington won the Indiana state high school championship in 1941 and 1942. During the 1941 season, they

3. Petersburg High School basketball team, 1940–41: Gil Hodge(s), #11; Bob Hodge(s), #7. Courtesy of Sandy McBeth.

routed Petersburg, 37–19. Two black players, Chuck Harmon and his brother William, were the stars of the Washington team. Chuck was such a gifted basketball player that as a freshman he led the 1943 University of Toledo team to the semifinals of the National Invitational Tournament, then the premier college basketball tournament. But Harmon was also an outstanding baseball player; years later he could still recall playing sandlot baseball games against Gil Hodges's Petersburg team. In southern Indiana there were few blacks, and inter-town baseball games were generally lily-white affairs, so competing against Harmon provided Hodges with a firsthand lesson in the unfairness of Major League Baseball's then existing whites-only policy.

The Hodges brothers played baseball on Sundays for a sandlot team, the Petersburg Independents, but only after attending morning mass at Saints Peter and Paul Catholic Church in Petersburg, the only Catholic Church in the county. They were also the two best players on Petersburg's Conrad Post 179 team in the American Legion circuit. Gil played shortstop, Bob pitched.

On July 21, 1939, when Gil was only fifteen, the Petersburg American Legion team came within a single victory of reaching the regionals of a statewide tournament. But Evansville, the largest city in southwest Indiana, trounced them, 12–0. Bob, who had started the game at first base, came in to pitch in the third inning after the starter gave up six runs. Bob gave up six more runs in the fourth, but settled down and shut out Evansville for the rest of the game. Bob's inconsistent pitching against Evansville was typical for him. Jim Kelley, who batted against Bob in American Legion games, recalled, "Bob could throw as hard as anyone I ever saw at that age." But as is not uncommon for a young, hard-throwing left-handed pitcher, control was an issue. "I was scared to get into the batter's box against him," Kelley added. "Bob could throw it through a brick wall, but he could also stick it in your ear."

During his high school years, already a tremendous power hitter, Gil developed the habit of "stepping in the bucket." When a right-handed hitter puts his foot "in the bucket," he's moving his left foot (the foot closest to the pitcher) toward the third base line as he swings and moving away from, rather than into, the pitch. Lonnie Spade, Gil's coach with the Independents, came up with a solution. During practice, Spade placed a foot-high wooden board that ran the length of the batter's box immediately behind Hodges's heels as he stood at the plate. When Gil moved his left foot back toward the third base line, his foot hit the board. It worked; but resisting the urge to bail out would be a challenge for Gil throughout his career, especially against right-handers with an effective curve ball.

In high school Gil was more athlete than scholar: his grades were average. Bob was the only one of the two Hodges brothers to earn any academic mention at graduation, receiving a certificate stating that in four years of high school he was "neither absent nor tardy." A fellow member of Gil's 1941 graduating class, Mildred Hisgen, couldn't recall Gil volunteering to answer a single question in class.

As a young boy, one of Gil's first interactions with the young ladies of Petersburg took place on Higgins Field. Wayne Malotte's sister, Mary, asked him if she could play baseball with the boys. In an era far removed from ours, Gil shook his head no.

"This," Gil said, "is a boy's game."

Over time, Gil became more interested in the ladies. As star athletes, Bob and Gil attracted a good deal of attention. But in Gil's case, when it came to the ladies, he had better success as a matchmaker.

When he was a teenager, Gil's closest friend in Petersburg was his fellow classmate Bob King. During their high school years, King told Hodges that he wanted to date a young lady named June. Unfortunately, June had little interest in King. After school, while making deliveries for the Home Grocery (by then Hodges was driving its delivery truck), Hodges began to pay daily visits to June at Buchanan's Drug Store, where she worked. Ostensibly, the visits were for June to cook a muriatic acid concoction and apply it to warts that Hodges had on his index finger and thumb. Every visit, the routine was the same. June applied the muriatic acid with a toothpick, and Hodges would tell her what a nice fellow King was and how she should "go with him." June finally got the point and went on a date with King.

Although Gil didn't have a steady relationship in high school, he did have his eye on one particular young lady. When they were teenagers, Gil took Barbara Vance on a date to Jimmy's Café outside of town down by the White River. He didn't have a car, so they walked. Barbara didn't mind. "We walked a lot back in those days," she told me well over a half century later. Jimmy's didn't serve alcohol, but there was a jukebox, and they danced the night away to the tunes of Glenn Miller and the Dorsey Brothers.

"Bud was an excellent dancer," Barbara said. (Everyone I spoke to in Petersburg who had known Gil Hodges still called him Bud.)

Gil took Barbara to Jimmy's twice. In the unwritten social etiquette of Petersburg in 1941, a third date would have sent a message that Gil was seriously courting Barbara, intending marriage. But Barbara was Protestant, and her father wouldn't let her marry a Catholic. A little more than a decade after Al Smith became the first Catholic to run for president—but two decades before a Catholic (John F. Kennedy) won a presidential election—religious differences of this nature were common. They never had that third date. Barbara told me, "Bud was the nicest guy you could ever meet, but we were just good friends."

Gil graduated in the spring of 1941 with varsity letters in football and track, and a place on the Indiana All-Sectional basketball team. The graduating class motto fit Hodges, who always got to work early and was never one for late nights out: "Not evening, but dawn."

In the summer of 1941, for fifty cents an hour, Gil worked at the Ditney Hill Mine (but only "up top") digging out and lining a water cistern. The work was done entirely by hand using a pick, a shovel, and a hand-pulled winch to lift the dirt out of the hole. Gil was seventeen and already "very strong," said George Harris, who also worked on the job. That summer, Gil received an offer to sign a professional baseball contract with the Detroit Tigers, who were impressed with his home-run power and wanted to start him as a short-stop at the Class D level. Instead, anticipating he would end up a high school or college basketball coach, Gil took, in his own words, the "more sensible" approach and accepted an athletic scholarship to St. Joseph's College. Bob also received a scholarship to St. Joseph's, and that fall, they were off to the all-male Catholic college located two hundred miles away in the northern Indiana town of Rensselaer.

At St. Joseph's, Joe Dienhart, who had played football at Notre Dame under Knute Rockne, coached the football, basketball, and baseball teams. As a fresh-man, Gil played on all three as well as the track team. By the spring of 1942, with so many young men in the military, there was no longer a freshman baseball team, and Gil played on the varsity squad. He was switched from shortstop to third base because St. Joseph's best fielder, Frank Staucet, who later played in the Pittsburgh Pirates' Minor League system, played shortstop. As he had in the American Legion circuit, Gil impressed everyone with his power. Legend has it that he once hit a home run over a row of trees that served as the baseball field's boundary and into the College's Reflecting Pool, a distance of nearly five hundred feet. As with similar legends, no one ever hit one that far again.

In 1942 and 1943, in large part due to Bob and Gil, St. Joseph's baseball team won the Indiana Collegiate Conference title. This was quite an accomplish-ment, since they competed against much larger universities such as Indiana and Purdue.

In those years, St. Joseph's was also a football power and reached the final game of the 1942 season with twenty straight victories. But the week before, in a game against Butler, St. Joseph's starting fullback and his backup were both injured. That year, Dienhart had allowed Gil to skip the football season so he could be in better shape for basketball. But due to the injuries, and with only one week of practice, Gil started at fullback and scored a touchdown as the Pumas defeated Valparaiso to finish the season undefeated. Football was a two-way sport back then, and Gil enjoyed the physical aspect of defense even more than offense.

On Thanksgiving Day in 1942, Gil wrote to his parents and sister, who were living in a tin-roofed house they rented at 404 Cherry Street in Petersburg. From the opening of his letter, handwritten in a neat script, it's clear Gil had not mastered what would later be his formidable skill of using as few words as possible. "Well, I am getting ready to go to bed, so I thought I would write before going to bed." The letter gives insight into his concern for his family's modest financial circumstances, reveals a hint of sibling rivalry, and suggests that even with no school the next day, Gil was not one to sit around idle. Unlike Bob, Gil had decided to stay at St. Joseph's and not come home for Thanksgiving.

> I guess Bob is home by now, isn't he? If he isn't he should be. What time did he get home last night? I was coming home, but I thought it would cost entirely too much money for both of us to come home and since I was home just about a week ago I thought I would stay up here. We had a nice dinner up here today. Everything imaginable. I ate so much I didn't even go to supper. Bernie [a fellow student] and I are going to work tomorrow out in a corn field. I don't know how much we will make, but whatever it is, it will be better than laying around up here.

On that long holiday weekend, even with extra time, Gil didn't have much interest in doing his own laundry, and showing how inexpensive postage was back then, he mailed his laundry home for his mother to do. And when Irene mailed it back, she always enclosed one of her home-baked cookies.

But Gil had a lot on his mind. When the Japanese bombed Pearl Harbor, he was only seventeen. But having turned eighteen in April of 1942, he was giving serious thought to enlisting: "Have there been any more fellows left for the Army down home? I imagine there will be a lot of 18 & 19 year-old boys going before long. I am going to see about getting in the Marines before long. Answer soon. Love, Bud." And, with what would become his trademark, self-deprecating humor, he ends, "ps: Isn't a very long letter is it?"

In his sophomore year, Gil starred on the baseball and basketball teams. After playing in only that one football game, he was in such good shape that he could jump high enough to touch the basketball rim with his forearm. That winter, the only thing that stopped him from excelling on the basketball court was his grades. Back then, the "student" part of "student-athlete" came first: if you didn't pass your classes, you didn't play or even travel with the team. On a snowy Saturday in February 1943, Gil wrote to "Mother, Dad, and Marj":

> I'm very sorry I couldn't make the Terre Haute trip last week. I really wanted to make it and I would have if it hadn't been for Father Speckbaugh. I thought I would pass in his class and I did in my final exam, but my other grades brought me down. I just needed two points to pass and he wouldn't consent to give them to me. . . . Joe [Coach Dienhart] has been talking to him, so I might be able to play again soon. I know I could have done better, but I just didn't do it. I guess I didn't spend enough time on it but I thought I did. If I am up here for quite a while yet, I'm sure I will get along all right. I guess everyone makes mistakes during their life and I can see that was one of mine.

But Gil's main concern was the war, and he already knew ("If I am up here for quite a while yet . . .") that he would be unable to finish college before enlisting.

In the summer of 1942, Bob and Gil had both worked in a factory in Indianapolis and played baseball in the city's industrial league. But Bob joined the army in the spring of 1943, leaving Gil on his own that summer. He worked as a drill press operator for the P. R. Mallory Company, a dry-cell battery manufacturer, and played shortstop in the industrial league.

In late August of 1943, an Indianapolis sporting-goods-store owner, Stanley Feezle, approached Gil and asked him if he was interested in trying out for the Dodgers. Feezle was a part-time scout with an eye for talent; a few years later he signed Carl Erskine, who lived in the nearby town of Anderson and became a key member of the Dodgers' pitching staff in the 1950s. Feezle sold sporting equipment to St. Joseph's and had been watching Gil for over a year. With the Dodgers finally willing to pay the travel expenses of Midwest prospects to participate in a try-out camp in upstate New York, Feezle seized the moment. So did Gil. Despite having already committed to joining the marines (and still believing basketball was his best sport), Gil packed a few days' worth of clothing and boarded a bus heading east toward a town called Olean.

2

THE TWIG, THE BRANCH, AND THE LIP

Though I was with him a short time, Durocher had an effect on me. . . . If a player was with Leo for one day, Durocher had an effect.

Olean, New York, was something "straight out of Andy Hardy." Victorian houses with wraparound porches. Three movie theaters, one of which still ran vaudeville shows. And on summer afternoons, you walked over to Bradner Stadium to cheer for the Oilers, the Dodgers' Class D Minor League team managed by Jake Pitler.

At forty-eight, Pitler was a rare commodity: a Jewish baseball lifer who had spent a quarter of a century kicking around the Minors, as a player and then a manager. The highlight of his career came in 1917 when he spent his only full season in the Majors and was a teammate of Honus Wagner. Pitler, who had been managing in Olean for four seasons, put the fifty players who had come from all over the East and Midwest through two days of running, hitting, throwing, and fielding drills. Branch Rickey Jr., the director of the Dodgers' Minor League operations, was also there.

Rickey Jr. was called the Twig—but never to his face. He hated the nickname. Rickey Jr. had the misfortune of working as a baseball executive in the formidable shadow of his already legendary father, Branch Rickey. Prior to joining the Dodgers organization, as the general manager of the St. Louis Cardinals, Rickey Sr. had successfully established the concept of Major League teams owning their own farm system to develop players, enabling the Cardinals to become the best team in the National League: from 1926 to 1946, the Cardinals played in nine World Series, winning six.

As the tryouts began, no one took much notice of Gil Hodges, who was unimpressive in the field. But years later, Rickey Jr. could still recall seeing Hodges's first at bat. "Hodges hits one," he said; "it reaches the cinder track beyond the outfield. The second time he hits it over the track, and the third time the ball lands in the same place. In those tryout camps you see a lot of kids who can run like the dickens . . . [and] throw hard, but it's a rare thing to find a kid who can shillelagh a ball. Hodges just beat the ball to death. I saw him and I said: 'Hornsby or Foxx.'"

Rickey Jr. was prescient in comparing Hodges to Jimmy Foxx. Nineteen years later, after Hodges's last full season as a player (1962), Foxx would be the only right-handed hitter in baseball history who had hit more career home runs than Hodges. It was equally clear to Pitler that Hodges was the only player at the tryout who had Major League potential, and he urged the Oilers' general manager, Spence Harris, to sign Hodges to a Minor League contract with Olean.

"Don't let him get away," Pitler said.

Rickey Jr. decided that his father, then in his first full season as general manager of the Dodgers, should have a look at Hodges before any contracts were signed. At the time, Rickey's decision seemed inconsequential, but it would have a profound impact on Hodges's career. Together, Rickey Jr. and Hodges boarded a train for Grand Central Station. Hodges couldn't believe he was going to have a private tryout with the most famous executive in baseball.

He spent his first night in New York City at the Hotel New Yorker at Thirty-Fourth Street and Eighth Avenue. "I'd never been in Manhattan before. That night, with the big buildings and all, I didn't go further than a block from my hotel," Hodges recalled. Rickey Jr. called Hodges the next morning and told him to take the subway to Borough Hall in Brooklyn and walk to the Dodgers' offices at 215 Montague Street. But Hodges got on an uptown train and was in the Bronx before he realized he was heading the wrong way and asked for directions to Brooklyn.

In 1943 the Brooklyn Dodgers were a team in transition. In the first two decades of the twentieth century, Charlie Ebbets, a man who loved both baseball and Brooklyn, owned the Dodgers. Ebbets fought to keep the team in Brooklyn and in 1913 built a new ballpark for them on land he had purchased. His players rewarded him with pennants in 1916 and 1920. But Ebbets died in 1925, and by the mid-1930s, with no one person owning a majority interest in the team, the rudderless Dodgers were bankrupt and the brunt of New York Giants manager Bill Terry's sarcastic comment, "Is Brooklyn still in the league?"

At the end of the 1930s, after the Dodgers were acquired by their largest creditor, Rickey Sr. was asked who would be the best person to lead the Dodgers toward respectability. He recommended Larry MacPhail, a charismatic, manic marketing genius then running the Cincinnati Reds. MacPhail took the job and spent large sums of money purchasing veteran players, refurbishing Ebbets Field, and acquiring two of the best young players of the era, Pee Wee Reese and Pete Reiser. MacPhail hired Rickey Jr. to head up the Dodgers' Minor League operations, and a sweet-talking southerner named Red Barber to be the Dodgers' broadcaster. From high up in the catbird's seat, Barber brought Dodgers games alive with his idiosyncratic vernacular: fly balls were caught like an easy can of corn, fights between the Giants and the Dodgers were rhubarbs, and blow-outs produced victories sewed up in a croker sack. By 1941 the Dodgers had won a pennant; in 1942 they won 104 games; and in 1943 the Dodgers were poised to eventually replace the Cardinals as the league's best team. But MacPhail had left to join the military, and Rickey Sr. was again approached regarding the general manager's position. This time, he took the job for himself, and Rickey Jr., who had come to Brooklyn to get away from his father, was again working for him.

But for Hodges, the arrival of Rickey Sr. was a godsend. Like Hodges, Rickey was cut from deeply religious Midwestern cloth. He wasn't just interested in a player's abilities; he wanted to learn their personalities, which he was convinced impacted their chances for success. For Rickey, a family man made a more stable player.

Hodges experienced Rickey's standard interview: Son, tell me about your father, what does he do? How about your mother? Do you have any brothers or sisters? Do you attend church? Where did you go to school? Are you married? No! What about a girlfriend? Do you drink? You can tell me, son.

Rickey would so indoctrinate Hodges with the importance of a player being married that in the 1960s when Hodges was managing the Washington Senators, he said that the play of his newly married third baseman, Ken

McMullen, would improve because as a married man, "He'll apply himself more diligently now."

Although Hodges was neither married nor a Methodist (as was Rickey), he passed the interview with flying colors. Hodges fit in perfectly with Rickey's goal to fill the Dodgers' Minor League system with as many talented ballplayers as he could find. For Rickey, quantity accumulated during the war years—when many others teams were cutting down on the size of their farm system—would produce postwar quality.

Hodges's tryout at Ebbets Field lasted three days, from August 28 through August 30. The Dodgers were then in Philadelphia for a four-game series with the Phillies, so for the tryout, local kids were brought in to pitch and shag fly balls. First, Rickey had Hodges hit, as Hodges recalled, "until his hands were sore." The combination of Hodges's power and a bandbox like Ebbets Field convinced Rickey he had found his right-handed slugger for the postwar period.

The only question was where to play him. Rickey systematically moved Hodges through every position except pitcher and catcher. Hodges spent hours shagging fly balls and fielding grounders until he was worn out. Rickey claimed to see a flaw in Hodges's throwing motion and ruled him out at his usual shortstop position. (The likely flaw was that Pee Wee Reese, then only twenty-five, had already established himself as the Dodgers' shortstop for the long term.) After the workout, Rickey told Hodges his future was behind the plate. Rickey made this decision based upon the size of Hodges's huge hands and the fact that those hands were lightning fast. And no one was going to question Rickey, who was often referred to as the Mahatma (after Mahatma Gandhi), "an incredible combination of Jesus Christ, Tammany Hall, and your father." But Rickey had another nickname, El Cheapo.

Rickey proved himself gifted at two things: accumulating ballplayers and making money. The problem was, he didn't like to mix the two. (Under Rickey's contract with the Dodgers, he received a percentage of the team's net profits, so the less he paid his players, the more money he made.) In retrospect, the gyrations Rickey went through to keep salaries low seem comical; but to the players trying to get a raise, they were not so humorous. In St. Louis, future Hall of Famer Johnny Mize was Rickey's star. After leading the league with a .349 batting average in 1939, Mize sat down with Rickey to talk contract

4. Hodges had huge hands: from the tip of his thumb to the tip of his pinkie finger measured nearly twelve inches across. Brooklyn Public Library—Brooklyn Collection.

and Rickey made no mention of Mize's batting average. Instead, he said, "Well, your home run production stayed pretty much the same." The next season, Mize led the league with forty-three homers, but his average fell to .314. Rickey said to him, "Well, your batting average wasn't so good. Would you be willing to take a cut?"

"The only way to get the best of Rickey," Casey Stengel once said, "is to listen to him talk for three hours, then when he asks, 'Is it a deal?' yell, 'NO' and walk out."

If Rickey could bamboozle a veteran like Mize, Hodges was a lamb to the slaughter. Rickey offered Hodges a signing bonus of $1,250. At the time, a new Ford cost $800, so $1,250 sounded like a lot of money to the coal miner's son. But knowing Hodges had committed to joining the marines in October, Rickey said he could only pay half the bonus up front—his sonorous voice no doubt rising to a plummy crescendo as he said, I'm sure you understand why, young man.

Hodges telephoned Charlie, who spoke directly to Rickey. The apple had not fallen far from the tree; Charlie wasn't any better a negotiator than his son. For an upfront payment of $625, Hodges signed a contract that legally obligated him to the Dodgers—without any recourse—until he was waived, traded, or retired. Within a decade, that contract was estimated to be worth $150,000.

With Major League rosters expanded at the end of the season, Hodges was sent to Philadelphia for the final game of the Phillies series, where he met Dodgers manager Leo Durocher for the first time. Durocher, who once appeared on the cover of *Time* magazine, was a nationally known figure. His long-term claim to fame originated with his pointing at a lackluster New York Giants team managed by the beloved Mel Ott and saying, "The nice guys are all over there, in seventh place." That was quoted in the papers as the phrase that would long outlive him, "Nice guys finish last." Ironically, considering Hodges would come to be viewed as the ultimate nice guy, beginning that season, and at several critical junctures in his career, his success or failure would be inextricably entwined with Durocher.

For his entire professional career, from 1925 when he played his first game with the New York Yankees until his last game as manager of the Houston Astros in 1973, winning was all that mattered for Durocher. As he wrote in the first sentence of his autobiography, "I never had a boss call me upstairs so that he could congratulate me for losing like a gentlemen. 'How you play the game' is for college boys. When you're playing for money, winning is the only thing that matters. Show me a good loser . . . and I'll show you an idiot."

To win, Durocher had his pitchers well-schooled in the art of throwing at opposition batters, intending not just to back them off the plate, but to hit them. When Durocher signaled his pitchers with a slow jerk of his thumb upward in a hitch-like motion toward his forehead, opposition batters knew they were in trouble. In one game, after the Phillies' Del Ennis was hit in the wrist, the Phillies' manager screamed at Durocher, who replied, "What are you crying about? It's lucky it didn't hit him in the head!" But Durocher produced winning results and not even Rickey short-changed him. Durocher was paid $50,000 a year to manage the Dodgers. Except for superstars like Joe DiMaggio, that was one of baseball's highest salaries.

Off the field, Durocher was just as aggressive. A writer once asked Durocher how he had such success with the ladies. Durocher replied, "Kid, when you pick one of them up at 7:00 . . . you make sure you put your hand on their snatch at 7:05. 7:05! Now, one of two things can happen . . . they can knock your hand off. All right. It's 7:05. No go . . . it's still early yet. Plenty of time to call another broad. But suppose she don't knock your hand off. Well, then hello dear. You know you're in . . . you'd be surprised. Some damn famous broads don't knock your hand off."

Now, imagine if you will, entering stage right, Gil Hodges, the devout Catholic teenager from the all-male St. Joseph's College, shaking hands with Durocher, a man who spoke in sentences filled with, as Red Smith once wrote, "short, indelicate words."

The Lip, as Durocher was called due to his combative nature, and Hodges prayed from very different hymnbooks. As far as baseball rules go, Durocher believed in them because, as he said, "if there weren't any rules, how could you break them?" When an umpire made a close call against his team, Durocher's approach was to "squawk loud enough" in the belief that the next close one would go his way. Showing up an umpire by kicking dirt at him was standard procedure for Durocher; and when he retired, only one other manager in baseball history, John McGraw, had been thrown out of more games. In contrast, Hodges would come to pride himself on thoroughly understanding and following the baseball rule book. Hodges wanted to win as badly as Durocher, but he believed umpires were just men doing their jobs as best they could and if you showed them up, you accomplished nothing.

Durocher's focus was also more about himself than his team. In later years, Durocher would say of Hodges, "If he'd ever blow up, if he'd push an umpire around, Gil would be the greatest!" If you want to get noticed and build up a Hall of Fame reputation, Durocher was correct—getting noticed was the way to go. But as sportswriter Arnold Hano would conclude of Hodges near the end of his playing career, "Clean living isn't exciting."

In 1943 the Dodgers were a typical World War II mix of veterans nearing the end of their careers, Minor Leaguers who would never have made the Majors but for the war, and teenagers straight off the sandlots. Durocher was impressed watching Hodges hit batting practice shots off the outfield fence at the Phils' Shibe Park, but Hodges didn't play until the season's final game.

The war was on his mind on Monday morning, September 13, 1943, when Hodges, still signing his letters home as "Bud," wrote to his parents from the Copley-Plaza in Boston during a series against the Braves: "They are having me catch batting practice once in a while now and I am getting out of the habit of ducking my head and closing my eyes. I guess Stan [Feezle, the scout that signed him] told you about him getting me a two week deferment. I think Stan fixed it also for me to take my exam [his physical in preparation for joining the marines] on the 25th in the city where we are. I don't know where that will be right now."

Hodges was back at the Hotel New Yorker on Saturday morning, September 18, 1943, when he again wrote to his family:

I got the package with my coat and other clothes in it yesterday. I went over to the office today and got my first pay. We are playing the Giants here in New York at the Polo Grounds. We had to pay our own expenses here though. We lost yesterday but should have won it. . . . I have been catching quite a bit now and am getting to do it pretty good. How is everyone down there? I haven't written Bob yet but I am going to do it tonight right after the game today. I should have written him sooner but I have been rushing from one place to another and I can't seem to find any time. You don't need to send me my top coat. I think I can make it all right without it till the end of the season.

Hodges played in his first Major League game on October 3, 1943, in Cincinnati. After the first inning, when Durocher learned the Phillies had defeated the Pirates, he knew the Dodgers were guaranteed a third-place finish (ahead of the fourth-place Pirates). Players then received a payment—in addition to their salary—depending on where they finished in the standings, and the difference between third and fourth place could mean an extra few hundred dollars to each player. With money no longer an issue, Durocher gave his youngsters a chance. Hodges went in to play third base. On his eighteenth birthday, Chris Haughey came in to pitch his Major League debut (and also finale), allowing only five hits but walking ten. In the fifth, Hodges made an error on a double-play grounder, which allowed two runs to score. Hodges later started a double play, but made another error in the eighth when the Reds scored four runs. The Dodgers lost, 6–1.

Things were no better for Hodges at bat. Johnny Vander Meer, the only pitcher in Major League history to throw two consecutive no-hitters, was pitching for the Reds. In 1943 he led the National League in strikeouts for the third consecutive season. Vander Meer had an outstanding fastball and he simply overpowered Hodges, who struck out twice. The only pitch Hodges hit sharply all day landed in foul territory. In later years, Durocher would tease Hodges, telling him he looked like a man swinging an axe when Vander Meer threw a curve ball.

But Hodges was also watching Durocher. Every time a Dodgers player reached first base, Durocher signaled for him either to steal second or to move on the pitch as part of a hit and run. (After drawing a walk, Hodges even stole a base that day.) Durocher's instructions had nothing to do with his team winning; they were entirely self-serving. Durocher wanted his players to run only to deny the Reds a chance to break the National League record for the most double plays in a season. In 1931 Durocher, playing shortstop, and Tony Cuccinello, at second, had turned 128 double plays to set the record, and Durocher wanted to keep his name in the record books. The Reds turned two double plays that day, finishing with 127. Hodges later said, "The Reds were throwing guys out at second right and left, but of course they didn't get the opportunity for double plays, so the record stood up."

In contrast to Durocher, what mattered to Hodges was how he affected his team. If a sacrifice bunt was what was called for to win, that was what he did. Records were never his priority.

But there was another significant aspect to Hodges's persona; and in that regard, it's ironic that one of the umpires in Hodges's first game was Larry Goetz. After the war, Goetz became Hodges's favorite umpire. He appreciated Goetz's sense of humor and his commanding presence. When Larry Goetz was umpiring, Hodges wrote, "you never forgot that he was the man in charge. He was the boss." As a manager, Hodges would be no different. And the seeds of his I'm-the-man-in-charge persona would be sown over the next two and a half years when he served in the Marine Corps.

AWAY

The Pacific (1944–45);
Newport News (1946)

3

OKINAWA

Sitting around in those foxholes out on Okinawa . . . I had to have something to do, so I started smoking.

After the war, Hodges never discussed his military service with his family. He deflected the press's questions as well. When writer Roscoe McGowen made inquiry, Hodges stated only his itinerary: boot camp in San Diego in 1943, Hawaii in 1944, Tinian in 1945, and then Okinawa as a member of the Sixteenth Anti-Aircraft Artillery (AAA) Battalion. With the where, when, and with whom set, McGowan pushed for the what. He had good reason to ask. More people died during the Battle of Okinawa than in the bombings of Hiroshima and Nagasaki combined.

But as Hodges would do throughout his managerial career when he didn't want to answer a reporter's question, he took control of the interview by ceasing to speak. And very few could endure Hodges's silences. McGowen was not one of them. "Anybody who wants to know what happened at Okinawa," McGowan wrote, "will have to read the history of WWII in the Pacific. Hodges just says he is not a fighting man."

Some writers had better luck. Herb Goren got Hodges to recall "that on Okinawa he slugged it out with ack-ack fire against some Jap Betsies [a type of bomber], but most of the time he had it pretty good."

Into the void created by Hodges's silence stepped Dodger teammate Don "Tiger" Hoak. A former boxer, Hoak could be counted on to knock out a quote unburdened by facts. Without a clue as to what Hodges really did on Okinawa, Hoak issued the line that became the prevailing legend of Hodges's war years: "We kept hearing stories about this big guy from Indiana who killed Japs with his bare hands."

Nothing could be further from the truth. In interviews with surviving members of the Sixteenth AAA Battalion, and in a review of Hodges's personnel records as well as the battalion's after-action reports, there was not a single reference to Hodges engaging in any hand-to-hand combat. Rather, Hodges's comment to Goren that "he had it pretty good" is the one that merits closer analysis because, beyond being classic Hodges-speak, minimizing his own accomplishments, it reveals Hodges's view of the risks he took on Okinawa.

In Hodges's mind, since he was in an anti-aircraft artillery battalion and not in an infantry combat unit, he had it "pretty good." But everyone on Okinawa faced the very real possibility of death on a daily basis. During the Okinawa campaign, popular war correspondent Ernie Pyle was killed by Japanese machine gun fire. Japanese artillery killed the commander of the U.S. Tenth Army, Lieutenant General Simon Buckner Jr., the highest-ranking American officer killed during the entire Pacific campaign. James H. Powers, a marine who served in a position similar to Hodges's in the intelligence and operations section of the Eighth AAA Battalion, told me, "On Okinawa, you were either bored to death or blown sky high."

Even if Hodges had it "pretty good," it was highly unusual for a member of an artillery battalion to win a commendation, and Hodges earned a Bronze Star on Okinawa. Hodges was recommended for that medal at the end of the war, but the story of his military service begins on December 7, 1941, with the Japanese attack on Pearl Harbor where many combat ships were sunk or damaged. But not the USS *Phoenix*. A light cruiser, the *Phoenix* survived unscathed because she had arrived when all the docking berths in battleship row were occupied, forcing her to anchor on the other side of Ford Island. Aboard the *Phoenix* was a twenty-three-year-old marine second lieutenant, Robert A. Merchant. By the end of the war, Merchant was the head of the intelligence and operations section of the Sixteenth AAA Battalion and Hodges was his aide-de-camp.

When President Roosevelt declared war on Japan, Hodges was seventeen and ineligible for military service, but the decision about when to enlist was soon in his thoughts. Like most of those who joined the marines, Hodges didn't wait to be drafted. He enlisted on September 27, 1943, in Indianapolis as the Dodgers were traveling on their way from Chicago to Pittsburgh. When asked to list his current job, Hodges wrote that he was a college student—not a ballplayer.

After the Dodgers' season ended, Hodges returned to Petersburg to say goodbye to his family. On the night before he left for basic training at Camp Elliot in San Diego, he went to the movies to see *Phantom of the Opera* starring Nelson Eddy. For Hodges, accustomed to the Dodgers' first-class traveling accommodations, his four-day trip across the country on a military train was a rude awakening. "We really had a terrible trip out here," he wrote home after arriving at Camp Elliot. "We couldn't get any berths and we had to sit up all the way from Indianapolis." After three nights of little or no sleep, Hodges's review of the western states was mixed. "There sure are a lot of mountains out here," he wrote, "and also a lot of ground that isn't worth a penny."

His train arrived in San Diego at midnight and he didn't get to sleep until 1:30 a.m. Reveille sounded at 5:45 a.m. By noon, he had had breakfast, heard "a few speeches," and taken a written exam. Although the first song Hodges would teach his children on family road trips was "The Marines' Hymn," getting used to marine discipline was not easy. In his first letter home, Hodges wrote, "Boy you sure have to be able to take it out here. They really shove you around."

And Hodges's indoctrination into military life proved to be physically, as well as mentally, challenging. Since Hodges was going to serve in the Pacific, many vaccinations and injections were required, and they were administered with rapidity to long lines of marines. In *With the Old Breed*, a memoir of his Marine Corps service in the Pacific during World War II, E. B. Sledge wrote, "Our arms were sore, and many men became feverish. The troops hated getting injections, and the large number . . . before Okinawa made us crotchety. The plague shot burned like fire."

Soon after receiving his shots, both of Hodges's ankles were "swollen just about twice as they should be" and he could barely stand. Hodges had had an acute allergic reaction to the inoculations, but he didn't make the connection. Of the injections, Hodges would write while in sickbay, "It isn't so bad, but they sure make your arms sore." But for a tired nineteen-year-old, anxiously awaiting the arrival of a doctor to "x-ray them [his ankles] or something to find out about them," it was a long afternoon. Hodges ends his letter promising "to write again as soon as the doctor gives me the once over."

Hodges recovered and, despite those difficult first few days, he learned to comply, receiving the highest possible scores in obedience and sobriety. In San Diego, Hodges saw how an organization responsible for focusing a group of young men on a single purpose went about its business. Years later, the methodology the marines used—the importance of the organization over the individual, teamwork, and firm discipline uniformly applied—became bedrock principles in Hodges's managerial handbook.

Hodges was in San Diego for Thanksgiving, while his brother, Bob, got a furlough from Camp Davis in North Carolina and came home for the holidays. By the time Hodges was landing on Okinawa, Bob, then a corporal, was in Germany with the Ninth Army.

Hodges completed his basic training on December 21, 1943. Promoted to private first class, he was assigned to Company A, Infantry Battalion, for eight weeks of training as a rifleman using a Browning Automatic Rifle (BAR). There were no rifles in the house when Hodges was growing up, so that was the first time he ever shot a rifle with regularity. In February of 1944, he qualified as a marksman with a rifle score of 271, below the level of sharpshooter (292 to 305) or expert (306 to 340). That month, Hodges joined the Forty-Fourth Replacement Battalion awaiting deployment overseas.

The Corps believed that a marine would be most effective performing a task of his own choosing and, where possible, they met a new recruit's job request. Hodges's preference was to be in the military police. For a man who would become known for breaking up baseball fights, it seemed a natural, but he was assigned duty as a rifleman.

Hodges's letters home reveal a young man who put the needs of his family first. In one letter, postmarked February 29, 1944, the week before Hodges was sent out for active duty in the Pacific, he arranged to send his family twenty-five dollars a month from his pay: "I won't need it while I'm over there." Hodges broke the news of his going overseas to his family as gently as possible: "I guess you will be shocked at what I am going to say but I might as well tell you and there really isn't anything to worry about, so don't start worrying about it."

Hodges knew his family. When his letters arrived, Irene and Marjorie would sit at their kitchen table crying. "Dad," Marjorie said years later, "just didn't know what to do for us." Hodges's follow-up letter attempted to allay their fears: "I know I will be all right. I have learned enough here to take care of myself and I'm in a good outfit."

In a letter to Marjorie dated February 28, 1944, Hodges, who years later didn't want to leave Brooklyn for Los Angeles when the Dodgers moved, wrote, "It wouldn't be bad out here in California in civilian life but I can't say I care for it too much being in the Marine Corps."

After Marjorie wrote about her struggles in algebra and biology; her brother responded, "I know you can get them [good grades] if you just get in there and set your mind to it. 85 isn't a bad average for the month. I know I didn't do that good very many times."

At the end of the letter, he added, "Pardon my writing."

In his March 3, 1944, letter home, Hodges wistfully wrote that he hoped to be home in time for next year's Petersburg Indians' basketball season so he could "see a few games." He notes how fast the time was passing before he had to ship out: "Well, here it is Friday again and this week sure has gone fast. I went to Mass last night and to Communion and I am going again tonight. They have a Mass at 4:30 and today will be the last time I will get to go for a while. The time has just about got here for us to shove off so this will be the last letter I will be able to write for some time."

On March 5, 1944, Hodges boarded the ss *Santa Monica* to join the Fifth Amphibious Corps in Hawaii. Because of military security, the next correspondence Irene and Charlie received was a postcard from Marine Headquarters in San Francisco, informing them that their son had safely arrived at his overseas destination. Due to military security, they were not told where that destination was, and thereafter Hodges's letters home spoke only of his life back in Indiana, since he couldn't mention his location or activities.

Hodges arrived in Pearl Harbor on March 11. At the Transient Center tent camp outside of Honolulu, he soon met Chuck Askey, another marine who was awaiting orders to join a unit. Hodges was working in the mess hall and Askey was assigned to Hodges's pot walloping (cleaning) detail. The first thing

Hodges ever said to Askey was to ask if he played softball or baseball. Hodges had formed a team at the Transient Center that played against other units.

In April, Hodges joined the newly created Sixteenth AAA Battalion, and a transport ship brought him from Pearl Harbor to Kauai, another island in the Hawaiian chain, where the Sixteenth would train. Askey was also ordered to the Sixteenth, and the two Midwesterners (Askey was from Ohio) became friends.

Marine AAA Battalions defended airbases from Japanese bombers. At full strength, a battalion had 60 officers and 1,300 enlisted men. Each battalion was like a small town, with its own trucks, tractors, trailers, mechanics, welders, radar technicians, radio operators, drivers, meteorologist, cobbler, and barber.

AAA Battalions previously had their own infantry, but in 1944 they began operating as part of the Tenth Army, eliminating the need for the AAA units to have riflemen. In May of 1944, Hodges was reassigned to work as a clerk at the Sixteenth's company headquarters where, after transferring from the USS *Phoenix*, Colonel Robert Merchant was now the chief operations and intelligence officer.

Hodges and Merchant were a good fit. Like Hodges, Merchant had attended college, graduating from the Virginia Military Institute with an electrical engineering degree. Both men had a wry sense of humor. In reviewing Merchant's personal military files at the U.S. Marine Library in Quantico, I found a "Memo to All Staff Officers" that Merchant either wrote or appreciated enough to save: "The typical staff officer is a man past middle age, spare, wrinkled, intelligent, cold, passive, non-committal; with eyes like a codfish, polite in contact, but at the same time unresponsive, cool, calm, and as damnably composed as a concrete post or a plaster-of-Paris cast; a human petrification with a heart of feldspar and without charm or the friendly germ; minus bowels, passions, or a sense of humor. Happily they never reproduce and all of them finally go to hell."

On Kauai, as Merchant's clerk, Hodges compiled reports, answered phones, and distributed mail. Hodges's position didn't require the use of a typewriter. But he could "operate a typewriter deftly, accurately, and at stenographer's speed" and was soon promoted to operations assistant, which required that he be "thoroughly familiar with the organization of the various types of units within the command" and "their tactical employment."

5. Colonel Robert Merchant. Courtesy of Virginia Merchant.

The Sixteenth reached its full combat strength on August 1, 1944, and that month it landed near Port Allen, Kauai, to practice defending against night attacks simulated by the U.S. Air Force, 494th Bomber Squadron. On December 22, the Sixteenth AAA Battalion set out for Tinian, a tiny island in the Marianas. By the time they arrived in early January of 1945, Hodges had been promoted to the rank of corporal.

U.S. forces had captured Tinian in the summer of 1944, and active combat was over before the Sixteenth arrived. The battalion set up their guns on Mt. Lasso, which overlooked the B29 airstrip, and remained on alert for Japanese bombing raids. During the Sixteenth's two months on Tinian, Hodges assisted Merchant in preparing for the most efficient unloading of the unit's equipment on Okinawa. Unlike Tinian, Okinawa was within easy flying range from Tokyo, making it imperative that the anti-aircraft batteries be established quickly to defend against air raids.

On March 13, Hodges left Tinian on LST 803 for the neighboring Marianas Island of Saipan. LST stood for landing ship tanks, sea-going vessels whose drafts were shallow enough to anchor close to shore so that at low tide trucks could pull the unit's anti-aircraft guns onto shore. Two weeks later, LST 803 left for Okinawa as part of the largest Pacific armada of the war.

D-day was Easter Sunday, April 1, but the Japanese put up only scattered resistance that day. Their strategy was to concede the beaches and save their efforts for the southern third of the island where the crevice-filled terrain gave them clear sight lines from well-entrenched positions in the cliffs. The heaviest fighting, and the greatest number of marine casualties, occurred there.

In one of his longest letters home, written after combat had ended and military censorship no longer applied, Hodges wrote:

We arrived here [Okinawa] the first of April and things really cut loose. We were always having air attacks and the ships were really knocking down the planes. It's just like being tied down when you're on board a ship because you can't do a thing but just stand there and wait for something to happen. One Jap plane, a Zero, came circling around where we were anchored and when everyone saw it they really cut loose. I don't see how it was possible for him to escape with so much firing being done at that time. He was the plane that really gave all of us a scare. He started to pull away from the firing and then he got hit and started circling around, then into a suicide dive. He started coming down and boy he was really moving. He crashed on the bow of another LST not very far from our ship and exploded. I don't know how many got hurt but I'm sure there were quite a few. Well, that's just one incident and I don't want to go into any other at the present time because I could probably sit here and write all day and still not be through.

Hodges was standing on the deck of LST 803 waiting to disembark when the Zero hit the nearby ship. Someone from the Sixteenth Battalion had to do advanced reconnaissance to determine exactly where the AAA guns should be set up, and Hodges was a member of the reconnaissance party of six officers and twelve enlisted men that went ashore later that day to do just that. By then the beaches had been secured but inland positions were still in flux. Only two days before, a marine had been shot and killed in the same area the reconnaissance party scouted. It must have been an emotional day for Hodges. The next day was his twenty-first birthday.

The Sixteenth set up several miles north of the heaviest fighting that would take place on Okinawa. Their mission was to provide air defense in the Yontan-Kadena area where the island's two airfields were located. On Okinawa, the airfields were the primary targets for Japanese bombers. From April 8, when the Sixteenth's guns were in place, until August 8, when the last enemy attack took place, there were 131 separate bombing raids. Of these, Corporal Lester Foster, a member of the Sixteenth's Charlie Co. 90mm gun crew, said, "When they got through, they worked us over pretty good."

In addition to frequent bombings, the Sixteenth was subject to sniper and mortar fire. The boldest enemy attack came on the night of May 24 when five Japanese planes, with eighty Special Attack Corps troops armed with explosives, attempted to crash land at Yontan Airfield. All but one of the planes was shot down. That night, two members of the Sixteenth were killed. Over the course of the entire engagement on Okinawa, five members of the Sixteenth died.

Hodges slept in a tent with five other marines. One was Romeo Paulino, the battalion's barber. Cutting Hodges's hair, Paulino noticed a bump on the back of his head, and, in deference to Hodges working with "the top echelon," Paulino dubbed it "the bump of knowledge."

As Merchant's assistant, Hodges was with him in the Sixteenth's filter center during bombing raids. The filter center was a rectangular-shaped trailer made of corrugated steel that served as the tactical headquarters of the battalion and was set up between the two airfields. Information from radar stations and any visual identification reports were charted in the filter center on two maps. One covered an area 150 miles in diameter around the airfields, the second a 50-mile area. Based upon the information obtained, the filter center would supply positioning data to the units manning the artillery pieces so they could accurately target enemy planes.

Working in the filter center required mental toughness. While the AAA batteries could shoot back at the enemy planes, all you could do in the center was sit tight and hope you made it through. All AAA filter centers had two backup centers set up at least 250 yards away from the operational one. During enemy bombing raids, the backup filter centers were fully manned in the event the primary was "blown sky high."

By the end of June, more than 1,547 Japanese planes had been destroyed in the Okinawa area, and 75 percent of the planes that sortied for Okinawa never returned to Japan. The Sixteenth destroyed or damaged more planes than any other AAA unit.

In addition to his duties as Colonel Merchant's assistant, Hodges was also assigned to guard duty in those foxholes he spoke of after the war. That was why all recruits were trained in the use of the marine fighting knife, or KA-BAR, because at some point it was assumed that either you or the marine in the next foxhole would need to use it. Hodges joked about starting to smoke in those foxholes out of boredom, but the truth was that he, like so many marines, smoked to allay his anxieties. New recruits—who had been adamant that they would never smoke—would yell out after being in combat for the first time, "Somebody gimme a cigarette." Hodges left Okinawa physically intact, but for the rest of his life he was unable to stop smoking.

Hodges received a Bronze Battle Star for his "excellent service while serving as a member of the operations and intelligence section." His commendation read, "Landing with the assault echelon in the Hagushi Beach area, by his outstanding professional attainments and tireless devotion to duty throughout extensive periods of enemy aerial alerts and extensive bombing attacks, he diligently collected data and prepared vital combat records, thereby contributing materially to the successful accomplishment of the battalion's mission."

But in his letters home, Hodges never mentioned his Bronze Star.

With the island still a dangerous place due to sporadic bombing raids, on June 21 primary hostilities on Okinawa ended. That summer the marines got a chance to interact with the Okinawan children. The kids won their hearts. The children were not as fearful of the marines as the adults were, and they made the marines laugh. The marines responded by giving the children any candy or rations they could spare. In addition to interacting with the children, the marines relaxed by playing baseball and "laughing and running like a bunch of little boys."

Hodges organized those baseball games for his battalion. He also played. At bat, "Moose," as the marines called Hodges, often bunted so he didn't hurt any of his fellow marines with a line drive. Hodges played catcher, but threw with his left arm to avoid injury. Except for the day Yankees star Bill Dickey flew in with a team of Major League players, Hodges faced mediocre competition.

Back in Brooklyn, Leo Durocher, fighting his own private war, assaulted a fan named John Christian, who had been heckling him. After a Dodgers security guard brought Christian behind the stands at Ebbets Field, Durocher hit him with a blackjack. Christian was hospitalized with a broken jaw and Durocher was charged with second-degree assault; but a jury acquitted him after Durocher testified that Christian's broken jaw was the result of his slipping and falling down.

Hodges had a harder time getting off Okinawa than Durocher did getting acquitted. On October 9, Hodges was still on Okinawa when a typhoon with 130 mph winds struck. U.S. forces had only a few hours' notice to strike all tents, lash down wooden structures, and, for fear of tidal waves, move all heavy equipment inland. Some took refuge in corrugated-steel Quonset huts, but the wind blew off a portion of the roof of one and rain poured inside. The typhoon severely damaged military installations, but no one was killed.

On Okinawa, Hodges developed a lifelong bond with his fellow marines. E. B. Sledge wrote that marines who participated in the war's terrible carnage later "had an intangible air of subdued, quiet detachment." As Riley Marietta, a driver for the Sixteenth, recalled, "I remember seeing dead Japanese officers . . . they were booby trapped and I saw a few blow up. I saw plenty of dead and wounded. . . . You had to be a little bit on the hard side or you might wind up

6. With the Giants' Alvin Dark talking to a group of marines wounded during the Korean War, April 20, 1951, the Polo Grounds. National Archives and Records Administration.

being a mess." Years later, in a darkened movie theater in Louisville, Hodges was seated next to *Long Island Newsday* writer Jack Lang as they watched a movie about the marines in the South Pacific. Lang recalled that every time a marine or an enemy soldier was killed, Hodges would silently mutter, "Amen."

On February 3, 1946, Sergeant Gil Hodges was honorably discharged. In his separation report, he no longer listed himself as a student; instead, under "occupation," he wrote, "Pro-baseball, Brooklyn." His locality preference, however, was still "Petersburg."

Under "reason," he needed just one word: "Home."

4

NEWPORT NEWS

Fitz was our manager at Newport News. . . . We were all kids and what we needed most was patience and encouragement. Fitz gave us both, and some laughs.

After Hodges was demobilized, Charlie drove to the railroad station at Vincennes to pick up his youngest son and bring him home to Petersburg. After two years of dehydrated potatoes, weevil-infested bread, and Spam, Irene's navy bean soup must have tasted especially good to Gil Hodges.

When Hodges left Petersburg for St. Joseph's, he was seventeen and had never been away from home before. Now he was a twenty-one-year-old marine ready to make up for lost time. When I asked his sister, Marjorie, how the war changed her brother, she said, "He partied more."

The first night Hodges was back in Petersburg, he borrowed Charlie's car to go to a dance in Jasper, about twenty miles away. When he was driving home, another car hit his. No one was hurt, but the driver's side door of his dad's car no longer opened. Hodges nervously waited up until Charlie awoke at 4:30 a.m. to go to work. When Hodges told his father what had happened, Charlie laughed, got into his car—through the passenger door—and drove off.

Hodges borrowed the car again the next night. "I was in Evansville," he later recalled, "and darned if some Marine doesn't run right into me. Now I couldn't get the door on the other side open. I went home and waited for dad to get up at 4:30 again. I told him the story, almost the same story I had brought home the night before. He was a little mad this time because he had to crawl through the window to get into the car. But he never said a word. He crawled through the window and drove off to the mine. . . . Not another word about the accident was ever mentioned."

Hodges's explanation of the accidents indicates that the other drivers were at fault. But according to Don Drysdale, who would be Hodges's roommate on the Dodgers, Hodges was a terrible driver. Hodges often drove Drysdale from Brooklyn to the Polo Grounds when the Dodgers played the Giants, and in his autobiography Drysdale wrote, "God Almighty! How could a man who was so smooth and graceful in every other aspect of life be so clumsy behind the wheel? He was one of those people who had the right foot on the accelerator and the left on the brake, usually at the same time. It drove me bananas."

Bob Harris, who lived next door to the Hodges family home on Fourteenth and Main in Petersburg, was seven years old when Hodges returned from Okinawa. Years later, Harris could still recall seeing the damage Hodges had caused to Charlie's car. Luckily, Hodges wasn't in Petersburg long enough to get into a third accident; by the end of February, he had left for the Dodgers' spring training camp.

In the spring of 1946 in Sanford, Florida, 150 young men, most of them returning soldiers, got a chance to show their skills; and if they made the cut, they received a Branch Rickey baseball education. Legend has it that Rickey sought Hodges out the day after he reported to camp. "What kind of glove did you bring along, young man?" Rickey asked. "I hope it was a catcher's mitt."

One thing that was surely not apocryphal from Hodges's first days in Sanford was his scouting report. From its very first words, it typecast Hodges for the rest of his life: "Nice guy. Should go all the way. Start him low. Is ahead of the ball a lot, but will learn. Great possibilities. Must smarten up with the bat. Only thing can keep him out of big league is physical mishap."

In Sanford, Rickey immersed Hodges in the catcher's position. He even assigned Hodges three roommates, all catchers: Ed Nulty, Charlie Ferrell, and Bruce Edwards. Less than a year older than Hodges, Edwards was the best of the three and by 1947 he would be on the National League All-Star team.

Unlike Edwards, Hodges was a work in progress. That spring, a veteran catcher from the Deadball Era, Bill Killefer, taught Hodges the fundamentals. Killefer was impressed that Hodges could squeeze his catcher's mitt with such control that he could direct the ball into his throwing hand to save a fraction of a second when he threw out a runner attempting to steal second base. After only a few weeks, Hodges was sent to Daytona Beach to finish spring training with the Montreal Royals, the Dodgers' top farm team, where Jackie Robinson was in his first season in the Dodgers organization. Beginning the following season, Robinson and Hodges would become Dodgers teammates for a decade. But in 1946 Hodges was not experienced enough to play at that level. He was sent on an exhibition tour with the Dodgers' B squad, managed by Dodgers coach Chuck Dressen. A decade later, Dressen would consider Hodges one of the best players in baseball—the kind one builds a team around—but in 1946 he didn't play Hodges much; and after Hodges hurt his shoulder in a collision at home plate in a game in Macon, Georgia, against the New York Yankees' B squad, Hodges didn't play at all as the team barnstormed north to Brooklyn.

Also traveling with the Dodgers was the team's batboy, Tod Parrott, the eight-year-old son of Dodgers traveling secretary Harold Parrott. Over the years, Hodges became one of Tod's favorite players. Tod had begged his mother to stay with the team after they broke camp in Daytona Beach, and his dedication to the Dodgers did not go unnoticed by the Yankee players when the two teams met in an exhibition game in Baltimore. The Yankees' second baseman, Joe Gordon, capturing the quaintness of the era, asked Tod to become the Yankees' batboy. "If you come over to us," Gordon said, "we'll give you a bat and a ball—and all the ice cream you can eat."

"No," replied Tod, "I'm a Dodger."

The Yankees and Dodgers didn't compete just when it came to batboys. On April 13 Hodges was on the bench at Ebbets Field getting a taste of just how hard fought any game—even a preseason exhibition game—was between the Dodgers and the Yankees. Hodges watched as Joe DiMaggio homered into the upper deck in the eighth inning to give the Yankees a 2–0 lead. But the Dodgers came from behind to win the game in the twelfth inning on a steal of home by Carl Furillo, who would one day be Hodges's road roommate. But Hodges was not close to being Major League–ready as a catcher, and after that game he was optioned to the Dodgers' Minor League Class B team in Newport News, Virginia.

The Dodgers' Newport News team played in the six-team Piedmont League (with Lynchburg, Norfolk, Portsmouth, Richmond, and Roanoke). Rickey sent Hodges to play at Newport News because their manager, John Fitzpatrick, was a former catcher with decades of experience. Rickey's instructions to Fitz, as the players called him, reveal how valuable Hodges's home run swing had made him. Rickey told Fitzpatrick that it didn't matter where his team finished in the standings; his only goal that season was to turn Hodges into a serviceable catcher.

Fitzpatrick followed orders. He sent off his best fielding catcher, Sam Calderone, to another one of the Dodgers' Class B teams and installed Hodges as his everyday catcher and eighth-place hitter. Calderone had been the starting catcher for Newport News in 1945 and was good enough to eventually make it to the Majors with the Giants.

As the season began, Hodges's fielding was terrible. Catching at a professional level was a lot more complicated than crouching down and catching his brother's fastballs under his dad's watchful eye. "For the first couple of weeks," Fitzpatrick said, "the fans threw stones at me from the stands. They hollered for Calderone."

Hodges asked Fitzpatrick to come to the ballpark early to teach him, and it was rough at first. Pitches down in the dirt gave Hodges "fits." Playing at night, under lights, was also a new experience and that took getting used to as well. Foul pops were a major challenge. But Fitz gave Hodges a simple rule to follow: "When the ball is hit in back of you, turn your back to the plate and keep the ball out in front of you. Its rotation will cause it to drop in towards you as you advance on it. If the ball is hit straight up over the plate or in fair territory, get directly under it with your hands outstretched and it will fade down and out into your hands."

Despite missing several games after a foul tip dislocated his right thumb against Norfolk on June 25 and after he was injured sliding into home plate on August 15 against Portsmouth, Hodges persevered. By season's end he was, according to Fitz, "pretty good" behind the plate. Rickey must have agreed. The next season when Hodges was catching for the Dodgers, Rickey sent Fitz a telegram congratulating him on a job well done. Even more than teaching Hodges the fundamentals of catching, Fitz had taught Hodges the value of patience. Decades later when Hodges managed, he and his coaching staff were willing to arrive early to work with any player who wanted to learn.

Hodges's roommate that season was a pitcher who never did make it to the Majors, Preston Elkins. But the player Hodges would come to know best from that team, and who would become his teammate for over a decade, was another pitcher, nineteen-year-old Clem Labine. When I spoke with him sixty years later, Labine joked, "Hodges befriended me that season because I was the only one on the team with a car."

Although it was clear to Labine that Hodges was still learning how to field his new position, Hodges's leadership skills—honed by his time in the Marine Corps—were already in evidence. If Hodges had personal doubts about his abilities, he kept those tucked away. The face he presented to his teammates— and especially his pitchers—was one of confidence and strength. Even at the age of twenty-two, no one was going to shove Gil Hodges around. "We looked up to him even then," Labine said. "He demanded attention, and people paid attention."

Hodges may have been the guy in charge on the field, but on team bus rides and late-night bull sessions the Newport News player you noticed was the first baseman, Kevin Joseph Aloysius Connors, a crew-cut, six-foot-five-inch string bean from Brooklyn. He was noted for flashing a calling card reading, "Kevin (Chuck) Connors, Affiliate Brooklyn Dodgers Baseball Club, Recitations, After-Dinner Speaker, Home Recordings for any Occasion, Free-Lance Writer." Connors could also hit: batting .293 that season, he led the league with seventeen home runs.

For Chuck Connors, life was theater, and he excelled at keeping his teammates in stitches. The man had "a gag for every situation and a ceaseless line of [banter]." Connors gave a spirited rendition of "Casey at the Bat," acted as a make-believe master of ceremonies for toasts while getting his fellow ball-players to pretend they were celebrities receiving some honor, and recorded it all on a reel-to-reel tape recorder so he could play it all back for his laughing teammates. And on those long bus rides back to Newport News after night games at Lynchburg, Roanoke, and Richmond, Connors would sit up front, entertaining his teammates with songs and jokes.

"Some of those trips would last all night," Hodges said. "The bus had hard seats with straight backs, and you couldn't sleep in them. Usually there would be a scramble to see who got into the bus first, and those that did would grab the aisle space and lie down. . . . I wouldn't like to do it again for $300 a month, and that was more than most of them got."

After the regular season ended, Newport News played the Roanoke Red Sox in a seven-game series for the 1946 Piedmont League championship. Roanoke won the first two games, but the Dodgers took the next four to win the title. The Dodgers won the final game, played in Roanoke on September 26, 4-1. In what would typify his career, Hodges played a crucial—but unspectacular—part in that game. In the top of the seventh, with the score tied 1-1, Hodges beat out a hit to deep short to lead off the inning, advanced to third base on two consecutive misplayed bunts, and scored what would prove to be the winning run on a sacrifice fly to left field.

The league's managers unanimously selected Hodges as the catcher on the Piedmont League All-Star team. Of the four unanimous selections—Hodges, shortstop Virgil Stallcup of the Roanoke Red Sox, pitcher Al Papai of the Lynchburg Cardinals, and outfielder John Zontini of Portsmouth—all but Zontini made it to the Majors. Although the Newport News team had several All-Star players (Hodges, Connors, second baseman Stan Wasiak, left fielder Maurice Santomauro, and pitcher Wayne Johnson) only Hodges and Connors played in the Majors.

Hodges merited selection to the All-Star team because his fielding had improved dramatically. Hodges led the Piedmont League catchers in assists (90) and fielding percentage (.983). In addition, despite his size, Hodges proved to be a heady base runner. For example, in the first game of a double-header against Lynchburg on July 11, Hodges noticed a flaw in either the pitcher's delivery or the catcher's technique and put on a running display to rival Ty Cobb. After singling to left field in the fifth inning, Hodges methodically stole second, stole third, and finished with a steal of home.

Hodges could surely run the bases, but his hitting power won ball games. On July 20 his three-run homer was the difference in a 7–4 win against Norfolk. And in two consecutive games late in the season, Hodges drove in the winning or tying runs. First, on August 28, in the eleventh inning against Norfolk, he hit a two-run walk-off home run for a 4-2 win. The next night, Hodges went three for four, including a lead-off bunt-single in the fifth inning (he scored on a Connors double) and a two-run double down the third base line in the eighth that tied the game at 5–5 and was the crucial hit in a rally that gave Newport a 6–5 win.

Hodges was batting over .300 early in the season, but his average dropped over the course of the hot southern summer as he caught almost every game. Hodges hit a respectable—especially for a catcher—.278 for the season with eight home runs. After the season, the Dodgers' scouting report on Hodges read: "Is good receiver, must learn to hit curve ball, but know he will in time. Great prospect. Smart. Great temperament. Has all the physical tools, and should make a great catcher. Has improved 200%. A great pupil, came out early to practice catching fouls."

Expanding on Hodges hitting liabilities in Newport News, Clem Labine said, "Hodges left the outside part of the plate open and didn't hit the other way." But despite his continued frustrations trying to hit a curve ball, Hodges's "temperament" kept him on an even keel. The bus rides, the lack of sleep, the monotony of a long season far away from home were only minor inconveniences for Hodges. He didn't want to play in the low Minors again, but life on the road with Chuck Connors was a lot more fun than having bombs dropping all around you. And in Newport News, Hodges' quiet but upbeat disposition radiated brightly enough for the fans to notice. That season, the Newport News fans voted Gil Hodges the team's most popular player.

In a ceremony before the team's last game of the regular home season, the legend of Hodges as both a nice guy and a strong hitter grew as he received a prize for being "the most popular" and gave the fans something back, going two for three with a home run and three RBIs.

For all but the greatest hitters, 1,000 to 1,500 Minor League at bats (two to three seasons) are needed to gain the skills to perform on a Major League level. But because Hodges had been on the Dodgers' Major League roster at the end of the 1943 season, his Minor League career would be limited to the 406 at bats he accumulated in 1946 in Newport News, and he never learned to hit a curve ball in the Minors.

During World War II, to protect players who went into military service, Major League Baseball established a rule that after three years had passed since a player first was placed on a Major League roster, he could not be optioned to

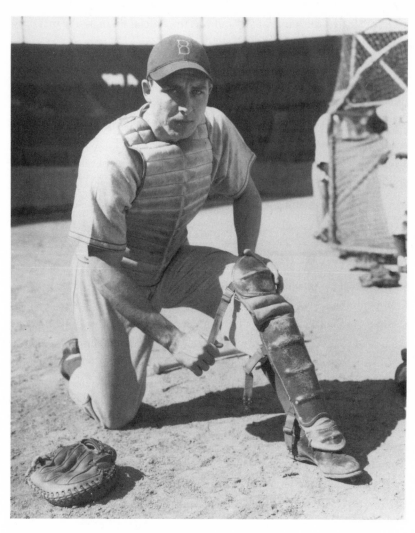

7. As a catcher, 1947 or 1948. Author's collection.

the Minors without first being subject to waivers. Hodges's month with the Dodgers in 1943 meant that he spent the first two years (1944 and 1945) of this three-year period in the Marine Corps, and his third in Newport News. Because Branch Rickey Jr. had insisted Hodges not sign a Minor League contract with Olean, the Dodgers had to keep Hodges on the Major League roster or risk losing him on waivers.

In the winter of 1946-47, whenever the Dodgers tested the waters and asked revocable waivers on Hodges, another club claimed him. As a result, to avoid losing him, Rickey Sr. was forced to promote Hodges to the Majors prematurely. For the 1947 season, rather than having the opportunity to play regularly in the Minors, Hodges was heading back to Brooklyn, where his immediate role would be more spectator than player.

HOME
Brooklyn (1947–57)

5

HANGING ON

In 1947, I had a great seat on the bench.

The three-year rule gave Gil Hodges admission to a remarkable era in New York City baseball history, when either the Dodgers or the Giants played the Yankees in the World Series seven times in the ten-year period from 1947 to 1956 and Jackie Robinson became the first black player in the Major Leagues in the twentieth century.

In the spring of 1947, the Dodgers and their top Minor League team, the Montreal Royals, trained in Cuba, where Rickey hoped the lack of Jim Crow restrictions would reduce the chances of a racial incident that might derail Robinson's transition into the Majors. But Rickey misjudged the intensity of the reaction of the Dodgers' southern players.

Although Robinson was still on the Royals' roster, the players sensed that he would start the season with the Dodgers. As a result, when the Dodgers and Royals played some exhibition games in Panama, at least three of the Dodgers' players (All-Star right fielder Dixie Walker; his roommate, backup catcher Bobby Bragan; and pitcher Kirby Higbe) signed a petition saying they would not play if Robinson was their teammate. Of the three, Dixie Walker— the older brother of Harry Walker, whose racist views motivated Clendenon to play for Hodges in 1969—was the most popular.

Hodges refused to sign the petition. Thanks to his teenage friend Chuck Harmon, playing baseball with a black man was nothing new to Hodges. And, from the very beginning of the ten years they would spend as teammates, Jackie Robinson "liked and admired Hodges."

Unlike Durocher, who saw Robinson as his meal ticket ("He's going to put money in your pockets and money in mine"), Hodges developed a relationship with Robinson based upon mutual admiration. Hodges wrote that Robinson was "the most complete offensive player" he ever saw. Robinson, in turn, disliking vile language and the cruder forms of locker room behavior, appreciated Hodges's clean-living ways. In his autobiography, Robinson wrote, "I listened to Gil because I had a tremendous amount of respect for him."

In 1955, in a heated moment in the Dodgers' locker room, that respect would be put to the test. Back in 1947, according to Dodger press secretary Harold Parrott, "A lot of the players, Reese and Hodges particularly, respected what . . . [Robinson] was doing. They were polite and cordial, but definitely not pally with him."

After games, Robinson and his white teammates went their separate ways. But at some point early in their friendship, and especially after Hodges married in 1948, the Robinsons and Hodgeses began to spend time together away from the ballpark. Like Hodges, Robinson was no night owl, and the two men had much in common.

"Gil was one of the first and only ones we socialized with," Robinson's wife, Rachel, told me. "He was quiet, friendly, warm—you could count on him. And you didn't have to ask for help from Gil . . . he anticipated what you needed and was there for you."

Even in their first season together, Hodges felt close enough to Jack, as Hodges called Robinson, to needle him. During a Dodgers road game at Wrigley Field in 1947, thousands of black men and women proudly came up to Chicago's largely white North Side dressed in their Sunday best to see Robinson play. Before the game, standing next to Robinson, Hodges nodded up toward the stands. Straight-faced, Hodges deadpanned, "All your friends in on passes you left for 'em, Jack?"

After the 1953 season, when Robinson put together an integrated team to barnstorm in the South in defiance of Jim Crow laws, out of Robinson's then current white Dodgers teammates only Hodges joined him on that tour. A few years before, when the Dodgers were playing in Cincinnati and Hodges received an anonymous letter criticizing him for "living in the same hotels,

8. With Branch Rickey, Jackie Robinson, and Gene Hermanski, late 1940s. AP Photo/stf.

using the same showers . . . with a bunch of 'niggers,'" Hodges told Sam Lacy of the *Baltimore Afro American* that he deposited that letter where it belonged, "in the toilet."

A one-two punch knocked out the Panama petition. First, in a late-night team meeting, Durocher gave his players a verbal shellacking, "I don't care if the guy is yellow or black, or if he has stripes like a fuckin' zebra. I'm the manager of this team, and I say he plays." The next day, Rickey met with the protestors one-on-one vowing to trade them as soon as practicable unless they relented. Higbe was soon playing in Pittsburgh; and after the season, Walker was there as well. Bragan remained with the Dodgers organization, becoming the manager of their Ft. Worth, Texas, affiliate in 1948.

On April 14, the day the Dodgers' 1947 season opened, a New Yorker had numerous entertainment choices: hear Cab Calloway and his band perform on Broadway; read Laura Hobson's best-selling novel, *Gentlemen's Agreement*; or watch Jackie Robinson step onto the field to play first base at Ebbets Field,

9. At Ebbets Field, late 1940s. Brooklyn Public Library—Brooklyn Collection.

breaking baseball's gentlemen's agreement to ban blacks from participating. Hodges was watching from the dugout as the Dodgers beat the Boston Braves, 5–3.

Although Hodges spent most of his time on the bench that year, Petersburg was proud. When the Dodgers visited St. Louis to play the Cardinals that season, Petersburg residents purchased 455 tickets to see one of the games, and many cars "made the trek" to St. Louis. The tradition continued for several seasons. Even with the hometown support, the 1947 season was a long one for Hodges. As the third-string catcher behind Edwards and Bragan, Hodges appeared in only twenty-eight games, accumulating just seventy-seven at bats. Yet he had his moments—good and bad.

On May 11, in the fifth inning of the first game of a double header in Philadelphia, with the Dodgers already trailing 6–0, Hodges replaced Edwards behind the plate. On the first pitch thrown, Hodges tried to pick off the Phillies' runner on second but heaved the ball into right-center field, and the runner scored. In the *Daily News*, Dick Young, near the beginning of his influential career covering the New York sports scene, wrote that it was good Hodges was put into the game, because "the boy could use a few lessons."

In June, after the Dodgers had lost seven of eight games and appeared to be fading out of pennant contention, Edwards injured his hand and couldn't play. As a result, from June 16 until June 30 Hodges got his only chance of the season to play consistently. During that stretch, the Dodgers won eleven of fourteen games. The founder of *The Sporting News*, J. G. Taylor Spink, wrote, "Without anyone shouting about his work, Hodges held the [eventual] pennant winners up."

Three games behind the National League lead when Hodges started to play regularly, the Dodgers were in a virtual tie for first place when Edwards returned. But, as would be typical throughout his career, Hodges was given little credit. Because he was surrounded by dynamic players like Robinson, whose twenty-one-game hitting-streak coincided with Hodges's presence in the starting lineup, few took notice of him.

Given a chance to play regularly, Hodges's hitting improved. On June 18 at Wrigley Field in his first two at bats facing the right-hander Hank Borowy, Hodges failed to get a hit and struck out once with Borowy throwing mostly curves. But in the seventh, Borowy became the first of many pitchers to learn that it was not easy to throw a fastball past Hodges, as he hit the first home run of his career, a 370-foot drive that landed fifteen feet behind the ivy-covered wall in left field. The homer, which proved to be the game winner, was particularly impressive because the wind was blowing in from left field that day.

On June 26, Hodges had two doubles in an 8–6 Dodgers win over the Boston Braves, but Edwards soon returned and Hodges was back on the bench.

That season Hodges shared a room with another young Dodgers player who also spent most of the season on the bench, the left-handed-hitting Duke Snider. Sensing their frustration, Rickey called them into his office and told them to be patient, to continue to work hard, because they were "the Dodgers' power combination of the future." After leaving Rickey's office, Hodges said to Snider, "If we're so good, how come we're not playing more?"

However frustrating the 1947 season was for Hodges, it was torture for Durocher. Before the season started, Commissioner Albert "Happy" Chandler had suspended him for one year for "conduct detrimental to baseball." Supposedly, Durocher had been consorting with gamblers. Durocher compared his feelings watching his replacement, Burt Shotton, manage the Dodgers to the pennant to "watching your mother-in-law go over a cliff in your new car."

In 1947 Hodges had ample time on the bench to watch Shotton. At sixty-two, wearing street clothes during games (which prohibited him from going onto the field during a game to change pitchers or argue a call), Shotton was often described as "kindly" and "old." But Shotton "knew how to reach a player with his sharp tongue," which, according to Hodges, "helped some players, and didn't help others."

On September 26, to celebrate the Dodgers' winning the 1947 National League pennant, a motorcade watched by a cheering crowd of nearly half a million drove down Flatbush Avenue from Grand Army Plaza to Borough Hall where Brooklyn Borough President John Cashmore presented each player with an engraved watch. Standing on the podium, all the Dodgers appear solemn except one, Hodges, who, contrary to his classic visage as a manager, was smiling from ear to ear.

Perhaps the other Dodgers players weren't smiling because they knew their Series opponent, the Yankees, with stars like DiMaggio, Phil Rizzuto, and Tommy Henrich, were a great team. Several players (Hugh Casey, Cookie Lavagetto, Pete Reiser, Reese, and Walker) had been with the Dodgers in 1941 when they had lost the Series to the Yankees. The 1947 Yankees not only had the best record in baseball but also tied an American League record for consecutive wins with nineteen, and unlike most of their subsequent

Series match-ups, the Yankees' pitching advantage over the Dodgers was not in their starters but in their bullpen, as the Yankees' star relief pitcher, Joe Page, proved to be the difference in a thrilling Series that went the full seven games.

Hodges didn't play in the first six games. Finally, in the seventh inning of the seventh game with the Dodgers trailing by two runs and two out and no one on, Shotton sent Hodges in to pinch-hit against Page, a dominating left-handed power pitcher. Although Hodges feasted on left-handers later in his career, he was still a neophyte then, and Page was at the height of his prowess with "the guts of a burglar, and for emergencies . . . a supply of graphite oil on the inner side of his belt."

Page's best pitch was his fastball, but against Hodges—a pure fastball hitter— Page threw his only slider of the game. Hodges struck out, one of thirteen successive batters Page set down in five innings of relief to preserve the win and to give the Yankees another championship.

After the Series, Hodges returned to Petersburg, where he attended the high school football team's last home game of the season; at halftime he was presented with a shotgun for hunting (a hobby he had come to find relaxing) and a set of luggage for his travels as a Major Leaguer. That winter, hoping to complete his college degree, Hodges took classes at nearby Oakland City College where, despite being a professional baseball player, he played on the college's basketball team. In a sociology class he took that winter, Hodges didn't say much. Yet, according to Donald Hume, who sat next to Hodges, when the instructor called on him, he was "pretty sharp." In between classes, they would go outside, Hodges would take out his catcher's mitt, and Hume would pitch to him while they shared their concerns about their fathers, who were both miners. Between his two years at St. Joseph's before the war and his part-time study at Oakland City, Hodges would accumulate three years' worth of course credit, but he never completed his college degree.

During spring training in 1948, it was reported that Hodges injured his ankle in a play at first base, but Dodgers batboy Tod Parrott told a reporter that Hodges had really been hurt playing a game of pickup basketball. Tod's dad, Harold, still the Dodgers' press secretary, was not pleased when the *New York Post* ran a headline with Tod's injury correction. Parrott and Durocher, now back from his suspension, gave Tod a stern talking-to. Hodges told Tod "to forget about it because it was okay by him."

Despite going through an 0 for 32 slump in spring training, Hodges proved to be an excellent fielding catcher, and with Bruce Edwards experiencing arm problems, Durocher installed Hodges as his starting catcher. Hodges, usually batting seventh or eighth, hit well enough in tantalizing bursts to keep the job: in a two-day period in early June, Hodges drove in seven runs, including a three-run homer off the upper-left-field façade in Ebbets Field.

But on June 30, after nearly a decade in the Negro Leagues, Roy Campanella was called up from the Dodgers' Minor League affiliate in the American Association, and from day one he was the best catcher in baseball. In his first twelve Major League at bats, he had nine hits, including two home runs. Over the next nine seasons, Campanella was the league's MVP three times.

Despite publicly stating he "wouldn't trade Hodges for any two catchers in baseball," in private Durocher had been pushing Rickey to bring Campanella up to the Majors since the beginning of the season. With Durocher lobbying for Campanella, rather than simply bench Hodges, or lose him to another team via waivers, Rickey started to talk up Hodges, hoping to increase his sale or trade value. "Hodges . . . [is] going to be one of the greatest catchers of all time. Nobody can say that he isn't a $300,000 ballplayer. . . . He's going to win the Most Valuable Player Award," Rickey said. "Campanella's a fine boy, too."

Durocher won the battle but lost the war. That July, in no small part because Durocher forced Rickey's hand regarding Campanella, Rickey pushed Durocher out the door. Having seen Shotton lead the Dodgers to a pennant, Rickey figured he could save himself a lot of aggravation and money—Durocher was the highest-paid manager in baseball—and still win. Rickey talked New York Giants owner Horace Stoneham into assuming Durocher's contract and literally, overnight, the Lip was managing the Dodgers' bitterest rival. But that May, in one of his final player moves with the Dodgers, Durocher told Hodges to start working out at first base.

"That was it," Hodges wrote. "The whole speech." Hodges knew if he wanted to play regularly, first base was his best shot. Preston Ward had won the first base job in spring training, but by June it was clear he was a journeyman.

"Preston Ward can run like a frightened fawn," Bill Roeder wrote. "His trouble now, is that he's starting to hit like one."

There is a misconception that first base is an easy position to play; it's where you put the worst fielder on your little league team. But playing first base well in the Major Leagues is a formidable challenge, and catchers don't necessarily make the transition to first base well. Anyone who saw Mike Piazza, one of the best-hitting catchers in baseball history, struggle to make that transition can attest to this. Late in his career, Hall of Famer George Brett, a Gold Glove winner at third base, was asked to play first. "Whoever says this is an easy position doesn't know what he's talking about," Brett said. "Just getting your hands and feet to work right is tough enough."

Hodges's transition to first base succeeded because of his athleticism and attitude. Hodges told J. G. Taylor Spink, "I came to play, not to sit around. I want to play and play every day more than anything else in the world. And if I can help us win, I'll play anywhere."

Spinks was taken by Hodges's sincerity, especially when Hodges added, "Stan Musial was one of the finest outfielders in baseball, but I watched him teach himself to play first base because it would help his team win. If a player of Stan Musial's ability is willing . . . to play anywhere for the team's good, even though it's a little tougher for him, why should I think twice about it?"

Hodges's preparation at first base involved nothing more than having Ray Blades, a Dodgers coach, hit ground balls to him. Though no one gave Hodges specific fielding instruction, he soon proved to be a natural: his size made him an excellent target, he was surprisingly quick around the bag; and he brought a shortstop's mentality to the position, aggressively going after balls hit between first and second.

Durocher said, "I put a first-baseman's glove on . . . Hodges, and told him to have some fun. Three days later I looked up and—wow—I was looking at the best first-baseman I'd seen since Dolph Camilli." Jackie Robinson, the Dodgers' first baseman in 1947, made a more realistic comment, saying Hodges was playing first base "just like he'd been there all his life. . . . He's got a real stretch. He has a little trouble shifting his feet on bad throws and in picking balls out of the dirt. That's to be expected. But that stretch—it's the thing you need most at first. You either have it or you don't. And he's got it."

Those first few weeks playing first base were tough, but Hodges made light of it: "I had a [hard] time getting my bearings. My feet didn't know where to go on a lot of plays, and I couldn't tell them."

Hodges realized he was at a disadvantage being a right-handed first baseman, but said "there were plenty of right-handers doing the job in spite of that." For Hodges, playing first base presented two difficult elements: "One is the ground ball that is hit between me and the second baseman. I have to decide whether to field it or cover first base; and I still have trouble with that one. I don't go in the hole as often as I should. The other one is the first-to-second-to-first double play. For a right-handed first baseman, that is always a hard play."

The transition to first base didn't help Hodges's hitting: it took him seventeen at bats as a first baseman before getting his first hit. But in a doubleheader in Cincinnati on July 17, Hodges broke out with six hits (five consecutively), including two doubles. That night, Roscoe McGowen, who covered the Dodgers for the *New York Times*, wrote, "Gil's play at first base, while not too good since he took over the post, was next to extraordinary today."

Hodges also showed his baseball smarts that day. In the second inning of the second game, Hodges was at bat when Campanella attempted to steal second base. Hodges stepped across home plate just as Cincinnati catcher Dewey Williams tried, but failed, to throw Campanella out. Williams claimed Hodges should have been called for interference; but Hodges's maneuver was subtle enough to impact Williams's throw, but not so bold as to merit a call. Williams was so incensed he "laid his hands" on umpire Frank Dascoli, who threw him out of the game. Hodges's old nemesis, Johnny Vander Meer, was also tossed for arguing, as was Reds manager Johnny Neun. The Dodgers scored three runs that inning and won both ends of the doubleheader.

Although the Dodgers were in contention until late in the season (they finished seven and a half games behind the pennant-winning Boston Braves), 1948 was a transitional year for them. Rickey had amassed a core of outstanding players and had repositioned them to make the Dodgers the best team in the National League for the long term. After the 1947 season, Walker had been traded to Pittsburgh for pitcher Preacher Roe, who became a mainstay of the starting rotation, and shortstop Billy Cox. With Reese a fixture at shortstop, Rickey moved Cox to third base.

With a cannon for an arm, Cox was an outstanding fielder but had an annoying habit: after catching a hard-hit grounder, he would then "stand there with the ball and drive everybody nuts. . . . Hodges at first base would be yelling, 'Throw the ball!'" yet Cox would wait so he could "shoot the runner out by . . . one step. . . . He never missed."

Center fielder Carl Furillo moved to right to replace Walker and was soon playing Ebbets Field's multi-angled right-field wall with consummate skill. Duke Snider took over in center, combining with Hodges to form a lefty-righty hitting combination that would power the Dodgers. Although Eddie Mathews and Henry Aaron would eventually break their record, Hodges and Snider would combine to hit more home runs than any other pair of teammates in National League history.

Hodges was at first base because Robinson, who had played there in 1947 as a way of protecting him from being spiked by opposition base runners, had been moved to his more natural position at second base. Robinson replaced second baseman Eddie Stanky who—despite Durocher's protests—had been traded to the Boston Braves. Stanky was a smart, aggressive punch hitter with an uncanny ability to draw walks, and Durocher loved him.

The Stanky trade was Rickey's way of sending a message that he—not Durocher—was in charge. Reporters upset Rickey whenever they asked him what Durocher thought about a trade Rickey had made. Rickey replied, "If someone will tell me where he is, and how I can reach him, I might ask him. But it's not too important that I should. I am the winter manager. . . . Leo is a great tactician but hardly a trade-maker."

Hodges had a ringside seat for the battle between Durocher and Rickey over when to bring Campanella up and the trading of Stanky. But the lesson Hodges should have learned, had he not been so personally involved in the outcome, was that a manager with the goal of winning in the short term is not the person who should be making trade decisions. That is best left to a general manager with a long-term perspective—the winter manager—as Rickey had done in establishing one of the strongest catcher, second baseman, shortstop, and center fielder combinations in baseball history as Campanella, Robinson, Reese, and Snider all would be enshrined in Cooperstown. The only other team with equivalent strength up the middle was the pre–World War II Yankees with Bill Dickey, Joe Gordon, Phil Rizzuto, and Joe DiMaggio.

Nineteen forty-eight was a year of firsts for Hodges. He played first base for the first time in his Major League career, and on June 16 he was booed at Ebbets Field for the first time. That day, in the fifth inning against the Reds, Hodges was on first with a single. The next batter hit a grounder to the shortstop, Red Stallcup, who threw to Bobby Adams at second base. As Adams was about to relay a throw to first to complete the double play, Hodges, who outweighed Adams by thirty pounds, slid into the second baseman hard with a "football block." Adams had to be carried off the field on a stretcher and not only missed the rest of the series, but was unable to travel to Boston to play the Braves.

Cincinnati manager Johnny Neun rushed onto the field to argue that Hodges should have been called out for running outside the base path. Most of the players on the Cincinnati bench followed Neun onto the field. No fisticuffs resulted, but tensions were high since Adams had just returned to the starting lineup for the first time in a month after recovering from a twisted right knee and a pulled groin. When Hodges came out to play first base in the top of the sixth, the Brooklyn fans booed him for the first (and only) time in his career.

"I deserved it," Hodges said. "I saw that Adams was going to cross the bag after he got the throw, moving from second toward third. It called for me to slide on my left side, something I do badly. Just as I was about to slide, I decided I couldn't slide that way, and it ended up with me diving headfirst into the base. I hit Adams in a body block."

X-rays later showed Adams suffered no fractures, but Hodges was so concerned about Adams that he visited the Reds' clubhouse after the game to inquire about his condition. (Adams eventually recovered.)

Hodges felt he deserved to be booed not because he injured Adams—in Hodges's mind, injuries were part of the game—but because of the way he slid into him. "I will take out the second baseman on double plays every time, if I can," Hodges said. "I absolutely must do it; I must break up the double play. But it has to be done properly."

To Hodges, properly meant it was okay to hit the second baseman, but only from the thighs down. And it didn't matter how you hit him, Hodges said: "With your legs, your spikes, your body. Cut down the man. Use your foot to trip him up. Flip him in the air. If you can get him up in the air, he may throw the ball away."

The body block on Adams was not a one-time event. Despite his nice guy reputation, Hodges ran the bases aggressively, and by the mid-1950s Hodges, along with Willie Mays, Don Hoak, and Daryl Spencer, was one of the league's most feared base runners. But Hodges paid a price. Pitchers, especially the Giants' Sal "The Barber" Maglie, threw at him with impunity in retaliation.

That off-season, on December 26, 1948, Hodges married Joan Lombardi, and for the rest of his life Brooklyn would be home. Joan grew up in the East New York section of Brooklyn. The daughter of Francesco, a butcher, and Olga, a housewife, she graduated from Girls Commercial High School in 1947 and went to work at Macy's. Even before meeting Hodges, in her nightly prayers Joan, who was Catholic, asked God to help the Dodgers win.

On a rainy night in the spring of 1948, Joan visited the home of Peggy and Ben Chase, who owned a home on Hawthorne Street within walking distance of Ebbets Field and rented rooms to Dodgers players. Peggy, who worked with Joan at Macy's, was well acquainted with Ed Miksis, an outgoing player who was renting from them that season. But that night, Joan met Miksis's more subdued roommate, who, Miksis joked, was so "shy . . . the only reason he wears a glove is that he doesn't want to be different, and attract a lot of attention."

When Joan was ready to leave, Hodges wasn't so shy. "I'll take her home," he said, hailing Joan a cab and joining her for the ride back to East New York. Before the ride was over, Hodges had asked Joan for a date. Despite already being engaged, Joan agreed. On their first date, they saw singer Jane Frohman at the Riviera, a nightclub in New Jersey. Their next date was a movie, *The Bells of St. Mary*. After that, "it was a date almost every night." By Christmas, Joan had the kind of holiday present most Brooklyn girls could only dream of—the Dodgers' starting first baseman. Although Charlie, Irene, and Marjorie didn't attend the wedding, which took place in Brooklyn, Bob was there to serve as best man. (By then, Bob's hopes for a Major League career had ended when he developed a dead arm.)

In January of 1949 the newlyweds traveled to Petersburg so Charlie and Irene could meet Joan. In February, Mr. and Mrs. Gil Hodges left for the Dodgers' new training facility on a former navy base in Vero Beach, Florida.

6

BREAKING THROUGH

Hitting is a physical act, but it's also a mental one. The batter must use his brain to conquer ... fear, which, like all other fears, doesn't stand up too well against logic.

For Hodges, the former naval base in Vero Beach, with its palm trees, Quonset huts, and regimentation, was reminiscent of boot camp in San Diego. The commanding officer at Rickey University was a meticulous teacher who schooled his players in baseball fundamentals in an insular environment removed from Florida's Jim Crow laws.

The military-style surroundings were apropos for Hodges. He was in a battle to hold onto his job. In an era when twenty-seven Minor League players were clamoring for every available Major League job, Hodges's competitors that spring were Dee Fondy and Chuck Connors. After Hodges had hit just .249 with only eleven home runs in 1948, they had a chance, since Shotton, back as the Dodgers' manager, said he couldn't go with a .250 hitter at first base. It was not a good sign that in the final weeks of the 1948 season, Shotton had replaced Hodges with a left-handed pinch hitter when the Dodgers trailed late in games and a right-hander was on the mound.

That winter, Connors had sent Rickey a letter reading, "They say all men have blind spots; perhaps your blind spot is first base." But Connors was more entertainer than ballplayer and would have only one at bat during the regular season (he hit a dribbler to the mound for a double play), and he was in the Minors the next day. With Fondy also proving unsatisfactory, Rickey considered trading for a veteran first baseman such as his former St. Louis star Johnny Mize. When spring training ended, Hodges was still the starting first baseman, but it was more for a lack of a viable alternative than his having won the job. Yet Hodges had his supporters.

Clyde Sukeforth, the scout who was instrumental in Jackie Robinson's signing, was then a Dodgers coach. Sukeforth believed in Hodges's abilities. "I felt pretty low," Hodges later said, "but all the while, Sukey kept saying to me: 'You'll be the one. You'll be the regular first baseman.'" Most important, Rickey had faith in Hodges.

"I would like some first base insurance. But if Gil Hodges hits only .275 for us—not an unreasonable expectation—he will be a great first baseman. All he has to do is meet the ball a little oftener. He can play any place around the infield. If Reese should break a leg at short, I wouldn't be afraid to send Gil to shortstop. He would do well there, I'm sure. He was a third baseman when I found him. I made a catcher out of him, and now he's a first baseman."

Rickey brought one of his favorite former players, Hall of Famer George Sisler, to Vero Beach to work with Hodges. But the man Hodges would later give credit to for helping him improve his swing was, surprisingly, Burt Shotton.

"I'm anxious to work with Gil Hodges," Shotton told J. G. Taylor Spink, who had come down to Vero Beach that winter to fish with Rickey and Shotton. "Why should an agile, strong boy like that hit .290, with seven homers and 25 runs batted in during the month of June [of 1948]," wondered Shotton, "and then slump off? He got confused, and was changing his batting style too much, that was all. He will straighten out, and be one of the good hitters in the game."

As the team traveled back to Brooklyn that spring, an exhibition game in Macon, Georgia, proved transformative. While watching Hodges taking batting practice, Shotton noticed he was not keeping his eye on the ball as he started his swing. Shotton asked Hodges, "Do you know what you're doing?"

Hodges's head, along with his entire body, was pulling left as he swung. Hodges had fallen back to his old habit of stepping in the bucket. Shotton suggested Hodges hold his head rigid (to aid his focus on the pitch) as he strode to meet the ball. With that tip, Hodges's hitting improved. On April 17, in an exhibition game against the Yankees, Hodges hit a game-winning grand slam home run against Joe Page on a pitcher's count of one ball and two strikes. Only eighteen months before, Page had overpowered Hodges in the World Series.

Hodges soon came into his own as a hitter, especially against lefties. By mid-May he was among the league leaders with a .321 batting average and would soon embark on a nineteen-game hitting streak, the longest in the National League in 1949. And Hodges was not just stringing together meaningless hits. On June 1 in the ninth inning against the Giants, Hodges's home run into the upper deck at the Polo Grounds tied the game, and the Dodgers won in extra innings. On August 30 at Ebbets Field, the Pirates, leading by a run in the ninth, made the mistake of pitching to Hodges with one out and a runner on first. Pirates veteran pitcher Murry Dickson got Hodges to swing and miss two curve balls to start the at bat. After Dickson wasted a pitch, he tried another curve. This time Hodges was ready. He hit a towering drive into the lower left-field deck for a two-run walk-off home run to give the Dodgers the win.

Hodges's fielding prowess also won games. In St. Louis on May 9, the Dodgers held on to an 8–7 win thanks to Hodges's "miraculous catch." In the bottom of the ninth, with one out and the tying run on third, St. Louis pinch hitter Ed Sauer "walloped a screamer about three feet fair along the first-base line. It looked like a certain double but Hodges, with perfect timing, speared the ball. This was the game-saving play."

Hodges's improvement came just in time. On May 18, the day before Hodges's nineteen-game hitting streak began, Rickey traded for first base insurance in the form of the Pirates' veteran Johnny Hopp, a .296 career hitter; but the trade was soon voided and Hopp was sent back to Pittsburgh.

That June, in a game against the Pirates at Forbes Field, Hodges lead the Dodgers to a come-from-behind win while accomplishing one of baseball's most prized feats—hitting for the cycle. It was a significant victory because it moved the Dodgers into first place, ahead of the Cardinals, their rival in a pennant race that would not be decided until the final day of the season. In the first inning against right-handed starter Bob Chesnes, Hodges came to bat with the bases loaded and no one out; he struck out looking. But the Dodgers scored twice to take a 2–0 lead. It didn't last long. Brooklyn's starting pitcher, Ralph Branca, gave up five runs in the bottom of the first. In the third, a barrage of hits, including a single by Hodges, knocked Chesnes out of the game; the Pirates sent in a left-handed fastball pitcher, Cliff Chambers. Batting for the second time that inning, Hodges greeted

Chambers with a double as Brooklyn scored nine runs to retake the lead. In the bottom of the third, Pittsburgh scored twice, but Hodges responded with a three-run homer off Chambers to seemingly put the game out of reach. But Branca decided he could coast and just "throw it down the middle," and Pittsburgh scored two more runs to draw within striking distance. But in the seventh, Hodges tripled, driving in a run and sending Chambers to the showers. In the ninth, Hodges added a solo home run for his sixth RBI of the game. Branca—despite giving up five homers and ten runs—got the complete-game victory, 17–10. Shortly after this game, in a clear sign he had broken through, *The Sporting News*, then baseball's Bible, called him "one of the best first basemen in the league."

Despite his mild demeanor, Shotton was tough with his players. That August, Carl Furillo was in a hitting slump and asked Shotton for a day off. But with the Dodgers in a tight pennant race, Shotton initially turned Furillo down and embarrassed him publicly. "How does a man expect to make any money out of this game," Shotton asked the press, "when he doesn't want to play every day?"

Robinson, Reese, and Hodges all felt they needed of a day off, but after seeing Shotton's reaction to Furillo, "none would have dared to ask for it." Hodges and Robinson played in every game that season—two of only seven National Leaguers to do so. In early July, Hodges was fifth in the league in hitting with a .325 batting average but ended the season at .285. (Furillo, playing in 142 games, hit .322.) Seeing how Shotton treated his players as "unbreakable, untiring, uncomplaining mechanism[s]," Hodges would make sure to give his players an occasional day off when he became a manager.

In 1949 the All-Star Game was played at Ebbets Field. Although the midsummer classic was an exhibition game, winning it was a matter of fierce pride between the two leagues. The Dodgers proudly sent seven players to the game: Branca, Roe, Newcombe, Reese, Robinson, Campanella, and Hodges.

Johnny Mize, then playing for the Giants, started the game at first base but played only three innings, the minimum required of all starters. Hodges replaced Mize as a pinch runner in the third and played the rest of the game. Hodges handled himself adequately at bat, bouncing out in the fifth, singling in the sixth, and reaching base in the eighth on an error. But the at bat in that game that Hodges never forgot was not his own, but that of Stan Musial.

Hodges considered Musial to be the best hitter he ever saw and he watched Musial's at bats with care, hoping to learn from him.

Robinson led off the third inning with a walk and broke for second on an attempted steal with Musial at bat. When Robinson broke for second, American League shortstop Eddie Joost ran over to cover the bag. The American League's defensive play—to have the shortstop (as opposed to the second baseman) cover second base on a steal attempt—was the standard play since Musial (a left-handed hitter) logically would pull the ball to the right side of the infield if he made contact. But Musial shifted his feet to direct his swing toward the spot Joost had just vacated. The result was a single through the shortstop hole. "In All-Star games," Hodges later wrote, "there is very little use of strategy. Everyone is pretty much on his own." To Hodges, this made Musial's split-second reaction to Robinson's breaking for second all the more impressive because not only was Musial a power hitter with the ability to cut down on his swing and go the other way, but no one had called for a hit and run; Musial had just intuitively reacted.

Another great hitter, Ted Williams, made the defensive play of the game. In the second inning with the bases loaded, Newcombe lined a shot to deep left field that looked like a sure double that would score three runs. But Williams, considered an average fielder, caught it and only one run scored (tagging up from third base). Ironically, Williams's great catch would stand in memorable contrast to Hodges's play on a "freak hit" later in the game. In the fourth inning, with the National League leading, 5–4, and runners on first and second for the American League, Joost, fooled by a Newcombe pitch, managed to make contact with the end of his bat to produce "the luckiest hit ever made in an All-Star game." The ball "squirted off like a miscued billiard ball, did a dance towards Hodges at first base and then at the last moment—just as if it had eyes—ran away from Hodges, caromed off his fist and dribbled into right field, scoring both runners and putting the American League in front to stay." Joost's bouncer was ruled a hit. After the game, National League manager Billy Southworth said, "That thing Eddie Joost hit off Newcombe . . . was the break of the game. Nobody could tell which way it was going to bounce. Hodges made a great try for it and didn't miss by much." Those two runs gave the American League a 6–5 lead, and they went on to win the game, 11–7.

After the All-Star Game, the Dodgers and Cardinals remained in a close battle for the pennant for the rest of the season. On Friday, September 23, 1949, after defeating the Cardinals two out of three games in St. Louis, the Dodgers flew back to New York. Steak was served. Pitcher Rex Barney, an Irish Catholic, noticed Harold Parrott, then the team's traveling secretary, staring at his steak. Barney said, "My bishop said it's all right in cases like this when nothing else that gives strength is available." Parrott then noticed Hodges was nibbling fruit salad, not steak. Parrott told Hodges about Barney's bishop's exemption. Hodges asked, "At what altitude are we flying?"

"21,000 feet," Parrott said.

"I think I'll stick to this salad," Hodges replied, "We're a little too close to headquarters."

On that same flight back from St. Louis, many Dodger players criticized Cardinals outfielder Enos Slaughter for his "malicious attempt" to spike Hodges as he fielded Slaughter's sixth-inning bunt, when the Dodgers had an insurmountable 16-2 lead. While running to first, Slaughter made no attempt to touch the bag; he just tried to spike Hodges. Shotton disputed claims that Slaughter was a hustling ballplayer: "That wasn't hustle—what Enos tried to do to Hodges. It was just plain lousy. Slaughter's a dirty ballplayer—always has been."

Slaughter said, "I never deliberately tried to spike a guy in my life. Besides, Gil Hodges is a good guy. You'll notice he doesn't say a thing. Just the manager and a couple of humpty-dumpties." Slaughter was having a case of selective memory: his attempted spiking of Robinson on a similar play during the 1947 season was well documented as being not only intentional but also racially motivated.

Hodges's lack of reaction to the spiking is consistent with his role as a peacekeeper during baseball fights. Back then, the unwritten rules of the game required that benches empty during a fight. Invariably, Hodges would be among the first out onto the field but always under control, acting as the MP he wanted to be during the war.

The first time Hodges acted as a peacekeeper was in Texas, during a 1948 spring training game between the Dodgers and their Double A Minor League team, the Fort Worth Cats. On one play, the Cats' first baseman, Dee Fondy, slid into Pee Wee Reese trying to turn a double play, and the two started jawing at each other. In the "general melee on the field," someone jumped on Fondy's back to keep him away from Reese. Meanwhile, Hodges saw the Cats' player-manager, Les Burge, heading toward Reese. Hodges cut him off and with two hands grabbed Burge by "the loose folds of Burge's shirt front and lifted the 200-pounder clear off the ground. 'I don't know where you're going, Les, he announced calmly, 'but it won't be near Pee Wee.' The ruckus ended right there."

"He was the biggest and strongest guy out there," his teammate Preacher Roe said, "but he was always the guy breaking up the fight."

Hodges's approach was commendable, but he played in an era when macho reputations—and back-page headlines—could be made with a single punch. For example, in a July 4, 1932, game at Griffith Stadium in Washington DC, the Yankees' catcher, Bill Dickey, upset at the way the Senators' Carl Reynolds banged into him on a play at the plate, followed Reynolds toward the Senators' dugout and cemented his tough guy reputation by breaking Reynolds's jaw with a single punch.

Hodges was not the violent type but Durocher—although he was then managing the Giants—never gave up hope. In the 1950s, Cincinnati Reds first baseman Ted Kluszewski was often mentioned along with Hodges as being baseball's strongest player. Durocher loved to compare the physical prowess of Hodges and Kluszewski. "Boy, oh, boy," Durocher said, "would I like to get those two guys in a room, lock the door and throw the key away."

The Dodgers, who had been out of first place since August, regained the lead at the end of September and won the pennant on the final day of the season, when they defeated the Phillies in ten innings, 9–7. Hodges had a terrific game, going two for four with a walk, one run driven in, and scoring twice. When the Dodgers' train from Philadelphia pulled into Penn Station, twenty-five thousand Dodgers fans were there to meet them. The five-piece Dodgers Sym-phony "thumped and blared," joined by the wildest of the Brooklyn faithful, the Section 8 Club, named for the military code section used to discharge mentally unfit servicemen. The fans, held back by wooden barricades, screamed as each player walked past them. The high point came when Robinson appeared; fans burst past the wooden horses and had to be forced back by the police. Before Robinson's grand finale, the "roar . . . hit a new crescendo when Hodges and Branca walked . . . into the driveway."

According to Carl Erskine, either Hodges, Robinson, Campanella, or Reese could have been team captain, but Reese had the job because he was "the captain of captains." Yet Erskine referred to Hodges as the conscience of the team. To explain what he meant, Erskine spoke of the unwavering fairness Hodges showed during the meeting the players would have after winning a pennant to determine how they would divide up their share of the profits from the Series.

In an era when most players were paid only $10,000 to $20,000 a year, a World Series check represented a sizeable bonus (in 1949 the winner's share was $5,666; the loser's share, $4,273). But the greater the number of World Series shares issued, the less each player received. Usually, if a player was with the team for the full season, even if only in a part-time role, he was voted a full share. But if a player was with the team for only part of the season, he might receive a commensurate half share, quarter share, or no share at all.

An open vote was taken to determine which players received a share, and whether it was full or partial. All determinations had to be unanimous, and the meetings could get heated. Logically, Reese, as captain, would be the one running these meetings; Reese had an easy manner, enabling him to say anything to anyone on the team. But Hodges ran these meetings—not Reese. If a vote fell just short of unanimity, Hodges would give the holdout a long, cold, blank stare. Some players, such as Furillo, could be tight-fisted, but even the more unruly players came into the fold after Hodges gave them "the look."

Thanks to Hodges, Luis Olmo, a legendary player in his native Puerto Rico, but viewed in America as a refugee from the renegade Mexican League, was among the thirty-one Dodgers to receive a full World Series share in 1949 despite joining the team on June 29 and appearing in only thirty-eight games. Throughout his playing and managerial career, Hodges emphasized that winning a pennant required an effort from all twenty-five men on the roster. Despite limited playing time, Olmo was worthy, having hit .305 with numerous key hits.

The Yankees were favored to defeat the Dodgers in the Series. Yet, reputations to the contrary, that season the Dodgers hit with more power (a team-record 153 home runs) compared to the Yankees (115). The Dodgers also had better speed on the bases, setting a team record with 119 stolen bases—Hodges even stole ten bases. But the Yankees had confidence. As the Yankee outfielder Tommy Henrich said earlier that season from a hospital bed while recovering from an injury, "We've got to win. We're a team of destiny." And it's easier to be a team of destiny when you have three great starting pitchers like Allie Reynolds, Vic Raschi, and Eddie Lopat.

The first two games of the World Series were at Yankee Stadium, where it was difficult for the largely right-handed-hitting Dodgers to be successful. The original Yankee Stadium was built with a short porch in right field only 296 feet down the foul line. This provided a close target for generations of left-handed-hitting Yankee sluggers, but for a right-handed pull hitter like Hodges, the expansive distance to left-center (451 feet) was a nightmare. Over the five World Series ('49, '52, '53, '55, and '56) Hodges would play against the Yankees, he would hit several balls into the deepest part of left-center field that would have been home runs in most other ballparks, but which were just long fly-outs to a part of the stadium the players called Death Valley.

Several years before Jonas Salk perfected his polio vaccine, a nine-year-old polio victim, Bruce Howard, tossed out the ceremonial first pitch before the opening game of the Series. Then Allie Reynolds pitched a shutout as Henrich won it for the Yankees with a ninth-inning walk-off homer on Don Newcombe's 114th pitch of the game. Newcombe struck out eleven, walked none, and did not allow a single batter to reach a 3-2 count. But Reynolds was even better, allowing only two hits and striking out thirteen. Batting seventh in the order, Hodges went hitless, struck out once, and hit into a double play.

Driving from Brooklyn to Yankee Stadium for Game Two, Hodges was in a "slight" car accident. There were no injuries reported when Hodges's car hit a taxicab. Luckily, it wasn't Hodges's only hit of the day.

Game Two was another pitcher's duel, with Roe beating Raschi 1–0. It was the first time the Yankees had been shut out at home in 156 games. Significantly, in the second inning, with Robinson on third base, bluffing to steal home, Hodges drove Robinson in with a single to left field for the only run of the game. Yet Hodges's accomplishment was minimized. After the game, Raschi raved about Robinson, "I had just never seen anything like him before, a human being who could go from a standing start to full speed in one step. He did something to me that almost never happened: He broke my concentration and I paid more attention to him than to Hodges. He beat me more than Hodges."

The Series shifted to Brooklyn for Game Three. Branca pitched wonderfully—the game was tied 1–1 going into the top of the ninth—but the Yankees scored three runs to take a 4–1 lead. The key hit was a bases-loaded, pinch-hit single by Johnny Mize, that year's late-season veteran acquisition by the Yankees.

The Dodgers lost Game Four, 6–4. Afterward, with the Yankees holding what was then viewed as an insurmountable three-games-to-one lead, the only player with anything quotable to say in the solemn Dodgers' clubhouse was Hodges, who offered reporters a few well-worn clichés. "Well, it's another day," said Hodges as trainer Doc Wendler applied a bandage to his left ankle for a spike wound. "We're still in there until we're counted out, huh?"

In batting practice before the fifth game, Hodges was pounding the ball. He hit a line drive with such speed that the Dodgers' batting-practice pitcher, Dick Whitman, "never had a chance" and the ball struck him so hard it fractured his right arm. But in Game Five, with Roe sidelined by an injury, the Dodgers had to go to one of their least consistent starters, Rex Barney. The Yankees blew Barney out early, taking a 10–2 lead. Hodges hit a three-run home run in the seventh to rally the Dodgers, but it not only proved too little, too late, but brought Page into the game. The Dodgers trailed 10–6 in the ninth when Eddie Miksis doubled off Page. But after Snider and Robinson struck out and Hermanski walked, Hodges struck out to end the game.

Despite batting only .235 in the Series, 1949 was a successful year for Hodges. In an era when hitting twenty home runs was the threshold figure for a legitimate power hitter, Hodges's twenty-three home runs tied the Dodgers' team record for the most homers by a right-handed hitter in a season. He also had 115 RBIs—only six players in baseball had more. Yet Hodges's accomplishments were overshadowed by Robinson, who won the MVP Award that season.

That winter Hodges worked at a Brooklyn department store, Abraham & Straus, but he also had a night job. Beginning on December 18, Hodges along with four other Dodgers (Barney, Branca, Newcombe, and Miksis) each earned twenty-five dollars a game playing basketball against local semipro teams on Monday nights at the Paramount Theatre on Flatbush Avenue in downtown Brooklyn. Fearing injury to his players, Rickey ordered the team disbanded, but because there had been advance ticket sales, Rickey allowed a six-game schedule to be played.

Hodges would visit Petersburg once a year, but his parents were always in his thoughts. When Hodges learned that Amber, the mutt Irene had brought home, had died, he bought his mother and father a beautiful brown boxer, and for years afterward Charlie and the dog, named Roxanne, could be seen strolling down Main Street.

7

FOUR IN ONE,
ONE FOR FOUR

For that fourth homer. . . I never saw a curve that looked so good.

That winter the Dodgers mailed out player contracts for the 1950 season with the salary amount already typed in. That was standard practice. The agentless players had two choices: sign and mail, or mail unsigned. The latter branded you a holdout, never a wise choice when management could, and often did, influence fan opinion through the newspapers. Few players got a chance to negotiate face-to-face. But on January 26, 1950, Hodges was invited to visit the Dodgers' offices on Montague Street. Hodges was a rising star; and considering he lived in Brooklyn, he merited a chat with Rickey.

After leading all National League first basemen in fielding with only seven errors, finishing fourth in runs batted in, eighth in home runs, ninth in total bases, fifteenth in batting average, and seventh in steals, Hodges could have held out for a significant increase over his 1949 salary of $8,000. But Hodges was still no match for Rickey.

After meeting Rickey in his office (the players called it the "Cave of the Winds"), Hodges signed a contract for $13,000. Contrast Hodges's result to that of Carl Furillo, who refused to sign his contract and engaged in a well-publicized holdout. Despite hitting fewer home runs and knocking in fewer runs than Hodges in 1949, Furillo signed for $18,500.

Yet, even though signed, Hodges was not on board the Dodgers' train on February 27 as it pulled out of Penn Station for spring training in Vero Beach. With Joan nearing the end of her pregnancy with their first child, Hodges refused to leave Brooklyn until she gave birth. At a time when players were truly beholden to management, it was highly unusual for a player to report late to spring training just to stay home with his wife when she gave birth. For example, Hodges's teammate Ralph Branca was never home for the birth of any of his children.

Remarkably, the Dodgers didn't fine Hodges for failing to report to spring training. The reasons are understandable when one considers the parties involved. Rickey knew Hodges was a serious student of the game who followed orders. If family-first Hodges said he was at home looking after his wife, Rickey knew it was true. If Durocher had made a similar request, Rickey would have raised his bushy eyebrows and wondered what bad situation the Lip was making worse. Hodges had Rickey's trust. He had always reported to training camp on time and in shape. In an era when few players worked out, Hodges hit the gym over the winter. Even if Hodges was in Florida, he'd be thinking about Joan and would be of little utility, so Rickey allowed him to stay home until Gil Jr. was born. A year later, when Joan was pregnant with their second child, Hodges received a far different response after there had been a change in ownership and Walter O'Malley was in charge.

With Hodges still in Brooklyn, Shotton's best option at first base was a rookie named Wayne Belardi, so Shotton announced that third baseman Billy Cox would begin practicing at first, sending Hodges a subtle message that he had better get down to Florida if he wanted to keep his job. But Joan had fallen down a flight of stairs a few weeks before, and Hodges was not about to go anywhere.

Four days later, Shotton tried to create the impression that Hodges was leaving his pregnant wife and had boarded a plane heading south. "We wanted Gil to wait until the stork arrived," said Shotton, "but I guess he wanted to get down here and get to work." Although the next day's newspapers erroneously reported that Hodges was aboard a plane en route for Vero Beach, that was wishful thinking.

Before an exhibition game that spring, Shotton told the team's twenty-two-year-old rookie radio broadcaster to suit up and shag a few fly balls. "They didn't have a uniform," Vin Scully later said, "so I had to wear Hodges'. I was 140 pounds . . . Gil was a marble statue. I put his uniform on and *Dodgers* comes down to my belly." After shagging a few ("I've never felt a ball hit my

10. Al Roon's Gym, Brooklyn, January 1950. Brooklyn Public Library—Brooklyn Collection.

mitt with such impact"), "I head to the clubhouse and kids want Hodges' autograph. I'm telling them I'm not Gil, but these two kids stay with me the whole way, and I'm thinking what a sweet guy Gil is and these kids are going to think Hodges won't sign for them. So I signed Gil's name, remembering he made a little circle above the 'i' in Gil."

11. Steam Cabinet, Al Roon's Gym, January 1950. Brooklyn Public Library—Brooklyn Collection.

Gil Hodges Jr. was born on March 12, 1950, at Unity Hospital in Brooklyn. Joan remained in the hospital for several days after giving birth. Doctors assured Hodges "things were under control," but he still refused to leave his wife and son. "I realized that he wouldn't leave until I had gone home from the hospital," Joan said, "so I got up and left after four days. Then Gil went to Florida."

12. With Joan and Gil Jr., August 1950. Brooklyn Public Library—Brooklyn Collection.

On March 15, Shotton received a telegram from Hodges reading, "I'll be in tomorrow. Father and son doing fine."

As promised, on March 16—after missing seventeen days of spring training—Hodges arrived. Shotton "was highly impatient because of his tardiness," and to appease his manager, Hodges didn't ease into practice but immediately "cut loose, with the unhappy result that in two days he could hardly lift his right arm." Shotton didn't care and penciled Hodges into the Dodgers' starting lineup a day earlier than expected. On March 21, after only five days in camp, Hodges started a game against one of the Dodgers' top Minor League teams, the Fort Worth Cats. Hodges responded with two singles and a walk. Two days later, Shotton further tested Hodges's fielding and throwing abilities, moving him from first to third base in the eighth inning of a game against the Philadelphia Athletics. Hodges was up to the challenge, making "a neat pick-up" of a ground ball to start a game-ending double play to seal an 8–4 Dodgers win.

A few weeks later, Hodges was back at first base when the Dodgers opened their season in Philadelphia. Although the Dodgers were favored to win the National League pennant, in a foreshadowing of how the season would end, Hall of Fame pitcher Robin Roberts shut down the Dodgers, 9-1. Philadelphia fans joked that defeating the defending National League champions on Opening Day was the Phillies' version of winning the pennant, since the Phillies hadn't won one since 1915. But the 1950 team, dubbed the "Whiz Kids" because of an outstanding core group of young players led by Roberts and Hall of Fame center fielder Richie Ashburn, had a special season.

In the Dodgers' second game, Hodges, despite his truncated spring training, proved to be in midseason shape, as he led the Dodgers to a 7-5 victory with a home run, two doubles, and a single. Hodges's performance sparked the Dodgers, and they reeled off seven consecutive victories. As Memorial Day approached, Brooklyn seemed on their way to another pennant.

But a baseball season is more marathon than sprint. In the heat of summer, the "Whiz Kids," playing at well over a .600 clip in July and August, took over first place. Unlike the Dodgers, the Phillies had outstanding relief pitching, which proved crucial as the season wore on. The star of the Phillies' bullpen was a right-handed screwball pitcher, Jim Konstanty. That season he was so dominant he won the National League MVP Award. But Konstanty had a hard time pitching to Hodges. His screwball (in effect a reverse curve ball) broke inside on right-handed hitters, and that was Hodges's sweet spot.

The 1950 All-Star Game was played at Chicago's Comiskey Park, the site of the first All-Star Game in 1933. As tradition dictated, the previous season World Series' managers, Stengel and Shotton, opposed each other. The Yankees had eight representatives: starters Rizzuto and Berra and pitcher Vic Raschi, as well as alternates Jerry Coleman, DiMaggio, Henrich, and pitchers Tommy Byrne and Allie Reynolds. The Dodgers had seven: starters Robinson and Campanella and alternates Roe, Newcombe, Reese, Snider, and Hodges.

At midseason, Hodges was not only hitting for power but also batting over .300, but he didn't start the game. Stan Musial, who had been moved from the outfield to first base, had been voted the starting National League first baseman. But logic dictated that after the mandatory three innings that the starters were required to play, Musial would be moved to the outfield to keep his bat in the lineup and, as had been done in the 1949 All-Star Game, Hodges would come in to play first for his defensive abilities. Before the game, Shotton said this was what he would do. Yet, despite the game lasting fourteen innings, Shotton benched Hodges for the entire game.

On a hot summer afternoon in Chicago, the American League took a 3–2 lead in the fifth, but in the top of the ninth Pittsburgh's Ralph Kiner tied it with a home run. In the top of the fourteenth, the National League gained a 4–3 lead on a home run by Cardinals second baseman Red Schoendienst. But even in the bottom of the fourteenth, when the logical move was clearly to get Hodges on the field for his defense, he sat.

Although it frequently happens that a player named to the All-Star team doesn't play, as a matter of pride no player ever wants to sit one out. And for a player to stay plastered to the bench for an entire fourteen-inning game—by his own manager—was highly unusual. Since Stengel played all of his Yankee position players and Shotton managed to get both his other Dodger position players into the game, one wonders if he kept Hodges on the bench as payback for his spring training tardiness.

On August 31, 1950, after what was then referred to as a western road trip to Pittsburgh, Cincinnati, St. Louis, and Chicago, the third-place Dodgers returned to Brooklyn to play the Boston Braves. Hodges had promised to bring Joan a present from the trip, but had forgotten. Joan, who referred to herself as a "baseball widow" when her husband was away, told him off. "It was a pretty one-sided quarrel," Joan recalled. "I did all the complaining, and Gil just remained quiet, keeping everything bottled up inside him. Finally, as he went to leave for the ballpark, he kissed me goodbye and said he'd see me after the game that night."

"You've been away so long," Joan replied, "one more night won't make any difference."

Things may have been tense in the home the Hodges shared with Joan's parents in Brooklyn, but at Wilson's Pool Hall on Main Street in Petersburg, it was just another day. Down at Wilson's you could buy a drink, play some pool, or place a wager on a baseball game. Wilson's had a Teletype machine that kept everyone updated on the scores. Long before the Internet, in Petersburg in 1950, if you wanted to keep track of a game as it happened, you either had to mosey on over to Wilson's or give the boys down there a holler on the telephone.

In nearby Princeton, the Palace Pool Room served a similar purpose. There, a man named D. A. Keimer manned the Teletype machine writing an inning-by-inning account of the games on a blackboard that hung on the wall. In the 1940s, a young man named Dave Niehaus, who later became a Hall of Fame broadcaster for the Seattle Mariners, began his lifelong love of baseball watching Keimer chalk up the scores. On August 31, 1950, Keimer did a lot of chalking.

That day, a left-hander for the Boston Braves, Warren Spahn, was making a rare start against the Dodgers. Although Spahn was a future Hall of Famer, he had trouble against the Dodgers, especially in Ebbets Field where the Braves usually altered their rotation so Spahn didn't pitch.

Entering the bottom of the second, the Braves led, 1–0. But Hodges homered off Spahn with Furillo on first to give the Dodgers the lead. In the Palace Pool Room, Keimer picked up his chalk: BKLYN. Home Run. Hodges. Second/1 on.

The home run landed in the lower deck, down the left-field line. When Hodges returned to the dugout, pitcher Rex Barney jokingly told him, "You're gonna hit one good before the game's over."

In the third, Robinson and Furillo hit back-to-back singles, knocking Spahn out of the game. Normie Roy, a righty, in what would be his only season in the Majors, came in to pitch. Hodges greeted him with a three-run homer that again landed in the lower deck. Barney again teased Hodges about not getting good wood on it. With Carl Erskine pitching solidly for the Dodgers, the game was effectively over as the inning ended with the Dodgers leading, 10–1. BKYLN. Home Run. Hodges. Third/2 on.

In the fourth inning, against a veteran left-hander, Mickey Haefner, Hodges grounded out to third. But in the sixth, with Furillo on first, Hodges connected for his third homer off another journeyman pitcher, the right-handed Bob Hall. Like Hodges's first two homers, the ball landed in the lower deck and Barney again gave Hodges the needle. BKLYN. Home Run. Hodges. Sixth/1 on.

In the seventh inning, Hodges came to bat with a chance for his fourth homer, but hit an infield single. Luckily, the Dodgers batted around in the eighth and Hodges got one more at bat. It came against a lefty, Johnny Antonelli, a future twenty-game winner for the 1954 World Champion New York Giants. But in 1950 Antonelli, who had been signed as a bonus baby, should have been pitching in the Minors. In the seventh, Antonelli had given up the infield single to Hodges. This time, with Furillo again on base, Hodges hit a tremendous shot that landed in the back of the upper deck in left field. On Hodges's return to the dugout, he told Barney, "You were right." BKLYN. Home Run. Hodges. Eighth/1 on.

The Dodgers won easily, 19–3. Erskine even got four hits in the game—all singles. Hodges's nine RBIs set a Dodgers franchise record that would stand for fifty-six years, and his seventeen total bases tied the all-time National League mark. After the game, Reese stuck it to Hodges. "As far as I see it," Reese said, "all you did was prolong the game."

At the time, only one other player in modern baseball history, Lou Gehrig, had hit four home runs in a nine-inning game. Although only 14,226 fans witnessed it, Hodges's four-homer game resulted in frequent comparisons to Gehrig. In some ways it made sense. Hodges and Gehrig are still the only two players in baseball history to hit for the cycle in one nine-inning game and also hit four homers in another nine-inning game. Both were power-hitting first basemen with quiet demeanors. But the comparisons heightened expectations for the then twenty-six-year-old Hodges. Hodges was a far better fielder than Gehrig, but at the plate, Gehrig, a left-handed hitter, hit for both power and average. Hodges knew it and tried to downplay the comparisons. When asked to compare himself to Gehrig, Hodges said, "The only difference between us is he's a much better player."

Hodges's modesty was not an act. He did not feel the need to flaunt his abilities. Years later, in June 1964, during Hodges's first full season as manager of the Washington Senators, one of his players, outfielder Jim King, became the 152nd player in Major League history to hit three home runs in one game. After that game, someone asked Hodges if he ever hit three in one game. Hodges said only, "I'm not in the record books for three in one game." To avoid taking away King's spotlight, Hodges made no mention of his four-homer game. And until he later looked it up, Bob Addie, the *Washington Post* reporter covering the game, had no idea Hodges had once hit four home runs in one game.

Hodges's feat was immortalized in one of Dick Young's *Daily News* columns, titled "Hodges Hits 4 in 1 Tilt, Asks 1 Apartment for 4." With Joan pregnant again, the Hodgeses were soon to be a four-person family, so when asked what he thought his overnight fame would bring, Hodges replied, "I hope it brings us a place to live."

Joan added, "We've tried everything to get a decent home to rent. We're living here with my folks, and there just isn't enough room. We've advertised, but didn't have any luck. Maybe, now, something good will happen."

It did. After Young's piece was published, the Dodgers' office was flooded with calls offering the family a place to live. Eventually, they found one that was acceptable to Joan only a few minutes away from Ebbets Field near the intersection of Foster and Ocean Avenues.

The article was also memorable for Dick Young, who was marking another stage in a lifelong relationship with Hodges that would come to full flower when Hodges became the Mets' manager.

When Young asked how Hodges accounted for his improved hitting, Hodges mentioned Shotton's advice not to turn his head when he swung, Durocher's adjustment of his stride, and his work with George Sisler. Then the real reason hit him and he became animated. "I'd say that confidence is the big thing—in myself or in any other player's development," Hodges said. In that vein, Hodges recalled Clyde Sukeforth's belief in him and how much it meant to him.

"Yes," Hodges said, ". . . I'd have to say Sukey helped the most."

The Dodgers were in third place on September 19, nine games behind the Phillies. Young wrote that "barring a miracle," the Dodgers were just "playing out the schedule." But that month, Philadelphia lost several pitchers to injury and another (seventeen-game winner Curt Simmons) to military duty. The Phillies, who won on the strength of their pitching (they led the Majors in earned run average that season), could not compensate. In the final two weeks of the season, the Phillies lost 9 out of 12. At the same time, the Dodgers, the best-hitting team in baseball in 1950, won 14 of 17 and the pennant race tightened.

Desperate to clinch the pennant, the Phillies began overworking Robin Roberts. On September 23 the Dodgers faced Roberts at Shibe Park. A Phillies win would clinch the pennant. The game's crucial at bat came in the top of the second, with no outs and runners on first and second. Hodges, ordered to advance the runners with a sacrifice bunt, twice failed to do so and fell behind in the count, 0-2. But with the sacrifice off, Hodges recovered and put together a terrific at bat, working the count full. On the next pitch, Hodges's three-run homer produced the only runs the Dodgers needed for a 3-2 win. Four days later, in the seventh inning of a game against the Boston Braves, Hodges hit another three-run homer (his thirty-second of the season), giving the Dodgers a come-from-behind win, 9-6.

With only two games left in the season, the Dodgers were two games out of first place, and those final games were at Ebbets Field against the Phillies. If the Dodgers won both, they would force a three-game playoff to determine the league champion.

The Dodgers defeated the Phillies in the first game, their sixth straight loss; the Whiz Kids "were wheezing rather than whizzing," wrote Young. On the last day of the season, Newcombe faced Roberts. It was Roberts's fourth start in a week. Both pitchers had won nineteen games and were hoping they could make it an even twenty.

Roberts pitched magnificently. The game was tied, 1-1, going into the bottom of the ninth. Dodgers left fielder Cal Abrams led off with a walk, Reese singled, and on the first pitch, the next batter, Snider, with the Phillies expecting a bunt, hit a line drive to center field for a base hit. The largest home crowd of the season "exploded in a vast roar."

The Brooklyn fans knew the Phillies center fielder, Richie Ashburn, had a weak arm, and the winning run was sure to score from second base. But on the pitch, Ashburn was charging toward the infield to back up second base for a bunt attempt or pick-off play. Roberts either missed the pick-off sign or Snider fooled him by hitting away. In any case, Ashburn caught Snider's base hit in short center field on one hop and made a perfect throw to home plate. Abrams was out by fifteen feet. For the Ebbets Field faithful, shock replaced elation.

With Snider on second and Reese on third, Roberts intentionally walked Robinson to load the bases. Swinging on the first pitch, Furillo hit an infield pop-up. With two outs and the bases loaded, Hodges stepped to the plate. Since Hodges and Roberts played the bulk of their careers in the National League over the same time period (1948–61), and the Phillies and Dodgers then played each other twenty-two times each season, in his career Hodges probably batted against Roberts more times than any other pitcher. As a result, Roberts was well skilled in how to pitch to Hodges to minimize his ability to pull the ball to left field—where Hodges got most of his hits.

"Stay ahead of him [in the count]," Roberts told me, "and throw fastballs, low and away. You could get him out with pitches that weren't so good [out of the strike zone]. But he had a knack of hitting my breaking ball better than my fastball." Roberts's approach was exactly why Ralph Branca often implored Hodges to go with the outside pitch. "Gil," Branca said, "you're strong enough to hit homers to right field."

This time, Hodges listened and went with the pitch, driving a high fly to deep right. But Hodges didn't get all of it. A few steps short of the Schaefer scoreboard, Del Ennis caught the ball for the final out. In the tenth, the Phillies scored three runs on a Dick Sisler home run, and then the Dodgers went down 1-2-3 to lose the game and the pennant.

In Brooklyn folklore, Cal Abrams cost them the pennant. Dodgers third base coach Milt Stock was fired for waving Abrams home. To his credit, Shotton defended his coach ("Milt played it right") and was fired as well. Abrams, the Dodgers' fourth-string left fielder—who was in the game only because of injuries to Gene Hermanski, Tommy Brown, and Jim Russell—went from fan favorite (he was a graduate of Brooklyn's James Madison High School) to Cincinnati, via trade.

A photo taken after the game shows a disconsolate Russell and Hodges sitting next to each other in front of their lockers. Shirtless and glum-faced, Hodges stares off into oblivion, his pine-tar-stained fingers holding a cigarette burned down to the filter. After batting .380 against Philadelphia that season, Hodges's failure to get even one hit in such a crucial game deeply pained him. Usually when he came home, Hodges could separate himself from that day's game. But that night, Joan Hodges recalled, "he never saw me . . . . Dinner was prepared but he didn't eat. He went right up to bed."

The final game of the 1950 season was an example of how Hodges's failure to come through in one notable situation could overshadow his considerable hitting ability. That season, in Hodges's final 126 at bats—as the pressure mounted down the stretch—he hit thirteen home runs and drove in forty runs to keep his team in contention. But the lasting image fans would have

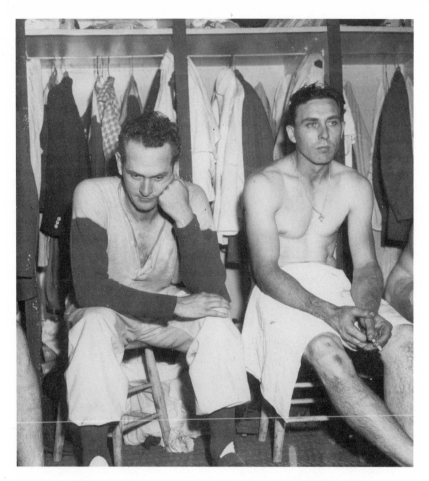

13. With Jim Russell after loss to the Phillies, October 2, 1950. Brooklyn Public Library—Brooklyn Collection.

of Hodges that off-season would be his hitting a fly ball to end the season's final game with the bases loaded.

The fact that the Phillies almost lost the pennant didn't matter to their jubilant fans or the manager of their World Series opponents. "So what?" Casey Stengel said. "It's like backing into a mansion, ain't it?" The Yankees beat the Phillies in four straight.

The day after Hodges's four-homer game, on the blackboard in the Dodgers' clubhouse, John Griffin wrote, "All players will report at 11 a.m., Wednesday, for group picture taking." The Dodgers had already gathered to take their annual team photo two weeks before on August 18. One player missed that photo session and management had previously decided to use the image anyway, deeming it sufficient to merely add the missing player's name to the photo and use an asterisk to indicate his omission. But an asterisk would no longer suffice.

"I just forgot the last time," said Hodges.

8

GREAT EXPECTATIONS

The ability to hit is a God-given talent.

Hodges wasn't the second coming of Gehrig. But Rickey was so sure he'd be the Dodgers' everyday first baseman for the long term, he traded Dee Fondy and Chuck Connors, both left-handed-hitting first basemen, to Chicago. That was Rickey's last major trade for Brooklyn. In the fall of 1950, with his days controlling the Dodgers numbered due to ownership changes, Rickey sold his 25 percent interest in the team and become the general manager of the Pittsburgh Pirates. Rickey was extraordinarily frugal, but as a former player and manager, he had a deep love for the game.

Walter O'Malley, the man who purchased Rickey's interest, did not. When the Dodgers first came into O'Malley's sights, it was as an asset in receivership—not a cornerstone of Brooklyn history. For O'Malley, then a successful bankruptcy attorney, the Dodgers were a business opportunity disguised as a baseball team. As a result of having to pay Rickey full value for his 25 percent interest, O'Malley despised all-things-Rickey and started to place his own spin on history. O'Malley told one reporter that he had seen Jackie Robinson play before Rickey purchased Robinson's contract from the Kansas City Monarchs. "From that evening on," wrote Red Smith, a Pulitzer Prize winner and one of the most respected journalists of the twentieth century, "the reporter had reservations."

O'Malley named Charlie Dressen as the Dodgers' new manager. Dressen, like his mentor Leo Durocher, thought highly of his managerial skills and would tell his players to just keep the game close until the final innings, because "I will think of something." Roger Kahn called Dressen "a man who had more explanations than newspapermen have questions." At his contract signing, when asked to comment about his new players, Dressen said that he had been managing in the Pacific Coast League and wasn't familiar with them, adding, "For instance, when I first saw Gil Hodges . . . he was a catcher and third baseman. Now he's just about the best first baseman in the majors."

With his new manager's supportive words, his four-homer fame, and the forceful Rickey out of the picture, Hodges was no longer a pushover in salary negotiations. On January 24, 1951, Hodges visited Montague Street to meet with Buzzie Bavasi, the team's new general manager. Hodges left without picking up a pen. It was reported that he was "not a holdout," but had decided to give management time to reconsider his abilities.

And they were considerable. In 1950 Hodges finished eighth—ahead of all his teammates—in the National League MVP voting. His 32 home runs and 113 RBIs were each third highest in the National League. More important, Hodges had hit in the clutch. Over two-thirds of his homers came with men on base. And approximately half had come off curve balls, a pitch that had often fooled him in the past. Hodges led all National League first basemen with a .994 fielding mark and set a record for first basemen, participating in 159 double plays. But Hodges was best at what today is a lost art: fielding bunts.

In a game against the New York Giants during the 1950 season, with the speedy future Hall of Fame outfielder Monte Irvin on first, Durocher sent his pitcher, Jack Kramer, up to bunt. But Hodges charged the plate so aggressively he was able to grab Kramer's sacrifice bunt on one hop, tag Kramer out, and then turn and throw to second base to double-up Irvin. A smart base runner, Irvin hadn't hesitated to take off for second, thinking Hodges had no chance to throw him out. During the 1951 season, Hodges once fielded a bunt, picked the ball up cleanly, but was out of position to turn and throw the runner out. "So he flicked the ball . . . [to pitcher Don Newcombe covering first base] through his legs, like a football center . . . to get the putout."

Hodges had other techniques to give his team an edge. After a put-out at first base, or whenever he came to the mound to talk to the pitcher, Hodges gave the ball a few good squeezes with his pine-tar-coated hands, and for the next several throws the pitcher had a better grip on the ball. "Hodges used more pine tar," Dodgers batboy Rene Lachemann told me, "than anyone else in the league."

In addition to his fielding, Hodges was the consummate team player. "If you had 25 Gil Hodges on your ball club," said Jake Pitler, then a Dodgers coach, "you'd never have to worry off the field or on it." Hodges knew when "to give his pitchers encouragement." Decades later, Dodgers pitcher Clyde King could still recall Hodges walking over to him on the mound in a crucial situation and calmly saying, "Clyde, just make him hit it, and we'll take care of it."

Hodges looked out for his teammates off the field as well. When Dodgers pitcher Roger Craig was a rookie, "The team was taking a train from Philadelphia to New York. . . . We had had a couple of beers and were playing bridge. I hear knocking on the door of the train as we're ready to pull out and there was Gil holding Pee Wee who had had a few drinks. Gil carries Pee Wee into the train and puts him into his bunk."

That story typifies the way Vin Scully, like Erskine, characterized Hodges within the constellation of the team's stars. "Pee Wee was the captain," Scully said, "Campanella was the mother hen. Robinson was the firebrand. Snider was the virtuoso. Hodges was the conscience."

But not all Hodges's teammates sang his praises. Dick Williams had his own Hodges train story. In 1951 Williams was on the Major League roster because he had been discharged from the military and could not be sent down to the Minors, since other teams had selected him on waivers. An outfielder, Williams wanted to be one of the boys, but his skills were not yet Major League ready, and the veterans resented him for taking up a roster spot. "Guys like Pee Wee and Snider and Gil Hodges and Carl Furillo and Carl Erskine would insulate themselves with their popularity," Williams wrote in his autobiography, "and turn their backs on the team's younger players, the ones like me who were dying for their leadership."

On one train ride Williams, who was six feet tall and 190 pounds, "jumped into the bottom bunk of a sleeper compartment" he shared with Hodges. Long-standing custom dictated that the regulars slept on the lower berths, with the second-stringers, like Williams, on the upper berths.

"I knew I was supposed to be in the top bunk, but Hodges was in a different car playing bridge with Pee Wee and Billy Cox and Preacher Roe. So I figured I'd lie there a minute and read a magazine. But no sooner did I focus my attention on a story than I felt two strong hands on my side. It was Hodges, and he was picking me up. Then he was dropping me on the upper bunk. 'That's where you sleep, rookie,' he said gruffly."

Williams had noticed Hodges as he approached; and well aware of the appropriate etiquette, Williams should have moved up to his bunk without having to be asked. But Williams, who liked playing the role of the wise guy, didn't move. Instead, with respect to the card game, he asked, "How did you do?"

A few years later, Bob Aspromonte, a rookie who was much more respectful toward the veterans, had a different take on Hodges. "When I came up ... I was just a wide-eyed kid out of high-school," Aspromonte said, "I didn't know which way was up, but Gil took me under his wing and helped me not only with baseball but with my social adjustment. What he did was give me direction. It's not something you easily forget."

But despite accolades regarding his persona, his feared home run power, outstanding fielding, and heady base running, Hodges's streakiness at the plate kept him from becoming a consistent .300 hitter in an era when mind-sets were stuck in the 1930s, when batting .300 was the standard for greatness. Attitudes regarding Hodges's abilities, even among some of his teammates, all too often focused not on what he could do, but on what he couldn't. When I asked Clem Labine what the one thing is I must include in a book about Hodges to make it complete, he told me, "I wish we had better hitting coaches."

After two weeks of not holding out, Hodges agreed to a $20,000 salary, a significant increase, but well below other Dodgers stars like Robinson, who had just signed for $36,000.

That spring, for the second year in a row, Joan was pregnant; and with her due date imminent, Hodges again failed to report for the opening of spring training. But O'Malley was in charge and he gave Hodges a few extra days, but announced, "[Hodges] definitely will report in time for the game with the Braves at Miami on Saturday."

When O'Malley spoke, people listened; Hodges later recalled, "The Dodgers ... put it to me to get down south."

On Thursday morning, March 8, with Joan still expecting, a reluctant Hodges flew from New York to Miami to join his teammates. "I'm here," Hodges said upon his arrival, "but my mind's in Brooklyn."

The next day, Hodges put on his uniform and practiced. But Hodges didn't feel pressure to throw hard from the get-go. To his credit Dressen—unlike Shotton—didn't rush Hodges back into the lineup. Instead, Dressen penciled in Hodges's backup, Wayne Belardi, for the Saturday, March 10, game against the Braves. Hodges didn't play against Major League competition until March 17, when he hit a line drive single off the left-field wall in Miami Stadium, driving in the Dodgers' first run. The next morning, putting aside thoughts of how "Joan cried and cried when [he] had to leave," Hodges and Robinson visited Miami's National Children's Cardiac Home and "made a lot of youngsters very happy."

Around 1 p.m. on March 20 at Unity Hospital in Brooklyn, Joan gave birth to an eight-pound girl named for Hodges's mother, Irene. At the time, Hodges was playing against the Philadelphia Athletics at Wright Field in West Palm Beach. When he came to bat in the fourth inning, the public address announcer played "Goodnight, Irene." That night, Hodges was on a plane back to Brooklyn. On the evening of March 24, satisfied that Joan and Irene were both well, a relaxed Hodges returned to Miami to help the Dodgers defeat the Cardinals 6–0, with a long home run over the left-field wall.

The Dodgers opened the 1951 campaign the same way they ended the prior season: losing to Robin Roberts and the Phillies. Despite motivation provided by a familiar sight at baseball games during the Korean War, a marine color guard participating in the flag-raising ceremonies, Hodges made a rare error when he booted a hard-hit grounder, and Del Ennis immediately followed with a two-run homer that proved decisive.

That season, Hodges began hitting home runs at the fastest pace of his career. He hit five in the first ten games. By the end of May, he was five ahead of Babe Ruth's 1927 pace when Ruth hit sixty, then the season record. Hodges set a National League record for the most home runs by July 1, with twenty-four. On July 6 he hit his twenty-eighth, putting him four games ahead of Ruth's record pace.

Less than a year after comparisons to Gehrig, Hodges was now being mentioned in the same breath as Ruth and was the subject of an inordinate

14. With Joan, Gil Jr., and Irene, September 1, 1951. Brooklyn Public Library—Brooklyn Collection.

amount of media attention. He was featured in a piece in one of the most popular national magazines, the *Saturday Evening Post*; the *New York Times* crossword puzzle listed clues like "Sultanate challenged by Gil Hodges"; and he appeared on the nationally televised *Ed Sullivan Show*. Even the staid Arthur Daley wrote, "How about Gil Hodges, the potential Babe Ruth of 1951?"

But one writer, John M. Ross, called the comparisons what they were, "out of focus and premature." But they were out there, and Hodges was often asked if he thought he would beat Ruth's record. In response, Hodges would drop his eyes "as if a deity had been mentioned" and proceed to answer the question, without really answering it. "I never saw Ruth play, but he must have been great to hit 60 home runs," Hodges would say. "When you consider slumps and injuries, gosh, that's an awful lot of homers. And the Babe only did it once. I guess my ambition in baseball is like most other players. I'd like to make enough money to feel secure when I get older, and in order to do that I have to improve a little bit each year."

The photographers even got into the act. In early June, when the Cardinals visited Ebbets Field, a photographer asked the great Stan Musial if he would pose for a photo with Hodges. Always the gentleman, Musial agreed and walked over to Hodges. "Ruth Jr., eh," Musial needled. Hodges asked Musial how many homers he had.

"Only twelve," Musial replied.

"This is the first time I ever heard anyone speak apologetically about twelve homers."

"You've got eighteen," Musial said.

Well aware of Musial's unique ability to hit for both power and average, Hodges replied, "And you've got a .380 batting average."

Despite Hodges's denials that he never swung for the fences ("Maybe I'll change," Hodges said that June, "but I never consciously go for home runs"), the record suggests the comparisons to Ruth had Hodges doing exactly that. In 1951 he struck out a league-leading ninety-nine times, the highest total of his career. His batting average suffered as well. Before the All-Star Game, Hodges hit twenty-eight home runs with a respectable .274 average; but in the second half of the season, Hodges hit below .250 with just twelve home runs. The only positive aspect of the second-half slump was that it enabled Hodges, whom one reporter called "almost painfully silent," to escape further attention from the national press. Hodges lost the 1951 National League home run crown to the Pirates' Ralph Kiner, forty-two to forty. They were the only two players in baseball to hit forty or more home runs that season.

Like Hodges, the Dodgers played impressively in the first half of the season. The Giants did not—at one point they lost eleven consecutive games. On August 8, after the Dodgers swept the Giants in a doubleheader, Brooklyn held first place by eleven and a half games, the largest margin in franchise history. After the second game, convinced his team was assured a pennant, Dressen stood outside the Giants' locker room yelling so Durocher could hear him, "Eat your heart out, Leo."

But Dressen had gotten ahead of himself. The Dodgers had weaknesses. After Roe and Newcombe, they lacked pitching depth. The Dodgers brought Clem Labine up from the Minors that season, but Dressen hardly played him. In addition, an ill-advised trade resulted in the regulars rarely getting a day off. The Giants on the other hand—at Durocher's urging—made two critical in-season decisions, both involving center field. First, they called up Willie Mays from the Minors, and he was soon playing center field as if he owned it. The second, as chronicled in Joshua Prager's *The Echoing Green*, Durocher illegally installed a telescope in a center-field window at the Polo Grounds to steal the opposing team's pitching signs. The telescope made a difference. The Dodgers' record against the Giants at Ebbets Field was 5-1 in the first half of the season and 4-1 in the second half. But at the Polo Grounds, before the telescope was first used on July 19, the Dodgers' record was 4-2; after that, the Dodgers didn't win another game there during the regular season, losing five in a row.

The Dodgers' ill-advised trade sent several key reserves to the Cubs for left fielder Andy Pafko (and three others). The trade made the Dodgers' starting team stronger—Pafko was a five-time All-Star—but weakened their bench. In the long term, the trade would benefit Hodges much more than the Dodgers. One of the three throw-ins the Dodgers received was Rube Walker, a backup catcher, who became Hodges's friend and later his pitching coach. Hodges needled Walker about his lack of foot speed, and Walker, with his distinct southern drawl, was fond of saying he was a champion wrestler back home in North Carolina. Hodges finally decided to take Walker up on it, and in a hotel room with all the furniture pushed against the walls and their teammates gathered in the hallway, they went at it. Hodges emerged first, stating that he was the new wrestling champion of North Carolina.

Hodges was well known for the lengths to which he would go to respond to children's autograph requests. Carl Esrkine recalled that after a game on a hot summer day in St. Louis, with the Dodgers' entire squad on the team bus waiting to leave, Hodges was still outside signing autographs for a group of children. Neither the heat nor his teammates' razzing mattered to Hodges. He didn't get on the bus until the last child had an autograph. Hodges viewed signing autographs for kids part of his responsibilities as a professional baseball player, but he also seemed to truly enjoy the time he spent with kids. Years later, after Father Vieck, the Hodges family's priest in Petersburg, watched Hodges interact with children on one of his visits home, he wrote, "For a man who was generally described as being shy, he had an endless variety of things he could say to youngsters. I had the impression that he was more at home with kids than the adults."

In May of 1951 when Hodges went to Wolf's Sport Shop on Sunrise Highway in Rockville Center, Long Island, to sign autographs, he was in a brief hitting slump, which writers blamed on Hodges's inability to get a good night's sleep because of infant Irene. At the signing, a young girl named Doris who had just won a contest that tested the participant's knowledge of catechisms gave Hodges her prize, a St. Christopher medal blessed by the Pope, telling him she hoped it would help him return home safely after his at bats. The people on line laughed at her rapid-fire speech—but not Hodges.

"He accepted the medal with great solemnity," she later wrote, telling her that he used to have a St. Christopher's medal blessed by the Pope, but gave it to his father so he would be safe working in the mines. Hodges shook the little girl's hand; like countless others, she never forgot how her fingers disappeared in Hodges's hand. Shortly thereafter, while on a road trip, Hodges began hitting again. Reporters credited the improvement to his getting more sleep. Doris knew better.

The 1951 All-Star Game was played at Detroit's Briggs Stadium on July 10. Hodges started the game and broke it open in the sixth inning with a two-run homer to give the National League a 6–3 lead. Musial, Kiner, and Bob Elliott also hit home runs for the National League, but Hodges's was the most impressive—the ball was still climbing when it landed in the left-field seats. The National League won, 8–3. After the game, Stengel said, "I didn't have a chance. They only used six Dodgers against me. I operate better against 'em when they use nine."

"Some people have street smarts," Dodgers pitcher Clyde King told me, but "Gil Hodges had baseball smarts." Never was that more evident than in a game against the Reds the week after the All-Star Game. King had walked Cincinnati's Johnny Wyrostek, and the next batter, Joe Adcock, attempting to bunt Wyrostek over, hit a pop-up. Hodges, anticipating the bunt attempt, charged the plate, but instead of catching the ball on a fly, he trapped it. With the ball in his glove, Hodges turned around and sprinted toward first, where he tagged Wyrostek out as he stood in the base path. Hodges then stepped on first base ahead of Adcock for an unassisted double play.

Hodges's heads-up play is even more impressive because in the previous inning Hodges had been hit in the face by a pitch from the Reds' Herm Wehmeier. The pitch dropped Hodges to the ground, his hand over his face, and concerned players from both teams surrounded him. But the brunt of the pitch was apparently absorbed by Hodges's left hand, which he had raised to protect his face. The next day on July 16, despite his left wrist being "stiff," Hodges "insisted" on playing. He went 2 for 3 and for the second straight day made a fine defensive play as the Dodgers won, ending a four-game losing streak.

The rivalry between the Giants and Dodgers reached its apex as the season neared its end. Bean ball wars became common due to Durocher's two-for-one rule: if you hit one of our guys, we're going to hit two of yours. Newly acquired Andy Pafko was amazed by the venom between the Giants and Dodgers. "Those games weren't baseball," Pafko said, "they were civil war." Yet, despite the animosity between the two teams, Bobby Thomson, the Giants outfielder, told me Hodges was the only player on the Dodgers who ever talked to him. "Hodges," Thomson said, "was the only guy on that team universally admired and respected for the type of person he was."

The Giants finished the regular season winning twelve of their last thirteen games, the Dodgers lost seven out of thirteen, and they ended the season with identical records, forcing a three-game playoff. The Giants won the first game; the Dodgers the second, 10-0, behind Labine's stellar pitching and Hodges's fortieth home run of the season. In the ninth inning of the deciding game—played at the Polo Grounds, telescope still in place—the Dodgers led 4–1, needing only three more outs to win the pennant. Never before—or since—has a team in the ninth inning of a deciding playoff or World Series game managed to overcome a three-run deficit and win. But Alvin Dark led off with a single off Hodges's glove.

With no outs, and a three-run lead, the first baseman normally plays behind the bag so he can be in a better position to make a play that produces an out. Even if the runner steals second base and scores on a base hit, the Dodgers would still be up by two runs. Where the first baseman should play with a runner on base was the manager's decision. Dressen decided to hold the runner. Over half a century later—with a pained look on his face—Carl Erskine showed me the signal Dressen used when instructing his first baseman to hold the runner. Erskine held his left forearm up and grabbed his left wrist with his right hand like a football referee calling a holding penalty. As a result of holding the runner, Hodges was only able to move a few feet off first base as Don Newcombe released the pitch and the next batter, Don Mueller, placed a perfectly hit grounder between first and second that went underneath the glove of a diving Hodges. Had he been playing back, Hodges would have easily fielded the ball. But now there were runners on first and second. Monte Irvin popped up to Hodges for the first out. Whitey Lochman doubled to drive in Dark. The score was 4–2. With runners on second and third and Bobby Thomson at bat, Branca replaced Newcombe. Then Thomson hit one of the most famous home runs in baseball history ("the shot heard around the world") and Giants broadcaster Russ Hodges was screaming over and over, "The Giants win the pennant!"

With the front page of the *New York Times* reading, "It's Like a Wake in Brooklyn," someone had to perish. Management decided on Clyde Sukeforth, the bullpen coach, because he had told Dressen that Branca (and not Erskine, who was also warming up) was ready to pitch. After twelve years with the Dodgers, the coach who was instrumental in helping Hodges believe in himself was fired.

That October, without any World Series money to divvy up, Campanella and Hodges formed two barnstorming teams—one white, one black—and traveled to the segregated South for a series of games. Upon his return, Hodges was selected to be an instructor in the not-for-profit American Baseball Academy, intended to combat juvenile delinquency in New York City. For twelve weeks, beginning in early November, youngsters ranging in age from ten to eighteen spent two hours, five days each week, in a gym, learning baseball fundamentals.

For Hodges, the Academy was a chance to make use of the teaching skills he had learned from his dad. "We're very careful in picking our teachers," the Academy's director, Malcolm Child said, "because their influence is the key to the whole enterprise. All they're told to do is teach baseball.... But it's noticeable how much interest they take in the boys.... Their prestige is so enormous that they can do about anything just by example. Boys get attached to one or another of them[,] ... imitate their heroes, get a new standard of behavior." Hodges returned to teach at the Academy the following winter.

In Petersburg, even without any mention of Bobby Thomson, the fall of 1951 was a challenging time for Charlie Hodges. He ran for a seat on the Petersburg city council on the Democratic ticket and lost. Not even his son's popularity could save him from a Republican clean sweep at the height of the "I like Ike" era. But Gil Hodges's appeal crossed at least one party line. Every day during the baseball season, Vic Colvin, who owned a tailoring/dry-cleaning business on Main Street, posted Hodges's updated batting average, home run, and RBI totals on a piece of cardboard in the front window of his store. That fall, another member of the Colvin clan, Fred, benefited from the publicity and won a council seat.

9

A BITTER UNIQUENESS

I'm an authority on slumps.

Charlie Dressen hit eleven home runs in his entire eight-year Major League playing career; Hodges hit forty or more home runs in a single season—twice. Yet, in the spring of 1952, Dressen was convinced he could improve Hodges's hitting. Unlike Rickey, who accepted Hodges's sub-.300 batting average as a consequence of his home run power, Dressen felt Hodges's home runs didn't justify his league-leading strikeout total of ninety-nine (forty-six on called third strikes) and hoped to cut down on Hodges's strikeouts with more bunting.

"If we can get Gil to where he can bunt . . . we'll drive those guys crazy," said Dressen. "Look, they gotta play him back on the grass. So we have him bunt, and if the third baseman has to come in and take two or more steps to field the ball, Gil's on first because he's fast. So next time Gil comes up, we do the same thing, and maybe by this time the pitcher is worried and so he doesn't get one where he wants it, but instead gives Gil a nice fat one. So Hodges has his home run."

"No one," wrote Arthur Daley, "can argue about the soundness of the theory, although some may be inclined to doubt the soundness of this application of it."

Red Smith later recalled "how everyone jeered at Dressen in the spring of 1952 for announcing that he was going to teach Hodges to hit to right field." Hodges was a streaky hitter due to his unwillingness, not inability, to hit to right, which accentuated Hodges's strength: his ability to pull pitches thrown anywhere from the middle of the plate in with power to left field. But Hodges played the part of the good soldier and followed orders. As a result he became one confused hitter, "holding his bat like a torcher in a torch-light parade . . . out and up. His elbows stuck out." In 1952 Hodges's batting average fell to .254, even lower than his .268 average in 1951.

In an era when a hitter usually attempted one bunt during batting practice and hit away for the balance of their at bats, a visitor to Vero Beach that spring noticed that on that particular day Hodges was only practicing bunting. Arthur Mann, Rickey's longtime assistant, wrote, "I see poor Gil as nothing more than another victim of those well-intentioned managers and coaches of baseball who are always eager to 'help the accomplished.' I've seen several fine examples of it in the past. It pops up whenever a hitter of high promise appears. It's a psychopathic weakness, an urge on the part of the mediocre to be a part of eventual greatness. It feeds the ego and, more importantly solidifies the self-appointed teacher's job."

Yet Hodges defended Dressen, saying that he was just trying to teach him something all good hitters must do: protect the outside corner of the plate. But Hodges, who could be as stubborn as his mother, believed that if he kept his strikeout to home run ratio below 4 to 1, his at bats would have the net effect of helping the team. His logic was simple: every home run he hit generated four total bases; every strikeout denied his team a base runner. When Hodges's playing career ended, his strikeout to home run ratio was slightly over 3 to 1 (1,137 to 370), well within the range he found acceptable. In addition, Hodges drew a high number of walks. In 1951 his 93 walks placed him sixth in the league. Over the course of his career, Hodges drew almost as many walks (943) as strikeouts. Preceded in the lineup by .300 hitters like Robinson, Hodges understood he was paid to drive in runs, not hit for average. Hodges viewed the difference between a .275 hitter and a .300 hitter as just one hit more a week, and he readily accepted a lower average as long as he was knocking in runs. For his career, Hodges batted .273. That was enough for Rickey, who understood that with Hodges at bat "the runner on first was always in scoring position."

In addition to wanting to change Hodges's hitting, Dressen wasn't happy with Hodges's failure to argue with umpires. Dressen preferred, as his mentor Durocher once said, "scratching, diving, hungry ballplayers who come to kill you." Hodges was an intense competitor, but for him angry was not usually

15. Working out with Chuck Dressen, early 1950s. AP Photo/JH.

better. But that didn't stop Dressen. In one game, when Hodges was called out on strikes on a bad call, Dressen offered him fifty dollars if he would "say something" to get himself thrown out of a game. For Dressen, if a hitter didn't argue a bad call, the umpire would subsequently favor the pitcher. For Hodges, the offer was "ridiculous."

"How about," Hodges suggested, "if I don't ask him how his wife and kids are?"

Hodges saw no benefit to offending umpires. First, they "are human beings," who shouldn't be abused. Second, "it didn't do any good." Later in that same game, Hodges thought he had Eddie Stanky picked off at first base, but umpire Bill Stewart ruled him safe. Stewart and Hodges had "quite a discussion." Dressen offered Hodges fifty dollars upon his return to the dugout. Hodges just shook his head.

When Hodges's favorite umpire, Larry Goetz, heard about Dressen's offer, he told Hodges the umpires would not only match it, "but better it."

Hodges replied, "They won't have to, Larry."

Those years cemented Hodges's reputation with the umpiring community, which was quick to spread the word on which players were pains-in-the-ass and which never caused you a problem. Goetz named "Stan Musial, Bill Terry, Carl Hubbell, and Gil Hodges as the kind of players it was a pleasure to work with." The good ballplayers, Goetz said, "never bother the ump." Goetz, Hodges later wrote, "couldn't care less" that the players didn't like him.

"What I do want," Goetz would say, "is their respect."

Hodges said those exact words about himself when he became a manager. And Hodges clearly patterned himself after Goetz; they both had no use for show-offs. "Hot dogs" earned nothing but "contempt" from Larry Goetz. "And although he was genuinely fond of people," Red Smith wrote, "he was capable of venomous dislike of a ball player who prolonged a protest or laid on the histrionics to show up the umpire before the fans. The players he detested had to be aware of it, for Larry was not one to disguise his feelings or reserve opinion."

If a player got too theatrical, Hodges put him in his place. The Boston Braves outfielder Sam Jethroe led the league in stolen bases twice. In one game, Jethroe was safe on a play at first base, fell down, and was "very slow getting up." Although Jethroe seemed "barely able to stand up," he stole second on the next pitch. The next time the Dodgers played the Braves and Jethroe was on first, Hodges went to the mound to confer with Erskine. When Hodges returned to first and Jethroe took his lead, Hodges pulled the ball out from his glove (the old hidden ball trick) and tagged Jethroe out.

In Vero Beach that spring, O'Malley allowed CBS to film an episode for famed journalist Edward R. Murrow's television show *See It Now* depicting the Dodgers as a corporation no different from General Motors. Ebbets Field was the "showroom" where customers came to purchase "the product"; Vero Beach, "the manufacturing plant" churning out Major League ballplayers; and there were the many costs of doing business: turnstile boys paid fifty cents a game, at least a thousand baseballs consumed in one season, and food for the players ("Pee Wee Reese likes his steaks extra rare"). And "the boss [O'Malley] has his headaches too . . . needing 1.4 million fans to support his business."

The camera peeked in on an instructional meeting where Dressen was teaching the players the signs the coaches would use that season. Hodges asked, "With these new signs, does a pinch runner and pinch hitter take the same signs?" Hodges's question implied a need to change signs on occasion so the opposition couldn't figure them out. But Hodges's point went right by Dressen; and in a response that would come back to bite him during that year's World Series, Dressen said, "Yes."

That season, near the end of May, the Giants had a two-and-a-half-game lead over the Dodgers. As was typical of Hodges's streaky hitting, immediately after he hit poorly in a series against the Giants at the Polo Grounds in which the Dodgers were swept, he went on a tear. From May 29 to June 1, Hodges hit four home runs, and the Dodgers swept a three-game set from the Braves and then defeated the Cubs to take over first place.

On July 8, the Dodgers took a four-and-a-half-game lead into the All-Star Game, which the National League won, 3–2. The fans had voted the Giants' Whitey Lockman to start at first; Durocher, managing the National League, selected Hodges as a reserve, but rain shortened the game and Hodges didn't play.

As Labor Day approached, the Dodgers led the Giants by eight games. On August 31 the Giants took a four-game winning streak into Ebbets Field, but the Dodgers won, 9–1, sending a message there would not be another late-season collapse. The key hit was a grand slam home run by Hodges, his twenty-eighth home run of the year. But Durocher's team didn't fold. On September 7 the Giants faced the Dodgers again. The Giants were on a five-game winning streak and had cut the Dodgers' lead to four games. But Roe threw a three-hitter and Hodges hit his thirtieth home run in a 4–1 Dodger victory. In the eighth inning of that game, trying to break up a double play, Hodges hit Giants second baseman Davey Williams with a hard—but legal—slide that knocked him out of the game. "Davey had a bad back, and I flipped him," Hodges said in a 1960 interview. "He came down and hit badly, and he was through."

"Would you do it again?"

"Yes," Hodges said, "a thousand times. As a matter of fact I did do it again the same day. Bill Rigney came in to play second, and there I was on first again, and another ground ball came down to short. As I ran down the line I could see Rigney's body stretched out toward third. I tried to hook his leg with my spikes and flip him. Instead I gashed him down the thigh. The Giants had to use three second basemen that day."

Robinson was also an aggressive base runner. In retaliation for being hit by a pitch, he would drag a bunt up the first base line so he could knock down the pitcher covering first. In those instances, Sal Maglie would often leave it to his second baseman to cover the bag. In 1954, on one such play, Robinson knocked down Davey Williams, who never again played second base on a regular basis for the Giants.

When the 1952 war between the Giants and Dodgers finally ended, the Dodgers had won the pennant by four and a half games. Hodges finished fourth in the league in RBIs with 102. He was the only Dodgers player to knock in over 100 runs, and he led the team in home runs (32) and walks (107).

The Dodgers faced the Yankees in the Series, and pitching would once again be their weak spot. Don Newcombe was in the military, and the only Dodgers pitcher who both was healthy and had previously started a Series game was Roe, who was nearly thirty-eight and could no longer pitch on three days' rest. The Dodgers had to rely on two rookies, Joe Black and Billy Loes. Black, pitching exclusively in relief until the last eight days of the season, had won fifteen games. But the Yankees, then winners of fourteen of their eighteen World Series appearances, still had Reynolds, Raschi, and Lopat. Yet it would be a close Series, with every game (but one) decided by two runs or less.

For Hodges, it would be a nightmare. He later said he "never felt sharper or more ready" when the Series began, but in the last ten games of the season, Hodges failed to hit a home run, and he brought an 0 for 10 slump into the Series.

In Game One the Dodgers' Joe Black, starting for only the third time in his Major League career, pitched a complete game, giving up six hits, for a 4–2 win. Hodges went hitless.

In Game Two Raschi limited the Dodgers to three hits, as Erskine struggled.

In the sixth, the Dodgers trailed by just one run, but Mantle reached on a bunt, Gene Woodling singled, and Berra walked to load the bases. Loes replaced Erskine. Collins then hit a grounder to Robinson. After tagging Berra out at second, Robinson fired to Hodges to complete the double play, but Hodges dropped the throw. In the thirty-nine World Series games of his career, Hodges made only two errors. This was the first, and it proved costly. The next batter, Gil McDougald, bunted down the first base line. Hodges fielded the ball but saw that he couldn't get Woodling at home and turned to throw to first. But Loes failed to cover. Billy Martin then hit a three-run homer to give the Yankees a 7–1 lead, tying the Series at one all. Hodges drew a walk in his first at bat of the game but went 0 for 3. In the ninth, Hodges grounded to Joe Collins at first. Although the Dodgers were down by six runs, Hodges, hustling all the way, tried a fallaway slide into first, but Collins tagged him out.

The Dodgers won Game Three, 5–3. Hodges again went 0 for 3 with a walk. The closest he came to getting a hit was in the eighth when he hit "a rap" off the right wrist of Yankee third basemen Gil McDougald (a righty), who was unable to accurately throw to first. The official scorer ruled it an error. Hodges was the only Dodgers regular who was still hitless but, pleased with the win, he said, "I'll get one tomorrow."

The Dodgers lost the fourth game, 2–0. Reynolds struck out ten, giving up only four hits. On only two days' rest, Black pitched well but gave up a home run to Mize. Hodges went 0 for 2 but did take part in the Dodgers' best scoring chance of the day. Down by one run, Pafko led off the fifth with a single, Hodges walked, and Furillo sacrificed the runners over. Black was the next batter. When the Dodgers were at bat, Dressen managed from the third base coach's box. A master sign stealer, that day Dressen was hoisted on his own petard. With the count 1-1 to Black, Dressen reached his hand up to his throat, signaling for the squeeze play. Black had to make contact on the pitch; otherwise Pafko, who would take off for home the moment Reynolds released the ball, would be an easy out. But Dressen had forgotten that when he managed in the Pacific Coast League, one of his players was Yankee second baseman Billy Martin and—despite Hodges's preseason suggestion—Dressen was still using "the same old squeeze sign." Martin read the sign and signaled Berra, who had Reynolds throw a fastball outside that

Black had no chance of reaching. Berra easily tagged Pafko out, effectively ending the game.

For the fifth game, vice presidential candidate Richard Nixon showed up late and became the "first Republican to be jeered by a World Series crowd since Herbert Hoover." Hodges again failed to get a hit but did reach base three times on two walks and a throwing error.

In the tenth, the Yankees' Johnny Sain hit a slow grounder to Robinson at second base, "and the vote of the witnesses was 70,536 to 1" that Sain beat out the throw and was safe at first. "The lone dissenter was Art Passerella, umpire at first." Photos showed Sain stepping on first before the ball reached Hodges's glove.

The Dodgers beat the Yankees in extra innings, 6–5. After the game, Arthur Patterson, the Yankees' press agent, "gave an exhibition of tasteless bellyaching that would have been considered bush in Horse Cave, Kentucky," wrote Red Smith. Larry Goetz, a member of the 1952 World Series umpiring crew, replied to Patterson's comments with "cold, Teutonic bluntness": "The Yankees," Goetz said, "won the crying championship."

Up three games to two, with the home field advantage for the final two games, the Dodgers were confident. The Yankees had not played a championship game on the brink of elimination since 1942, and the pressure was on them. After the game, reporters asked Hodges about his performance. Outfielder Gene Woodling had robbed him of a hit with a diving catch in the tenth, but Hodges was upbeat—his team had won. "It wasn't hit too well," Hodges said. "Sure he made a good catch. Maybe I'll get one tomorrow."

That night, the season premiere of the *Jack Benny Program* was televised nationwide. The program opened with a commercial showing a huge pair of hands gripping a baseball bat. The voice-over said: "Whose hands are these? They belong to one of the finest first basemen in all of baseball. Meet big Gil Hodges, the home run king of the Brooklyn Dodgers."

The spot cuts to a smiling Hodges, dressed in a long-sleeved plaid shirt, looking relaxed as he lights up a Lucky Strike. "I always felt Luckies were the best-tasting smoke I ever tried," said Hodges. "Luckies are made better and it figures they've got to taste better. They're a great cigarette." The commercial ends with a voice-over, "Be happy, go Lucky."

Raschi faced Loes in Game Six. With no score, Hodges came to bat in the second with one out and no one on base. Standing as far back in the batter's box as possible to maximize his time to read the pitch, Hodges fouled off Raschi's first pitch and took his second offering outside for a ball. Raschi then threw a curve ball for a strike that had Hodges so badly fooled he was backing away from the plate. With the count at 2-2, Raschi went back to his curve, and Hodges swung and missed for Raschi's first strikeout of the game.

Shadows covered home plate as Hodges came to bat in the fourth. The game was still scoreless, but Campanella had just singled with two outs. Yankee broadcaster Mel Allen noted that the Dodger fans gave Hodges "a big ovation," hoping to help him break out of his slump, another instance of the fans cheering Hodges even when he was hitting poorly, a phenomenon wrote Joe Durso, "rarely . . . rivaled in modern baseball," a player whose lapses "seemed to endear him to the public as human failings of a superman." Hodges struck out swinging.

With the game still scoreless, the Yankees' Irv Noren singled and Stengel ordered Raschi to sacrifice Noren to second. Raschi squared and bunted, but Hodges, forgetting his hitting woes and charging on the pitch, pounced on it and made a perfect throw to Reese covering second, who fired to Robinson at first for a 3-6-4 double play.

In the sixth, Snider hit a home run to give the Dodgers a 1-0 lead. But in the seventh, Berra led off with a home run to tie it. Woodling then singled and Loes balked him to second. With two out, Raschi's ground ball hit Loes's left leg and bounced just beyond Hodges into right field; Woodling scored to put the Yankees ahead, 2-1. It was "a hit off Loes," said Red Barber, "in every sense of the word."

After the game, when reporters asked Loes what happened on Raschi's ground ball, he said, "I lost it in the sun." Always the gentleman, Erskine later wrote that there were a few moments in the late afternoon when the sun shone through the stands at Ebbets Field blinding a pitcher to anything, even a ground ball.

Hodges led off the seventh. Up in the press box, the talk was of how many players had gone through an entire Series without a hit. Curve ball: swing and a miss. Fastball, high inside, but Hodges swung and missed. Another high inside pitch: ball one. Curve, fouled off. Curve outside, bringing the count to 2-2. Raschi had Hodges looking for another curve, but fired a fastball on the outside corner for strike three, Hodges's third strikeout of the game.

In the eighth, Mantle led off with a home run, putting the Yankees up 3-1; but Snider followed in the bottom of the inning with his second home run of the game, and the Dodgers trailed by one run.

In the ninth, Hodges was neither happy nor lucky. Scheduled to be the leadoff hitter against righty Allie Reynolds, pitching in relief of Raschi, Hodges was lifted for a left-handed pinch hitter, Rocky Nelson, who had only thirty-nine at bats all season. Nelson struck out. The Dodgers didn't score and there'd be a decisive seventh game.

Before that final game, Dodgers organist Gladys Goodding played (and sang) the National Anthem while umpire Larry Goetz stood at home plate. The night before, knowing he would be working home plate for the most important game of the season, Goetz hadn't slept. "A whole year," said Red Barber, "came down to one ball game." Mel Allen called the Series "one of the greatest and most dramatic of all time."

For the final game, each team started four future Hall of Fame players in the two through five spots in the order: Rizzuto, Mantle, Mize, and Berra for the Yankees; and for the Dodgers, Reese, Snider, Robinson, and Campanella. Hodges batted sixth; "his name was lost in the lineup," said Frank Graham Jr., the Dodgers' assistant publicity director. Dressen again called on Black to pitch on two days' rest. Stengel sent his best-rested starting pitcher, the lefty Eddie Lopat, to the mound. Lopat relied on deception and control to get hitters out and was the kind of pitcher that gave Hodges fits.

Black held the Yankees scoreless for three innings, but Lopat shut the Dodgers down as well. With one out in the second, Hodges batted for the first time. Despite his woeful 0 for 17 in the Series, the fans gave him an ovation. Hodges was "a sentimental favorite," said Red Barber, adding that unless he got a hit, Hodges would forever bear "a bitter uniqueness."

Hodges hit a long fly to straightaway center field. It was, said Barber, Hodges's "best-hit ball" of the Series, but the elements conspired against him. The wind was blowing in from left field at 22 mph and held the ball up.

Mantle caught it in front of the center-field fence, almost four hundred feet from home plate.

Trailing 1–0 in the fourth, the Dodgers loaded the bases. With no outs and Hodges due up, Stengel replaced Lopat with righty Allie Reynolds. "On the banks of the Gowanes, with the bases FOB (Full of Brooklyn)," Hodges hit a hard line drive to left field, but directly at Woodling. It wasn't a hit, but Hodges's sacrifice fly allowed the runner from third to tag up and score, which tied the game.

A home run in the top of the fifth gave the Yankees a 2–1 lead, but the Dodgers tied the game in the bottom of the fifth on a Cox double and a single by Reese. Mantle homered in the sixth to give the Yankees a 3–2 lead. But in the bottom of the sixth, Campanella led off with a single. Reynolds got Hodges to hit a hard ground ball to Rizzuto, who turned it into a double play. Shuba grounded out to end the inning.

The game's crucial play took place in the seventh with the Yankees leading 4–2. The Dodgers had loaded the bases with one out. Left-hander Bob Kuzava was called in to pitch to Snider, who made the second out. Robinson then hit a pop-up to the right side of the infield just beyond Kuzava. First baseman Joe Collins lost the ball in the sun and it appeared it would fall in for a single. With the runners moving on the pitch, two runs had already crossed the plate and a third was about to score to give the Dodgers a 5–4 lead. But Billy Martin made a lunging catch just before the ball hit the ground.

In the eighth, Hodges reached base when third baseman Gil McDougald fielded his grounder and made a high, wide throw that pulled Collins off the bag. The official scorer ruled it a throwing error. But the Dodgers couldn't bring Hodges home. In the ninth, they never even got a man on base, and the Yankees were again champions.

After the game, a writer told Hodges, he had gotten into the record books as the first regular in World Series history to play in a seven-game series without getting a hit. His 0 for 21 tied the record for most at bats in a Series without a hit. Hearing the inglorious details, Hodges said, "That proves I go from one extreme to another, eh?" The press noted his demeanor was a "trifle" sad.

Knowing that one hit might have resulted in a different outcome for his team, Hodges felt more than a "trifle" sad. "The agonized face of Hodges trying desperately for a hit" would remain so vivid to *Los Angeles Times* writer Cecil Smith that he listed it among a handful of the decade's television images "that left a lasting impression." Many years later, when a reporter asked Hodges about the 1952 World Series, Hodges responded with a blank look, "1952? . . . I don't remember anything special about that one."

Despite his ability to later joke about it, the 1952 Series would be the first thing many would think of when Hodges's name was mentioned. And it was an image burnished into the memory not just of writers but of his fellow players. When Hall of Famer Eddie Mathews went hitless through the fourth inning of the fourth game of the 1957 Series, he said his greatest fear was ending up like "poor Gil Hodges."

Despite his World Series debacle, UPI selected Hodges as the league's best first baseman; yet "the loftier intelligences in the Brooklyn organization," wrote Red Smith, "had grave doubts about Hodges. . . . He's an easy-going guy and . . . too tranquilly disposed towards the attitude that, 'oh, well, you do or you don't.' The amazing form reversal of Hodges in the World Series . . . encouraged the belief the Dodgers were prepared to part with the first baseman."

That winter, the Dodgers offered Hodges and Furillo to the Braves for Spahn, but the trade fell through. O'Malley then said, "We are not parting with the league's best first baseman. . . . And Robinson is not leaving, either. Any talk of their leaving Brooklyn is ridiculous."

Gussie Busch, the owner of the Anheuser-Busch Company, had recently purchased the Cardinals and asked his manager, Eddie Stanky, what they needed to win a pennant. Stanky said a power-hitting first baseman like Hodges. Busch then called O'Malley and their conversation became part of Hodges's legend.

"How much do you want for Hodges?"

"At least $600,000," O'Malley replied. "But don't tempt me. If I ever get rid of Hodges, the Brooklyn fans would hang me, burn me and tear me to pieces."

O'Malley understood the Brooklyn fans' passion: after Mantle's homer in the Series' final game, a solitary Yankee fan stood behind home plate at Ebbets Field and screamed out in celebration. A Dodgers fan in an open-necked Mackinaw told him to "go back where you belong."

"I got a right to cheer my team," replied the Yankees fan, "this is a free country."

"This ain't no free country, chum, this is Brooklyn."

That winter, things were neither free nor easy for Hodges. "Everywhere I went," he said, "people asked what had happened to me against the Yankees. The kids were the most persistent of all. The funny part was we all talked about it as something over and done with."

It wasn't.

10

SAY A PRAYER

I would appreciate anything you could tell me in this matter, Mr. Cobb.

That winter, at the New York Baseball Writers' Dinner, a parody poked fun at Hodges's World Series *non-hitting* record. Hodges, who was in attendance, "laughed along with the other guests." But Dodgers management was in no laughing mood. They felt that "Hodges is still a pretty good hitter against ordinary pitchers."

"That," Red Smith wrote, "isn't exactly the acme of praise."

In an attempt to rehabilitate Hodges's image, Frank Graham Jr., the Dodgers' assistant publicity director, called Jimmy Cannon, then the most influential sports columnist in New York, and asked him to write a piece on Hodges. Cannon agreed, and Graham, with Hodges in tow, visited Cannon at his favorite watering hole, Toots Shor's Restaurant. For a Dodger, it was a rare appearance in a place frequented by Yankee stars like DiMaggio and Mantle.

Cannon's piece bolstered Hodges's public image, but nothing could help him in contract talks, and his salary was reduced to an estimated $22,000. O'Malley gave Hodges his "assurance" that he would not trade him during the off-season; but once the season began, if Hodges didn't perform, all bets were off. Hodges toed the party line, saying he was "the happiest guy in Flatbush" and was ready for "the greatest year of my life, because nobody ever received better treatment from a ball club, and that goes for the fans, too."

But Gil Hodges was not naïve. "I'd be the first to understand," he added, "if they did make a deal that would help the club and I happened to be the guy they sent away. But what Mr. O'Malley told me did a lot to wipe out those bad World Series memories."

The *New York Times* announced Hodges's new contract: "Despite his usual September slump . . . the big first baseman came up with some impressive figures." In 1952 Hodges was fourth in the league in runs batted in, was second in walks, and led all first basemen in assists. He was the Dodgers' team leader in home runs, doubles, runs batted in, walks, but also strikeouts.

A few days after signing his new contract, Hodges was back at the American Baseball Academy in Brooklyn when Dick Young paid him a visit. On January 7 Carl Furillo had eye surgery at St. Clare's Hospital in Manhattan, but he had neglected to tell management. Young, a master at unearthing a headline-worthy story, got Hodges to mention Furillo's eye surgery, and the next day the story broke in the *Daily News*, alongside quotes from O'Malley saying that nothing of note was happening regarding the Dodgers. After reading Young's piece, O'Malley was not happy. "It looks like we don't know what's going on in our own ball club—and by golly," he said, "I guess we don't."

Hodges arrived in Vero Beach on the last day of February, looking "as pale as a ghost" and doing "nothing of note in spring training games." By March 23, Hodges was so troubled by his lack of production in a game against the Philadelphia Athletics in which he went hitless, he publicly vented his frustration when first base umpire Larry Napp called a Phillies base runner out but then reversed his call, claiming Hodges's foot was off the bag. Hodges gave Napp "quite an argument." Hodges's reputation for integrity was already so well entrenched that his vehement arguing "convinced most observers that Hodges must have been right."

That spring, in response to criticism that he wasn't seeking enough advice to get out of his slump, Hodges contacted two of baseball's greatest hitters, Rogers Hornsby and Ty Cobb. Hornsby told Hodges, "The main thing about hitting is to watch the ball until it hits the bat."

In a letter to Cobb, Hodges wrote:

I'm strictly a pull hitter and hit very few balls to right field up to last season; sacrificing my power to get a base hit to right. As I am a hard swinger it was difficult to cut my swing down to try and punch the ball to right. I can hit one pitch well to right and that is the letter high ball over the plate.

16. Arguing with umpire Larry Napp, March 25, 1953. Brooklyn Public Library—Brooklyn Collection.

I would appreciate anything you could tell me in this matter, Mr. Cobb. I am willing to try anything that might help me improve.

I consider it an honor hearing from you and would greatly appreciate it if you could write to me at Vero Beach, Florida very soon.

How, or if, Cobb responded is unknown, but Hodges's fans offered encouragement. Mrs. Joseph Mitchell, wife of the famed *New Yorker* writer, told

Hodges she would pray for him. Aware that Mr. Mitchell's vision was failing, with characteristic compassion Hodges replied, "And I'll remember you and your husband in my prayers."

Just when things seemingly couldn't get worse, Hodges developed a painful growth between his right thumb and forefinger that made it hard for him to grip the bat, as well as a "mysterious ailment in his right foot" described as "cramped toes, a bruised instep, and inflammation of the foot," leaving him unable to play against the Yankees in St. Petersburg on March 30.

As the Dodgers headed north, they stopped in Mobile, Alabama, where X-rays were taken of Hodges's legs. They proved negative. A local physician, Dr. Joseph Little, thought the "pain in both ankles and lower legs" indicated arthritis and suggested Hodges "rest indefinitely."

The Dodgers flew Hodges back to New York where he went to Long Island College Hospital for testing. Dr. Herbert Fett, the son-in-law of the Dodgers' treasurer, Harry Hickey, concluded Hodges had had an allergic reaction to penicillin administered at the end of March to reduce the infected growth on his hand. "They had me scared when they were talking about arthritis a few days ago," Hodges said. "But the doctor . . . said it wasn't arthritis, so that's a big relief. I feel better today and I don't think it's anything serious."

At the same time Hodges was in Long Island College Hospital, Dr. Fett successfully removed bone chips from the left elbow of the Dodgers' other first baseman, Wayne Belardi. After they returned, Dressen sometimes played Hodges in left field and Belardi at first against right-handed pitching. And later that season, after Furillo broke his hand hitting Durocher during a Dodgers-Giants melee at the Polo Grounds, Hodges replaced Furillo in right field.

Playing right in Ebbets Field was an adventure. The bottom portion of the concrete outfield wall in right was concave, the top a ninety-degree vertical, and above that there was a wire fence. Balls hitting off any one of the surfaces bounced onto the playing field in wildly different ways. Hodges's willingness to switch playing positions—and possibly look foolish doing so—"reflects the genuinely cooperative spirit of a sincere and popular team player," wrote Red Smith. "Where the Dodgers can use Hodges to the greatest advantage, he will cheerfully play. What needs most to be done for the success of the team, he will do to the best of his very considerable ability."

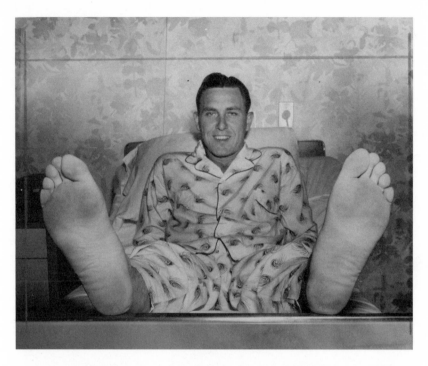

17. In Long Island College Hospital, April 2, 1953. Brooklyn Public Library—Brooklyn Collection.

When Hodges was managing a new generation of players in the 1960s, it was this attitude that made it difficult for him to understand a player's reluctance to switch positions when it was in the team's best interests. But no matter what position he played, after recovering from his allergic reaction, Hodges performed no better than he had in spring training. On May 5 a Dodgers home game against the Braves was rained out. With the day off, Hodges went to Ebbets Field and took extra batting practice to break out of his slump. Dodgers relief pitcher Bob Milliken pitched Hodges outside, where opposing teams had been successful against him. The extra practice helped; the next day Hodges went 2 for 4, hitting his first extra-base hit of the season, a "towering clout into the upper left-field deck" in the sixth inning of a 7–3 Dodgers win over the Cardinals. But that didn't lead to sustained improvement.

"A slump like mine," Hodges said, "is hard to describe, even after you've licked it. At first you just think: Well, tomorrow is another day. But tomorrow

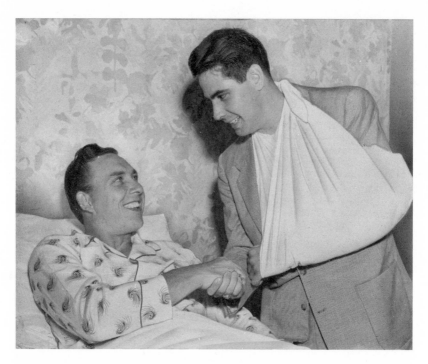

18. With Wayne Belardi at Long Island College Hospital, April 3, 1953. Brooklyn Public Library—Brooklyn Collection.

comes and goes and nothing happens. Day after day, week after week, nothing happens. You wonder if you're all through. 'What happened?' you ask yourself. 'I had it—where did it go?'"

But despite his slump, when he came up to bat at Ebbets Field, Hodges was cheered and fans even began a "Save Hodges" campaign. The advertising agency that handled the Dodgers' fan mail reported that over half the letters they received dealt with Hodges's slump. Hodges later said, "The way Brooklyn fans backed me when I couldn't buy a base hit is my biggest baseball thrill. Their support helped me recover as much as anything else. . . . It made me feel I was part of Brooklyn. . . . This is my home now. I'm proud to say so."

The "Save Hodges" campaign reached its apex the first two weeks of May when Hodges's fan letters jumped from thirty a week to thirty a day. It was the first time in five years that any Dodgers player received more fan mail than Robinson. One letter suggested that carrot juice would help. Another asked

19. Packing up his mail with Senator Griffin, October 1950. Brooklyn Public Library—
Brooklyn Collection.

for custody of Hodges for ten days, after which time he would be "a boy who could hit most anything."

"I suppose some of the letter writers might be called cranks," Hodges said, "but not in my book. They were kindhearted people who felt sorry for me. Mostly, they sent encouraging messages instead of suggestions. Many sent religious articles—rosary beads, scapulars, medals and mezuzahs. Others sent good-luck charms—rabbits' feet, four-leaf clovers, miniature horseshoes. . . . It was a comfort to feel that the fans were with me, but it couldn't keep me from worrying."

Hodges worried. His teammates joked that he worried himself into shape. But as Hodges did throughout his career, he internalized his frustrations. Furillo, then Hodges's roommate, was amazed by it. "I've had slumps in my time, too," said Furillo, "but I never could hide my feelings like Gil. He never reached the point where he would growl at waiters or porters as some guys do."

The Hodgeses' next-door neighbor in Brooklyn, Howard Luebke, agreed. "That's the way Gil is," Luebke said. "He never shows anything."

Roger Kahn, the *Herald Tribune*'s Dodgers beat writer from 1952 to 1953, later wrote in his classic book *The Boys of Summer* that Hodges "built an outer barrier of calm, but . . . churned beneath the way the sea churns below a pale, rippled surface."

In contrast to Hodges, Dressen's emotions were often on display. Dressen grew so frustrated with Joan Hodges who, Frank Graham Jr. told me, "would call constantly to the clubhouse" asking her husband to "bring home a quart of milk" or some other item, that legend has it Dressen ripped the phone off the clubhouse wall. Graham doesn't recall that, but he does remember that Dressen felt the calls were "a distraction and made it harder to get to the phone."

Through the first twenty-four games of the season, Hodges batted .187, and with the exception of his lone home run, all of his hits had been singles. So, on May 16, when the Dodgers-Reds game in Cincinnati was rained out, Hodges must have been churning as Dressen concluded the only way to get Hodges "back on the beam" was to bench him.

With Hodges in a 0 for 19 slump, Dressen was considerate enough to first tell Hodges his decision prior to announcing that he wouldn't play in the next day's doubleheader against the Reds. Belardi started the opening game, Robinson the second game. Only Dick Young could spin Hodges's benching as a positive: "Such is the magnificence of Gil Hodges, that even when he's benched, it takes two men to take his place." Hodges sat out all three games in Cincinnati. But Dressen let Hodges know he was planning for his return. "If Hodges hits and Belardi hits," Dressen said, "I might put Gil out in left field. I think he can play any position."

Unbeknown to Hodges, during his hitting slump Dressen had team photographer Barney Stein take film of Hodges's game at bats from numerous angles, which showed that Hodges had reverted back to his old habit of stepping in the bucket. Rather than using a ten-foot-long board, Dressen instructed Hodges to place his right foot a few inches further away from the plate so when he moved his left foot away from the plate his left leg would align with his right leg. Hodges was still pulling away from the pitch, but the hope was that because of the new stance, the effect wouldn't be as detrimental to his swing.

If Dressen's attempt to get Hodges to bunt more contributed to his slump, Dressen also did all he could to undo the damage. Hodges's first at bat since being benched came on May 21, when the Dodgers returned to New York for two games at the Polo Grounds. Dressen gave Hodges a good chance to succeed by pinch-hitting him in the seventh inning in an unpressured situation (the Giants were ahead by five runs) against a second-tier left-hander, Dave Koslo. Hodges singled to center.

The next day, after leaving him out of the starting lineup for six games, Dressen penciled Hodges in at first against the Giants right-hander Jim Hearn. Hodges went 0 for 4, but Dressen kept him in the lineup when the Dodgers went to Philadelphia for a three-game series.

In the opener, Hodges went 0 for 3 against Robin Roberts, but he didn't let it affect his fielding, making an outstanding play in the eighth on a "vicious grounder" to the right side of the infield with two out and a runner on first to preserve the Dodgers' slim 2–0 lead. Despite "taking a collar" for two consecutive games, Hodges was not discouraged. "After all, Hearn and Roberts are a couple of pretty fair country right-handers,' Hodges said. "They're liable to blank anybody. I felt that I was seeing the ball better and that it was only a question of time before I'd bust loose."

Hodges finally broke through in the final two games of the series. On May 24 against lefty Curt Simmons, Hodges went 2 for 5. The next day he had 3 hits in 5 at bats and knocked in two runs. Hodges's confidence had returned. On May 29 he was 3 for 5 with three runs batted in to help the Dodgers defeat the Pittsburgh Pirates, 7–4. In the five games ending on May 29, Hodges had 10 hits in 23 at bats for a .435 average with seven runs batted in. The next day,

Hodges hit two home runs as the Dodgers defeated the Pirates in both ends of a doubleheader and moved to within a half game of first place.

The following week, on a humid Sunday in early June, Father Herbert Redmond was leading the ten o'clock Mass at St. Francis Xavier in Brooklyn. Father Redmond traveled to Roman Catholic congregations throughout the borough as the chaplain for the Nursing Sisters of the Sick and Poor. After the Gospel and announcements were read, Father Redmond looked at his perspiring listeners fanning themselves with their missals, handkerchiefs mopping their brows, and spoke the words that would do much to perpetuate Hodges's saintlike legend. "It is too warm this morning for a sermon," Redmond said. "Go home, keep the Commandments—and say a prayer for Gil Hodges."

Father Redmond had never met Hodges, and he later told reporters he decided to speak of Hodges because "he seemed like a decent boy who deserved a break." Whether it was the prayer, the new stance, or the carrot juice, Hodges was out of his slump.

Like Hodges, the Dodgers started the season slowly, but on June 28 they took over first place and never relinquished it for rest of the season. On August 17 the Dodgers won their tenth consecutive game, a 5–2 extra-inning victory over the Pirates, with Hodges hitting a game-winning three-run home run in the eleventh inning, giving him 101 runs batted in for the season, his fifth consecutive season with over 100 RBIs.

In Milwaukee on September 11, shortly after Furillo broke his hand, Hodges started the game in right field. Dressen wanted Hodges to get some experience playing right field if Furillo was unable to play in the World Series. In the second, the Braves' Joe Adcock hit a ball to deep right center that appeared headed over the outfield wall. Hodges crashed into the fence and deflected the ball back onto the field, holding Adcock to a triple, but severely bruised his left side as he "impaled himself on the low outfield fence."

Hodges had to leave the game, and it was reported that he probably wouldn't play the next day. But with Hodges saying, "It won't hurt me to swing unless I try to hold back," and his team on the threshold of clinching the pennant, Hodges started the next day. He had a hit in five at bats, scored a run, and knocked in another run to help the Dodgers defeat the Braves and win the pennant. Subsequent X-rays of Hodges's sore left side "indicated a fissure fracture of the eleventh rib," but the examining physician, Eugene Zorn, said, "If it is a fissure fracture, it isn't bad and Gil should be able to swing within two or three days."

With the pennant clinched, Dressen rested Hodges for the next eight games, next starting him on September 25 in Philadelphia. Hodges hit a triple and scored a run. He played in right field again the next day. But for the season finale, Hodges returned to first base and had two hits, two runs batted in, and scored two runs. Despite his early hitting slump, Hodges hit .302 with thirty-one home runs that season.

The 1953 Dodgers won 105 games, even more than the American League Champion Yankees, who won 99. The Dodgers lead both leagues in batting average, slugging average, stolen bases, runs batted in, runs scored, and fielding average. Pitching was another matter. With Newcombe still in the military, Loes still inconsistent, and Black suffering from the sophomore jinx, the Dodgers had only one solid starter, Carl Erskine. Erskine would give it his all in the Series, becoming the first pitcher to start three times in a six-game World Series. But the Yankees still had the firm of Lopat, Raschi, and Reynolds, bolstered by junior partner Whitey Ford, a future Hall of Fame pitcher. Before the Series began, a year after his 0-21 debacle, Hodges said "he was 'quite determined' that such a thing would not happen again."

And he made sure it didn't. In Game One Hodges hit a home run and two singles. But it wasn't enough. Since suffering an arm injury, Erskine knew that on the days his arm felt right, he was going to pitch well; but when he couldn't get loose, the Dodgers were in for a long afternoon. Erskine didn't have it that day and allowed four runs in the first. The Dodgers fought back to tie it up at 5–5; but in the seventh, with no outs, Hodges on second and Furillo on first, Dressen ordered Cox to bunt, and he laid down a beauty. But Berra pounced on the ball and made a quick throw to third that just beat Hodges. Instead of bases loaded and no outs, there was one out and runners on first and second. The Dodgers failed to score and the Yankees won, 9–5.

In Game Two, Hodges went 2 for 3, scored a run, and even stole third base, but the Yankees won anyway, 4–2. At that point (in its seven-game format), no team had ever come back to win the Series after losing the first two games. In the Dodgers' locker room, a showered and dressed Hodges sat in front of his locker with his head down, despite sporting a .625 batting average after the first two games, "Yes," Hodges said in response to questions asking if he was pleased with his own performance, "but we're two down—and that's no good."

For the third game, four hundred newspaper reporters were in attendance to document a day when Erskine *had it* as he set a World Series record with fourteen strikeouts, and the Dodgers won, 3–2. Hodges did his part, going 1 for 2, with a walk in the sixth when the Dodgers took a one-run lead.

In Game Four Hodges went hitless, but the Dodgers won, 7–3, to tie the series at two games each as a poised Billy Loes got the win.

Game Five was the Series' crucial game. With 36,775 fans setting an Ebbets Field attendance record, thousands stood for the entire game, which was tied 1–1 after two innings. The Dodgers' starter, Johnny Podres, a twenty-one-year-old rookie, walked Phil Rizzuto to open the inning. He was sacrificed to second. Gene Woodling grounded out as Rizzuto advanced to third base. Then Joe Collins hit a "scorcher" on the ground to the right side of the infield. Hodges was playing about ten feet off first base. Collins's hit didn't give Hodges time to position himself properly. The ball skidded off his glove as he tried to make a backhanded stop. It was one of those rare instances where, instead of the usually sure-handed Hodges playing the ball, the ball played him. The official scorer ruled it an error, but it was one of those plays that would have been considered an outstanding play if Hodges had caught the ball.

The "third-out error" proved costly. Not only did Rizzuto score on the play to give the Yankees a 2–1 lead, but Podres, the second-youngest player to ever start a World Series game, lost his focus, hit Hank Bauer in the arm, and walked Berra to load the bases. Dressen replaced the left-handed Podres with the right-handed Russ Meyer. It didn't matter to the switch-hitting Mickey Mantle. He hit Meyer's first pitch for a grand slam home run to put the Yankees up 6–1. The Dodgers lost, 11–7. Hodges went 2 for 4, but he couldn't overcome his fielding error.

In the 1952 World Series, Stengel had waited until the seventh and deciding game to give Dressen "the big wink," Stengel's way of saying the Series was over—the Yankees had won yet another championship. In the ninth inning of the fifth game of the 1953 Series, when Stengel went out to bring in Reynolds to close out the game, he gave Dressen "the big wink." Although the Yankees needed to win one more game to take the Series, with a four-run lead in the bottom of the ninth and his best pitcher on the mound, Stengel knew the Yankees were unbeatable.

And Stengel's confidence rubbed off on his players, who were jubilant after the game. Whitey Ford was named the Yankees' starting pitcher for Game Six. He decided to take things easy the night before. "I'm going to my mother-in-law's house," Ford said. "I'll watch television—Martin and Lewis, Red Buttons and Jackie Gleason and Jack Benny—all the comics." Ford allowed only one run in seven innings. Erskine, starting his third game in six days, gave up three early runs, but the Dodgers tied it up on Furillo's two-run homer. But in the bottom of the ninth, the Yankees scored the winning run on Billy Martin's single, his record-setting twelfth hit of the Series. Hodges went 0 for 4. He led the Dodgers in hitting in the Series, batting .364 and scoring three runs, but he knocked in only one run.

A few days after the Series, O'Malley announced that Dressen would not return as manager. Dressen wanted a multi-year contract, and the club's policy was for one-year contracts only. That month, Hodges was the only white Dodgers player to join Robinson on a month-long southern barnstorming tour. Robinson had led prior tours, but this time his team had three white players—Hodges, Branca (then with Detroit), and Bobby Young—on an integrated team that "broke daring new ground." Jim Crow laws made interracial play illegal, but Hodges, the lead attraction among the three whites, played on Robinson's team in Wilmington, Norfolk, Houston, and Jacksonville. But in Birmingham, Alabama, after city officials made their "opposition to interracial play clear," Hodges and the other white players "stayed away on their own, so as not to disrupt the tour." Some criticized Robinson for caving in to social prejudice, but the nonconfrontational approach produced results: later that year the ban on interracial play in Birmingham was rescinded.

A few weeks after Hodges returned, Walter Alston, who had won pennants at the Dodgers' top Triple-A farm team, was named to replace Dressen. Alston was "an island of silence in a sea of yakkety-yak ball players." Unlike Dressen, who barely finished high school, Alston was a former high school biology teacher from Ohio who "parried leading questions like a fencing master." But after Dressen, Alston's silence was "so unnatural as to be uncomfortable." At six

20. With Joan, Gil Jr., and Irene in Vero Beach, March 2, 1954. Brooklyn Public Library—Brooklyn Collection.

feet two inches tall and powerfully built, Alston was an imposing figure, with a habit of settling disagreements with the words "Let's settle this outside."

Alston confidently faced the pressures of managing a two-time pennant winner. "I realize that if I don't win, I will be blamed," he said. "But if I have the best club, there is no reason why I shouldn't win."

Hodges admired Alston for his ability to adjust his style to match his players. Unlike Durocher, Alston never insisted that management acquire "his kind of players." Alston won with power-hitting teams in the 1950s, as well as power-pitching teams in the 1960s. Hodges would pattern himself after Alston, a man whose managerial style was succinctly summarized by Hall of Fame manager Sparky Anderson, who said, "He knew exactly what he had and what to do with it."

Unfortunately for Alston, in 1954 the Giants, with Willie Mays back from two years of military service, were much improved and finished in first place, five games ahead of the Dodgers. The tone for the season was set on Opening Day when the Giants defeated the Dodgers, with Mays's sixth-inning home run the game winner. Mays won the MVP Award that season, leading the league with a .345 average, hitting 41 home runs, and knocking in 110 runs.

That September, before a game in the Polo Grounds, the Dodgers were warming up when two future Major League managers formed a battery. Tommy Lasorda, then a rookie pitcher for whom words came more fluidly than strikes, was throwing to an imaginary batter as Hodges served as his catcher.

"I got good stuff today," Lasorda said to Hodges. "When I get loose I pitch nothing but strikes. Watch me work on this hitter, a big powerful left-hander."

"You knocked him down with that pitch," Hodges said.

"That left-hander I already struck out. I'm working on a righty now."

Hodges said nothing; he just threw the ball back to Lasorda faster than Lasorda had pitched it to him.

In 1954 Hodges played in every game of the season, hitting .304, one of only twenty-three players in either league to hit .300 or higher. Hodges's RBI (130) and home run (42) totals were higher than every other player's in baseball except Ted Kluszewski and marked the sixth straight season Hodges had driven in over 100 runs, a record no other active Major League player could claim. It was also his fifth straight season with at least 30 home runs. To put his home run power in context, when Hodges hit the 200th home run of his career on August 15, 1954, he was only the thirty-second player to reach that total. And in a fitting statistic for a man who put team first, Hodges led both leagues in sacrifice flies with nineteen. Yet because the Dodgers failed to win the pennant—and Reese and Snider also had great seasons—Hodges finished tenth in the MVP vote.

Off the field, Hodges sometimes had a higher profile than he would have preferred. That July, Hodges showed up in traffic court for a speeding ticket he had received two years before. Magistrate James Lo Piccolo fined Hodges fifty dollars for reaching "home plate much too late."

Rather than paying for traffic tickets, it's easier to envision Hodges visiting sick children, something he did frequently. In January of 1955, a thirteen-year-old from Portland, Oregon, named Robert Gray was a patient in New York City's Rockefeller Institute, suffering from a rare heart disease. After the Oregon Heart Association informed Hodges that Gray wanted to meet him,

21. With Tommy Holmes and Philip Certilman loading up gifts for needy children, December 24, 1954. Brooklyn Public Library—Brooklyn Collection.

Hodges brought Gray a ball, a glove, and a book on how to play baseball. But Hodges was less inclined to make speaking appearances. As one commentator wrote, "Gil is no platform spellbinder." Yet, after his talks, in one-on-one interactions, Hodges's "lack of sham" came through, making "a fine impression with his cooperative attitude and straightforwardness."

22. With Tommy Holmes visiting Robert Gray at the Rockefeller Institute, January 9, 1955. Brooklyn Public Library—Brooklyn Collection.

Living in Brooklyn, though, made Hodges an easy touch for the Dodgers' publicity director, Irving Rudd. One winter, the Rochester, New York, branch of B'nai B'rith offered Hodges $2,500 to give a speech. But a trip to Rochester would require Hodges to be away from home overnight at a time of year he considered family time.

Rudd told Hodges, "There's a grand in it for me."

"I'll give you the grand," Hodges replied, "We'll stay home."

"What do you say about a guy like that? Gil was the one guy I could go to for anything," Rudd later wrote. "If I needed a player to visit a blind kid in the stands; a kid in a wheelchair. Gil this, Gil that . . . he'd be there."

11

THE DAY NEXT
YEAR ARRIVED

Jack, don't say anything else. Cool down, Jack.

With the constancy of Vero Beach's orange crop blossoming in the distance, the Dodgers began spring training on March 1, 1955. After finishing in second place behind Durocher's Giants the prior season, they were a driven bunch. "I've never seen a spirit to match the spirit this team has," said Dodgers vice president Fresco Thompson. "It's as if they're determined to make amends for last year." Jackie Robinson was more succinct: "We are proud men. We won't lose again."

In typical fashion, Hodges was both optimistic and pragmatic. "We have an excellent chance of over taking the Giants," he said. "To repeat the Giants will have to see more than half a dozen players, all who had great years in 1954, come through again. And that doesn't figure. The Dodgers, on the other hand, had a number of players who were playing sub-normal last year and should have much better seasons in 1955."

Hodges was right. In 1954 only he, Reese, and Snider had stellar seasons. But at thirty-six, with his physical skills on the wane, Robinson was receiving inconsistent playing time from manager Walter Alston, who was giving journeyman Don Hoak a chance to replace Robinson at third base. Robinson hated being benched. But Alston did what he felt was best for the team, saying he had "a pretty good idea" what his Opening Day lineup would be, "but I don't see why I should tell you fellows now."

Alston didn't want complacent players assured of a starting job; Robinson understood that. In mid-March, Robinson said, "There are only three positions

23. Buzzie Bavasi tossing Hodges his new contract, January 22, 1955. Brooklyn Public Library—Brooklyn Collection.

on this ball club absolutely safe—first base, centerfield, and catcher. And when someone comes after your job, your pride whips you to even greater effort."

On April 1 in Montgomery, Alabama, as the Dodgers headed north to begin the season, Robinson made the mistake of asking Dick Young if he knew what Alston had in mind for him when the season started. Young poured gas on the fire. "If Alston doesn't want to play me," Robinson was quoted by Young, "let him get rid of me."

A few days later, before an exhibition game in Louisville, in which Hoak was starting instead of Robinson, Alston called for a closed-door clubhouse meeting and gave his players a dressing-down for airing grievances to the press. Without any names being mentioned, everyone knew whom Alston was talking about, and Robinson responded by calling Alston uncommunicative. There was no love lost between Alston and Robinson. "We will win," Robinson once said, "despite the Minor League manager."

24. With Stan Musial being honored by the New York Press Photographers Association as 1954's "Most Cooperative" Sports Personality, January 25, 1955. Brooklyn Public Library—Brooklyn Collection.

Alston and Robinson started screaming at each other. Robinson stood up and a physical confrontation seemed imminent. But playing his usual role of peacemaker, Hodges intervened. He didn't confront Robinson head on; instead, Hodges repeatedly tapped Robinson's arm saying, "Jack, don't say anything else. Cool down, Jack."

Robinson, who "had a tremendous amount of respect for him," did as Hodges suggested, and an altercation was averted.

Few outside the locker room ever knew that Hodges had defused a potentially explosive situation. Decades later, Robinson, referring to the confrontation, said, "The thing that stands out is the quiet way Hodges interceded. . . . He leaned over and told me not to say anymore. I responded, and that was it."

Johnny Podres, who witnessed the scene, told me he couldn't recall Hodges's involvement but did remember Campanella stepping in between Alston and Robinson to keep them apart. Whether it was Hodges or Campanella who interceded, the next day, when the Dodgers moved on to Washington to play the Senators, Robinson was starting at third base.

But Robinson was not the only veteran Alston tried to motivate. Alston suggested Hodges and Campanella "cut down their swings," saying he would "like to see fewer home runs and more base hits." For the home opener, Alston sent a message, batting Campanella eighth, and he responded with one of the best seasons of his career.

Alston also found a way to motivate Hodges. That spring, the Dodgers traded for a right-handed journeyman first baseman named Frank Kellert. Alston played Kellert at first base "to see how he hits" and "to get a good look at Hodges as an outfielder." As always, Hodges played where asked and fielded his position solidly. That season, Hodges played sixteen games in the outfield, spending time at all three outfield positions. Kellert had only eighty at bats that season, but several of his hits were game winners.

On April 9 a highly motivated Dodgers team played the Yankees at Ebbets Field in their annual end-of-spring-training exhibition series. The Dodgers embarrassed the Yankees, winning by a football-like score of 14–5. Hodges and Campanella did not "cut down their swings," and both hit two home runs in the game. A few days later, on a cold, rainy afternoon at Ebbets Field, the Dodgers opened their season with a 6–1 win over the Pirates. Robinson started at third, Hodges at first. In a sign that the 1955 season would be different, Erskine got the win, his first Opening Day victory in four attempts. Hodges knocked in the Dodgers' first run of the season with a line single to right center. And as if to form bookends, he would also drive in the final runs of the season that October.

A week later the Dodgers won their ninth straight game, 3–2, over the Phillies. Hodges was the hero; his seventh-inning bases-loaded single drove in the tying and winning runs. The Dodgers defeated the Phillies the next day, their tenth win in a row, setting a National League record for most consecutive victories to start a season. Hodges again did his part, going 3 for 5 and scoring three times. At the end of that game, an announcement was made asking the 3,874 fans in attendance to mail in their ticket stubs so the Dodgers could send them a memento of the record-breaking game. O'Malley felt those few fans in attendance had "showed loyalty and should be rewarded."

After losing two out of three against the Giants, the Dodgers won eleven more games in a row for a phenomenal 22-2 season start. The Dodgers played well all season, finishing with a 98-55 record, clinching the pennant earlier than any team in National League history.

That season, nineteen-year-old Sandy Koufax, who had received a significant signing bonus, made his Dodgers debut. Most of the team's veterans ignored Koufax. In the mid-1950s, to prevent bidding wars that would drive up salaries, baseball owners established the "bonus rule," requiring that any player receiving a signing bonus over $4,000 had to be kept on the Major League roster for two years. Koufax, who should have started the season in the Minors so he could pitch regularly to hone his craft, was taking up a roster spot that would normally have gone to an experienced pitcher. As a result, for most of the 1955 season, Koufax felt he was "with the team, not of it."

The next season when Mike McCormick, another highly regarded left-handed teenage pitcher, joined the Giants, Hodges revealed his feelings about "bonus babies." Before the first Giants-Dodgers game after McCormick's signing, Hodges walked up to the seventeen-year-old pitcher, enveloped McCormick's left biceps with both of his huge hands, and said, "So this is what they paid all that money for."

For most of the 1955 season, Koufax told me, "My contact with Gil was negligible. He hardly talked to me." But on August 27, Koufax shut out the Reds, allowing just two hits and striking outs fourteen—the highest one-game total in the National League that season. Koufax proved that was not a fluke when he shut out the Pirates in his next start a week later. After that, "things changed," Koufax said, "I was part of the team."

Hodges and Koufax were teammates from 1955 to 1961. During much of that period, Koufax showed flashes of his immense talent, but his greatest seasons were still ahead of him. It was in those challenging years that Koufax came to appreciate Hodges. "His smile," Koufax said, "lit up the room. Joan and Gil were good to me. They invited me to their home many times for card games. They were kind to me."

Hodges had an outstanding season in 1955. He hit .289 (only twenty players in baseball hit over .300 that year) with 27 home runs. He knocked in 102 runs, his seventh straight season of at least 100, one short of Mel Ott's National League record of eight. He also showed why the Dodgers rarely faced left-handed pitchers; Hodges batted .477 against southpaws that year. But Hodges's accomplishments were overshadowed by his superlative teammates: Snider lead the league in runs batted in and Campanella won his third MVP Award. The only individual hitting category Hodges led the league in was, once again, sacrifice flies.

On September 16, having clinched the pennant, the Dodgers players, dressed in their home uniforms (but wearing shower sandals), marched from Ebbets Field to nearby Grand Army Plaza. Their twenty-four-year-old batboy, Charley DiGiovanna, the married father of three, led them. A fixture at Ebbets Field since he was a kid working as a turnstile boy for fifty cents a day, DiGiovanna had been promoted over the years and became the first batboy with an annual salary. The dean of his profession, DiGiovanna, called "The Brow" because of his bushy eyebrows, paraded down the Brooklyn streets holding a baseball bat aloft as if it were a baton. At Grand Army Plaza, the players boarded open cars for the two-mile ride to Brooklyn's Borough Hall for a ceremony in their honor. When they arrived downtown, each of the players was introduced by John Cashmore, the borough president, and presented with a four-piece silver service set, paid for not by Dodgers management but by the fans. "The warmest applause from the 20,000 in the [downtown] plaza came for Reese, Robinson, Snider, and Hodges."

The Yankees won the American League pennant in 1955. Although their three gifted pitchers Reynolds, Raschi, and Lopat were gone, the Yankees still had Whitey Ford, but they lacked pitching depth. The Dodgers' starters, Newcombe, Loes, Erskine, and Johnny Podres, had started the season well, but injuries had curtailed their effectiveness in the second half of the season.

In Game One, Ford outlasted Newcombe and the Yankees won 6-5. The game's indelible image was of Robinson, with the Dodgers trailing late in the game, trying to push his team to victory with a successful steal of home. Hodges had a single in four at bats but did little of note other than starting a 3-6-3 double play.

Neither Hodges nor the Dodgers did better in Game Two. The Yankees got to Loes with four runs in the fourth and won, 4-2. Hodges went hitless, and in the game's final at bat he struck out swinging. Hodges did save a few runs with his fielding. In the fourth inning, after a Gil McDougald single, Irv Noren hit a "scorcher" down the first base line; Hodges snared it, stepped on first, and fired to Reese at second to complete the double play. As a result, no one was on base when Loes then allowed four singles, a walk, and a hit batsman.

At that point, the Dodgers' chances appeared slim. No team had ever come back to win a best-of-seven Series after losing the first two games. But before Game Three, in a move much against his character, Alston called a team meeting and told his players they were as good as the Yankees and that he had faith in them. More significantly, Alston selected Johnny Podres as his starting pitcher. Podres was an unusual choice: he had been injured for much of the season and had not pitched a complete game since June 14, and when he had pitched, he was inconsistent, finishing the season with a losing record. But Alston's role of the dice worked. The Dodgers won, 8-3, as Podres, pitching on his twenty-third birthday, held the Yankees to seven hits. Hodges caught the final out of the game, a pop fly near the pitcher's mound, and after the catch congratulated Podres by placing his huge right hand on the top of Podres's head and giving him a friendly pat that sent Podres's cap flying off.

In Game Four Hodges's old Newport News teammate Clem Labine came out of the bullpen to secure the Dodgers' 8-5 win. Hodges had his best game of the Series, going 3 for 4 and knocking in three runs. His fourth-inning, two-run home run gave the Dodgers a 4-3 lead, which they never relinquished.

In Game Five, Hodges went 2 for 3 and scored on a Sandy Amoros home run in the second. But Hodges's greatest contribution came in the top of the seventh, when Bob Cerv led off for the Yankees with a home run, Elston

Howard walked, and Irv Noren came to the plate representing the tying run. Alston called Labine in to relieve starter Roger Craig. Noren hit a grounder to Hodges who started his third double play of the Series to end the threat. Late in the game, hoping to expand on his team's one-run lead, Hodges dropped a sacrifice bunt down the first base line, advancing Furillo to second. He scored when Robinson followed with a single, giving the Dodgers a two-run lead, and they held on to win, 5–3, making them the first team in Series history to lose the first two games and come back to win three straight.

Back in the Bronx (Games Three through Five were played at Ebbets Field), Ford threw a four-hitter, making the Dodgers "look feeble and dispirited" as the Yankees tied up the Series with a 5–1 win.

At Yankee Stadium on the afternoon of October 4, an entire season once again came down to one game. It was not a good sign for the Dodgers that Robinson couldn't play due to a strained Achilles tendon and Hoak started at third base.

That morning, before the city turned its focus to the Bronx, Roy Rogers and his horse, Trigger, in New York City for the World Championship Rodeo's annual visit to Madison Square Garden, performed for thousands of disabled children on the grounds of Bellevue Hospital in Manhattan. Robust morning trading on Wall Street slowed down to a trickle by game time. In felony court, Manhattan Assistant District Attorney John A. McAvinue Jr. surmised the unusually light volume of criminal cases was due to the Subway Series having "ne'er-do-wells nailed to radios and television sets."

Podres took the mound for the Dodgers. After his Game Three performance changed the momentum of the series, Alston had confidence in him and his I-got-nothing-to-lose mind-set that made him well equipped to handle the pressure. It would be one of the best managerial decisions of Alston's career. After the game, Campanella said, "I caught him [Podres] without a sponge in my glove, and boy, am I sorry. My hand's as sore as it's ever been."

Stengel gave thirty-five-year-old left-hander Tommy Byrne the start. Early in his career, Byrne walked too many batters, but after a stint in the Minors, he developed a better command of his pitches and won sixteen games for the Yankees in 1955. In the second game of the Series, which had also been played at Yankee Stadium, Byrne became the first lefty to pitch a complete game against the Dodgers that season. Stengel was hoping the Dodgers' right-handed hitters would again be unable to pull the ball against Byrne and take advantage of the 301-foot distance down the left-field line at Yankee Stadium (even shorter than Ebbets Fields' 348-foot equivalent) but instead would hit long fly-outs to "Death Valley."

The temperature was around seventy and a gentle breeze blew over Yankee Stadium as the game began. Byrne did not allow a hit or come close to giving up a run for the first three innings. The best the Dodgers could do was Hodges's two-out walk in the second. Podres was shaky in the first few innings. In the third, Podres walked Rizzuto, Martin singled, and with runners on first and second, McDougald hit a slow grounder toward third base. Hoak had no chance to get McDougald and it appeared the bases would be loaded with no outs. But then came one of the three crucial plays of the game. The grounder hit Rizzuto as he slid into third base and he was automatically out. That erased the lead runner, and Podres got out of the inning without allowing a run.

In the fourth, Campanella hit a one-out double, his first hit at Yankee Stadium in the Series. Furillo grounded out; Campanella advanced to third. With two out, the lead run ninety feet from home plate, Hodges came to bat. It was a highly pressurized situation and a base hit would give Hodges the chance to atone for his prior Series' sins. With two strikes, Hodges powered a curve ball in on his hands for the crucial hit of the game, a single to left for a 1–0 lead.

In the top of the sixth, with one out, Reese at third, and Snider on second, Stengel ordered an intentional walk of Furillo to load the bases. With Hodges coming to bat, Stengel replaced Byrne with the right-hander Bob Grim. Hodges rose to the challenge, lifting a high outside pitch the other way. The ball was caught in deep right-center field in front of the 407-foot marker. Reese tagged up, scoring easily, and the Dodgers led 2–0. After Hoak walked, George Shuba, pinch-hitting for second baseman Don Zimmer, grounded out to end the inning.

A defensive change led to the game's third crucial play. To start the bottom of the sixth, left fielder Junior Gilliam moved to second base to replace Zimmer, and Sandy Amoros jogged out to play left field. Podres walked Martin. McDougald bunted his way on base. With no outs and runners on first and second, Berra, who usually pulled the ball to right, unexpectedly sliced a ball toward the left-field corner. Amoros had been playing Berra toward center field. But with the crack of the bat, Amoros sprinted toward the left-field line and arrived within a step of foul territory just as the ball came down. Amoros reached out his gloved right arm and caught the ball. Had Gilliam, a right-hander, still been playing left field, he would have been forced to attempt a difficult backhanded catch.

Amoros threw the ball to Reese, wisely standing just inside the foul line directly behind third base to shorten the distance Amoros had to throw to get the ball back to the infield. Reese caught the throw as he leaped in the air, landed, spun around, and threw to Hodges at first base. McDougald had been so certain the ball would fall in for a hit, he had already passed second base when Amoros made the catch. Hodges stretched and the throw just beat McDougald back to the bag. That was the Dodgers' twelfth double play, setting a record for the most double plays turned by one team in the course of a World Series.

In the seventh, Elston Howard singled, and Stengel sent Mantle up to pinch-hit. Mantle, who led the American League in home runs in 1955 with thirty-seven, hadn't been in the lineup because of a torn leg muscle. A home run would tie the game, but Podres got Mantle to pop up to Reese to end the inning. In the eighth, the Yankees put runners on first and third, but Podres struck out Hank Bauer on a high fastball to end the threat. With two out in the bottom of the ninth, no one on and the Dodgers leading 2–0, Elston Howard came to bat.

The symbolism was perfect. Eight years after Robinson had integrated the game, Howard was the Yankees' first black player. With the count 2 and 2, Howard fouled back two pitches. Then he hit a ground ball to Reese, who fielded it cleanly and threw to Hodges. For years afterward, Hodges loved to tease Reese that his throw bounced, forcing Hodges to make a spectacular pickup in the dirt. In reality, the throw was low but right on target; the ball never hit the ground, and Howard was out.

It was 3:43 p.m. Fearing that if he said anything lengthy his emotions would overwhelm him, Vin Scully, in the calmest of voices, announced, "Ladies and gentlemen, the Brooklyn Dodgers are the champions of the world." After losing the World Series in 1916, 1920, 1941, 1947, 1949, 1952, and 1953, next year had finally arrived in Brooklyn. Red Smith wrote that Podres was "lost from sight in a howling, leaping, pummeling pack that thumped him and thwacked him and tossed him around, hugged him and mauled him and heaved him about until Rocky Marciano [then heavyweight boxing champion], up in a mezzanine box, paled at the violence of their affection."

As the players took the ramp into the clubhouse, Carl Erskine recalled, "we were more reverential than boisterous." As he entered the clubhouse, Erskine thought about asking his teammates to take a knee or bow their heads to thank God for their victory, but decided against it. Nonetheless, for Reese, who had lost to the Yankees in five previous Series, emotions ran deep. "I looked at Pee Wee, and he had a tear in his eye. So did Jackie and Gil."

The veteran players may have disliked the way Walter Alston had treated them, but he had accomplished something no other Dodgers manager had ever done—win a championship. And Alston faced dissension by exerting his authority. The man was not out to win any popularity contests. When Newcombe, his best pitcher, refused to throw batting practice, Alston not only suspended him but fined him three hundred dollars. Newcombe got the message; his record improved from 9-8 in 1954 to 20-5. When journeyman pitcher Russ Meyer complained to Alston about not getting enough work, he was soon pitching for Chicago. And after winning the 1955 Series, Alston was in control, his authority unchallenged, and the press began referring to him—as they would to Hodges during his managerial career—as the "Quiet Man."

In the winning clubhouse, Hodges, the goat of the 1952 Series, modestly accepted congratulations for knocking in all the runs either team scored that day. Hodges batted .292 with one home run and five runs batted in and set a record for the most double plays started by a first baseman during a World Series with three. Amoros, a huge cigar in his mouth, smiled and chattered away in a mixture of English and Spanish. Podres's father, Joseph, an iron miner from the small upstate New York town of Witherbee, had to compose himself before entering the clubhouse to embrace his son. Labine, tears of joy running down his face, said, "Imagine a grown man crying." Koufax described the scene as joyful, "but not nuts."

After the Dodgers showered and dressed, the players took the team bus from the Bronx back to the County of Kings. "No one realized how important it was to Brooklyn," Koufax recalled over half a century later, "until the bus came over the bridge . . . and we saw the people in the streets, the honking car horns."

The players may not have been *nuts*, but the fans were. Downtown Brooklyn was one big block party. Fans surrounded the Dodgers' team bus, impeding its progress. The volume of phone calls into Brooklyn from 3:44 to 4:01 p.m. was the highest recorded since the day Japan surrendered to end World War II. At 3:45 p.m., Brooklyn police headquarters issued a bulletin for policemen to remain alert to the lawlessness that might follow the end of over half a century of frustration. But there was nothing illegal about the flying confetti, joyous dancing, exploding firecrackers, and clanging pots and pans. At 324 Utica Avenue, Joseph Saden, the proprietor of Joe's Deli, set up a stand outside his store and gave out hot dogs for free. "This, for a Brooklyn merchant," wrote Meyer Berger in his famed "About New York" column in the *Times*, "is but one step removed from total numbness."

Hodges joked that the Dodgers' accomplishment was reduced to its "proper perspective" when he came home after the game and five-year-old Gil Jr. looked up from watching television and said, "Gee, Daddy, you missed *Captain Midnight*."

That night in downtown Brooklyn, Walter O'Malley threw a victory party for the team in the Hotel Bossert. During the festivities, someone told Frank Graham Jr. that a huge crowd of fans was downstairs on the street outside the hotel screaming for Podres and Hodges. Graham rounded the two players up and took them outside to wave to the crowd. But when Hodges saw a little boy standing near the police barricades asking him for an autograph, he walked over to oblige. With that, the huge crowd surged forward, knocking over the barricades and swallowing up Hodges, who had to fight his way through the crowd, "like a swimmer in heavy seas," back into the hotel as the police struggled to move the crowd back. Afterward, a police sergeant glared at Graham through the glass front door of the Bossert. "Try that again, buddy," he growled, "and I'll have you locked up."

Upstairs, far above the frenzied crowd, Brooklyn Borough President John Cashmore promised a survey would be done for a new ballpark at the corner of Atlantic and Flatbush Avenues.

Asked about such plans, Walter O'Malley said, "Right now the matter is pretty much out of our hands. But I don't see the Dodgers leaving Brooklyn."

12

WHERE IN AMERICA WOULD YOU SEE THAT?

You know me. I'm likely to go the other way tomorrow.

Eight days before the veterans were required to be in Vero Beach to begin spring training for the 1956 season, Hodges reported for duty with the pitchers, catchers, and rookies. Alston let Hodges (and Furillo, who was also in camp) know that if they were going to work out with the team, they had to go through the full practice and not just pick and choose when they wanted to participate.

"That's not good for the rest of the fellows," Alston said.

Hodges said he would comply; but the very next day, he and Furillo failed to show up for practice. But winning a World Series had mellowed Alston. "Those fellows are on their own," Alston said, "They don't have to work out every day until March 1st."

When the Dodgers flew to Tampa to play an exhibition game that spring, the bus driver, Joe Garvey, who drove them from the airport to the ballpark, had gotten permission for his seven-year-old son, Steve, to be the Dodgers' batboy for the day. Over the next six years he continued to serve as their batboy whenever the Dodgers came to Tampa, and he watched how Hodges always seemed to have time for autograph requests; and in particular, how Hodges showed an interest in him, asking him how he was doing in school and in Little League, and even taking a few minutes to play catch with him. Hodges became the player Steve wanted to emulate.

But kids didn't have to know Hodges personally to admire him. In 1956 twelve-year-old Kenny Ofshe pitched for the Hawks, a Little League team in

25. With his parents, Charlie and Irene, and his children, Gil Jr. and Irene, on a visit to Petersburg prior to the 1956 season. Photo courtesy of Art Miley. Credit: *Evansville Courier & Press*.

Fresh Meadows, Queens. Ofshe wore jersey No. 14 to honor his favorite player, Gil Hodges. Why Hodges? "He's a good sport," said Ofshe, "never gets into arguments and is a good fielder and hitter."

That same year, Don Drysdale, a rookie pitcher from California, also came to appreciate Hodges. In prior years Hodges had roomed with Furillo, but beginning in 1956 Drysdale was Hodges's road roommate. Management paired them up, hoping Hodges would have a calming influence on the nineteen-year-old Drysdale, who tended to wear his emotions on his sleeve. It worked. Decades later Drysdale would have trouble describing the ineffable quality that enabled Hodges to make him feel better about himself with his mere presence.

Despite having won the World Series, the Dodgers were viewed as a team on the wane. Robinson and Reese were nearing the end of their careers, and two more youthful teams were on the assent. Milwaukee had two future Hall of Famers entering their prime years, Hank Aaron and Eddie Mathews; and in Cincinnati, Frank Robinson, the Mets' nemesis years later in the 1969 World Series, would set a rookie record with thirty-eight home runs.

Hodges's timing was off that spring, and early on the morning of May 13 he was at Ebbets Field for solo batting practice. Before each swing, Hodges yelled out, "One, two, three," trying to force himself to hold up on his swing. When asked what he was doing, Hodges replied, "This is a state secret. No one knows that I'm swinging ahead of the pitch except . . . every pitcher in the National League. If this ever gets known in the other league I'm sunk."

That season would prove to be an off year for Hodges. He hit 32 home runs, his sixth season with 30 or more homers, but his batting average fell to .265. In addition, Hodges's 87 RBIs was his lowest total since 1948.

In the field, Hodges again showed his versatility, playing the outfield for several games. In addition, in a game against the Giants, Hodges filled in as an emergency catcher for two innings. A few days later, before a game at the Polo Grounds, the Giants' catcher, Bill Sarni, asked Hodges, "What do you do when you find runners on the bases?"

"Tremble," said Hodges; but he added, showing his understanding of a position he had not played in years, "I really didn't have much to worry about. . . . There were only two runners. One was the result of a triple and he couldn't steal on me. Later Bill White walked with two out. Since Willie Mays was the next hitter, I didn't think he'd steal. He didn't."

Thanks largely to the starting pitching of Don Newcombe and Sal Maglie, the former Giant who was acquired that May and won several crucial games down the stretch, as well as Snider's league-leading forty-three home runs, the Dodgers did better than expected, staying within striking distance of the first-place Braves for most of the summer, and pulling to within a half game on September 8 when they defeated the Giants, 4–3, in a come-from-behind victory at Ebbets Field.

For Hodges, that game would be best remembered as the day he engaged in a glove exchange. At the start of the Giants' half of the eighth, Hodges went to take the field, but his glove was not in its usual place on top of the

Dodgers' bat rack. After a frantic search, the glove still didn't turn up. Bat-boy Charley DiGiovanna emerged from the Dodgers' locker room with a brand-new first baseman's mitt. But in a tight game with pennant implications, Hodges didn't want to take the field with a glove that had not been broken in. Then, in one of those moments that could only happen in Brooklyn, the public address announcer, Tex Rickards, said solemnly, "Ladies and gentlemen, if anyone knows where Gil Hodges' glove is, will they please return it to the Dodgers' dugout."

No one turned it in. Hodges took the field with the new mitt on his left hand. Then, before the start of the ninth, Rickards tried again: "Ladies and gentlemen, Gil Hodges has asked me to announce that if anyone will return his glove, they will receive a brand new one in exchange . . . no questions asked."

Shortly thereafter, "a dark visaged adult, wearing a sports shirt under a blue jacket, appeared somewhat sheepishly at the box-seat railing at the inner edge of the Dodgers dugout." He handed the "lost" mitt to Rickard, who announced the games from next to the Dodgers' dugout and not up in the press box. Rickard gave the fan the new first baseman's mitt and a new baseball. Measures were even taken to prevent a freelance photographer from taking a picture of the exchange, and the glove-returner remained unidentified.

For the rest of that month, the Dodgers and Braves took turns at the top. On September 11 Maglie allowed eight hits (but no walks) as the Dodgers beat the Braves to move into a first-place tie. Hodges's "towering home run" into the left-field stands in the eighth gave Maglie a three-run lead, which he needed, as Joe Adcock led off the ninth with a home run to make the final score 4-2. After the game, Maglie shook Hodges's hand, saying, "Thanks for that homer, buddy, that was a big run."

The next day, Pee Wee Reese and Billy Herman teased Hodges about his home run. "All the hits you could have made to right field last night," Herman said. "It was wide open for you."

"But not him," Reese added, "He wants to hit one down the wind tunnel that leads into the left field stands."

The Dodgers lost to the Braves that day and fell back into second place, but Hodges kept things in perspective. "All is not lost," he said, "We have our health—and fifteen games left."

That September, despite his reputation for failing to produce after Labor Day, Hodges started swinging a hot bat. On September 5 he hit his twenty-sixth home run of the season (his first in nineteen games) as the Dodgers defeated Pittsburgh, 4–3. Hodges went on to hit seven home runs that September, including two in an 8–3 victory over the Pirates in a rain-delayed game that began on September 23 but didn't end until the ninth inning was completed the next day. Hodges hit a two-run home run in the regularly scheduled game on September 24 that tied it at 5–5 in the eighth, but the Pirates scored in the bottom of the same inning and held on to win 6–5.

Hodges's fielding was clutch as well. In the eighth inning of a tie game with the Cubs on September 14, with the go-ahead run on first, the next batter tried to sacrifice the runner into scoring position. But Hodges made "a spectacular play" on the bunt that had flown into foul territory "in a low arc towards the right side. . . . Gil, racing in, nabbed the ball inches from the ground." The Cubs failed to score and the Dodgers won. Hodges made the key fielding play in Sal Maglie's no-hitter against the Phillies on September 25. With one out and a runner on first in the eighth, Solly Hemus "hit a hot grounder over the first base bag," which Hodges grabbed and threw to Reese at second to start a double play to end the inning.

The Dodgers were a half game behind the Braves when the Pittsburgh Pirates arrived at Ebbets Field for the season's final three games beginning with a doubleheader on September 29. Maglie pitched the opener; Hodges went 2 for 4 with an eighth-inning two-run homer to give the Dodgers a 6–2 win. It was Maglie's thirteenth win with the Dodgers.

The second game was crucial. A win guaranteed the Dodgers at least a tie for first place and would place them in control of their own destiny. No matter how the Braves did in their final game of the season, a Dodgers win the next day would give them the pennant. Clem Labine, in his sixty-second appearance of the season—but only his third start—threw a complete game, allowing only seven hits. But the Pirates' Ron Kline gave up only one run through five innings. With one out in the sixth and runners on first and second, Gil Hodges got the game's key hit, a line-drive triple down, surprisingly, the right-field line; two crucial runs scored and the Dodgers went on to win, 3–1. The next day, the Dodgers won, 8–6, to win the pennant.

Despite the Dodgers having the home field advantage for four of the seven games, the Yankees were favored to win the Series. Mantle was healthy and led MLB with a .353 average, 52 home runs, and 130 runs batted in.

It was also an election year, and the Series brought both presidential candidates to Ebbets Field. Before Game One in which Maglie faced Whitey Ford, wanting to favor neither team by wearing one of their caps, a bare-headed President Eisenhower threw out the first pitch. Maglie gave up a two-run homer to Mantle in the first, but settled down to limit the Yankees to only one more run. Ford allowed five runs, and Stengel was forced to pull him out of the game after only three innings. Hodges went 2 for 4, including a three-run homer off Ford that gave the Dodgers a 5–2 lead. Maglie, at age thirty-nine, had the first World Series win of his career. In the next day's papers, Hodges was referred to as the "quiet hero" of the game in contrast to Maglie, who "has been interviewed more often in the past two weeks than Eisenhower."

Before Game Two, the Democratic candidate, Adlai Stevenson, looked foolish as he posed for photographers wearing both a Yankees and Dodgers cap on his head at the same time. Hodges again had the crucial hits: a fourth-inning two-run double that broke a 7–7 tie and a two-run fifth-inning double off the left-field wall that gave the Dodgers an 11–7 lead. It was a great win for the Dodgers, who had trailed 6–0 before they had even come up to bat in the second inning, when they knocked Yankee starter Don Larsen out and tied the game at six all. After the game, Hodges, surrounded by reporters after driving in seven runs in just two games, was asked if he was going to break Lou Gehrig's record of nine runs batted in during a World Series. "I wouldn't say," Hodges answered. "You know me. I'm likely to go the other way tomorrow. But I feel good today—real good."

The loss marked the first time a Yankee team had lost the first two games of a World Series. After the game, outside the Yankees clubhouse, the Dodger fans were chanting, "The Yankees are dead. The Yankees are dead."

They weren't. Enos Slaughter, the Yankees' latest midseason, future Hall of Fame player acquisition, won the third game for them with a three-run homer. In the seventh, Hodges did some heady base running as he moved from first to third on an infield single and then scored on a grounder to third base, sliding under Berra's tag for the Dodgers' third run of the game. The

Yankees won anyway, 5–3. After the game, Ford admitted he had pitched well enough to win at spacious Yankee Stadium, but not if the game had been played at Ebbets Field.

The Yankees won Game Four, 6–2. Mantle and Bauer both homered and the Dodgers managed just six hits off the Yankees' Tom Sturdivant. Hodges had one hit, an RBI single in the fourth that tied up the game, but that would prove to be Hodges's final hit of the Series.

The pivotal fifth game was a classic, as Larsen threw the only perfect game in World Series history. It was also the first perfect game thrown in the Major Leagues since 1922. Twice, Hodges came close to ruining Larsen's masterpiece. Once was in the eighth. After letting two pitches go by that were, according to home plate umpire Babe Pinelli, only inches outside, Hodges hit a "tricky, low liner" to the left of Yankee third baseman Andy Carey. The ball initially looked like a base hit, but Carey "lunged for the ball and caught it inches off the ground." Of all the catches Carey made in his eleven-year Major League career, that was the only one that merited mention in his obituary. As a result, Hodges was unintentionally kind to Pinelli. In the last few innings, Pinelli knew history was on the line and he anguished over every ball and strike call, later writing, "Hodges let me breathe again by lining out to third base."

The first time Hodges had been so generous was in the fifth when he came to bat with one out. In center field, Mantle took a few steps back and toward left and was well positioned when Hodges (on a 2–2 count) hit a fly ball to deep left-center. Mantle started to "run like hell" and caught up with the ball four hundred feet from home plate just in front of the auxiliary scoreboard in "Death Valley." Mantle extended his left arm and reached out his glove as far as he could, catching the ball backhanded. Instead of ruining the perfect game, Hodges had launched what Mantle later called "the best catch I ever made."

After the game, while Hodges sat forlorn in the Dodgers' locker room, Walter O'Malley—always one to know a good investment when he saw one—went to the Yankees' locker room to get Larsen to sign a ball for him. "Mickey would have had to climb mighty high," Hodges said, "if he'd caught that one in Brooklyn."

Back at Ebbets Field, with their backs against the wall, down three games to two, Labine threw ten innings of shutout baseball and Robinson knocked in the game's only run to tie the Series up.

In the deciding Game Seven, the Yankees jumped out to an early 5–0 lead. In the seventh, the Yankees right-handed-hitting Moose Skowron came to bat with the bases loaded. Stengel told him, "Take two shots to right." Instead, Skowron pulled the ball into the left-field stands for a grand slam home run, icing yet another Yankee championship. When Skowron returned to the dugout, Stengel told him, "That's the way to pull the ball, big fella."

Hodges led the Dodgers in runs batted in and tied Duke Snider for the highest batting average on the team during the Series (.304). Despite Hodges's fast start, Yogi Berra ended up being the one to break Gehrig's World Series RBI record.

After the bitter loss, the Dodgers had no time to recuperate. The day after losing the Series, a dejected group of players left for Japan to play a twenty-game exhibition series against local All-Star teams. For Walter O'Malley, the publicity generated from the trip was incalculable. And with a stop in Los Angeles, already the object of his desires as a possible home for his team, it was quite a windfall.

Better yet, O'Malley didn't have to pay for the travel, lodging, or food for anyone on the trip. With the exception of certain "reciprocal functions," *Yomiuri Shimbun*, one of Japan's largest newspapers, covered all expenses. But O'Malley made sure to hedge his bets when it came to deciding who got to travel to Japan.

One member of the Dodgers family that very much wanted to go to Japan was Harry Hickey, the team's former treasurer and a longtime member of the board of directors. Hickey had been very ill, but had sufficiently recovered to make the trip. When finalizing the team's plans, the Dodgers' travel secretary, Harold Parrott, told O'Malley about adding Hickey to the travel roster.

"Have you stopped to think," replied O'Malley, "what it would cost to send a body home from Japan?"

Apparently, O'Malley had. Hickey stayed home.

On October 11, 1956, most of the players (and some of their wives, including Bev Snider, Betty Erskine, and Rachel Robinson) as well as Alston, O'Malley, Scully, DiGiovanna, and even a few influential season ticket holders, boarded a Pan Am DC-7C at Idlewild Airport in Queens, bound for Haneda Airport, Tokyo.

Harold Parrott decided not to make the trip and was replaced as travel secretary by Dick Walsh, who had spent the past year as farm director Fresco Thompson's assistant.

Joan Hodges stayed home. As Walsh recalled, "For Joan, anything west of the Hudson was Indian Country." That may have been the case, but a month was a long time for both parents to be away from their three young children, especially when one of them was a newborn. (That past summer, the Hodgeses' second daughter, Cynthia, had been born on August 19.) In addition, there was a financial incentive for Joan not to go: players traveling alone were paid $3,000, but if their wives joined them, they were only paid $1,500.

On board, a stewardess welcomed the sixty-two members of the Dodgers' party: "If there is anything we can do to make your flight more pleasant, please let us know. By the way, my name is Miss Larsen."

The Dodgers groaned; someone joked, "We ought to have a perfect flight."

After a three-day stay in Hawaii, the Dodgers flew to Wake Island, where Hodges mailed a postcard to his parents:

> We just landed here for refueling and a cup of coffee. It's five A.M. here today which is Thursday. We just lost a day going over date line. Weather has been nice. Flying had been real nice. Hope everyone is feeling fine. Will write again from Tokyo.
>
> Love,
> Gil

The postcard reveals Hodges's ability to roll with the punches. The flight had not been "real nice." The nose wheel of their plane had broken upon landing in Wake. Before the plane could take off for Tokyo, a new wheel had to be flown to the island. The Dodgers spent eight hours at the airport at Wake Island and by the time they arrived in Tokyo, they had spent seventeen hours in transit since leaving Honolulu. Hodges's postcard was typical of his appreciative, let's-look-on-the-bright-side approach. "If you gave some of the other players a turkey sandwich, when they had wanted a roast beef club, you'd hear about it," Dick Walsh told me. "Hodges accepted whatever you gave him in an easy way. He was a class act."

After they finally landed in Tokyo, forty actresses from the Daiei Motion Picture Studios presented them with bouquets as thousands of children waved greetings. When the team arrived at the Imperial Hotel, their rooms had "flowers everywhere," recalled pitcher Fred Kipp. Although Kipp had not yet pitched in the Majors, he was viewed as an up-and-comer and had been asked to join the team for the trip. The Japanese hitters were most effective hitting fastballs, and Kipp, who threw a knuckleball, would pitch quite often on the tour.

That trip was the first time Kipp met Hodges. He was impressed by the way Hodges was "totally respected" by the other veteran players: "No one fooled with him." By the same token, Kipp said, "Hodges didn't bother anyone. He just loved baseball." And on a trip where there were many temptations and "it didn't take much to ruin your reputation," Hodges was, Kipp recalled, "morally strong . . . . He never did anything to ruin his reputation."

Their first night in Tokyo, despite being worn out from their long flight, the players enjoyed "a giddy round of parties." Most didn't get to bed until early the next morning. That same day, the Dodgers played the opener of their exhibition series against the Yomiuri Giants, the champions of the Central League, before a crowd of twenty thousand at Korakuen Stadium. Drysdale started. On the Japan trip, Hodges roomed with Reese, not Drysdale, which may explain why Drysdale gave up two home runs in the first three innings and was quickly replaced. In the fourth, Hodges "whacked one of the longest homers ever seen here," but the Dodgers lost, 5-4. The Japanese, not known for their slugging, hit four home runs in the game, the Dodgers only two. Although the Dodgers would finish the tour with a record of 14-4 (with one tie), the Dodgers lost two of their first three games and the Japanese were initially not impressed. "I can sympathize that the Dodgers are in bad condition from fatigue after a hectic pennant race, the World Series, and travel to Japan and that they are in a terrific slump," said Masao Yuasa, a former manager of the Mainichi Orions, after the Dodgers lost again, this time by a lopsided 6-1 margin. "But they are even weaker than was rumored at bat against low, outside pitches and we are very disappointed to say the least. . . .

It would not be an overstatement to say that we no longer have anything to learn from the Dodgers."

The Dodgers' pitching was no better. In his first appearance in Japan, Don Newcombe was pulled from the game before getting a single batter out. The Dodgers had committed what to the Japanese was an unpardonable sin, not making an effort, of losing face; "We hope they [the Dodgers] will recover their form as soon as possible and display their full strength," concluded Yuasa.

Relying on rookies hoping to play their way onto the Major League roster, the Dodgers improved. In Shimoneski, Kipp threw a two-hit shutout for the Dodgers' fifth win in six games. Hodges, playing the outfield, had an RBI single.

After leaving Tokyo, the Dodgers played in several smaller towns in northern Japan. During one game, with the Dodgers leading by a wide margin, Hodges, playing left field, gestured to the fans asking their advice as to where he should position himself for the next batter. The fans pointed in numerous directions. Hodges began wandering around frantically pretending to be completely baffled. The fans roared with laughter. Then Hodges began mimicking every move the pitcher made. "He would bend down to get the sign, rub up a new ball, pretend to be holding the runner close to first, go into an exaggerated windup and shake his head in sorrow if he didn't get a strike."

Hodges expanded his routine. As a former catcher, Hodges gave an "uncanny imitation of Roy Campanella." Hodges would also "imitate the hitter[,] . . . stagger around rubber-legged under fly balls and catch them with a last-minute lunge."

Dick Walsh recalled, "The Japanese loved Hodges."

By the time the Dodgers traveled to one of Japan's larger cities, Osaka, the Dodgers' improved play had also helped to change perceptions. Perhaps because the Dodgers were winning regularly, Hodges did not feel the need to put on his clown routine in Osaka, especially after the Dodgers hit eight home runs in a 14–0 win before forty thousand fans at Namba Stadium. That day, the manager of the losing team, Azuhito Yamamoto, said, "That terrific hitting showed the Dodgers in their true form. I just have nothing else to say."

During the Dodgers' three-game series in Osaka, Walsh noticed Hodges had mostly played it straight, but also saw that the few times Hodges put on his routine, "almost every fan had leafed through his program to read the sketch on Hodges." By the time the Dodgers reached their next stop, Nagoya, Walsh "encouraged Gil to go ahead with this tremendous act after realizing that he is making us thousands of friends in every town."

In Nagoya, before a crowd of twenty-five thousand, "Hodges pantomimed the action of the pitcher, the catcher, and the umpire. When a Dodger made an error, Hodges glowered and pointed his finger. At various times he made his legs quiver, shook his fist, stamped on the ground, swung his arms, frowned, and smiled."

Hodges's performance at bat that November day in Nagoya was also showy. Hodges came up to bat in the fourth with the bases loaded and the Dodgers trailing 2-0. Hodges doubled to tie the game. The Japanese team immediately removed their starting pitcher and called in Kazuhisa Inao of the Nishitetsu Lions, Japan's champions. Inao's first pitch sailed over the catcher's head and what proved to be the winning run scored. After Hodges left the game in the eighth, he was called back onto the field to take a curtain call amid the cheers.

During one of the Dodgers' first games back in Tokyo, Hodges again returned to his comic routine. But in a game played on November 10, he hit a pair of 400-foot home runs that helped the Dodgers win, 8-2. In the Dodgers' final game, "The crowd of 30,000 stirred as Hodges slammed Takehiko Bessho's pitch over the top of the left-field stands in the fourth." The Dodgers won, 10-2.

During one of the games in Tokyo, Hodges was playing first when one of the smallest players on the Japanese team reached base. Rather than hold the runner on, Hodges "crouched directly behind him, mimicking each of his movements. . . . The crowd screamed in laughter as the runner, his eyes riveted on the pitcher, tried to figure out what was so funny. When he finally caught on, he retreated to first base, stepped up on the bag[,] . . . put his hands on his hips and looked Hodges in the eye angrily. Then both players broke up laughing and, as the crowd roared its approval, Gil lifted him in the air and held him up to the stands. When Hodges left the game, the crowd cheered so loud and long that he had to return for a curtain call, tipping his cap and bowing from the waist in a Japanese gesture of appreciation."

But Hodges's greatest contribution toward establishing the Dodgers as crowd favorites came when he helped an umpire save face. After one of the Dodgers' players was called out on strikes, "in a childish display of petulance," the player threw his batting helmet onto the ground with such force that it bounced up on top of the Dodgers' dugout.

The Dodgers player had embarrassed the umpire. In Japanese culture, this was unacceptable. "The fans were shocked. . . . [They] sat in stunned silence." Hodges sensed the problem and immediately came up with a way to correct it. "Gil suddenly appeared, jumped up on the dugout roof and approached the helmet as if it were a dangerous snake. He circled it warily, made a couple of tentative stabs at it, then quickly pounced on it, tossed it back on the field and then did a swan dive off the top of the dugout. The fans beat their palms and shouted until they were hoarse."

Near the end of the tour, a Japanese high school student asked Jackie Robinson whether baseball was more popular in Japan or in the United States. Robinson replied diplomatically, saying that when he and his teammates were out early one morning to play golf they drove past a field where four baseball games were going on at once. "Where in America would you see that," Robinson said, "at 7 A.M. in November?"

Robinson's question—*Where in America would you see that?*—was just as applicable to describing Hodges's humorous behavior on the baseball fields of Japan. Unfortunately, the answer was "nowhere." It wasn't in his nature to intentionally draw attention to himself. Hodges played to win, never for show. And that's why his behavior in Japan, as Carl Erskine said, "was so totally out of character."

"Hodges," said Walsh, "had a great sense of humor."

But not in America, where, as Johnny Podres told me, "Hodges tended to be all business in the summer."

As a result, only his teammates knew that when Hodges smiled and doled out his dry brand of humor, "his eyes danced."

13

THE LAST SEASON

No way.

Despite helping the Dodgers win another pennant, Hodges faced trying contract negotiations. Buzzie Bavasi said that certain players "who didn't do so well" would be "shaved down a bit." Roy Campanella, one of the greatest catchers in baseball history, but whose batting average plunged while playing the entire 1956 season with an injured hand that inhibited his ability to grip the bat, was expected to take a pay cut. Hodges, because "he had failed to reach the 100-mark in runs batted in," was "in the same boat." In January of 1957, Hodges signed a contract for $35,000, the same salary he was paid the prior season.

Hodges's salary was static, but the Dodgers were in transition. Jackie Robinson had retired. Pee Wee Reese and Campanella were nearing the end of their careers. Carl Furillo, Hodges, and Duke Snider remained solid, but Don Newcombe and Carl Erskine were limited by injuries. Meanwhile, in Milwaukee, all the pieces had come together and the Braves won their first pennant since moving from Boston. Henry Aaron led the Majors in home runs and RBIs; and Cy Young Award winner Warren Spahn, along with Lew Burdette and Bob Buhl, formed an outstanding rotation. In the 1957 World Series, the Braves defeated the Yankees thanks to Nippy Jones's precedent-setting use of the shoe-polish trick. The Dodgers finished in third place, eleven games back.

Yet Hodges had one of his best seasons, finishing with a .299 average. Hodges was outstanding from the Dodgers' home opener, when he went 3 for 4 with a single, double, and home run, until mid-June, when he was leading the league with a .365 batting average. He finished the year with 27 home runs and 98 RBIs. Aaron was the league's MVP; Hodges finished seventh in the voting. But after the Dodgers' final game of the season, instead of focusing on Hodges's accomplishments, a paragraph in the *New York Times* describing his statistics was titled "Hodges Misses Goals."

In addition, despite Hodges's "practically . . . carrying a faltering ball club on his back," Stan Musial was voted as the National League's starting first baseman in that year's All-Star Game. Shirley Povich, the dean of Washington DC sportswriters, disagreed with the fans' choice, writing that no one could play first base better than Hodges due to his "special skill at shagging wild throws and making the first to second to first double play."

A few days after the All-Star Game, in a game against the Braves at Ebbets Field, the Dodgers were trailing by one run in the bottom of the ninth when Hodges came to bat with a runner on first to face Bob Buhl, who had already struck Hodges out twice. On Buhl's first pitch, Hodges homered into the left-field stands to give the Dodgers a come-from-behind 3–2 victory, a highlight in a season in which the Dodgers had little to celebrate. The entire team greeted Hodges as he crossed home plate, including the usually laconic Walter Alston, "wearing a grin broad enough to threaten his ears."

On July 17 Hodges hit the twelfth grand slam home run of his career, tying him with Rogers Hornsby and Ralph Kiner for the most by a National League player. The grand slam was not window dressing in a blowout, but the key hit in a come-from-behind victory against the Cardinals in a game at Ebbets Field. It was also redemption for Hodges, who had made a crucial error in the top of the inning when, with one out and a runner on first base, he tried to make a throw to second to get the lead runner before he had a handle on the ball, allowing the Cardinals to take a 9–4 lead with seven runs in the top of the ninth.

In the bottom of the ninth, Hoyt Wilhelm gave up an infield hit and two walks. Fred Hutchinson, the Cardinals' manager, made the logical move and brought in the southpaw Wilmer Mizell to face the left-handed Snider. After Snider hit a run-scoring infield ground out, the right-handed-hitting Gino Cimoli walked. With the bases loaded, Hutchinson made the mistake of allowing Mizell to stay in the game and pitch to Hodges, who was a devastatingly good hitter against left-handers. Hodges made up for his fielding miscue with his grand slam home run that tied the game. The Dodgers won it in the eleventh inning.

After the game, rubbing salt in Hutchinson's wound, Hodges said, "I was very surprised—and pleased—to see Mizell."

Late that night as the Cardinals left Penn Station on a train bound for Pittsburgh, "Hutch lurched like a drunken bear from one side of the Penn Station platform to the other, his sorrow pronounced dead."

"That," Hodges would later say to the writer Bob Broeg, "is one I'd like to see."

Two days later, on the evening of July 19, nearly thirty thousand fans came to Ebbets Field to pay tribute to the native Hoosier who had become their hometown favorite. The timing of Gil Hodges Night produced the bittersweet highlight of a lackluster season. The Dodgers defeated the Cubs in both ends of a doubleheader that night, but New York Giants owner Horace Stoneham's recent admission that his team would not be playing in New York in 1958—in combination with rumors of the Dodgers moving to Los Angeles—put a damper on the proceedings. Interestingly, although the tradition of honoring a beloved player was long-standing, the idea of honoring Hodges had not come from management, but from two fans, Joann Duffy, the president of the Gil Hodges Fan Club, and Al Bonnie, chairman of the committee for Gil Hodges Night.

In between games, Hodges was presented with dozens of gifts, ranging from a sleek Dodge convertible to a lifetime supply of dill pickles to a silver serving tray engraved with the signatures of all his teammates. Hodges also received hundreds of telegrams, including ones from President Dwight Eisenhower, Vice President Richard Nixon, Admiral William F. (Bull) Halsey, New York governor Averill Harriman, Indiana governor Harold W. Handley, and New York City mayor Robert Wagner.

President Eisenhower's telegram gave equal emphasis to Hodges's personality and his baseball ability: "I have learned of the tribute to be given Gil Hodges by his friends in baseball and it is a pleasure to join in this occasion. As a distinguished player and an outstanding gentleman, Gil Hodges makes a splendid contribution to the game. His quality of sportsmanship is an example to the youth of the land. Please give my congratulations to Gil Hodges and my best wishes to all gathered in his honor."

Admiral Halsey wrote, "He is an outstanding ball player and also was a fine Marine and member of my team in the South Pacific."

After forty-five minutes of tribute, Hodges, "gracefully and in control of his emotions," gave his reply, which lasted all of one minute: "Thank you very much. I'd like to take this opportunity to thank Joann Duffy and Al Bonnie. To all my friends, all I can say is I thank you from the bottom of my heart for making this a wonderful evening for me and my family. May God bless you."

Charlie, Irene, Marjorie, and Bob had all traveled to Brooklyn to be there. Charlie threw out the ceremonial first pitch (to his son) to start the second game. In that game, Hodges's single to drive in the game's first run was the one thousandth RBI of his career. At the time, only two other active National League players, Stan Musial and Del Ennis, had more.

That summer, with Hodges at the height of his popularity, the *New York Times* assigned its metropolitan reporter, Meyer Berger, to do a piece about Hodges for their "About New York" column. Hodges is depicted wheeling his youngest child, Cynthia, down the street in her baby carriage, picking up groceries on Nostrand Avenue, and taking Gil Jr. and Irene to church. Yet, despite all Hodges's accomplishments, wrote Berger, he was a man who "never talks himself up."

That season also marked the deepening of Hodges's friendship with his roommate, Don Drysdale. Back then on long road trips when teams still traveled by train, the players used a heavy trunk-like suitcase that was cumbersome to carry. After playing a game in St. Louis, Hodges and Drysdale went up to their room at the Chase Park Plaza Hotel, but Drysdale couldn't push the door open. Apparently, when their trunks had arrived that afternoon from the train station, the bellman had left them blocking the door and exited through an adjoining room. Drysdale was six feet five and a physical force in his own right. Hodges asked Drysdale to step aside and pushed the door open, "which was no small task." Hodges had had a poor game that day and was "hot"; without using the handles, Hodges picked up each trunk, putting "his hands around them like you would put your hands around your thigh," and "just tossed them" across the room.

"Now," Hodges said, "we can get into this cotton-pickin room."

Drysdale was not surprised that Hodges didn't curse—he never swore—but

Drysdale couldn't believe Hodges could toss the two heavy trunks across the room "like they were nothing."

But it wasn't just Hodges's strength that impressed Drysdale; it was Hodges's demeanor, which sent an unspoken message: always be a gentleman, since you're a Dodger, a professional; after dinner have a few drinks, but not too many (Hodges preferred Jack Daniel's); get a good night's sleep, because you have to keep your strength up over the long season; eat a good breakfast to keep your weight up over the course of all those afternoon games in the heat of the summer; and always stay in control, and carry yourself the right way. And if teaching by example didn't work, Hodges would give Drysdale the needle.

On occasion, Drysdale would get that "gleam" in his eyes and stay out late. On those nights, Hodges made sure to close their room from inside with the chain lock. As a result, Drysdale had to wake Hodges up to get into the room, and the next morning over breakfast Hodges would invariably ask Drysdale, "What time was it you got in last night?"

"Right about twelve-thirty, maybe one o'clock."

"Really? Geez, I thought it was a little later than that."

In those moments, Drysdale wrote, Hodges could make you feel "about six inches tall."

Drysdale got the message and later admitted that Hodges "probably prolonged" his career.

On those nights when Drysdale didn't go out, he and Hodges would sometimes stay up reading a book called *Knotty Problems of Baseball*. The book, published by *The Sporting News*, contained stories that raised obscure baseball rules that Drysdale and Hodges would discuss at length and solve by taking out a copy of the baseball rule book. It's a quaint image: Hodges, who could have easily ended up a college coach, teaching a young Drysdale the importance of knowing the rule book backward and forward.

But Drysdale also saw that Hodges could lose his temper. Most of the time, Hodges would make his point with his dry humor, but Drysdale noted, "If you didn't know Gil, there were times when you thought he was so mad at you that you wanted to run away and hide."

This is a crucial point in understanding Hodges. As Hodges's roommate for six seasons, Drysdale knew Hodges as well as anyone. But for most others, whether they were the out-of-town sportswriters who saw Hodges only a handful of times each season, or his players (Tom Seaver could count on one hand the number of times he engaged in a lengthy dialogue with Hodges), or even the Mets announcers (in all the years Hodges knew Ralph Kiner, other than team functions, the two men never went out to dinner), he was a tough read.

But that was by design, and Hodges played it to full effect. It made those rare moments when a flash of anger from the usually placid Hodges was a powerful motivational device. Once in Pittsburgh, the Dodgers were at the bar at the Hotel Shoenly late in the afternoon on the team's "getaway day" waiting to go to the train station to leave town. The bartender was moving very slowly and the players were growing impatient. "Finally, Gil had enough. He slammed his fist onto the bar and everybody's drinks . . . jumped."

"Now," Hodges said to the bartender, "start here with another drink and go all the way around to the end with drinks for the rest."

The bartender "hurried as he'd never hurried before in his life."

Drysdale had a much shorter fuse than Hodges. By his own admission Drysdale could be "a miserable person at times, a no-good SOB," especially after losing a game. At those times, Hodges sensed Drysdale "needed to let off some steam" and was there for the young pitcher. "He knew just how to handle me," Drysdale wrote, "sometimes better than I knew how to handle myself."

Hodges helped Drysdale on the field as well. When Hodges sensed Drysdale was getting too emotional during a game, Hodges would call time out and walk over to the mound. Calmly, with only a few words, Hodges would get Drysdale refocused. "Roomie . . . settle down . . . don't let this game get away from you."

Hodges also stood up for Drysdale in the locker room. One season before Opening Day in their clubhouse at Ebbets Field, the Dodgers players were asked to complete forms regarding their pension plan. Benefits varied depending on what age a player decided to start to receive them, and Drysdale asked Hodges, "Hey roomie, what age should I figure on retiring at? 45?"

Before Hodges could answer, pitcher Ken Lehman said, "45, Drysdale? Are you crazy? You're not even 21 yet. You might get hit with a truck before you're 45."

To which Pee Wee Reese added, "Or a line drive."

Hodges said, "Don, fill it in for whatever you want, because you're going to be around this league for a long time."

That season Drysdale got a chance to pitch regularly and won seventeen games. Drysdale later wrote that Hodges was "the greatest thing that ever happened to me in baseball."

In addition to giving Drysdale confidence, teaching him when to call it a night, and monitoring his temper, Hodges impressed his roommate with the importance of family. "As a professional ballplayer, living in that bubble," Drysdale wrote, "you can lose touch with reality. . . . But Gil always had his priorities straight, and whenever we returned to Brooklyn, where Joan and the kids were waiting, you could see how important his family was to him. Gil was a great husband and father. He was a real homebody."

Drysdale developed his own needle after being the brunt of many of Hodges's jokes. Once during spring training, when the two were discussing knocking down a hitter, Hodges asked Drysdale if he would feel bad if he hit a guy in the head and seriously hurt him. "No," said Drysdale, "It's his job to protect himself up there."

Hodges took Drysdale seriously. Hodges then asked his roommate if he would regret it if he killed a batter. "No," Drysdale said, "I wouldn't regret it."

"It was funny," Drysdale later said. "I really had Gil going. I'm sure he thought I meant every word of it."

The reality was, as a rookie in 1956, Drysdale had come under the tutelage of Sal Maglie, who had indoctrinated Drysdale in the importance of having the "respect" of the hitters. And that led to a situation where Hodges had to rescue Drysdale from physical harm.

In a game on June 13, 1957, at Ebbets Field against the Braves, Drysdale pitched poorly. The Braves' lead-off hitter, Bill Bruton, hit a home run to start the game and belted another in the second inning. In between the two homers, Drysdale had allowed two doubles and a single. After giving up five hits and four runs in two innings, Drysdale decided to send a message and hit the next batter, shortstop Johnny Logan, in the back with a one-strike fastball. Logan was a proponent of the Leo Durocher I-came-to-kill-you style of baseball. The man never backed down to a challenge. But Drysdale, in only his second season in the Majors, had already established himself as an equally tough competitor who threw at opposing batters with regularity.

From first base, Logan screamed at Drysdale, "I'll get you when you come into second base."

"If you got a beef, come on and get it over with now," Drysdale screamed back.

Logan accepted the offer and charged the mound. Ever the peacemaker, Hodges ran after Logan to grab him before he reached Drysdale. In baseball fights, Hodges's usual approach was to step in between the two combatants and physically separate them. Hodges's preference was to grab his teammate and hold him so he couldn't throw a punch. But he was not always able to get to his teammate in time and sometimes had to resort to restraining an enemy combatant.

Before Hodges could get between Logan and Drysdale, the Braves' first base coach, John Riddle, grabbed Hodges from behind. At this point, Walter Alston, who had been walking out to the mound to change pitchers, grabbed Logan. The on-deck hitter, Eddie Mathews, a powerfully built six-foot-one 200-pounder, was a man with few inhibitions. "I didn't mind starting fights," Logan said. "Mathews was always there to finish them for me."

Mathews raced to the mound, knocked Drysdale down, and proceeded to pummel him. Luckily for Drysdale, like the cavalry in old westerns, after shaking Riddle off his back, Hodges came to the rescue.

"I don't exactly look for any trouble," Hodges once said, "but if it happens . . ."

In his autobiography, Eddie Mathews wrote, "The next thing I knew somebody had a hold of my ankles and was dragging me, face down, away from the mound area. It was Gil Hodges, who was a pretty tough hombre."

The newspapers reported that "baseball's most forceful pacifier" dragged Mathews "halfway to third base," collecting "a couple of spike scratches in the process." According to Drysdale, Hodges told Mathews, "Stay right there and don't come back!"

Mathews didn't return to the fight.

Hodges pulling Mathews off of Drysdale was all the more impressive because he did it with severely bruised ribs from a collision with the Braves' backup second baseman, Bobby Malkmus, that took place the day before when Hodges slid into Malkmus as he successfully prevented a double play. X-rays had revealed no fractures, but after the game against the Braves, Hodges sat out the Dodgers' entire next series against the visiting Cardinals. When Hodges was hitting well—which he was that June—he was rarely held out of a game, so he must have been pretty banged up "to beg off playing."

Drysdale was also looking out for Hodges. In a game against the Phillies, after Robin Roberts hit Hodges in the ribs with a pitch, Drysdale reciprocated by hitting Roberts with a pitch in his next at bat. As Roberts stood at first base, Drysdale glared at him. Finally, Roberts told Hodges to tell Drysdale he "got the message."

Because of his work on the Dodgers' trip to Japan, Dick Walsh had been promoted to serve as Walter O'Malley's Los Angeles representative regarding the Dodgers' move to the West Coast. Walsh spent much of the 1957 season in Los Angeles and had an intimate knowledge of O'Malley's negotiations to acquire both the Cubs' territorial rights in Los Angeles and the land to build a new ballpark in Chavez Ravine.

Late that season, when Walsh was back in Brooklyn to meet with O'Malley, he dropped by the Dodgers' clubhouse. On the Japan trip, Walsh and Hodges had developed a rapport: Hodges referred to the bespectacled Walsh as "Clark Kent." Knowing how much playing in Brooklyn meant to Hodges, Walsh decided to tell him the truth.

"This is the last season you'll see Brooklyn," Walsh said.

"No way," Hodges replied.

The idea of the Dodgers leaving Brooklyn was ludicrous—not just to Hodges but to the fans. Brooklyn and baseball had a long and memorable history. It was in Brooklyn (in 1858) that for the first time anywhere an admission fee was charged to watch a baseball game. A Brooklyn team made the first road trip. A Brooklyn journalist invented the box score. A Brooklyn pitcher threw the first curve ball. A Brooklyn player laid down the first bunt. Two Brooklyn players inaugurated the first double play. But the Dodgers were also the first team to travel in their own airplane, and in 1958 they would fly away for good.

As they spoke, Hodges started to believe Walsh. The clincher came when

Walsh told Hodges that if O'Malley ran into political problems acquiring the land in Chavez Ravine, his backup plan was to move the team to Minneapolis—not stay in Brooklyn.

Half a century later, Walsh could still recall the look on Hodges's face as reality set in.

"It was a cross," Walsh said, "between shock and horror."

Hodges was the only player Walsh told.

"The others," Walsh said, "didn't care as much."

Hodges knew Joan had never lived anywhere else but Brooklyn and saw her mother or sister almost daily. A family move to Los Angeles would be, at best, problematic, and there was the real possibility that Hodges would be separated from his family not just for road games, but for most of the season. Hodges's 1943 letter from San Diego that read in part, "It wouldn't be bad out here in California in civilian life," had come back to haunt him.

Much has been written about who was to blame for the Dodgers' move to Los Angeles. Was it Walter O'Malley, who ruled the Dodgers, or Robert Moses—though never elected to any office—who ruled New York? Or, as might be closer to the truth, a bit of both? In the end, it didn't matter. The loss was immeasurable. Ebbets Field was the place where a diverse community of two million people—black and white, Jewish and Catholic, Italian and Irish—came together to share the one thing they all had in common, their beloved Dodgers.

On September 24, 1957, the Brooklyn Dodgers played their final game at Ebbets Field. A left-handed pitcher named Danny McDevitt defeated the Pittsburgh Pirates, 2-0. Organist Gladys Goodding played "Don't Ask Me Why I'm Leaving," "After You've Gone," and "Thanks for the Memories." Gil Hodges was the last Dodger to ever come to bat at Ebbets Field. He struck out swinging.

The next season, the Giants and Dodgers began playing on the West Coast, and New York was without a National League team for the first time since the 1882. But despite the family challenges the move created for him, Hodges dutifully headed to Los Angeles in October to help promote what was being billed as a cross-country hit from Brooklyn to Los Angeles resulting in, from California's perspective, "The Greatest Catch in Baseball."

On October 28 Hodges, along with Roy Campanella, Duke Snider, and Pee Wee Reese, attended a welcome luncheon for 1,100 fans in the Pacific Ballroom of the Statler Hotel in downtown Los Angeles. A band played "California, Here I Come" as the Dodgers contingent marched into the room. Retired umpire Beans Reardon yelled, "Play ball!" and "Dodger Pot Roast" was served. Casey Stengel, a California resident in the off-season, gave a welcome speech, letting everyone know the Dodgers' move was great for Southern California and that he was "in the banking business in Glendale." Reese and some of the other players engaged in humorous banter with comedian Joe E. Brown, the master of ceremonies. Walter O'Malley signed autographs.

Gil Hodges said little, appearing to be "just along for the ride." Later on the trip, when asked if he would move to Los Angeles, Hodges visibly "shuddered" and said, "I'm a Brooklyn resident. My wife's a Brooklyn girl. Can't take everything away from those poor fans."

Then, trying to sound hopeful, he added, "Still, she might like it. This is my third trip—when I was in the Marines in 1943, and last year, en route to Japan. We'll probably rent a house here."

Thanksgiving brought more bad news. That fall, while working at Ditney Hill, Charlie Hodges was injured yet again when some slate fell on him and broke his leg. After surgery, he was immobile and forced to recuperate at home. On the evening of Friday, November 22, while watching television in his Petersburg home, Charlie Hodges suddenly died. As is not uncommon after surgery, following a period of inactivity, a blood clot had formed in Charlie's leg, broken loose, and traveled to his lungs. The cause of death was listed as pulmonary embolus due to venous thrombosis. Charlie was fifty-six.

Hodges immediately drove to Petersburg, stopping in Philadelphia to pick up his sister, Marjorie. Upon arriving, Hodges went to the Harris Funeral Home to make arrangements for the burial. Bob Harris, whose family owned the funeral home, and his wife, Sonny, who had recently given birth to a daughter, were both in the funeral home's office when Hodges arrived. After greeting everyone, the first thing Hodges did was look directly at Sonny and say, "I want to congratulate you on having Lisa." Sonny Harris was impressed that Hodges, in a time of personal loss, had bothered to learn—and remember—her newborn daughter's name. Hodges bought eight funeral plots at the nearby

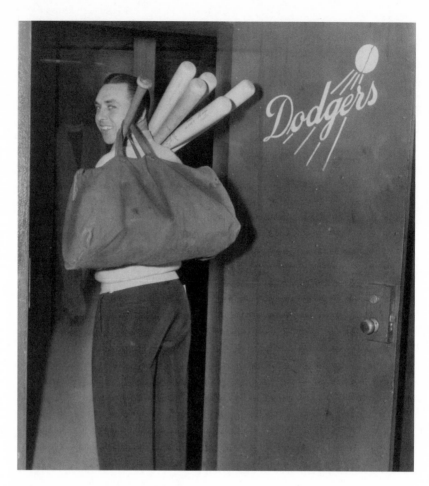

26. Leaving Brooklyn on a barnstorming tour with Jackie Robinson, October 1953. Brooklyn Public Library—Brooklyn Collection.

Walnut Hills Cemetery: two for Charlie and Irene, two for himself and Joan, and two each for his brother and sister.

The night after Charlie's funeral, John Drof, the editor of the *Petersburg Press*, knocked on the back door of the Hodges residence to pay his respects. Only the screen door was closed; Drof had a clear view inside. At the kitchen table writing thank-you cards to those who had sent telegrams or flowers or brought food over for his family, a fountain pen in his huge right hand, Gil Hodges sat alone.

AWAY

Los Angeles (1958–61)

14

THE WORST PLACE EVER

If I hit one ball to the right of second base all year, I'm to quit and go home.

That winter, still mourning the loss of his father, Hodges received some positive news, winning the inaugural Gold Glove for first basemen. In 1957, following the success Hillerich & Bradsby enjoyed promoting their Louisville Slugger bat by awarding a Silver Bat to the top hitters in baseball each season, Rawlings, a leading baseball glove manufacturer, established the Gold Glove. That year, one player in baseball was selected as the best fielder at his position and presented with the award. Hodges would win again in 1958 and 1959, but in those years two Gold Gloves (one in each league) were presented per fielding position.

In part, Hodges's greatness as a fielder was a product of his baseball intelligence. On every pitch, Hodges was consciously thinking of what he would do when—not if—the ball was hit to him. In this regard, by carefully watching the opposing team's third base coach to determine their signs, Hodges elevated knowing how and when to anticipate a play into art. To Carl Erskine, Hodges had a deeper understanding of the game than anyone else he ever saw. When Hodges believed the bunt signal had been given, he would call time out, walk to the mound, and tell Erskine not to throw over to first base because he would be charging the plate on the next pitch. Hodges was fearless. If the sign had changed and the batter was hitting away, Hodges risked serious injury on a line drive hit to the first base side. But Hodges persisted, and his kamikaze-style charges forced batters to adjust and bunt toward third base. Stan Musial wrote that Hodges "revolutionized bunt defense," making it much harder for opponents to successfully sacrifice runners into scoring position, forcing them away from a station-to-station approach and having to "go for the long ball." Musial called Hodges a "remarkable first baseman," adding that had Hodges "been left-handed, he might have been remembered as the most efficient first baseman ever."

A left-handed first baseman has numerous advantages over a righty. The most significant one involves throws to second base. On a bunt or other hit down the first base line, a right-handed first baseman has to catch the ball, stop, turn, and then throw to get the lead runner. This is because a right-hander charging a ball is naturally suited to throw to his left. To understand this, imagine a right-handed third baseman bare-handing a bunt and firing to his left toward first without having to break stride. Now, reverse the same concept and apply it to a lefty first baseman naturally predisposed to fielding a ball and throwing to his right in one fluid motion. Don Mattingly, a nine-time Gold Glove winner at first base, said, "It's a pretty tough position right-handed. You've got to rotate on that throw to second."

Hodges took full advantage of his sign-stealing ability to gain an edge, and it became part of Hodges's legend. In the 1950s, twin brothers Eddie and Johnny O'Brien played for the Pirates. After one of them singled (no one seems to recall which one), Hodges was holding him on at first. The situation called for an attempted steal. But after the next batter took several pitches, O'Brien remained on first. At that point, Hodges leaned over and said, "I don't want to interfere, son, but your coach has just given you the steal sign three times."

Hodges did not consider fielding percentages an accurate measurement of a fielder's abilities. A fielder who always tries to make the difficult play will end up with more errors but will prove far more valuable to his team for the hits he does prevent. This is another example of Hodges's focus on team success rather than his individual accomplishments. Another reason Hodges didn't value fielding percentages was because they do not take into account mental errors (such as forgetting how many outs there are). The mental error, Hodges wrote, "will beat you just as often as the physical error."

Hodges also used his thorough understanding of the rule book to take advantage of mental errors by the opposition. For example, Hodges knew that when there was a runner on first base, it was not uncommon for a hitter attempting a bunt to advance the runner, to pop up. Sometimes the frustrated hitter would lose control of his emotions, smack his bat into the ground, and forget to run to first. Hodges worked out a plan where he would let the ball bounce, field it, and throw to second to get the lead base runner to start a double play. From the time Hodges first came up with the strategy, it took him three years before the right situation arose for him to use it.

"Hodges," said longtime New York sportswriter Dave Anderson, "made everything look easy." Opposing players were well aware of Hodges's fancy footwork as well. Jim Bouton, a pitcher for the Yankees, wrote, "Routine ground balls are not exactly the most thrilling things that ever happen in a baseball game. But a bit of spice can be added if you watch a good first baseman . . . taking his foot off first base before the ball actually arrives in his glove. Gil Hodges . . . was a master at this deception. It's an important move because the umpires watch the feet, too. But if the first baseman takes his foot off the bag with aplomb the umpire can easily delude himself into thinking he heard the sound of ball in glove at the same time. Thus many runners who are actually safe at first base are called out."

One of the people who saw Hodges play regularly was *Long Island Newsday* reporter Jack Lang, whose career began with him covering the Dodgers in the 1940s and didn't end until the 1980s when he watched the Mets and their great-fielding, left-handed first baseman, Keith Hernandez. "Gil Hodges," Lang told me, "was the best-fielding right-handed first baseman I ever saw."

But no one respected Hodges more for his fielding than his fellow first basemen. Frank Torre, who played first for the Milwaukee Braves in the 1950s, was such an outstanding defensive player he was often put into games as a late-inning defensive replacement. Torre considered himself "a pretty good fielding first baseman," but after he came up to the Majors and saw Hodges play on a regular basis, he began to understand what it meant to be a truly great fielder at first. "Hodges," Torre told me, "was in a class by himself . . . far and away the best first baseman that I ever saw. He covered more ground than any other first baseman . . . and was one of the few right-handers who made the throw to second. He positioned himself in such a way that he acted like a left-hander. I can't tell you how many runs I saw him save for the Dodgers."

Early in 1957, Charlie Dressen, then recently rehired by the Dodgers as

27. Diving catch, March 8, 1952. Brooklyn Public Library—Brooklyn Collection.

their third base coach, was asked who was the best player on the Dodgers—
"the man you would pick first if assembling a team?"

"Gil Hodges," he said.

In their final season in Brooklyn, Hodges had led the team in almost every
offensive category: runs scored, hits, doubles, triples (tied), runs batted in, and

average. The Dodgers signed him to a new contract "in the neighborhood of $35,000" and immediately put him to work helping promote their move to the West Coast. In early February, Hodges flew to Los Angeles to participate in what was being billed as the biggest baseball clinic in Southern California history. Twelve hundred local coaches participated. Of the Dodgers players attending, Hodges was the only star. Roy Campanella was also supposed to attend, but a car accident that January left him paralyzed for the rest of his life.

But 1958 would be a miserable year for Hodges both on and off the field. He rented a home in Los Angeles for the season, but as he anticipated, Joan missed her family back east. When the Dodgers were on the road, she often flew back to Brooklyn.

As he had during his military service, Hodges enjoyed the Southern California weather, and when members of the Dodgers' executive staff like Fresco Thompson and Al Campanis were purchasing half-acre lots to build homes in the Sunny Ranch development in Fullerton, Hodges, practicing wishful thinking, said, "This country estate living is ideal for my three young children. My wife will be out as soon as school is over in Brooklyn to pick up our half acre and get our home construction started."

That never happened. And Hodges had more on his mind than his homesick wife. He felt guilty over his father's death. When Charlie had injured his knee, the doctors told him they could repair it with "some simple surgery." Charlie was hesitant, but Hodges encouraged his dad to have the procedure done, comparing it to surgery baseball players have for a "trick knee." As a result of his son's encouragement, Charlie had the surgery that may have caused the blood clot that formed in his leg and ended up killing him.

Although doctors told him that was not the case, Hodges linked the knee surgery to his dad's death. As Hodges wrote, upon hearing the news of his dad's death, "I felt unmistakable pangs of remorse. Had I talked Dad into the operation? The doctors said it wouldn't have made any difference. The blood clot could have formed at any time, operation or no operation. But if I had gone home, I would at least have been there when it happened. Why wasn't I there?"

Hodges's genius was compartmentalizing his job from his family. Generally, he didn't bring his problems (whether they be hitting slumps or, in later years, his managerial frustrations) home, and vice versa. In 1958 this proved to be a challenge. More time at the ballpark helped Hodges stay focused on his work. In Los Angeles, one way he did this was spending time teaching a local high school kid Charlie Dressen had signed to a Dodgers' contract how to play first base. When Wes Parker wasn't throwing batting practice for the Dodgers, Hodges taught Parker two key rules of how to play first base.

Some first basemen vary which foot they use to touch the bag: for throws from the right side of the infield, they use the left foot; for throws from the left, their right. Hodges referred to this as the twinkle-toes approach, and it was to be avoided. On quick throws to first there is no time to think about which leg should be used to touch the bag, and the result is needless errors. Hodges's rule was simple. If you're right-handed, always touch the bag with your right foot; left-handed, your left foot.

Hodges's second rule was "Be smooth." When Hodges first told Parker this, he didn't understand what Hodges meant, and it would take years for him to develop this skill. But finally, the thought that Hodges planted in Parker's head "just sprouted." Being smooth meant to always be conscious of your movements and keep them under control: "Don't be jerky [in your movements]."

For example, Hodges advised waiting until the last possible second before going into your stretch at first base. By keeping your weight balanced and your legs parallel, you were in a better position to move left, move right, or jump if necessary to catch an off-line throw. In addition, Hodges advised to always move your glove slightly toward you as you catch the throw. This way, the direction of the throw would match the motion of your glove, reducing the likelihood of the throw popping out. This was part of the reason, as George Sisler, the Hall of Fame first baseman, said, "[Hodges] had great hands and never missed a ball thrown to him."

In 1958 Hodges's challenges were far greater in the batter's box than in the field. Walter O'Malley had decided the Dodgers would play their home games in the Los Angeles Coliseum, a ninety-thousand-seat football stadium, rather than Wrigley Field, the Minor League baseball stadium located near Hollywood that O'Malley had acquired from the Cubs in order to secure the Dodgers' right to play in Los Angeles. Not to be confused with its namesake in Chicago, this Wrigley Field was even smaller than Ebbets Field, with only twenty-two thousand seats. To maximize revenue, the Dodgers spent the next four years playing at the Coliseum.

The Coliseum was barely big enough for a baseball field, resulting in distorted outfield dimensions. The left-field fence was only 252 feet away from home plate, but right-center was 440 feet away. (Upon seeing the Coliseum for the first time, Willie Mays told the left-handed pull-hitting Duke Snider, "You couldn't reach it with a cannon! You're done, man!") To compensate for the short distance in left, a 42-foot-high fence was put up. As a result, a wind-blown pop fly to left that would be an out anywhere else would carry over the fence for a home run. On the other hand, a rising line drive that might have gone 400 feet would hit the fence and land on the playing field for a single. The Coliseum was as well suited for baseball "as a bowling alley is for tennis."

Dodgers pitcher Ed Roebuck called the Coliseum "the worst place ever." Warren Spahn described it as a "pitcher's nightmare." Bob Feller summed up the feelings of most pitchers: "There's going to be a lot of grumbling. . . . They should let O'Malley pitch on opening day."

With such favorable dimensions for right-handed hitters, some predicted Hodges would lead the Majors in home runs. Although Hodges was already planning to pull everything to left field to take advantage of the short distance, he did his best to temper expectations, saying, "Ebbets Field was the easiest park in the National League for right-handed hitters to hit home runs and the Polo Grounds and Connie Mack Stadium . . . were next. . . . So, what the power hitters gain in Los Angeles, if anything, they'll lose by no longer playing in Brooklyn or New York."

Pee Wee Reese teased Hodges, telling him, "You're a cinch to break Babe Ruth's record."

"The only record I'll break," Hodges replied, "is Tommy Brown's." Brown was a former Dodgers utility player who kept count of his batting practice home runs, once hitting 285 in a season. But Hodges's self-deprecating humor was about to be put to the test. Starting from Opening Day when Hodges went 0 for 4, the Coliseum's dimensions got the better of him. Trying to pull everything to left ruined his hitting. Walter Alston told Hodges to forget about the left-field screen. But he couldn't.

In 1958 Lee Walls, a journeyman outfielder for Chicago, hit more home runs in the eleven games he played in Los Angeles that season than Hodges hit in seventy-seven. At season's end, Hodges had a .259 batting average, 22 homers, and 64 runs batted in, his worst statistical season since 1948. Although Hodges's 22 home runs tied him with Charlie Neal for the team lead, Hodges struck out 87 times, leaving him at the top of the National League list for most career strikeouts with 934. (Snider was right behind him with 933.)

Amid the disappointment, Hodges had one moment of triumph. He hit the 300th home run of his career in the seventh inning at the Coliseum on April 23 against Chicago, which briefly gave the Dodgers the lead. But the Cubs came back to win the game, 7–6, on a ninth-inning, two-run double by longtime Dodgers killer Bobby Thomson. Hodges was the fifteenth player in baseball history to hit 300 home runs.

Playing in Los Angeles was not without its benefits for Hodges. There was the adulation of the Hollywood elite. On Opening Day at the Coliseum, the 78,672 fans included Gene Autry, Jimmy Stewart, Burt Lancaster, Jack Lemmon, Nat King Cole, Danny Thomas, Groucho Marx, Joe E. Brown, and Ray Bolger. After the mandatory star gazing, they even played a game. The Dodgers beat the Giants, 6–5.

That summer the Dodgers held what was billed as the first night clinic "in the history of major league baseball" at Wrigley Field. Hodges was the featured attraction of the free clinic jointly sponsored by the Dodgers and various recreational departments in city of Los Angeles and Los Angeles County. With Joan and his children often in Brooklyn, events such as the night clinic made the time go faster for Hodges, who preferred night games to day games so he was less likely to be alone in the evening. After day games ended, the nights dragged on for Hodges, who rarely accompanied his teammates on late-night sojourns on the town. "Hodges was not in the bars much," Johnny Podres said. "He was a social drinker. He might put a few dollars down and say, 'Okay boys, have a few on me.'"

Hodges tried everything he could think of to improve his hitting that season. For many years, Hodges had ordered a Hillerich & Bradsby model H138 bat that was 35 inches long and 35 ounces, the same model that a long-forgotten player named Bill Hart used when he was with the Dodgers during World War II. In 1958, like many older players trying to quicken their swing, Hodges began ordering the same length bat, but reduced the weight to either 33 or 32 ounces.

By mid-June, hoping to end his hitting slump, Hodges was coming to the Coliseum early in the afternoon to take extra batting practice. After spending forty-five minutes in the batting cage on the afternoon of June 11, that night Hodges hit a double and a home run to knock in three runs and helped Don Drysdale defeat the Phillies, 7–4. As they had done when Hodges went through his horrific slump in the early part of the 1953 season, the Dodgers' coaching staff suggested he alter his batting stance. But this time, instead of having Hodges move his right leg further away from the plate, he was asked to move his right foot closer to the plate so he had a more open stance. Hodges had used this new stance against the Phillies. "I didn't feel too comfortable," said Hodges, "but I guess you can't knock results."

But Hodges couldn't sustain it. "I'm just not hitting. I don't know why and nobody seems to know why," Hodges said. "I've snapped out of slumps before, though, and I'll whip this one."

In order to change his luck, he even visited the racetrack, picking what appeared to be a sure winner. Although he was no gambler, Hodges enjoyed an occasional day at the track, so placing a wager was not unusual for him. "[But] in LA, when he had been going bad at the plate," recalled Johnny Podres, who was with Hodges that day, "he put two dollars down on a horse with 1–9 odds. But the horse got beat."

Even Pee Wee Reese, who usually enjoyed teasing Hodges, felt sorry for him. A few days after the Phillies game, Hodges came to bat in the eighth inning against the Pirates. The Dodgers were trailing, and the bases were loaded, but he failed to deliver. After the game, Reese, who ended up the hero with a game-winning double, said, "Gil has been having such a tough time getting going that a big blow right then would have done him a world of good."

Trying to pump up Hodges, even the usually subdued Walter Alston told the Dodgers' announcer, Jerry Doggett, that Hodges "has become more offensive-minded lately. He's taking fewer called strikes and swinging the bat more like he used to."

But after the Dodgers lost the final game of the home stand against the Pirates by a lopsided score of 12–1, Alston changed his tune. Hodges's batting average had fallen to .255, well below what was then his lifetime batting average of .279. Hodges had hit nine home runs, but his thirty-five strikeouts led the team. Hodges's strikeout to homer ratio, at nearly 4 to 1, was higher than usual. Hodges had played in all but one of the team's fifty-seven games so far that season, but had only twenty-three runs batted in. "Gil is having such a rough time with the bat," Alston said, "that I'm thinking of benching him for a few games and using Norm Larker at first base."

At twenty-seven, Norm Larker, a left-handed first baseman who had hit over .300 the previous three seasons for the Dodgers' Minor League team in St. Paul, was in only his first season in the Majors. Like so many first basemen before him, Larker knew the reason. "I got in the wrong organization," Larker said, "with Hodges."

Benching Hodges on the road (and not in front of the hometown fans) would have made sense, but Alston gave Hodges one more chance, playing him in the first two games in Philadelphia, the team's first stop on the road trip. Hodges went 0 for 9; Larker started the next two games.

"Gil agreed that a rest might help him snap out of it," Alston said, "I told him not to even pick up a bat for a couple of days. We've all been trying to help him and now he's really fouled up."

After Philadelphia, Hodges sat out the opening game in Pittsburgh, but Larker didn't impress, and Hodges started the last three games there. He managed only two hits in twelve at bats. The Dodgers' next stop was Cincinnati, where an electronic scoreboard had recently been introduced at Crosley Field. It was then considered a modern marvel that a batter could step up to the plate and the scoreboard would instantaneously show his uniform number and current batting average. "That Cincinnati thing," Hodges said, "is awfully embarrassing to a man with a batting average as low as mine."

Hodges was in for more frustration when the Dodgers returned to Los Angeles. In the sixth inning of a game against Pittsburgh on July 15, Duke Snider hit one of the longest home runs of his career, a 430-foot blast that cleared the top of the fence in deep right-center field. In a season when Dodgers fans had little to celebrate, it was a moment to cherish. In the eighth, trailing 6–2, with two men on base, Snider was again due up but Pittsburgh brought in a left-hander to pitch, and Alston pulled Snider and sent Hodges in to pinch-hit.

Alston's logic was sound: Snider rarely hit well against left-handers, and Hodges enjoyed great success against them. But Hodges struck out swinging, which "evoked much booing from the crowd."

For a man who had never been booed at Ebbets Field during some horrendous slumps, it was a rude awakening. In that same game, which the Dodgers ended up losing 6–2, Alston took Don Drysdale out in the eighth inning. In that era, it was a matter of pride for a pitcher to throw a complete game, and in a display confirming why they had Drysdale rooming with Hodges, Drysdale angrily threw his glove into the dugout, knocked all the batting helmets off the rack, and "generally raised Cain."

Alston later said that was okay with him. "I don't care whether Don's mad at me or the Pirates or what. I'd rather have 'em full of fight, fighting mad, than with no spirit."

Alston's comment is consistent with his later position that Hodges was not the man to replace Pee Wee Reese as team captain because Hodges was not the type to appear "full of fight." Although Hodges's poor hitting had him "eating his heart out," *Los Angeles Times* reporter Frank Finch noted you could never tell that from his demeanor.

But due to injuries to other players, Alston kept Hodges in the lineup, playing him in a variety of positions. In a game in Cincinnati on August 1, for example, Hodges started in left field, then played two innings at first base, and finished up behind the plate. "Hodges can play anywhere," Alston said. "Maybe I should try pitching him."

No matter where he played, Hodges, like many of his teammates, was no longer the player he once was. At thirty-eight, Reese retired at the end of the season. After hitting forty or more home runs for five consecutive years, Duke Snider hit only fifteen. Carl Furillo led the team in runs batted in but was in his last season as an everyday player.

With an aging core group, the Dodgers spent much of the season in the cellar, an unfamiliar place for a team that had not finished in last place since 1905. The season ended with the Dodgers in seventh place, twenty-one games behind the pennant-winning Braves and just two games ahead of the last-place Phillies. Yet the fans flocked to the Coliseum. The Dodgers' 1958 home attendance represented an increase of more than one million from their final season in Brooklyn. Including road games, more than three million fans saw them play that season. Such support provided hope, but Hodges was making no predictions about his own play. He did say, "Next year I'm going to forget all about fences and try to do what comes naturally when I go up to the plate."

Alston agreed, saying, "I can't believe Gil is over the hill."

Despite his struggles, Hodges was still the best-fielding first baseman in the league. Hall of Fame pitcher Dizzy Dean, then a broadcaster, was asked to name his personal All-Star team. "I'd want Hodges on first base," Dean said, "because there ain't no first basemen in the last ten years done what I seen him do game after game."

But unless Hodges improved at the plate, the words of another man, the one with the final say on Hodges's future, sounded ominous. "Management had mistakenly decided to let Los Angeles see the old-timers, whose names were legend," Walter O'Malley said, "instead of starting the youth movement."

At the end of the season, there was no "half-acre" talk from Hodges. In the *Los Angeles Times*, Frank Finch wrote, "As soon as the season ends, Gil Hodges will hustle back to his family in Brooklyn. His winter plans are indefinite."

But throughout that long first season in Los Angeles, despite his reputation for being solemnly serious, Hodges maintained his dry sense of humor. And it came with an edge: his teammates referred to him as "the great needle."

In 1958 the Dodgers were Hollywood's newest novelty act. Bing Crosby, Danny Kaye, and Jerry Lewis regularly visited the Dodgers' clubhouse. And like his teammates, Hodges befriended the Hollywood celebrities who flocked down to the field during batting practice.

Gil Hodges's pals included a diminutive makeup man named Jack Barron. As makeup men went, Barron was top-notch. He often worked for Alfred Hitchcock. But for reasons no one could figure out, Barron was convinced he could improve Hodges's hitting. He pecked away at Hodges with unsolicited advice on his stance, his swing, even his position in the batter's box. Eventually, Hodges had enough. But it wasn't his style to tell Barron off. Instead, Hodges offered Barron his bat: "Show me."

As Hodges anticipated, Barron grabbed the bat and stepped into the batter's box. The Dodgers players knew the coming proceedings would be worth watching, and they gathered around the batting cage.

"Sandy," Hodges said to the batting-practice pitcher, "would you mind throwing a few to my friend Jack?"

The first pitch was a *pea*. That's what hitters called it, because that's what the ball looked like when Sandy Koufax was throwing it. Jack Barron didn't see the ball whiz past him. Koufax threw again: another pea. The bat never left Barron's shoulder. Then, without saying a word, Barron stepped out of the batter's box and handed Hodges back his bat.

The Dodgers doubled over in laughter.

Jack Barron never offered Gil Hodges hitting advice again.

15

WORLD CHAMPIONS

This is more gratifying, more of a triumph, than anything I've ever experienced as a Dodger.

Buzzie Bavasi waited until after Christmas to mail the Dodgers players their contracts for the 1959 season. Otherwise, he said, "I'd spoil the Yuletide holiday for a few guys." Hodges was one of them and his salary was reduced.

That season, as Walter O'Malley had indicated, the Dodgers retooled with younger players. By the end of the season, rookies like pitcher Larry Sherry and shortstop Maury Wills would be making significant contributions. The Dodgers also acquired veteran left-handed-hitting outfielder Wally Moon, who developed an inside-out swing well suited for popping balls over the Coliseum's left-field fence that came to be known as "Moon Shots."

Walter Alston remained undecided about whom to name as Reese's replacement as team captain. "You need a man like a Reese, a Stanky or a Dark to be a good infield leader," Alston said. "Nobody is smarter, baseball-wise, than Hodges, but he's not the fiery type. However, it might help restore his confidence if he was given the responsibility of leadership."

Considering Alston's own demeanor, his focus on "fiery types" seems odd. Although Alston never named a captain for the 1959 season, with Pee Wee Reese's retirement Hodges became the de facto team leader. "Hodges commands the utmost respect of his teammates without goading them by loud words or violent actions," wrote Frank Finch.

The regular season began in Chicago. Don Drysdale was the Dodgers' Opening Day pitcher. The night before—thanks to Hodges's mantra "Sleep is very important to a ballplayer. It gets you through road trips"—Drysdale and Hodges had dinner at 5, took a walk, and were back in their hotel room at 7:30 and in bed by 9:30. It didn't do much good. Drysdale lasted just five innings, giving up six runs, and the Dodgers lost.

But 1959 would be one of Hodges's most satisfying seasons. He left his hitting woes behind him, supplying numerous game-winning hits propelling the Dodgers into a three-way pennant race with Milwaukee and San Francisco.

In a July 23 game against the Cubs, Hodges hit a two-run home run to give the Dodgers a 2–0 lead. It was Hodges's team-leading nineteenth home run of the season. But in the sixth, after drawing a walk, Hodges tried to tag up on a fly ball to center field. As he slid into second, his spikes caught, severely injuring his right ankle, and he had to be carried off the field on a stretcher. At first, it appeared he had broken his fibula just above the ankle, but X-rays proved negative. At Daniel Freeman Memorial Hospital, the injury was deemed "a severely pulled muscle," and Hodges would be out for a week to ten days.

But Hodges had "heard something pop" when his spikes caught in the dirt, and in an era when the true extent of a player's injuries was often kept from him (the Yankees once neglected to tell Roger Maris he had a broken bone in his hand), Hodges did not know he had suffered more than just a pulled muscle. Less than a week later, Hodges took batting practice. He hit the first seven pitches thrown against the screen in left. The eighth pitch was inside. Hodges turned his right ankle to avoid being hit, and the Dodgers soon announced that he would be out for at least another week.

Trailing by a run in the seventh inning of a game in Chicago on August 11, Alston sent Hodges up to pinch-hit. He took one swing and reinjured his ankle. Hodges was in so much pain, he was unable to finish the at bat. The next day, with more wrapping on Hodges's ankle "than a mummy's torso." Writer Frank Finch asked Hodges when he would return.

"I don't know, maybe I'll never play again," Hodges replied—"testily," noted Finch.

The next day, wearing tennis sneakers, Hodges took batting and infield practice. He looked, according to Finch, "fairly spry."

Like many newspaper writers with the coveted job of covering their city's Major League Baseball team, Finch was loyal to management. A week later, in Cincinnati, Finch wrote,

No matter which town we visit during this current Dodger junket, the home town ballplayers invariably inquire (a bit apprehensively we might add) as to when Gil Hodges will return to the regular line-up. It is quite a compliment to the moon-faced slugger. . . . The injury came at the worst possible time, for Gil was in the throes of his hottest hitting streak of the year. . . . At the time Gil was injured L.A. had won four of the last six games. . . . Since the mishap, which could cost us a pennant, the Dodgers barely have managed to stay above the .500 mark by winning 13 and losing 11. This is not intended as a rap at Hodges' hustling understudy, Norm Larker, but there's no gainsaying that Larker can't hit or field with the veteran star.

On August 21, Hodges had a pinch-hit single during a four-run, seventh-inning rally in a win over Pittsburgh. A few days later, Hodges returned to the starting lineup. "Although the veteran still [had] a slight limp," wrote Finch, he told Alston he was "anxious to rejoin the troops."

Two days after returning, Hodges drove in five runs, including his twentieth home run of the season, to provide Koufax with enough run support for an 8–2 win over Philadelphia. The next day, Hodges homered off his old nemesis, Robin Roberts, in another Dodgers win. And on August 30, against the first-place Giants, Hodges hit a two-run home run in a 7–6 Dodgers win.

San Francisco had been in first place since July 4, but on September 20 the Dodgers completed a three-game sweep in San Francisco, knocking the Giants into third place. That left the Dodgers and Braves in a two-team pennant race in the season's final week.

The Dodgers' flight back from San Francisco arrived in Los Angeles at two in the morning. Although it was a day off for the team, after going hitless (0 for 14) in the three games against the Giants, Hodges went to the Coliseum to take batting practice.

The Dodgers then flew to St. Louis for two games against the Cardinals. In the first game, the Dodgers took a 3–0 lead, but Sandy Koufax gave up a grand slam home run and was knocked out of the game early. Heading into the third inning, the Dodgers tied it up at 4–4. Then, with a man on base, Hodges hit a 425-foot home run to center, one of the longest home runs hit in St. Louis all season, giving the Dodgers a 6–4 lead. But the Dodgers lost, 11–10.

The next day, Roger Craig threw a five-hit shutout to defeat the Cardinals, 3-0, putting the Dodgers in a first-place tie. In the first inning, of that game, Cardinals rookie right-hander Bob Miller hit Hodges on his left forearm with a pitch. Hodges stayed in the game until the seventh, when his arm became too badly swollen for him to continue. X-rays proved negative, and Frank Finch once again began lobbying for Hodges to keep playing. "Any prolonged absence of the great first baseman," Finch wrote, "a case-hardened veteran of pennant dog fights and World Series, would be a stunning blow to Los Angeles' chances."

The Dodgers were still in a first-place tie with the Braves when they finished their season with three crucial games in Chicago. Dodgers trainer Bill Buhler gave Hodges's left forearm ultrasonic treatments and deemed him fit to play. Before the first game against the Cubs, after Hodges hit several balls over the fence in batting practice, Hodges grinned and said, "Guess I haven't got an alibi now."

With both his right ankle and his left arm taped, Hodges played one of the best games of his career. In the top of the first, the Dodgers took a lead on a Wally Moon home run, but the Cubs tied it at 1-1. In the fifth the Dodgers took a 2-1 lead with a walk, stolen base, ground out, and sacrifice fly. The Cubs rallied and would have taken the lead were it not for Hodges. With runners on first and second, he charged home plate and fielded a bunt attempt so quickly he was able to throw out the lead runner at third base. As a result, when Chicago's George Altman hit a two-out single to center field, only one run scored. In the sixth, with two outs and runners on first and second, Hodges doubled to drive in two runs for a 4-2 lead. But the Cubs tied it to force extra innings. With one out in the tenth, Hodges bobbled the ball when he tried to make a one-handed pickup of an easy roller. After the runner was advanced to second, Hall of Famer slugger Ernie Banks faced twenty-four-year-old rookie Larry Sherry. A hit would win the game for the Cubs. In a tense at bat, Sherry struck Banks out looking. Finally, in the eleventh inning, with one out, Hodges hit his twenty-fifth homer of the season to give the Dodgers a dramatic 5-4 victory and move them one game ahead of the Braves.

In the next day's *Los Angeles Times*, Hodges's career was accurately described as "brilliant" but "up 'n' down."

The Dodgers split their final two games in Chicago, but the Braves won their last two games of the season. The two teams finished in a first-place tie resulting in a three-game playoff to determine the National League pennant winner.

Game One was played in Milwaukee. With the Braves up 2–1 in the third, Hodges's two-out single drove in the tying run, and in the sixth, Johnny Roseboro's solo home run gave the Dodgers a 3–2 win.

The Dodgers trailed 5–2 in the bottom of the ninth in Game Two, played in Los Angeles. But Lew Burdette gave up singles to Wally Moon, Duke Snider, and Hodges. The tension mounted as the Braves' best relief pitcher, Don McMahon, came in to pitch to Norm Larker, who hit a line-drive single off the left-field screen that scored two runs. Warren Spahn replaced McMahon and Alston sent Carl Furillo in to pinch-hit. Hodges scored on Furillo's sacrifice fly and the game went to extra innings. After a scoreless tenth and eleventh, with two out in the twelfth, Hodges drew a walk and advanced to second on a single. Furillo then hit a sharp grounder over second base. Shortstop Felix Mantilla made a great play to stop the ball from getting through the infield, but his off-balance throw to first bounced past Frank Torre and Hodges scored the winning run. The Dodgers mobbed Hodges as Vin Scully said, "We go to Chicago."

The Dodgers were the first seventh-place team to come back to win the National League pennant the following season. The fact that no one expected the Dodgers to compete for the pennant made the victory special. Some credit belonged to Walter Alston. During the season, many suggested he reconfigure his infield so Norm Larker could play first base to add another solid hitter to the lineup. But that would require moving Hodges to third and Junior Gilliam from third to shortstop. Since the Dodgers led the league in runs scored at the beginning of July, Alston concluded that on balance, "defense was far more important than any additional hitting power." As a result, the Dodgers committed the fewest errors of any team in the National League and Alston was named the National League Manager of the Year. But much like Hodges when he managed the 1969 Mets, Alston took a modest approach, insisting "that a manager is no better than his tools."

The Chicago White Sox were the Dodgers' World Series opponent.

The *Go Go* Sox won with speed (they led the American League in stolen bases), pitching (with three outstanding starters, Bob Shaw, Billy Pierce, and Early Wynn), and defense (anchored by a pair of future Hall of Fame middle infielders, Luis Aparicio and Nellie Fox).

Before the World Series began, the Dodgers players held a team meeting to determine how to divide their share of the Series proceeds. Under Hodges's usual direction, they were "most liberal in cutting the melon." Several players who were not with the team for the entire season, such as Larry Sherry, Maury Wills, and even Art Fowler, who was no longer with the team, received at least a partial share; and a surprisingly large number, thirty-five, a full share of the World Series payout.

Roger Craig faced Wynn in the first game. A future Hall of Famer, Wynn, with a record of 22-10, would win the Cy Young Award that season, and Craig was overmatched: after only three innings, the White Sox led 9-0. In fact, the entire Dodgers team looked out of sorts. The Dodgers not only failed to score but, uncharacteristically, made three errors. And they looked old. Duke Snider made two errors, both in the same inning; and Hodges looked foolish when he tried to cut off a throw from the outfield and fell backward on his rear end, allowing a run to score. Some West Coast fans lost faith, calling the Dodgers a "bunch of erroring bums."

Hodges showed leadership. "You hate to take a beating like that," he said, "but the guys aren't down. We still have our confidence . . . you can't lose a World Series on the first game, or the first two games. Remember, we dropped the first two to the Yankees in 1955 and wound up winning the whole thing. Don't count us out."

Hodges was right. The Dodgers won Game Two, 4-3. And with the next three games in Los Angeles, momentum had swung their way. So did the fans. Setting a still existing World Series attendance record, over 92,000 people attended each game at the Coliseum. In Game Three Carl Furillo's two-run single was the key hit, and starter Don Drysdale, with Larry Sherry in relief, pitched well enough for a 3-1 win.

In the pivotal fourth game, Wynn again faced Craig. This time, Craig pitched well and the Dodgers knocked Wynn out in the third inning, scoring four runs.

That inning, Hodges had a run-scoring single and came around to score on a passed ball. But in the seventh, Craig tired and the Sox tied it at 4-4.

Gil Hodges led off the eighth inning thinking home run. White Sox right-hander Gerry Staley started Hodges off with a curve ball. Hodges swung and missed. Behind in the count, Hodges switched strategy and just wanted to make contact. Staley's next pitch was a sinker that broke inside. That was all Hodges needed.

Hodges was the kind of hitter that a great first baseman of a later generation, Keith Hernandez, would refer to as a "cripples hitter," a player who could look foolish on a pitch one minute, but if the pitcher made a mistake and threw one in the hitter's sweet spot, the hitter had the ability to drive the ball for an extra-base hit and *cripple* the pitcher. Hodges's sweet spot was inside, and he drove Staley's pitch over the screen in left-center field. And it wasn't a cheap home run, the kind the fans called a "Screeno." The ball traveled 360 feet and "probably would have landed in the upper deck at Ebbets Field." White Sox manager Al Lopez knew it was gone the minute Hodges hit it, and just stood on the steps of the dugout holding his head in his hand. Lopez, a future Hall of Famer manager, knew that thanks to Hodges's crucial home run, the game was effectively over.

The Sox couldn't score on Larry Sherry, who had come in to pitch in relief in the eighth, and the Dodgers took a 3-1 Series lead. After the game, Joan Hodges gave her husband a congratulatory kiss through the screen behind home plate. On the blackboard in the Dodgers' dressing room, someone wrote, "One to Go-Go-Go."

After the game, his hands black and sticky from pine tar, wearing a patch on the palm of his left hand due to a skin fungus, Hodges answered questions in a soft-spoken voice. Never one to gush over anything, Hodges was asked to rate the importance of his home run. Hodges downplayed it, saying his eleventh-inning winning home run against the Cubs in the final series of the season was "a mighty big thrill, too." Some reporters, not used to Hodges's appearance, commented that his "pale skin makes him look unlike most base-ball players." He also sounded different. The Associated Press pointed out that Hodges "rarely if ever uses profanity, selects his words carefully and uses excellent grammar." But Hodges's genuine modesty further distinguished him. On the day he hit the game-winning home run in the World Series, Hodges said, "You've got to be lucky to hit."

For sportswriters, all too familiar with the typical baseball star who could be quite full of himself, Hodges's humility was a revelation. Veteran *Los Angeles Times* writer Jim Murray called Hodges "easily one of the nicest human beings in the whole fabric of baseball."

That night, on the popular *Steve Allen Show*, after comedians Don Knotts and Buddy Hackett did a skit about beatniks and Teresa Brewer sang "The Party's Over," Allen was joined on stage by Walter Alston.

"So Walter," Allen said, "I've heard you're quiet and when you do talk you use as few words as possible."

Walter Alston said nothing and just shook his head no.

Steve Allen then introduced all of the Dodgers players, ending with Hodges. Calling him the hero of today's game, Allen said of Hodges, "He could be elected mayor." Some players briefly spoke with Allen, but Allen didn't even try to get a yes or no out of Hodges. But each of the players had been scripted to tell a joke.

Hodges's joke, in tune with his preference for double-entendre-filled, self-deprecating humor, related to his weaknesses as a hitter and a driver. "I used to hit 300 every year," Hodges said. "Then I sold my cab and went into baseball."

The next day, Sandy Koufax allowed five hits and only one run, but the Dodgers, despite nine hits, couldn't score. With one out in the fourth, Hodges tripled to deep right-center field but was left stranded. In the eighth, with the Dodgers trailing 1–0, one out, and Wally Moon on first, Hodges hit a long fly to left field. The crowd roared as it appeared Hodges had hit another game-winning home run. But it flew into the left-field stands in foul territory. White Sox manager Al Lopez immediately ran out of the dugout to confer with his pitcher, Bob Shaw. The pitch Hodges had fouled was letter high, a perfect pitch to drive into the air. Lopez then told Shaw to keep his pitches low. On a 2-2 count, Hodges hit his second single of the game, but the Dodgers again left him stranded and they lost, 1–0.

The White Sox were confident they could win the final two games of the Series back in Chicago. Early Wynn, scheduled to start Game Six, had noticed

Hodges kissing Joan after the fourth game. "We're going to take you guys back to the big porch," Wynn said. "It looks like Hodges will have to take mamma back to Chicago, anyway." Hodges strained his right shoulder in the eighth inning of Game Five when he threw off-balance after fielding a bunt. "It may affect my throwing some, but it won't bother my swing," Hodges said.

Back in Chicago for Game Six, the Dodgers' bats came alive. Snider, who had only been able to pinch-hit during the games in Los Angeles due to an injured knee, had asked Alston if he could start Game Six. Snider said, "I want to play against Wynn. I feel . . . that I am going to get a hit that will help us win."

And he did. Snider hit a two-run home run to give the Dodgers an early lead. Making his third start of the series, thirty-nine-year-old Early Wynn was "throwing rather than pitching"; but even after Snider's home run, Lopez left Wynn in the game, and in the fourth the Dodgers scored six times to put the game out of reach. Larry Sherry, in relief of Johnny Podres, got the win and the Dodgers were World Series champions. What had taken over half a century in Brooklyn had been accomplished in Los Angeles in only two seasons.

The scene in the Dodgers' dressing room was a far cry from the tears shed in 1955: "Picture six cans of sardines squeezed into one. Add pandemonium, hysteria, screams, shoving, and joyous back-slaps." Walter Alston was ecstatic. "This is the greatest team I've ever been connected with," he said, "This team never quit."

Hodges said, "It was a thrill just to play with this team. Most of the old Dodger teams went into the season picked first or second, and came through mostly by overpowering the opposition. This one got no attention from the sports-writing experts last spring—and that was understandable the way we flopped in 1958. But this team fought against great odds to win the pennant, the playoff and now the series. What more can you ask?"

The 1959 Dodgers lacked a great everyday player in the prime of his career and won with team effort. As a mix of former stars at the end of their careers (Carl Furillo, Duke Snider, and Hodges), players on the edge of greatness (Sandy Koufax, Don Drysdale, and Maury Wills), and a veteran enjoying his career season (Wally Moon), the 1959 Los Angeles Dodgers were the weakest championship team in baseball history, according to statistical guru Bill

James. But for Hodges, it was a lesson in how a manager makes the most of his entire twenty-five-man roster.

For example, a rookie pitcher named Gene Snyder started just two games for the Dodgers that season, winning once in what was the only win of his Major League career. A decade later, Hodges still appreciated the importance of Snyder's contribution. Considering that the Dodgers finished the 1959 season tied with the Braves, Hodges noted, "without Gene Snyder's victory we wouldn't have been in the playoff." Although he would not always succeed in doing so, Hodges used Snyder to make the point that a manager's job is to make all of his players, even the last man on the bench, "feel important."

Hodges had led the Dodgers in World Series hitting for the third time with a .391 average (1953 and 1956 were the other years), but Larry Sherry, who had won two games and saved two, was named the most valuable player of the Series. The only award Hodges won that season was for his character, receiving the Lou Gehrig Memorial Award.

But injuries and age had finally caught up to Hodges; 1959 would prove to be his last season as a full-time player. Yet Buzzie Bavasi rewarded Hodges for his leadership with a contract for $39,000, making him the highest-paid Dodger.

During the 1960 season, with his family usually in Brooklyn, Hodges's Los Angeles hotel, the Mayfair, was a lonely place. Time passed much faster at the Coliseum, where Hodges made sure to give his autograph to any child who asked for it. No line of kids was too long. Decades later, Norm Sherry, then a catcher on the Dodgers, could still recall the image of children crowding around Hodges thrusting baseballs and scorecards at him, and Hodges's only request being, "Please don't step on my toes."

In 1960 and 1961, the Dodgers were unable to repeat their championship success, and Hodges's utility was as an instructor to young players like a first baseman named Frank Howard. In the spring of 1960, Hodges tutored Howard on playing first despite the fact that the better Howard did, the more time Hodges would spend on the bench. That spring, when Howard, who then tended to answer questions with a curt "yes, sir" or "no, sir" response, was asked about Hodges, he suddenly became talkative. "They don't come no better than Gil," Howard said, "That sonovagun is a great guy."

But Howard, at six feet seven, lacked the agility to play first and was moved to the outfield. Hodges initially won the starting first base job, but by early May, Norm Larker became the starter, hitting .323 for the season. Hodges took his demotion well. "Anything Skip wants to do," Hodges said, "is all right with me."

There is a story from Hodges's final years in Los Angeles that may be apocryphal but no doubt harbors a kernel of truth. Hodges asked Walter Alston if he was in the lineup that day and Alston snapped at him, "No, you're not." Annoyed at what he considered an impertinent question, Alston asked Hodges why he wanted to know.

"I thought if I wasn't in the lineup, I'd pitch batting practice," Hodges replied, hoping to give one of the team's pitchers a break from a chore they all considered onerous.

In 1960 supporters of John F. Kennedy asked Hodges if he would endorse his fellow Catholic for president. Hodges felt it was not a professional athlete's place to support one political candidate over another, so he turned them down. Stan Musial felt differently and traveled all over the country in support of Kennedy.

That year, Hodges participated in a television show called *Home Run Derby* in which two players competed head-to-head to see who could hit the most home runs in a simulated nine-inning game. In his first home run derby, Hodges competed against Willie Mays. The program began with the host, Mark Scott, explaining the contest rules. After Scott finished, he asked, "Any questions?"

Hodges replied, "How do you get the ball over the fence?"

Hodges defeated Mays and moved on to compete against Ernie Banks. While one participant was at bat, the other would sit next to Scott and answer his questions. Early in the contest, after Hodges hit a home run, Scott asked about it. Hodges said he was "lucky enough to get one." But when asked about Banks, Hodges said Banks was "one of the outstanding shortstops in baseball" and had "one of the most beautiful swings in baseball." Late in the contest Hodges hit three home runs to draw even with Bank's total of six. But on the very next pitch, Banks hit a homer to retake the lead. Hodges smiled and said, "That didn't take very long, did it?" Banks won. Hodges's cigarette smoking habit was catching up to him. In the last few innings, when he returned to his seat next to Scott, he was out of breath.

In 1961 Hodges's greatest contribution to the team came before the season even started. Before a Dodgers B-team road game against Minnesota that spring, Hodges, who was managing in Alston's absence, noticed that the Dodgers had brought only two pitchers for the game. Sandy Koufax was scheduled to start; if he was wild and walked too many batters and had to be replaced, the Dodgers wouldn't have another pitcher. To avoid that problem, before the game Hodges told Koufax he had to pitch seven innings. (The game was scheduled for only seven innings.) Because of Hodges's request, Dodgers catcher Norm Sherry told Koufax not to throw so hard but instead focus on just throwing strikes. Koufax pitched seven innings of no-hit ball and later commented how that particular game showed him that he didn't have to overpower hitters with every pitch to win.

Buzzie Bavasi signed Hodges to a 1961 contract so he would be available for the National League expansion draft to be held later that year to stock the rosters of the new expansion teams: the New York Mets and the Houston Astros. Hodges was a perfect fit for the Mets. The previous summer, in late June of 1960, when the Dodgers had returned to New York for an exhibition game against the Yankees, Hodges's continuing popularity in New York was clear. Over 53,000 fans showed up at Yankee Stadium, most rooting for the Dodgers. When Hodges was thrown out at the plate trying to stretch a triple into an inside-the-park home run, the fans gave him a standing ovation and the "rafters reverberated."

"Never seen anything like it," Casey Stengel said. "First time I ever felt like a total stranger in my own ballpark."

In 1961 Hodges's bat speed had slowed and he started to use a 31-ounce bat, the lightest of his career. But when he did play, he still had his baseball smarts. Against the Phillies that July, Dodgers relief pitcher Dick Farrell threw a wild pitch with a runner on second base. Catcher Johnny Roseboro chased after the ball but home plate was uncovered because Farrell had forgotten that on a passed ball it was the pitcher's responsibility to cover the plate. But Hodges raced to home plate to take Roseboro's throw and tag the runner out. The Dodgers lost the game anyway and few noticed Hodges' heads up play. But Hodges filed away Alston's reaction to a mental error. "I fined Don

Drysdale for the same sort of thing earlier this season," Alston said, "so there's no reason I shouldn't fine Farrell."

In Los Angeles, Hodges was the team's representative in the fledgling players union, and he spoke out in support of his fellow players. From 1959 to 1962, two All-Star Games were played each summer, and player sentiment was against it. "A second game seems to be anticlimactic. It has no impact," said Hodges. "I think it would be to the classic's best interest to return to the old one-game-a-year policy." Eventually the former policy of one All-Star Game each year was reinstated. After Wally Moon was suspended for touching an umpire while arguing a call, Hodges, despite having never been fined or suspended as a player, began a campaign to require that players be entitled to a hearing prior to any suspension. When Don Drysdale pitched poorly and the fans at the Coliseum began booing him every time his name was announced, Hodges defended his roommate. "Back at Ebbets Field the fans could get pretty rough at times," Hodges said, "but Don never received the abuse he's gotten in his home town. . . . No ball player likes to hear himself razzed all the time, particularly on those occasions when it's not even justified. Anybody who really knows Don knows he does not deserve such treatment."

In February of 1961, hoping to take advantage of the nation's bowling obsession, Hodges opened Gil Hodges Lanes in Brooklyn, a state-of-the-art facility with forty-eight lanes. To give back to the community, bowling competitions were arranged between former Dodgers and Giants players with the proceeds going to the Brooklyn Cancer Fund. Beginning that winter, Hodges's off-season time was largely spent with family or at the bowling alley where children would unhesitatingly run up to him shouting, "Gil, I bowled 182."

HOME
Manhattan (1962)

16

CASEY

A lot of Stengel's influence rubbed off on me. He was around so long, he knew so much, he noticed everything—and there were things about handling men, which is an important part of managing, in which he helped me.

The New York Mets' founding owner, Joan Whitney Payson, owned a fifty-room mansion on 110 acres on Long Island, a summer home in Maine, a winter home in Florida, and "cottages" in Saratoga and Lexington where she kept her eye on her Belmont Stakes-winning thoroughbred racehorses. When Mrs. Payson wanted to see a Gauguin, a Renoir, or a Van Gogh, she perused the walls of her houses. But Mrs. Payson was no stuck-up society matron. Ever since she was a little girl, she loved to go to the Polo Grounds, fill out a scorecard, eat a hot dog, and root for her beloved Giants. And when they moved west, she missed them so much that when a lawyer named Bill Shea gave her the chance to bring National League baseball back to New York, she made the multimillion dollar investment. As a result, the pleasantly plump, jovial woman Mets players would come to refer to as "mother dumpling" gave birth to a financially secure team.

Payson installed her stockbroker, M. Donald Grant, as the Mets' chairman of the board. Grant knew little about baseball but had always dreamed of managing a team. In later years—often to the Mets' detriment—Grant would exert his authority over baseball decisions; but in 1961 he limited himself to hiring George Weiss, the Yankees' former general manager, to run the team. Weiss in turn hired the Mets' first manager, Casey Stengel.

Fearing the fans would not come out to watch a team of unknowns, Weiss paid the Dodgers $75,000 for the right to select Gil Hodges in the expansion draft. Al Wolf, a writer with the *Los Angeles Times*, predicted Stengel would manage the Mets for one season and then turn the job over to Hodges. Wolf understood Hodges's long-term goal: to manage on a Major League level, preferably in New York. But managers, like players, hold on as long as they can, and Stengel would manage the Mets until the summer of 1965 when a broken hip forced him to retire.

Arthur Daley, in his welcome-back-to-New York piece, wrote that Hodges had been homesick and unhappy in Los Angeles "because he is a devoted family man of rare intensity." Hodges said, "It's wonderful to be back. Within 24 hours, I changed ball clubs to come back to New York and my wife presented me with our fourth child, a daughter [Barbara]. My association with the Dodgers was long and pleasant. In a way, I hated to leave but there's nothing like being home with my family. This change should give me the lift I've been needing. I felt better physically this season than I have since we left Ebbets Field but we had so many talented kids on the club that I didn't play as much as I would have liked. I welcome the chance to play regularly—although that holds no guarantees. Ballplayers always say, 'If the manager had used me more, I'd have hit .300.'"

That winter, at the New York Chapter of the Baseball Writers' Association dinner, Roger Maris and Mickey Mantle received an award as co-players of the year after their outstanding performances in 1961. That night, Dick Young presented Hodges with the "Good Guy Award" as the "baseball man most cooperative with the press, friendly and available in good times or bad and frank and honest in his remarks."

The press largely appreciated Hodges as a player and in later years he continued to have a forthright relationship with established writers like Young and Jack Lang—men who knew him since his early days in Brooklyn. But among younger writers earning their first assignments in the 1960s as generational differences were widening, Hodges's tight-lipped, cryptic style never earned him a lot of votes as "most cooperative" during his managerial years.

That winter, Hodges negotiated his salary with George Weiss, a man with a well-deserved reputation for frugality. Despite Hodges being the Mets' star attraction in their inaugural season, Weiss wanted him to take a pay cut, and Hodges contacted Buzzie Bavasi for help. But Hodges was on the outside looking in at the old-boys' network. In early 1962, Bavasi wrote Hodges a letter dripping with cynicism: "I talked to George Weiss today and I guess other clubs are not as generous as the Dodgers." The letter implies that Hodges and Bavasi had a prior agreement that if the Mets cut Hodges, the Dodgers would reimburse him based upon an annual compensation of $44,000. Bavasi wrote, "I have no intention of getting into your salary problems with the 'Mets.'"

Hodges signed with the Mets for about $2,000 less than his 1961 contract with the Dodgers and proceeded to heartily promote his new team. When asked if the Mets didn't have a chance, Hodges said, "I don't think this club hasn't a chance. We have a number of first-division players and if we get the pitching, we will have a chance."

Reality would prove otherwise. Hodges's return to New York brought him happiness at home, but a new set of challenges at work. The 1962 Mets were one of the worst teams in baseball history, winning only forty games. To put it in a historical perspective, the Mets' 120 losses are still the highest single-season total since 1900. For Hodges, having experienced only one losing season in his sixteen seasons with the Dodgers, it was a dramatic change. The writer Robert Lipsyte, who covered the Mets in 1962, said, "Those guys were not happy being on a terrible team." Hodges was one of those unhappy players.

Hodges, like Casey Stengel, was not a man who took losing lightly. Yet the two men could not have been more different in personality. For Hodges everything was internal; for Stengel nothing was. But despite their vastly different demeanors, Stengel and Hodges formed a bond rooted in their love of the game and how it should be played. Stengel lived for two things: baseball and to be noticed. Yogi Berra wrote, "You never heard anybody say Casey was not interested in himself. He was, and he could make you interested in him. He could make the whole room interested in him." Or as Stengel's biographer, Robert Creamer, pointed out, "Casey did a lot to create his own legend."

And it was quite a legend. As an outfielder with the Brooklyn Dodgers, Stengel, after making a catch during a regular season game, once lifted his cap to let a bird fly out. Stengel had earned a master's degree in baseball playing for the Giants' Hall of Fame manager John McGraw, who saw the substance behind Stengel's clown act, and the two men spent many nights talking baseball. In 1923 Stengel hit the first World Series home run at Yankee Stadium. He hit a second home run in that Series and thumbed his nose at the Yankees' bench as he rounded the bases, insulting the Yankees' owner, but not Babe Ruth, who said, "I don't mind. Casey's a lot of fun."

By 1962, after winning five consecutive World Series with the Yankees (1949–53), Stengel was destined for the Hall of Fame. His reputation was like Teflon. No matter how badly the Mets would play—and over the years Stengel would manage them, they were by far the worst team in baseball—all he had to do was be his charming self and he was doing his job, taking the pressure off his players. It worked. In 1962 the Mets drew more fans than the Giants had in their final season in New York. In contrast, Hodges let his largely silent demeanor forge his legend. Unlike Stengel, Hodges was never going to charm the press, but Stengel respected him. "No one," Stengel said, "will have to tell Gil Hodges what to do at first base."

It wasn't just Hodges's fielding ability that Stengel appreciated, but his baseball smarts. One of the few umpires enshrined in Cooperstown, Jocko Conlan, considered Hodges the best of any player he saw when it came to knowing baseball rules, and Stengel "particularly admired people in the game who knew what they were doing and why they were doing it." And on a team filled with young, inexperienced players and many long-in-the tooth veterans that "Casey couldn't wait to get rid of," Casey had his kind of player in Hodges, despite his being a shadow of the great fielder and slugger he once was. Casey "had [a] keen awareness of other people's dignity—those whose dignity, or right to dignity, he respected." And when it came to Hodges, Casey treated him with the utmost respect "despite knowing that Hodges was hurt and didn't want to play anymore."

Although Casey told reporters that Hodges was so strong "he could squeeze your ear-brows off" (Stengel said "ear" not "eye"), he would never have dreamed of embarrassing a fellow student of the game like Hodges. This speaks volumes. Stengel was never shy about whom he showed up. In 1950 Stengel knew it would embarrass Joe DiMaggio if he moved him from center field to first base—even for just one game—but that was exactly what he did.

Hodges in turn appreciated Stengel. "As an older player," Hodges later wrote, "and . . . with a bad knee to boot, I was a liability to Casey. . . . Yet, his treatment of me was something that I'll never forget."

Stengel was famous for giving long, convoluted speeches that somehow managed to relate back to the original topic. But if you didn't know the topic, Stengel was hard to understand. During spring training, Stengel began one of his talks. Norm Sherry, a backup catcher in his first season with the Mets, was sitting next to Hodges during Stengel's lecture. Sherry and Hodges had been teammates in Los Angeles, so when Stengel finished, Sherry, unsure of what Stengel had been talking about, turned to Hodges for guidance. "Don't ask me, Norm," Hodges said, "he lost me too."

On the Mets' first day of spring training, forty-two Mets players began their routine by jogging around the field. Only thirty-nine finished. Hodges wasn't one of them. He was sweating heavily and limping and was soon lying on his back in left field leading two other Mets players in calisthenics. "Every spring it gets harder," Hodges said when he left the field. "But not too bad for the first day."

The first game ever played between the New York Mets and the New York Yankees took place on March 22, 1962. Hodges played first base. It was a meaningless preseason game, but Stengel and George Weiss, both of whom had been fired by the Yankees, wanted to win. Hodges did his part, starting a 3-6-3 double play to kill an early Yankee scoring chance. Roger Angell, who was at the game, wrote that Hodges's "stance and his mannerisms at the plate" were a comfort "to those with memories: The bat is held in his left hand while he fiddles with his eyelashes with his right hand, then settles his helmet, then tucks up his right pants leg, then sweeps the hand the full length of the bat, like a duelist wiping blood off a sword." The Mets scored the winning run in the bottom of the ninth for a 4-3 victory. In retrospect, that was the high point of their season.

Hodges injured his left knee during spring training, but he was in the starting lineup for the first regular season game in Mets history as the Cardinals blew the Mets out, 11-4. Hodges hit the first home run in Mets history that day, the 362nd of his career, moving him ahead of DiMaggio for eleventh place on the career home run list.

Although Hodges would miss more games than he played that season,

Madison Avenue knew his popularity in New York had not diminished, and he could do a lot more than sell root beer as he had in Los Angeles. Merrill Lynch used Hodges for a print ad that appeared in the *New York Times* on Opening Day at the Polo Grounds, asking, "Gil should help the Mets. Should we be helping you?"

But six years before his first heart attack, Hodges was also plugging cigarettes. That season, while Hodges was being photographed for a cigarette poster, an advertising executive told Robert Lipsyte of the *New York Times*, "Quality men use quality products. If Hodges smokes Viceroy, it might do something for you, too." Ironically, in the clubhouse after games, Hodges would cup his burning cigarette in his hand and hide it behind his back when photographers appeared. With the Dodgers, Hodges had also smoked during close games, and Duke Snider had a lasting image of Hodges's hands shaking so badly "he could hardly light the cigarette."

When the Mets' starting lineup was announced on Opening Day at the Polo Grounds, Hodges was named as the starting first baseman. But Hodges asked out of the lineup because of his painful left knee. In light of the muddy field and a right-handed Pittsburgh pitcher, Stengel acceded to Hodges's wishes. As a result, when the Mets took the field, Jim Marshall, a former Giant, ran out to play first. But the fans had come to see the man whom Howard Cosell, on his *Clubhouse Journal* show prior to the very first Mets broadcast, called "perhaps, and this is no exaggeration, the most popular player ever to wear the spangles of the Brooklyn Dodgers, still number 14, Gil Hodges."

When the fans realized that Hodges would not be playing, they let Jim Marshall hear it the minute he stepped onto the field. Years later, Marshall recalled, "The boos are still ringing in my ears."

When Hodges did play, he could still hit with power, but he was no longer consistent defensively. In a game against the Phillies in early May, Hodges's error allowed a runner to reach base, and he eventually scored; the Mets lost the game by one run. During the same series, Hodges redeemed himself with a twelfth-inning, two-run single for the first extra-inning victory in Mets history. A week later, back in the Polo Grounds, Hodges's ninth-inning home run in the second game of a doubleheader against the Braves broke a 7–7 tie and gave the Mets their first doubleheader sweep.

In the first few months of the season, despite his physical limitations, Stengel used Hodges as a late-inning defensive replacement. In the late innings of a close game against the Mets, Chicago Cubs manager Charlie Metro looked across the field into the Mets' dugout where Stengel appeared to be sleeping. Suddenly, Stengel jumped up and began shouting for his "glove." This was Stengel's way of calling for Hodges to go in as a defensive replacement at first. In June, against the Braves, with the Mets leading 6–4, Stengel put Hodges in as a defensive replacement in the ninth. With two out and a runner in scoring position, the Braves' Gus Bell "obligingly hit the ball to the sure-handed if not sure-legged Hodges and Gil retired him unassisted."

During a Memorial Day doubleheader against the Dodgers at the Polo Grounds, in front of one of the largest crowds that season, Hodges enjoyed one final day of glory. Before the game, while the Mets were taking batting practice, the crowd booed as the Dodgers players and coaches walked out onto the field. At one point, the intensity of the booing grew to a crescendo. Without seeing who it was, Hodges said, "That has to be Leo." He was right. Leo Durocher, then a coach for the Dodgers, was crossing the outfield. Durocher's main activity that season was trying to undermine Walter Alston, hoping to get him fired so he could reclaim his old job as Dodgers manager.

That day, nearly fifty-six thousand fans saw Hodges hit three home runs: one in the opener and two in the nightcap. Although the Mets trailed the Dodgers by a 10–0 score, when Hodges hit a home run in the first game against Sandy Koufax, it brought an "explosive roar" from the crowd, followed by chants of "Let's Go Mets." Koufax allowed thirteen hits and two walks, but the Dodgers won, 13–6. "That wasn't a game I was particularly proud of," Koufax told me.

In the second game, both of Hodges's home runs came against Johnny Podres; the next day, Stengel teased him with gusto. "Podres, you know that outside pitch?" Stengel said, "Well, Hodges can't hit it."

After losing the second game of the doubleheader, the Mets had a ten-game losing streak, the Dodgers ten straight wins. Hodges's former team was on the rise, the Mets hopelessly weighted down by players Branch Rickey would refer to as "anesthetic" because "they looked better than they were and . . . deadened club officials to the realities of their limitations."

Although Hodges was batting .316 with eight home runs at the end of May, when the Giants visited the Polo Grounds for a four-game set, Stengel played Hodges only once, and that was as a pinch hitter. "First base is serious," Stengel said, "because that feller is a cripple. He ketches a ball like a jai-alai player. There's not a stain on him. No one ever says, 'I hate Hodges.' He kin come over here from Brooklyn and they love him."

The Mets traded for a new first baseman, "Marvelous" Marv Throneberry, who would be immortalized in Mets lore as a symbol of their daffiness. In a testament to Hodges's self-effacing humor, he later wrote that however poorly Throneberry played, he was good enough to keep Hodges on the bench. And Throneberry committed mental errors Hodges wouldn't have made in his sleep. In a June 17 game at the Polo Grounds against Chicago, in a rundown between first and second, without possession of the ball, Throneberry collided with the Chicago base runner; instead of an out, the interference call allowed the Cubs to score four runs. In the bottom of the same inning, Throneberry drove in two runs with what appeared to be a triple. But Throneberry had failed to touch first base and was called out. Stengel didn't bother arguing— Throneberry had also missed touching second base. The game ended with Throneberry striking out and the Mets losing by one run.

Despite his inadequacies, "Marvelous Marv" received regular playing time. Hodges was placed on the disabled list on July 15 and missed the next two months of the season as he recovered from kidney-stone-removal surgery. After losing eleven pounds due to the surgery, Hodges came off the disabled list on September 12 looking thin and gaunt, but hoping to play in a few games to see if he would need knee surgery after the season. He did. That fall at Roosevelt Hospital, torn cartilage was removed from Hodges's left knee. The operation, said the Mets' physician, Dr. Peter LaMotte, "was satisfactory."

Although the season had been a disappointing one for Hodges, he did reach a significant milestone. At the Polo Grounds on July 6, he hit the 370th and final home run of his career. It was also a rare day for the Mets—they won. And for two Stuyvesant High School students, Wayne Block and Bill Feldman, sitting in their favorite seats in the first section beyond the foul pole in left field, it was also special. After Hodges's home run hit off the left-field façade and bounced back onto the field, Cardinals left fielder Stan Musial picked the ball up as Block and Feldman yelled, "Hey, Stan, throw it up here."

Musial did, but the two high school seniors had no idea of the ball's historical significance. They just wanted a home run ball. A little later, a Mets representative approached them and asked them to come to the press box to watch the rest of the game. After the game, they, along with Hodges, appeared on Ralph Kiner's television show. Kiner had made the home run call on the Mets broadcast that night. All of this was because, in a strange coincidence, the home run had moved Hodges into tenth place on the career home run list ahead of Kiner, the former Pirates slugger, who hit 369 home runs.

After their television appearance, Block and Feldman walked out to center field where the Mets' clubhouse entrance was located, and they were introduced to the Mets. Decades later, Block could still recall how gracious Hodges was as he made small talk with the two young men. But Block's lasting recollection of the evening, like countless others, was not Hodges's words, but his "enormous and strong hands."

In an era long before baseball memorabilia had much value beyond the pure joy of the experience, in exchange for Hodges's home run ball, Block and Feldman each received two autographed baseballs signed by the entire Mets team.

One of the players on that team was Rod Kanehl, a one-time Minor League player in the Yankees' system, where he had impressed Stengel with his hustle and outgoing personality. In 1962 Hodges befriended Kanehl and once, while talking with Hodges, Kanehl referred to his father as "my old man." Hodges didn't like that. Hodges was only ten years older than Kanehl, but his attitudes about what was respectful behavior came from an earlier generation. Hodges told Kanehl that when he spoke about his father with him he should never refer to him as "the old man." Another time, Kanehl's young son referred to Hodges as Gilly. In Hodges's mind, Stengel or one of the Mets' players could refer to him as Gilly, but not a young boy. Hodges asked Kanehl, "Don't you think your son ought to call me 'Mr. Hodges'?" Several weeks later, when Kanehl's son saw Hodges, he said, "Nice game, Mr. Hodges." With that Hodges turned to Kanehl and winked. Hodges's interactions with Kanehl are indicative of the challenges Hodges would face relating to some of the young players he would soon be managing: free-spirited and unafraid to challenge authority, for whom Hodges would seem old-fashioned, rigid, and inflexible.

In June of 1962, the Mets signed Ed Kranepool, a seventeen-year-old first baseman out of James Monroe High School in the Bronx, where he broke Hall of Famer Hank Greenberg's single-season home run record. On such young shoulders much hope was prematurely placed. But Kranepool's signing enabled Hodges to make his greatest long-term contribution to the 1962 Mets.

Hodges taught Kranepool "the fundamentals and secrets" of playing first base: how to position yourself based on where the ball was hit in the infield, how to always use proper footwork, how to block and scoop up throws, how to keep your hands loose as you catch the ball, how to stretch, and when to stretch to be able to adjust and catch off-line throws. Kranepool later said, "Gil polished me into a good first baseman." On September 22, 1962, Kranepool, the youngest Met, made his Major League debut as a late-inning replacement for the thirty-eight-year-old Hodges, the oldest Met.

In addition to teaching the intricacies of playing first, Hodges liked to tell riddles. That season, he posed one: "A yacht has a ladder with rungs one foot apart. At low tide two rungs are in the water. At high tide, when the water rises three feet, how many rungs are in the water?" To one of the young writers covering the Mets, Leonard Shecter, the riddle was "so simple-minded" he did a column about it, facetiously writing that if any one solved it correctly, he would send them "an autographed copy of Marv Throneberry."

On August 24, 1962, before a game at the Polo Grounds against the Dodgers, despite still being out of the lineup as he recovered from surgery, "the pride of the Mets" was honored on "Gil Hodges Night." M. Donald Grant presented Hodges with a plaque commemorating the evening, the Mets players gave Hodges a motorized golf cart, and Duke Snider, on behalf of the Dodgers organization, presented Hodges with a shotgun. "Gil," said Snider, "it was a pleasure playing with you all those years, and I want you to know that we sure miss you."

Fans made donations to the Gil Hodges Foundation "to further the education of needy boys." And near the end of the season, in honor of Hodges being named the most popular Met, a local supermarket gave him a car. But in light of Hodges having missed most of the season due to injury, one reporter wrote, "Could it be that the fans voted for Gil because he has contributed so little to the Mets misadventures?"

No matter, on his night Hodges tipped his cap to acknowledge the fans. "It was a tremendous thrill being honored in Brooklyn," he said, "and doubly so this time. After all, not many ballplayers get two of these things. It's especially gratifying because I've been away from Brooklyn four years ... and I haven't played much this year."

That night, many were conjecturing what Hodges would do for an encore. Roger Craig, Hodges's teammate with the Dodgers and the Mets, said, "Gil Hodges will never be a manager. He doesn't want it. Being a manager means he'll have to talk to people at banquets and things like that. It's the only thing he really hates."

Craig was wrong. Although Hodges never enjoyed public speaking, as a manager, Hodges would have far more trouble interacting with the press than with the people of Brooklyn. Never was this more the case than when a Brooklyn postal worker named Alvin Miller read in the newspaper that the wife of Sam Terranova had died. Terranova had been close friends with Alvin's deceased father, Jack. Wanting to pay his respects, that night after work Alvin took the bus to the Torregrosso Funeral Parlor in the Gravesend section of Brooklyn for the wake. After arriving at the funeral parlor, Alvin stood outside, waiting for someone from among his father's friends to walk into the funeral home with. As he waited, a tall man and a woman passed him as they headed into the funeral home. The man turned to Alvin and asked," Are you coming in also?" It was dark and Alvin didn't recognize him. But after they walked inside, Alvin saw it was Gil Hodges.

Gil and Joan knew the Terranova family and were also there to pay their respects. Inside, Hodges asked Alvin what his connection was to the deceased and they talked about baseball. After about forty-five minutes, Alvin left and went outside to wait for the bus on Avenue U. A few minutes later, a car Alvin didn't recognize pulled up to the bus stop. Gil Hodges rolled down his window. "You want a ride, Alvin?" Hodges drove miles out of his way to take Miller to his home in the Mill Basin section of Brooklyn.

In February of 1963 Hodges was back in Florida for spring training. But his knee problems were chronic and he was concerned about his future. When asked for a prediction for himself and the Mets, Hodges said, "Last year, I predicted the Mets had a good shot at sixth place. I also predicted I'd have a good year—and I wound up twice in the hospital. What could I possibly say now that the people would believe?"

Soon after the regular season began, Hodges was back on the disabled list. "I'm grateful that the club decided to handle it this way," Hodges said. "Did I think I might simply [be] dropped? You never know . . ."

AWAY
Washington DC (1963–67)

17

IN THE CELLAR

I appreciate this nice-guy routine everybody gives me, but managing a ball club has nothing to do with being a nice guy. You have to get the most out of the 25 guys available, keep the players' respect, and make the right moves in a game.

In early May of 1963, a Little League ballpark located on McDonald Avenue in Brooklyn opened. It was a tiny jewel with concrete stands that could seat 1,250, a clubhouse with showers, water fountains in the dugouts, and a playing field with sprinkler and drainage systems. Hodges was instrumental in getting it built and the field was named for him. Beyond any award or honor he ever received, "nothing," he wrote, "has given me the same degree of pride that I get every time I see that field. I just wish that my father was able to share that feeling with me."

Opening day began with 350 children from the South Highway Little League parading up Coney Island Avenue as "drum and bugle corps blared." The day was memorialized in a photo in the *New York Times* of an amused Hodges reaching down to shake the hand of one of the Little Leaguers, seven-year-old Nicky Lipariti. Little Nicky stares up at Hodges open-mouthed, revealing several missing teeth.

Later that month, Hodges was on the disabled list again and his thoughts turned to how he could remain in baseball after his playing career ended. Unlike Pee Wee Reese, Hodges knew he was never going to be a broadcaster, but in 1955 on a visit home to Petersburg, when Hodges was asked if he would be interested in managing, he replied, "Very much so. Baseball has been extremely good to me, and . . . I would like to continue in some capacity." But, as Clyde Sukeforth, the coach who had been supportive of Hodges's switch to first base, once said, "You've got to have the right temperament to manage a big league ball club"; and Reese, who knew Hodges as well as anyone, didn't think he had it. "Of all the guys on our ball club, Gil would be the last . . . I'd think of in terms of becoming a successful manager," Reese said, "He's the nicest guy in the world and is so good-natured, so kind and so gentle that he doesn't fit the managerial description."

Buzzie Bavasi hoped that Hodges would take a job as a Minor League manager in the Dodgers organization. Teaching young players the fundamentals would fit perfectly with what Hodges had been training for back at St. Joseph's. Bavasi said, "He can have a job in our organization any time."

But there was one man who wanted to give Hodges a chance to manage in the Majors immediately, Washington Senators general manager George Selkirk. That spring, our nation's capital was living up to its long-standing reputation for lousy baseball. In 1960 the original Washington Senators had moved to Minnesota and were replaced by an expansion team that finished last in 1961 and 1962 and by May 22, 1963, after losing nine out of ten games, were heading to a third consecutive cellar finish. But Selkirk, who had replaced Babe Ruth in right field for the Yankees in 1935 and played on five pennant-winning teams, had no patience for losing or careless play or lack of hustle.

"Sloppy ball players," Selkirk said, "make me sick."

Selkirk was new to the general manager's job and was not happy with Mickey Vernon, the manager he had inherited. Vernon had spent the bulk of his playing career with the sad-sack Senators and had too tepid a reaction to losing. But when Selkirk fired Vernon and suddenly signed Hodges to a two-year contract to manage the Senators, most questioned his decision. Vernon and Hodges were both former first basemen with reputations for being amiable. As beloved as Hodges had been in Brooklyn, Vernon had been in Washington where he was President Eisenhower's favorite player. To most it seemed that Selkirk had replaced a left-handed nice guy with a right-handed nice guy. But Selkirk had delved beyond Hodges's image enough to know that Hodges wasn't crazy about sloppy ballplayers either.

"I'll tell you about Hodges," Selkirk told Shirley Povich. "He's a nice guy, but only when things are going nicely for him. He's a Jekyll and Hyde, and he can adapt to whatever the situation calls for. Gil has two natures."

Up until two days before he signed Hodges, Selkirk admitted that Hodges was "a complete stranger" to him. But, Selkirk said, "I asked baseball people about Hodges. These were men I respect. I told them to forget the nice-guy aspect. I asked, 'Can he get tough with ball players?' and 'Will he lower the boom on the loafers?' That's when I learned about the other side of Hodges and was satisfied with what I heard."

One of the people Selkirk no doubt spoke with was Johnny Murphy, then the Mets' chief scout. Selkirk and Murphy, an outstanding relief pitcher during his playing career, had been Yankee roommates for six years. Murphy had seen that Hodges was no different with the Mets than he had been with the Dodgers where, as Rube Walker once said, "He'd get mad . . . once in a while." Johnny Podres told me, "Hodges was the best agitator on the team. With just a smile he'd make you know you weren't doing your job. You'd walk away and a few minutes later you'd say, 'He was right.'"

Hodges paid a steep price forgoing any Minor League apprenticeship. Washington had not won a World Series since 1924 (the year Hodges was born) or a pennant since 1933, nor had it finished in the first division since 1946. But Hodges was not naïve. He knew what he was getting into. At the press conference introducing him, he said, "I believe in fitting the strategy to the material. You obviously can't hit and run or get too fancy with players that can't do the job."

For his first two seasons in Washington, Hodges would rely on the coaches he inherited: Sid Hudson (pitching), George Susce (bullpen), Danny O'Connell (first), and Eddie Yost (third). Of the four, the only one Hodges would come to rely on in the long term was Eddie Yost. A graduate of NYU, Yost was—like Hodges—both a student of the game and a straight arrow off the field. Yost had played in the American League for almost two decades, mostly as the Senators' third baseman, and he led the league in walks six times. As a player and coach, Yost was not flashy, just solid.

In Baltimore, on May 23, Hodges made his managerial debut. The Orioles' starting pitcher was Hodges's old nemesis, Robin Roberts. More significantly, despite the fact that the Orioles had an 11-1 record against southpaws, Hodges named a twenty-three-year-old lefty named Claude Osteen as his starter. Osteen was knocked out in the third and Roberts pitched a complete-game shutout, but from his first game as manager Hodges viewed getting Osteen as much experience as possible a key to the Senators' long-term success. And after that game, Hodges also established his tight-lipped approach with the press. "There's not much you can say after a game like that," he said.

The Senators then traveled to New York to play a four-game series against the Yankees. The Senators lost the first three but came back to win the last 7-6, the first win of Hodges's managerial career. During their stay in New York, Hodges appeared as a contestant on the popular television show *What's My Line?* Four judges had to determine the occupation of a contestant by asking a series of yes or no questions. Usually the contestants were not famous, but once a week there was a well-known "mystery guest" and the panel had to wear blindfolds. On May 26, a show with a mystery guest who had recently changed jobs was aired. One of the judges, Bennett Cerf, a founder of Random House, figured out it was Gil Hodges. After the judges took off their blindfolds, Cerf asked Hodges, "Who would win a game between the Mets and the Senators?" Hodges had new loyalties. "The Senators," he said.

Hodges tried everything he could think of to improve his team. If players did not perform up to his standards, he benched them. "Our fellows realize they're not going to be handed any job on a platter," Hodges said. Immediately after games in which the Senators did not hit well—no matter if they won or lost—Hodges sometimes had the entire team take batting practice. Poor fielding could result in a four-hour drill on nothing more than rundowns and relay throws.

This was a big change from Vernon. When Hodges wasn't around, all the players referred to him as the "D.I."—for drill instructor. "He doesn't demand respect," Senators outfielder Ken Hunt said. "He commands it." Don Zimmer, who had been traded to the Senators from the Dodgers, said of Hodges, "Ain't nobody goin' to run over him."

Having reached a position of unquestioned leadership, Hodges had reverted back to his marine training. But now, by the sheer force of his personality—and his still imposing physical presence—Hodges was the guy doing the shoving. Not literally, but figuratively, and his players developed a healthy respect for him. That respect was "rooted in a sort of fear of him." Hodges could, Povich wrote, "drill a ballplayer with a mere look of displeasure."

Reporters always knew when Hodges had entered the clubhouse—all the players grew silent.

Despite Hodges's efforts, the Senators again finished last in 1963 with a record of 56-106. With the exception of the solid-fielding shortstop Ed Brinkman, the Senators lacked infielders one could envision as building blocks on a contending ball club; the outfielders had power but were inconsistent; and the starting pitching was a hodgepodge due to injuries and inexperience.

But publicly, Hodges hid his doubts. "I don't see the Washington picture as hopeless. Naturally we lack a few things," Hodges said that June. "For instance, I could use a good right-handed pinch-hitter." The Senators needed a lot more than just a right-handed pinch hitter, and Hodges knew it. That summer, when someone again asked him to compare the Mets and Senators, his response had changed since his May television appearance. "I refuse to answer," Hodges said, "on the grounds that I might incriminate myself."

That season, when the team was in Boston, Hodges learned that the curfew he had set—midnight following day games and two hours after the conclusion of a night game—was not being observed. Hodges called a team meeting and told his players, "It's going to start costing you money for any violation. When you abuse the curfew, you let down yourself and your team. I've played ball too long not to know that the season is a grind and you must be in shape to play your best. I'm asking only that you give me your best and you can't do that if you don't get proper rest and follow a proper routine."

Hodges never announced the name of a player he had fined for breaking curfew. This was not something he wanted his players' wives reading in the papers or hearing about from the wives of other players. This produced a story that became part of Hodges's legend. One night, after seeing a player return to the team's hotel after curfew, Hodges announced that he had seen an unnamed player out late and asked that he leave a check for $100 on his desk. The next day, seven players left a $100 check on Hodges's desk.

As a first-year manager, one of Hodges's most difficult jobs was learning how to handle his pitchers. When do you pull a pitcher? A pitcher says his arm aches, but is he injured? Hodges would make mistakes, but in his first few seasons in Washington, his greatest success was the development of Claude Osteen.

When Hodges arrived, Osteen was at the crossroads of his career. As a

28. With Casey Stengel and umpire Al Salerno (the first umpire to ever toss Hodges from a game), annual Hall of Fame Game, Cooperstown, New York, 1964. Courtesy of Al Salerno.

teenager, Osteen signed with the Cincinnati organization, but they gave up on him and traded him to Washington, where he continued to struggle. But timing is everything and Osteen got lucky. Hodges believed that pitching—as opposed to hitting—can be taught. Assuming a player has the arm strength to throw with a certain modicum of speed, he could be taught how to throw various types of pitches, the importance of getting ahead in the count, and the strengths and weaknesses of the hitters. (It didn't hurt Hodges's belief that by 1967 American League batting averages were at their lowest point since 1908.) Hodges taught Osteen that to be a successful Major League pitcher, ability alone wasn't enough. You had to always be thinking and acting in a professional manner.

But exactly what does it mean for a pitcher to act in a professional manner? In 1963 Osteen learned the answer on a cool, windy September day in Yankee Stadium as he faced the Yankees' Jim Bouton. Osteen pitched well; the Senators led 4–3 in the top of the ninth. With his team at bat, Osteen sat in the dugout thinking he was going to win the game. But with a Senators runner on first, hoping for an insurance run, Hodges sent Minnie Minoso up to pinch-hit for the catcher, Ken Retzer.

Osteen trusted and was familiar with Retzer, a veteran catcher. That day, Retzer had called for Osteen to pitch sliders away from the Yankees' left-handed slugger Roger Maris, who was 0–3 and had been unable to pull those outside pitches for home runs. But as soon as Hodges called for the pinch hitter, Osteen knew the Senators' backup catcher, Cal Neeman, who had been acquired from Cleveland that season, would come in for the bottom of the ninth. Osteen didn't say a word but thought to himself, "There goes my catcher." Osteen didn't stand up or make a face. All he did was raise his head and look up.

Minoso struck out and Osteen took the mound still holding a one-run lead and facing the heart of the Yankee batting order beginning with Elston Howard, that season's eventual MVP Award winner. Osteen walked the right-handed-hitting Howard on a 3-2 pitch.

Then, only two seasons after breaking Babe Ruth's single-season home run record, Roger Maris came to bat. Earlier in the game, Ken Retzer had told Osteen that a smart hitter like Roger Maris would be looking for the outside pitch in his final at bat, and they should jam him inside with a fastball. But Neeman put down the sign for a slider away and Maris hit a game-winning, two-run homer.

Well after the game had ended, with emotions less raw, Hodges called Osteen into his office. Hodges began with a positive, telling Osteen he had thrown a good game. Then he asked, "What were you thinking when I called for a pinch-hitter for Retzer?"

Although Hodges had only been managing the Senators for a few months,

Osteen already knew what all his players throughout his managerial career would come to know: you don't lie to Hodges. "Hodges," Osteen recalled, "never missed a trick on the bench. He saw every emotion. If you were on one end of the bench chewing gum, and he was on the other, he could tell you how many pieces you chewed."

Osteen admitted he was upset when Retzer came out. Hodges told Osteen that he couldn't let that bother him; that it was a common strategy to pinch-hit for a weak-hitting catcher late in games.

Osteen was amazed: "It was as if Hodges read my mind."

But Hodges wasn't finished: "What were you thinking pitching to Howard with the count full?"

"I wasn't going to let him beat me."

In other words, Osteen had decided to walk Howard rather than let him get a hit.

Hodges asked, "What was the worst thing Howard could do?"

"Tie the game."

"But by walking him, you allowed the winning run up to the plate. That was a mistake."

"Losing that game," Osteen said, "may have been the best thing that ever happened to me. I learned."

After the season ended, Hodges was asked about Osteen. "He has matured as a pitcher and with a little improvement could be a star," said Hodges. "He has the right mental attitude now."

Hodges remained consistent throughout his managerial career. Mets shortstop Bud Harrelson said, "He would call me into his office and ask why I'd done something in a game the day before. He'd let you discover the truth, until you realized there was more to this game than just ability. There was thinking. Professionalism."

On July 23, 1964, Osteen was back in Yankee Stadium, holding a 2–1 lead in the late innings, again facing Maris, Mantle, and Howard. Osteen didn't walk anyone and the Senators won. In 1964 Osteen's record improved to 15-13, a tremendous accomplishment on a team that lost thirty-eight more games than they won. After that, when other teams contacted George Selkirk seeking a trade, Osteen was the first player they mentioned.

Hodges's approach didn't work with everyone: case in point was the Senators' best player, outfielder Chuck Hinton. In 1962 Hinton batted .310, with 17 home runs, 75 runs batted in, and 28 stolen bases. He had power, speed, and unlimited potential, but struggled to meet high expectations.

In a game against Kansas City, with the bases loaded, Hinton caught a deep fly ball for what he thought was the final out of the inning, and with his head down, he began jogging back toward the infield. But it was only the second out. The runner on third would have scored anyway (by tagging) up on the deep fly, but a wise veteran, Ed Charles, who would be a key player for the Mets in 1969, was on second and realized Hinton's mistake. Charles ran back to second, tagged up, and was crossing home plate before Hinton could react. Hinton's mental error cost the Senators the game. Hodges not only benched Hinton after the inning was over, but fined him $100.

A few days after that game, Hodges said, "We all know what a fine ball player Chuck is but he must apply himself every minute. This is not a sometimes game. It is an all-the-time game." It didn't help that Hinton was the team's highest-paid player. Selkirk gave Hodges a mandate to "shake up" Hinton: "Make him play to the best of his abilities or bench him." Of Hinton, Hodges said, "I doubt if he has the right viewpoint. He could become one of the game's great players. But he must make up his mind. . . . He's got to fight for it."

In contrast to Hinton, Fred Valentine, a player with less ability but more focus, thrived under Hodges. The Senators had acquired the switch-hitting Valentine from the Orioles in 1963. In an early indication that Hodges had great sway with Selkirk on trades, Valentine believes that Hodges was "instrumental" in the Senators acquiring him. By 1966 Valentine was playing regularly and—considering the dominance of pitching in that era—hitting with power (sixteen home runs) as well as average (.276) and stealing bases. He was one of the few players on the team that always had the go sign from Hodges to steal bases at will.

Valentine flourished under Hodges's approach. "Give him 100% at all times," Valentine would recall years later, "and he would be satisfied of the outcome." To Valentine, Hodges was a "tremendous person" and "a generous manager when it came to dealing with the players." On more than one occasion, Valentine "played hurt out of respect for Hodges."

In 1968, after Hodges left to manage the Mets, Valentine ended up back in Baltimore playing for Earl Weaver. For Valentine, the contrast between Weaver and Hodges was striking. "Both were aggressive and wanted to win, but they were totally different. Weaver just exploded. He never held anything back.

"Many times," Valentine said, expressing a thought many of Hodges's teammates and players would repeat, "I felt Hodges should have exploded more, especially when mistakes were made."

Hodges maximized the abilities of his players, but only if they were willing to do things his way. And that meant doing what was best for the team, not the individual. It was this conflicting dynamic that led to Hodges's greatest misstep during his years managing the Senators—his treatment of veteran pitcher Tom Cheney.

A member of the Pittsburgh Pirates' 1960 championship team, when Cheney was "in his groove," wrote Povich, "he conjures a composite of Sandy Koufax, Whitey Ford, and Warren Spahn." But Cheney was also strung tighter than a brand-new baseball still in the box. "He didn't just smoke cigarettes," said Cheney's former Pirates teammate, Dick Schofield, "he ate them."

The Pirates gave up on Cheney and he ended up in Washington. On September 12, 1962, Cheney pitched a sixteen-inning complete-game victory against the Orioles, setting a still-existing Major League record for most strikeouts in a game with twenty-one. Cheney threw 228 pitches in the game, a pitch count that seems inconceivable today when pitchers are often pulled after 100 to 120 pitches. Don Lock, Cheney's Senators teammate, believed throwing those 228 pitches was the beginning of the end of Cheney's career.

Sure enough, early in the 1963 season, Cheney won his first four starts (two by shutout) but then, as if someone turned off a light switch, "the sharp edge was gone from his pitching." By then Hodges was managing the Senators and even though Cheney had lost effectiveness, he was still one of Hodges's best starters. When Cheney defeated Kansas City on July 4, his eighth win of the season, the victory represented his career high, and he said he hoped to win "at least 15 and keep going."

In Baltimore on July 11, playing in their first game back after the All-Star break, the Senators had a seven-game winning streak. Cheney got the start. In the sixth inning, after throwing a pitch, Cheney felt a sudden, searing pain down his forearm that forced him from the game. The Senators' team physician, George Resta, said Cheney had a strained arm and needed only rest and a cortisone shot. The reality was Cheney had torn ligaments in his elbow and should have immediately been placed on the disabled list. Cheney, however, told Hodges that he could still pitch, but only for a few innings at a time because after that his arm swelled and he was in too much pain to continue. Years later, Cheney said Hodges refused to send him to the bullpen where Cheney could pitch effectively for short bursts given his limitations. But lacking starting pitching and already having a reliable reliever in Ron Kline, Hodges cautiously tried to nurse Cheney back as a starter. Despite Dr. Resta saying Cheney should be ready for his next turn, Hodges gave him two weeks' rest. "Cheney was throwing half-speed," Hodges said, "and he didn't appear to be too loose. . . . I thought it would be better to rest Cheney."

Hodges used Cheney for a total of less than ten innings over the rest of the season, alternating him between starts and relief appearances, and finally shut him down for the season in August.

In 1964 Hodges hoped that after an off-season of rest, Cheney's arm would strengthen, and in spring training Cheney threw hard for periods of twenty to twenty-five minutes for two consecutive days. At the time, Cheney said, "I wouldn't say I could do that if I had a bad arm. I went to Gil Hodges this morning and told him I was ready to work. I didn't feel a bit of pain today after my hard workout. The arm wasn't swollen or anything. I'm ready to cut loose and I'm ready to pitch."

"I think Tom Cheney has come along much faster in the last two weeks." Hodges said, "but he's still not right."

Hodges put Cheney in fifteen games that season, including six starts. On June 9, 1964, in a start against Kansas City, Cheney pitched well but was in excruciating pain by the sixth inning when he told Hodges he couldn't continue. According to Cheney, Hodges replied, "Ah, go out there, you can do it." Cheney finished the game; the Senators won. Afterward, Hodges congratulated Cheney, who replied, "Yeah, you son of a bitch, that was the last game I'll ever pitch."

Five days later, Hodges started Cheney against Minnesota, who pounded him; he lasted only three innings. On June 21, after the pain in Cheney's pitching arm had persisted for almost a year, the Senators finally sent him to the Mayo Clinic in Minnesota for a "thorough examination." A few days later, he was placed on the disabled list with "an injured elbow," his career over.

Another Senators pitcher, Dave Stenhouse, was also having arm problems in 1963. But Stenhouse was more straightforward than Cheney had been. "I think I'm done for the season," Stenhouse told Hodges. "The arm is worse and I'm beginning to feel pain down to my fingers. I can't even hold a baseball—no less throw it. Maybe the best thing would be to have the elbow operated on for bone chips, I won't be able to pitch any more this season but at least I'll be able to work out in September and get the muscles back in shape." Although Stenhouse had been an All-Star, Hodges placed him on the disabled list, ending his season. "Hodges was very patient with me," Stenhouse said years later, "He gave me every opportunity to recover. I never had any issue with Hodges' decision."

Watching Hodges, Stenhouse learned that how aggressive a manager could be was a direct function of his player's abilities. As the Senators improved, Hodges's strategy would evolve; but in Hodges's first few seasons in Washington, Stenhouse said, "You couldn't count on our hitters."

There were also times when Hodges couldn't count on his pitchers. In a home game against the Orioles on June 28, 1964, the Senators' starter was pulled and Stenhouse came in, and he held the Orioles scoreless as the Senators scored four runs to take a one-run lead going into the seventh. With two outs and no one on and shortstop Bob Johnson at bat, Stenhouse decided to throw a pitch he had never thrown before. Johnson hit it for a home run to tie the game. The Senators lost—their sixth straight defeat.

In the dugout after the game, the Senators' catcher asked Stenhouse what pitch he threw to Johnson. "A spitter," Stenhouse said. Hodges overheard him. Stenhouse, who had attended the University of Rhode Island, had never heard Hodges "blow his stack," but at that moment "he raised his voice to me."

"What the hell were you doing [throwing a spitter]?"

Before Stenhouse could respond, Hodges added, "You college boys are all alike."

Hodges faulted his pitchers for throwing a spitball, not because it was illegal, but because it was a hard pitch to control. Hodges believed unless you threw it with regularity, you're better off not throwing it at all. For Stenhouse to throw it for the first time in the late innings while protecting a one-run lead was foolish.

Stenhouse also noticed that Hodges was particularly good about instructing his second-tier players. Where most managers, Stenhouse said, "only helped the good player," Hodges was adept at maximizing the abilities of the entire roster, "especially struggling players." After seeing how much of a difference Gene Snyder's lone career win made for the Dodgers in 1959, Hodges planned accordingly.

But no matter what Hodges did in 1963, the Senators didn't have enough good players to win consistently. And it wore on him. After his first season in Washington, his honeymoon period over, Hodges would be under constant pressure to turn the Senators into winners. As a result, Hodges brooded over his team's play.

"Do I replay the games over and over? Sure I do," Hodges said. "That's the only way to learn from your mistakes."

And it was harder than his playing days. "Now I worry about every man on the squad," Hodges said. "Defeats are harder to take as a manager but victories are sweeter. Every time the club wins, I get the greatest feeling in the world. Nothing, not even playing in a World Series, can equal the thrill of managing a winning ball club."

But there was also the constant hum of the fans who, Hodges wrote, "had the benefit of the second guess." Once, after a tough loss, Hodges was sipping a beer with a friend in a hotel lounge when a fan approached. "You're Gil Hodges, aren't you?"

Hodges, who would have never dreamed of telling off a fan, knew what was coming. He smiled, but his shoulders sagged.

"You don't mind if I sit down for a minute . . . ," the fan said. "I don't know much about baseball . . . but . . . why do you keep a guy like Valentine? What about Zimmer?"

18

OFF THE FLOOR

In football, when you lose you have to wait seven days before you have a chance to win again. But if you lose a baseball game today, you can come back and win tomorrow.

In 1964, because he would be managing the Senators from the beginning of the season and could select, train, and learn the capabilities of the twenty-five players he would go to war with, Hodges was confident his team would win more games than they had in 1963.

The Senators' spring training facilities were in Pompano Beach, Florida, where the players lived in an oceanfront hotel. That was the first year the black players could also reside there; previously, they had lived in the homes of black families in the area. But the white guests complained about the black players using the pool. Hodges's response was to try to "smooth things out as quietly as possible." That didn't work, so Hodges's Solomon-like solution was to place the pool off limits to all players, white as well as black.

Unlike the hotel, on the practice fields of Pompano Beach, Hodges was in complete control. You had to be "in uniform and on the field" on time, recalled Mike McCormick, the former Giants bonus baby who played for Hodges for two seasons in Washington, because "he would be sitting there . . . watching" and "when he took off his cap, and started scratching his head, you hoped you weren't the one he was upset with."

No time was wasted. Hodges held a chart that told him exactly where each player should be at any particular moment. He even sent a subtle message about where his players should be before practice began on Sundays by delaying the start of practice until 1 p.m., "in deference to the church going members of the squad."

Fundamentals were stressed and Hodges supplied verbal motivation to implant the basics. "Our bunting and base running were terrible last year," Hodges said. "All pitchers should know how to bunt because they never know when it may be the difference between staying in the game or being taken out. Of course, everybody should know how to bunt.... As to base running, we didn't have too much of it last year. At least, what we had wasn't good."

While one group of players practiced bunting, Eddie Yost shot baseballs out of a bazooka so catchers could practice catching sky-high pop-ups, and Hodges would supervise lengthy workouts that drilled it into his pitchers' heads that on grounders to the right side of the infield that had even a remote chance of pulling the first baseman off the bag, they had better get off the mound and cover first.

During games, Hodges would approach a player sitting on the bench—often when he was making small talk with a teammate—and ask what the pitch count was. Even if you knew the answer, Hodges was intimidating. And if you didn't, Claude Osteen recalled decades later, "You better level with him, because he had the goods on you."

Hodges viewed defense as the key element of a winning team. But practicing fielding was tedious and the players disliked it. But for Hodges fielding was where players could improve their skills most easily. In an era when weight training was rare and steroids were given only to horses, no amount of practice could help you gain strength, but you could always improve your fielding. During spring training, Hodges sometimes had his pitchers practice fielding by playing them at other positions such as the outfield or third base.

When it came to instructing hitters, Hodges's advice was usually more cerebral than physical. Although Hodges would sometimes change a batter's stance (to give him more bat control or better leverage), he emphasized "concentration on the strike zone," saying he was "disappointed to put it mildly, at the number of times my batters have struck out at bad balls which would have been ball four and would have put the batter on base." To correct this, Hodges used Rickey's technique of having batters stand at home plate without swinging, and just call each pitch a ball or strike.

That spring, Hall of Fame manager Bucky Harris—the last man to lead a Senators team to a championship—visited Pompano Beach. "This camp," Harris said, "has a professional air ... an air of competence I haven't seen in a Washington camp for many years. He [Hodges] has everybody hustling and working hard. Nobody tries to be a goldbrick and the enthusiasm is catching."

But practice can only take you so far. On opening day at D.C. Stadium, in front of a crowd of more than forty thousand, including President Lyndon Johnson, the Senators were shut out, managing just one hit off the Angels' Ken McBride, a pitcher "with three diminishing speeds, beginning with slow." During the game, the Senators' public address man, Charlie Brotman, announced there was a Senate quorum call on the civil rights bill, and "like little boys caught playing hookey," Senators Mike Mansfield, Hubert Humphrey, and Everett Dirksen left for Capitol Hill. "The wrong Senators," reporters wrote, "were asked to leave the ballpark."

Those years in Washington were a form of on-the-job training for Hodges, and in a game in Baltimore on July 26, he learned the shoe-polish trick. In the eighth, with two out and a runner on first and the Senators ahead 4-1, Baltimore's Willie Kirkland substantiated his claim that he was hit in the foot by a pitch in the dirt by calling for the black-stained ball and showing it to umpire Hank Soar, who awarded him first base. Hodges argued, claiming the ball had bounced in the dirt before it hit Kirkland. Hodges and Soar stood nose to nose for a full two minutes. Hodges, who had never been tossed from a game, was saved by the fact that he didn't make any gestures to show Soar up (when arguing with umpires, Hodges intentionally kept both his hands in the back pockets of his pants) and refrained from profane language. Hodges lost the argument but learned that it's best to be the one holding the shoe-polish-stained ball—not the opposing manager.

During Hodges's first few seasons in Washington, the Senators were desperate for competent players and often acquired veterans to fill specific needs. One such acquisition was former Yankee Moose Skowron. Skowron was an All-Star first baseman, but Hodges spent hours teaching him how to improve his fielding. Some players might have resented Hodges's efforts, especially one, like Skowron, with several World Series rings, but Skowron didn't. "I knew," Skowron said, "I was no gazelle around first base, but

Hodges taught me how to play the position better. Somehow it felt as if my glove expanded."

In addition to Skowron, another veteran Hodges brought to Washington was his former Dodgers teammate, relief pitcher Ed Roebuck. During one spring training game, Roebuck was hit hard and his career seemed over. But Hodges wanted to see for himself. When Roebuck pitched during practice the next day, Hodges got behind the plate as if he were an umpire and tried to figure out if Roebuck had anything left. Decades later, the unusual scene of a Major League manager, standing right behind the catcher, still amazed Roebuck. "That," Roebuck recalled, "was pressure." That spring, before Roebuck reported for training camp, he had been arrested for drunk driving. Since the DWI charge occurred before Roebuck reported, Hodges didn't fine him, but Hodges spoke to Roebuck "man to man," telling him to "take better care of himself."

As Hodges had predicted, the Senators got "off the floor in '64" and finished in ninth place, winning six more games than they had in 1963. And as the pennant race came down to the wire between the Yankees and Chicago, the Senators played spoiler, taking four out of five games from the White Sox. For a Senators team that lost 100 games, that effort against a 98-win team was a significant accomplishment.

That September, when the Senators were in Cleveland, they stayed at the Sheraton-Cleveland Hotel, where the Beatles, on one of their very first U.S. tours, were also staying. At one point, as thousands of fans stood outside the hotel hoping for a glimpse of John, Paul, George, or Ringo, Claude Osteen put on a black sweater, opened his window, and waved to the crowd. The fans thought Osteen was Ringo and screamed for more. Hodges called his daughters back home in Brooklyn and stuck the phone outside the window so they could hear. "I figured," Hodges said, "my kids would feel a little closer to the Beatles."

Hodges's contract ended after the 1964 season and rumors abounded that he would leave Washington to replace Walter Alston or Casey Stengel. George Selkirk didn't wait; on June 30 he gave Hodges a two-year contract extension through the end of the 1966 season. Hodges received a salary increase and, to pay for his frequent commutes back to New York to be with his family, "the largest managerial expense account in the American League." By way of contrast, after the 1964 season, both opposing managers in the World Series, Johnny Keane of the champion St. Louis Cardinals and Yogi Berra of the Yankees, were fired; yet Hodges kept his job despite losing 100 games. But Hodges knew that there would be little patience for continued failure. "There are only two kinds of managers," Hodges said, "winning managers and ex-managers. I like to work."

But Hodges could take the Senators' current roster only so far. "We need improvement at three or four positions," Hodges said after signing his new contract, "and I am certain that we'll produce the players who will provide such improvement."

The Senators needed help at first, third, catcher, and the outfield. With the exception of catcher Paul Casanova, their Minor League system had few players who projected out as Major Leaguers, and the frugal Senators were rarely serious bidders for top-rated high school players. The only way they could improve at multiple positions quickly was by trading what little quality they had for quantity.

But after having made some unsuccessful trades, George Selkirk was a bit gun-shy. In July of 1964, in what was called, "a Gil Hodges deal fully as much as a Selkirk deal," the Senators traded Skowron to the White Sox for the superior-fielding first baseman Joe Cunningham. That trade didn't provide the Senators with an everyday first baseman, but it showed that Selkirk was willing to take a risk if he had Hodges's support. As a result, Selkirk gave Hodges input in trade decisions, which did not always work out. A few seasons later, Hodges supported trading pitcher Mike McCormick to San Francisco for outfielder Cap Peterson. The very next season, McCormick won the Cy Young Award and Peterson provided the Senators with two seasons of pedestrian play. The concept of a manager having influence in personnel decisions was not something Hodges had learned from Branch Rickey, who viewed the general manager's job (the winter manager) as separate and distinct.

In Washington, and especially in New York after the Mets won the World Series, Hodges was, to some extent, both the winter and summer manager. But a manager wants to build a winner immediately so he can hold onto his job, an approach that could result in trades that mortgage a team's future.

Overall, Hodges did well in his dual role in Washington, but in New York his influence produced mixed long-term results.

Selkirk and Hodges agreed that because the Senators lacked pitching depth and had the lowest team batting average in the league, if the team was to make significant improvement, major trades were needed. They decided that Chuck Hinton was never going to meet their expectations. A comment Hinton had made, that "I can only be as good as my teammates make me," did not bode well and he was traded for a power-hitting first baseman, Bob Chance, and utility man Woody Held. Hinton never blossomed into a star, but Chance proved to be a bust.

If trading their best position player wasn't enough of a risk, the Senators also traded Claude Osteen, their best pitcher (and infielder John Kennedy), to the Dodgers for first baseman Dick Nen, third baseman Ken McMullen, pitchers Pete Richert and Phil Ortega, and outfielder Frank Howard. In one move, with Hodges's urging, Selkirk had upgraded the Senators lineup and replaced his one top-rated pitcher with two pitchers who might someday fill his shoes.

When Hodges urged the trading of Osteen, he was forsaking his personal preference for building a team around top-flight pitching. Hodges was once asked, if he was starting a team from scratch and had his choice of any two players in baseball, whom would he select? He picked Sandy Koufax and Juan Marichal. "If I have two pitchers like that," Hodges said, "I wouldn't worry about the rest of my lineup."

That spring, Hodges made no predictions for the 1965 season, promising only that the Senators wouldn't lose a hundred games. Privately, he would consider the season a success if the Senators won seventy games.

In addition to the trade with the Dodgers, the new season brought changes to the coaching staff as Hodges's former teammates Rube Walker and Joe Pignatano were hired as the pitching and first base coaches. Both men, like Eddie Yost, who remained as third base coach, were extremely loyal and protective of Hodges. Jack Lang referred to them as "soldiers" in the Hodges family.

Hodges was "not the best copy," but for one Washington reporter, he was a godsend. "He was," Russ White would say decades later, "the most decent, wonderful man I've ever met." As a young sports reporter with the third-ranked newspaper in Washington, the *Washington Daily News*, White lacked the

29. With (*from right*) Frank Howard, Bob Chance, and Ron Kline, January 12, 1965. Reprinted with permission of the DC Public Library, *Star* Collection, © *Washington Post*.

cache of a Shirley Povich, but for Hodges that made no difference. As a former navy man, a Catholic, and a young fellow just trying to make a living, White gained Hodges's trust. Hodges allowed White to work out with the team and he even had his own Senators uniform. On Sunday mornings, White joined Hodges and his coaches for breakfast followed by morning mass. It was the kind of relationship that would be impossible for a writer to have with a Major League manager today.

But the relationship didn't exempt White from Hodges's cutting humor. One day, White's typewriter disappeared. He eventually found it, but only after Hodges took it out of hiding and returned it. On a particularly bumpy flight to Kansas City, when many of the players were sick to their stomachs, White happened to be seated next to Hodges, who appeared remarkably calm as he read a paperback. When White took a close look, he noticed that Hodges was holding the book upside down and gave him "that little grin of his."

After Don Zimmer had a poor fielding game, White wrote, "Don Zimmer

30. With (*from right*) Joe Pignatano, Rube Walker, and Pete Richert, February 9, 1965. Reprinted with permission of the DC Public Library, *Star* Collection, © *Washington Post*.

brought his glove to DC Stadium and it stuck out like a sore thumb." The next day, Zimmer called White every name in the book and physically went after him. Hodges separated the two men and called them into his office, one at a time. Hodges told Zimmer, "We're not at war with the writers," and warned White, "You wrote a rough piece on him, so you've got to expect it."

Another Stadium regular Hodges had a friendship with was Charlie Brotman, the D.C. Stadium announcer and longtime master-of-ceremonies at presidential inaugurals. At one game, Hodges signaled to the bullpen for a relief pitcher and Brotman instinctively announced the name of the new pitcher. The next day, when Brotman was on the field getting the lineup before the game, one of the umpires got in his face and berated Brotman for announcing the prior day's pitching change before he had indicated it was official. The umpire towered over Brotman. "I thought he was going to put his foot down on my head," Brotman said. "I was scared to death." Brotman then felt a tap on his shoulder and a huge hand suddenly pulled him away. It was Hodges. "Don't you ever talk to Charlie Brotman that way again," Hodges—now standing nose-to-nose with the umpire—screamed. "He's the announcer here; a member of my team. If you have any problems with him, you come to me." To Brotman, "it felt like Hodges saved my life."

Hodges was also decisive in instilling the concept of family-comes-first. Before one game, the clubhouse man told Ed Brinkman that his wife had gone into labor and was at the hospital. In an era when it was still rare for a player to miss a ball game for any reason short of a severe injury, Brinkman, the team's starting shortstop, sat alone in front of his locker unsure of what to do. Hodges, upon hearing the news, walked into the clubhouse. "What are you doing here?" he asked Brinkman. "Get to the hospital where you belong."

On June 8, 1965, the Senators acquired the former Yankee All-Star relief pitcher Ryne Duren. On the field, Duren was known for his 100 mph fastball; off the field he had a drinking problem. That summer, Duren appeared in only sixteen games for the Senators, compiling a 6.65 ERA. One night, after another poor outing, drunk and despondent, Duren climbed to the top of the bridge over the gorge on Connecticut Avenue and threatened to kill himself. The bridge was then referred to as the "jumper's bridge." In Duren's autobiography, he recalled the police bringing Hodges to the bridge, where he told Duren, "Ryne, you're drunk. Come on down. We'll get you help. You're too good to do this to yourself."

Duren had only been with the Senators for a few months and Hodges could have easily told police he didn't know Duren well and an officer trained for suicide prevention would be the best person to respond. After all, in Duren's own words, he had already "put poor Gil through hell." But Duren was a member of Hodges's team, and Hodges went to the bridge himself.

The Senators immediately released Duren. Hoping to spare Duren further embarrassment, Hodges gave the writers his best poker-faced stare and skirted around the real reason for Duren's release, saying only, "The decision to put Duren on waivers was something that happened overnight." Out of respect for Hodges, the writers reported that because of a sprained ankle and sore arm, Duren was "unavailable for duty anyway," and his release didn't make any difference.

The Duren press conference was challenging for Hodges, but handling the press was part of his job. Hall of Fame manager Sparky Anderson, who, like Hodges, began his career with the Dodgers, felt there were four key elements to being a good manager: (1) staying alert in the dugout, (2) behaving in a manner that leads by example, (3) understanding your own players, and (4) dealing with the media.

In his view of what managing requires, Hodges listed the same first three items as Anderson, but there was no mention of the press. Managers like Anderson understood the need to not just be accessible, but quotable. Hodges wasn't built that way. His primary managerial mentor was Walter Alston. Hodges played for Alston longer than any other manager and saw him win pennants despite his stilted response to the press. Yet Hodges maintained good relations with the established baseball writers in Washington and, later, in New York. Bob Addie, who covered the Senators for the *Washington Post*, wrote early in Hodges's tenure in Washington, "Hodges is one of the genuinely decent men in sports. . . . He grows on you. . . . He never is too busy to be courteous. . . . Nothing ever is too much trouble for him to do."

But for some younger writers, especially those coming of age in the tumultuous 1960s, Hodges was from an older generation, and they couldn't relate. For those writers, like George Minot Jr. of the *Washington Post*, Hodges "spoons up enough sugar to make even Mary Poppins turn sour."

In Hodges's Mets years, a new generation of sportswriters, many of whom loved Casey Stengel, didn't know what to make of the tight-lipped Hodges. Although he appeared ill at ease with reporters, Hodges never failed to answer a question, however briefly or sugary, or vinegar-filled. The only demand Hodges made was that no tape recorders be used during a question-and-answer session.

During the 1964 season, the Senators acquired a pitcher named Alan Koch. That year his record with the Senators was a mediocre 3-10, but due to the poor state of the Senators' pitching staff, Koch was asked to report to Pompano Beach in 1965. That spring, with the recent passage of the Civil Rights Act, newspapers were filled with the racist views of Alabama governor George Wallace. An Alabama native and a graduate of Auburn University, Koch was appalled by Wallace. So much so that Russ White told Koch that if he wrote

31. Al Koch pitching on May 17, 1964. The batter, Floyd Robinson of the White Sox, hit a two-run homer on the pitch, and the Senators lost, 3–2. Reprinted with permission of the DC Public Library, *Star* Collection, © *Washington Post*.

an anti-Wallace piece, White would get it published under his byline in the *Washington Daily News*. White ran the piece, but it included the line, "I haven't been to a lynching in years."

A few days later, Hodges invited Koch to his office for a chat.

"Do you know anything about that article talking about lynching?"

"I wrote that line tongue-in-cheek," Koch said.

"What do you mean by tongue-in-cheek?"

"It's something so exaggerated, it can't be true."

"Trust me, here in Washington, it's not that funny. The NAACP is threatening to boycott Senators games. We're optioning you to our minor league team in Honolulu."

"Why Hawaii?"

"That's the furthest we can send you from Washington," Hodges said, "and still have you playing organized baseball."

Unlike Koch, Hodges needed Frank Howard, the key player in the Claude Osteen trade, to perform for the Senators—and perform well. Howard was not just strong but huge—six feet seven, 275 pounds. And after signing him out of Ohio State in 1958 for the then astronomical signing bonus of $108,000, the Dodgers' expectations for him had been just as large. But after a breakout season in 1962, when Howard hit .296 with 31 home runs and 119 runs batted in, his batting average had fallen to .226 and his strikeout totals were unusually high. In the outfield, Howard, by his own admission, "was not what you would call speedy"; and Howard had injured his throwing arm (which Hodges knew about prior to the trade), making him a liability in the outfield.

But Hodges wanted Howard anyway because, as Rickey preached, "you can't teach power"; and from his time as Howard's teammate, Hodges knew Howard was a humble, hard worker, and a far better home run threat than anyone he had on the Senators.

In spring training in 1965, his first with the Senators, Howard, wanting to strengthen his legs, placed weights in his cleats during exhibition games where he played left field and ran "like a man going through quicksand in iron boots."

"Howard really isn't as bad as he has looked in the field," Hodges said. And after taking a deep breath, he added, "I sure hope he isn't that bad." Hodges compensated for Howard's injured throwing arm by instructing shortstop Ed Brinkman to run out into left field on any ball hit to Howard to shorten the distance Howard had to throw. But at the plate, Howard was pounding the ball, hitting .452 early in the exhibition season. This gave Hodges hope. "I am not one to exaggerate," Hodges said that March, "but you must pardon me if I feel enthusiastic about this year's club. We really have a chance for a first-division berth. I'm not talking to sell tickets. I really believe this."

But after the Senators' 1965 home opener, Hodges saw he had his work cut out for himself with Frank Howard. In the fourth inning, the Senators had a chance for a big inning. With one out, Howard was on first and Bob Chance on second when Willie Kirkland hit a wind-blown pop-up near the pitcher's mound. Under the infield fly rule, Kirkland was automatically out. All Howard had to do was stay on first base. But when the Red Sox third baseman dropped the ball, Howard—forgetting one of the most basic rules in baseball—took off for second base where Chance, standing off the bag as Howard approached, was tagged out. The Senators' scoring threat was over and they lost their home opener.

32. Bob Chance being tagged out by Felix Mantilla (#12) of Boston after Frank Howard (standing on second base) forgot the infield fly rule on opening day at D.C. Stadium, April 12, 1965. Reprinted with permission of the DC Public Library, *Star* Collection, © *Washington Post*.

Howard may have been a veteran, but he had made a rookie mistake. "Gil is a patient man," Howard said. "I make a lot of mistakes out there. . . . Gil goes over those things with me. He's made me a better ballplayer, no question of that." But in transitioning to a new league, Howard struggled with his hitting. By 1966 his home run production had fallen to eighteen and he was striking out over a hundred times a season.

Hodges advised Howard to move closer to the plate, open his stance to force a shorter stride, and move his hands less rather than pumping while waiting for the pitch. The hope was to help Howard keep his head steady and produce a more level swing. Hodges wanted Howard to swing with an upper cut so his power would drive balls into the air where they could carry over fences. But the most significant thing Hodges did for Howard was to get him to start thinking like a professional. Unlike Claude Osteen, with Howard, Hodges decided an aggressive approach was best. One day, when Howard had come out early to practice his hitting from the iron mike (the pitching machine), Howard noticed Hodges was standing behind the batter's cage watching him.

"Frank," Hodges asked, "how much longer do you want to play in this league?"

Howard said, "Another five or six years."

"You have two more years, tops."

Howard turned and stared at Hodges, who stared right back. "Those blue eyes, like Superman—eyes of steel," Howard recalled, "looking right through you."

"Unless," Hodges added after a sufficient pause to act as a soothing balm, "you have a better idea of what those guys 60 feet away are thinking."

Hodges wanted Howard to study the pitchers to figure out what they were going to throw in certain situations: with men on base, when their team was ahead, or on specific ball and strike counts. This is what Hodges had done when he played, and he expected no less of Howard. Hodges would tell power hitters like Howard that they should aim to limit strikeouts to ninety a year—Hodges's goal in his playing days. For Howard, it was a wake-up call. It was one thing to hit against the iron mike, quite another to hit in a game. And Howard didn't have to reinvent the wheel: the Senators conducted meetings before every series to review the strengths and weaknesses of the opposition's pitchers. But some Senator players like Fred Valentine maintained a journal, noting the tendencies of all the pitchers they faced; that was the kind of dedication Hodges wanted from Howard. With one sentence, Hodges had taught Howard what it meant to be a professional hitter. After that, Howard developed a game plan for every pitcher he faced and his hitting improved.

Howard, after playing on a championship team in Los Angeles, had the utmost respect for Hodges and his struggles with less than stellar players. "When you manage a marginal club," Howard later said with respect to Hodges years in Washington, "you have to really manage."

In 1965 the Senators finished in eighth place with a record of 70-92. In retrospect, that might not seem like much, but back then, as Povich noted, "for Washington fans . . . eighth place is heady stuff."

Even former Brooklyn Dodgers fans like Marianne Moore, the Pulitzer

Prize-winning poet, still pulled for Hodges. When Moore came to Washington to give a reading at the Library of Congress, she was more interested in talking about baseball than poetry. "And how is Gil Hodges doing as Senators manager?" she asked. "He's a fine fellow."

The next day, the headline read, "Prize Poetess Moore Who Sang about Dodgers Now Dodges the Muse to Exult in Gil Hodges."

19

ON THE DOORSTEP OF RESPECTABILITY

Every time the club wins, I get the greatest feeling in the world.

In the spring of 1966, the fledgling players union was preparing to vote on whether or not a former steel-union executive, Marvin Miller, should represent them. Miller insisted that he visit with every player prior to the vote, and he undertook a tour of all the Major League training camps. He arranged to meet with each team prior to one of their preseason games when all their players would be available. When Miller arrived in Pompano Beach, Hodges came out to greet him. Although it was the first time they had ever met, Hodges asked Miller for a "personal favor." Would he mind speaking with the Senators players after the game against Pittsburgh?

"My team needs the practice," Hodges said.

Miller agreed and watched the game. Having worked in Pittsburgh, Miller loved watching Roberto Clemente play right field. Clemente was in fine form that day, making a throw that Miller later called "an arrow, knee high." After the game, when Miller met with the Senators players, he invited Hodges to join them. Hodges declined, but promised to later meet with Miller, privately.

In 1966, even with extra practice, the Senators again finished in eighth place, winning only one more game than they had the prior season. Hodges had expected better. As the season neared its end, it became apparent to the Washington writers that it was only a matter of time until Hodges's emotions boiled over during a game. First, in a sure sign he was more stressed than usual, Hodges publicly criticized his players in front of a reporter in early

September. And later that same week, Hodges was thrown out of a game for the first time in either his playing or his managerial career. The umpire who tossed him was Al Salerno.

After starting his career in the Red Sox organization, Salerno injured his pitching arm and ended up working as a New York State trooper. But the baseball bug never left him. After an apprenticeship in the Minors, Salerno became an American League umpire in 1961. Salerno and Hodges had first crossed swords at Yankee Stadium on July 17, 1965, when Hodges argued with the home plate umpire Ed Runge, who had ruled that a Ken McMullen drive that ended up in the left-field stands was a ground-rule double, not a home run. On his way out to argue with Runge, Hodges walked past Salerno. "It's still going to be a double, Gil," Salerno said. Hodges told him it wasn't his call and to "keep his mouth shut." Salerno "made a threatening move" toward Hodges, but the other umpires held him back.

About a year later, on September 6, 1966, in the top of seventh in Detroit, with one out and runners on first and second and the Tigers leading, 4–1, Ed Brinkman was called out by Salerno on a close play at first. After arguing with Salerno, Hodges returned to the dugout to determine whom to bat for his pitcher, Dave Baldwin, who was due up next. Hodges was slow sending up a pinch hitter and Salerno told him to speed it up. But Hodges knew it was the home plate umpire's responsibility to tell him if he was dawdling, not Salerno, who was umpiring at first base that day. Hodges told Salerno to mind his own business. Salerno persisted, "Are you going to send him out, Gil?"

"When I'm ready," Hodges said. Salerno told Hodges that if a batter wasn't out of the dugout by the time he walked back to first, he was going to throw him out of the game. With no batter in sight, Salerno gave Hodges the thumb. Hodges didn't take it well. "I think," Hodges later said, "that's the first time I've ever cursed a man in my life. I wouldn't have minded being thrown out if it had been by a good umpire."

More than four decades later, Salerno had forgotten Hodges's reaction. He told me, "Hodges never cursed. The worst you ever got out of him was damn."

At the time, Hodges said, "As a player, I had to protect only myself. As a manager, the entire squad is my responsibility." Hodges would be tossed from five more games during his managerial career, but never to draw attention and put on a show for the fans. Hodges said, "I don't believe in trying to be something I'm not."

After Salerno thumbed Hodges, Senators coach George Susce, a grizzled, former catcher with twisted, gnarled fingers who had been in baseball for nearly four decades, approached Salerno.

"You're going to get a lot of ink tomorrow, Al," Susce said.

"Why?"

"You just run the virgin."

The next time Hodges got the thumb was less than a month later. Hodges had come onto the field to support his second baseman, Bob Saverine, who had been tossed by umpire Bill Kinnamon for describing his call ruling a White Sox runner safe on a pick-off attempt as "horseshit."

A week later, Hodges and his coaches discussed that ejection in Hodges's office. After Hodges was tossed, another one of the umpires asked Rube Walker where Hodges was. Walker told him, "He's in the loving clubhouse where Kinnamon put him."

"You said I was in the loving clubhouse?" Hodges asked.

"Yea. . . . In the loving clubhouse," Walker repeated.

"I hope Kinnamon puts in his report what I said. I said you're full of it, an' I never considered *being full of it* cursing," Hodges said.

Joe Pignatano said, "That's 'cursin',' Gil."

"You're wrong there," Hodges said, "but do they put the actual words in the report?"

Pignatano said they did.

Hodges was incredulous. "Actual words? *Full of it?*"

The discussion ended with Hodges still insisting that *full of it* isn't cursing.

Before the World Series between the Orioles and Dodgers that October, Sandy Koufax was quoted as saying, "That Hodges is something, isn't he? What a man. I'll tell you. I was never so startled in my life as when I read that an umpire had run him. I couldn't believe it—not Gil Hodges, my patron saint. What do you guys feed them in Washington, Tiger meat?"

When I read this quote to Sandy Koufax, he told me, "You know a lot of the things people wrote that I said, I never really said."

Dave Baldwin, the pitcher Hodges had taken out of the Detroit game for a pinch hitter, was in the clubhouse when Salerno tossed Hodges and didn't even know that his Major League debut was also the first game Hodges was ever thrown out of until I interviewed him forty-three years after the fact. For Baldwin, that first Major League appearance had been a long time coming. He had spent the better part of eight seasons kicking around in the Minors, but after he began throwing sidearm in the mid-1960s, he became a much more effective pitcher. When Major League rosters were expanded after Labor Day in 1966, Baldwin, at twenty-eight, was finally called up to the Majors. Hodges sent Baldwin in to pitch the day he arrived, and he threw two innings of shutout ball in relief. Walker later told Baldwin he had done a good job. "If it came from Rube," Baldwin said, "that was as good as hearing it directly from Gil."

On one occasion, Hodges addressed Baldwin directly. In a game in Minnesota, with the score tied at 2–2, Dave Baldwin thought he could get cute. After all, he had retired the side in the seventh and gotten two outs in the eighth, including four consecutive strikeouts of Cesar Tovar, Tony Oliva, Harmon Killebrew, and Bob Allison—all outstanding hitters. But on his second pitch to the next batter, Rich Rollins, instead of using his sidearm delivery, Baldwin threw an overhand curve that hung. Rollins hit a home run and the Senators lost, 3–2. Hodges invited Baldwin into his office. "Throw another overhand . . . ," Hodges said, "you can pack up right after the game."

Baldwin credits Hodges and Walker with a masterful job of managing the Senators pitching staff:

> Not only did they know each pitcher's repertoire, but they understood the strengths and vulnerabilities of each pitcher's pitches. In the bullpen, they had a group of pitchers who varied greatly in style, repertoire, philosophy, and psychology. Gil and Rube had this figured out so that they could take advantage of each pitcher's strength and minimize exposing the pitcher's vulnerabilities. Before each series they sketched out a number of scenarios and made decisions for each, taking into consideration the opposing team's hitters, the ballpark, how much rest each pitcher had, the weather, and a lot of other factors. Gil and Rube never told the pitchers about this—we learned about it from one of the other coaches. But we could see the thought that had gone into decisions, and that gave the bullpen a lot of faith in their bosses.

Another Senators pitcher, Darold Knowles, who later pitched for Hall of Fame manager Dick Williams, agreed with Baldwin. "Hodges," Knowles later said, "handled pitchers as well as anyone I ever played for."

As a former catcher, Hodges also understood the fragility of pitchers' arms, so he was upset after the 1966 All-Star Game when Pete Richert, his best pitcher, was asked to warm up five times during the game. "I know Sam Mele [managing the American League team that year] is a nice guy and I like him," Hodges said, "but he had no business getting a starting pitcher up and down five times in a ball game. Richert could have permanent damage." Hodges suggested that at least two relief pitchers be selected to each All-Star roster to avoid the problem in the future. Hodges also criticized pitchers who came up with "instant sore arms" for the All-Star Game so they didn't have to play. "Richert won't tell you he shouldn't pitch," said Hodges. "He tries to be noble."

Jim Hannan pitched for four different Senators managers. "Hodges," said Hannan, "was the best, by far." And it was not because Hodges allowed Hannan to leave the team and visit his seriously ill father during the 1965 season. In fact, Hannan often frustrated Hodges. "Jim Hannan has everything to win with," Hodges said. "He is a graduate of Notre Dame and is taking his masters. He has been smart everywhere except on the pitching mound."

Even more important than playing "smart" was Hodges's immutable belief that his players perform their individual jobs within the context of the needs of the team as a whole. If a player's actions were selfish and detrimental to the team, Hodges's reaction could be terrifying. Never was this more evident than the day pitcher Phil Ortega showed up late for a game at Yankee Stadium.

That weekend the Senators were in New York to play a five-game series against the Yankees. The series began with a doubleheader on Friday, July 8, 1966. Hannan, who grew up in the New York area, wanted to start a game at Yankee Stadium in front of his friends and relatives. Hodges granted Hannan his wish, starting him in the second game. The Senators were leading 4–3 in the bottom of the fifth, and the Yankees' first batter was Mickey Mantle, who had already homered. "Mantle," Hannan said, "owned me." Hannan wanted to walk Mantle but Hodges told him, "If you walk him, you're out of here." Hannan pitched to Mantle, who singled, as did the next batter, and Hodges then came out to remove him. But Hannan was confident he could get the next batter, Elston Howard, and he wanted to keep pitching.

In spring training, one of the first rules Hodges established was that when he came out to make a pitching change, the pitcher immediately handed—not tossed—the ball to him. But Hannan decided he wasn't going to leave until Hodges spoke to him, and he turned his back to Hodges. Hodges grabbed Hannan's elbow and squeezed—hard. "If you don't give me that ball," Hodges said, "I'm going to fine you $500." Hannan figured that counted as Hodges speaking to him, so he handed the ball over.

That Sunday, the Senators played another doubleheader at Yankee Stadium. It was their fourth doubleheader in seven days. The pitching staff was worn out and Hodges was counting on his starters to give the bullpen a break. Phil Ortega, one of the pitchers acquired in the Osteen trade, was scheduled to start the second game. But Ortega had not only missed curfew the night before, but also missed the team bus that had taken the Senators from their hotel to Yankee Stadium that day. Although the reasons for Ortega's absence were never made public, the previous fall, in his hometown of Mesa, Arizona, Ortega had been charged with drunk driving on two separate occasions.

Before the game, Hodges came out of his office three times to see if Ortega had arrived. Finally, he asked twenty-nine-year-old reliever Bob Humphreys into the office. "What do you think about starting?" Hodges asked. Humphreys had never started a Major League game. "Well," Humphreys said, "I guess I have to start sometime." Hodges replied, "I don't expect nine, not even seven, just give me five." Hodges then called for a team meeting, something he rarely did.

Hodges started slowly, softly. But the longer he spoke, the angrier he became. Hodges told his players they were a team—not a group of individuals—and they must act accordingly. With the missing Ortega on his mind, Hodges told his players, "Your teammates are relying on you."

"He was pretty pissed," said Ken McMullen. When Hodges lost his temper, an artery in his neck rose up. "It looked like a huge muscle," McMullen recalled. At those moments, Hodges appeared much taller than his nearly six-foot-two-inch frame. A few minutes after Hodges began speaking, Phil Ortega walked into the clubhouse and started to put on his uniform. At first,

Hodges didn't see him. But when he did, Hodges screamed, "Take off that uniform and get out of here."

Hannan recalled that "Hodges pushing Ortega—but just a little."

Shortly after Ortega exited, backup catcher John Orsino walked into the Senators' clubhouse smoking a cigar. Orsino was on the disabled list and didn't have to be at the ballpark, but he lived in nearby Ft. Lee and wanted to support his teammates. Hodges forgot Orsino was on the disabled list and screamed at him to get out. Orsino followed orders.

Then, with the Friday night's elbow-grabbing pitching change still fresh, Hodges started in on Hannan for not consistently following the signs from catcher Paul Casanova. In the original Yankee Stadium, the visitor's locker room had support pillars, so as Hodges stood in front of Hannan, the two Senators players sitting on either side of Hannan were blocked from Hodges's view and they were teasing Hannan, trying to make him laugh. Rube Walker later told Hannan, "It was good you didn't. He would've killed you."

After Hodges's tirade, the Senators swept both games. Bob Humphreys threw five scoreless innings.

Sitting next to Hannan during Hodges's explosion was a player the Senators had recently acquired from the Kansas City Athletics, Ken "Hawk" Harrelson. A right-handed power hitter of little note, Harrelson was best known for being flamboyant on and off the field. He was among the first of a generation of athletes who realized the more you were noticed—no matter the reason—the greater the financial windfall.

Team-first Hodges and the attention-seeking Harrelson were two men cut from vastly different cloth. As a friend of Harrelson later said, between those two there was "a clash of life-styles." But compared to Hodges, whose range of managerial expression had been set in stone during the Eisenhower administration, Ken Harrelson was a quote machine, and the younger writers loved him.

In his autobiography, *Hawk*, Harrelson called Hodges "unfair, unreasonable, unfeeling, incapable of handling men, stubborn, holier-than-thou, and ice cold."

Hodges once told Harrelson if he did not get his hair cut, he couldn't play. Harrelson, who had previously vowed to get only one haircut that summer, returned the next day unclipped. Hodges told Harrelson to find a seat on the bench; but Bob Humphreys cut Harrelson's hair in the clubhouse and Hodges let him play.

Ken Harrelson was an excellent golfer. He believed if he dedicated himself to it, he could make the pro circuit. "Golfers," Harrelson said, "get to stay up late, play the night clubs, have a drink and relax. When you're a ballplayer you're supposed to live like a monk. But I don't." Hodges told Harrelson he should stop playing golf and focus on baseball. And despite saying, "I'm going to concentrate on baseball. I don't think it's fair to be distracted by golf," Harrelson resented Hodges for the limitation. "If I really make it big, with the golf life that is," Harrelson added, "then maybe baseball will have to worry about getting me back. I don't know if they can afford to lose a fellow like me."

But Hodges was only asking Harrelson what he expected of all his players: if you want to be a baseball player, forget about playing other sports professionally. Early in Hodges's Washington years, one of his outfielders, Tom Brown, who had been selected in the second round of the NFL draft, could not make up his mind which sport he wanted to pursue. When Brown was still undecided, Hodges was asked if Brown had a future in the Major Leagues. "Yes," Hodges said, "if he forgets about football." Hodges had it right. For Brown, football was a crutch; and after too many frustrating at bats, Brown's crutch became a self-fulfilling prophecy: he gave up his baseball career.

Although Harrelson was not Hodges's kind of player, Hodges saw he had potential. "Hodges," Harrelson wrote, "really worked at making a first baseman out of me." Hodges taught Harrelson "things about playing first base that most ballplayers never knew."

For someone who loved the limelight as much as Harrelson, nothing was more important than being in the starting lineup for the Senators' home opener, a game that drew the biggest crowd of the season in Washington and brought out President Johnson. The 1967 home opener was on April 10 against the Yankees and their outstanding right-handed pitcher, Mel Stottlemyre. Hodges decided to go with his lefty first baseman, Dick Nen, who had "enjoyed exceptional success against Stottlemyre in the past." But Harrelson had been the Senators' best hitter in preseason play, and he felt Hodges kept him out of the starting lineup to "hurt him."

33. Catcher Paul Casanova trying to tag out Al Kaline of Detroit, D.C. Stadium, June 23, 1966. Reprinted with permission of the DC Public Library, *Star* Collection, © *Washington Post*.

The following month, the Senators traded Pete Richert to Baltimore for Mike Epstein, a power-hitting first baseman. Shortly thereafter, Harrelson was shipped back to Kansas City.

Although Hodges felt Major League players, as a general rule, didn't need encouragement, on occasion—as Clyde Sukeforth had done for him—he offered some. Hodges told Mike McCormick, "From the second inning on, you're the best pitcher I've ever seen." And Hodges gave his catcher, Paul Casanova, a handshake after every game he played in order to boost his confidence. In 1967 Hodges's encouragement paid off. Casanova was named to the American League All-Star team. Even a curmudgeon like Hodges's former train-traveling companion, Dick Williams, who led the Red Sox to a pennant that season, said, "There are only two outstanding catchers in the American League—Bill Freehan of Detroit and Paul Casanova of Washington."

But Hodges's ability to get, as pitcher Pete Richert said, "a lot of mileage out of his players" was largely a product of the unspoken message Hodges conveyed: that he always had, said Dave Baldwin, "a firm hand on the steering wheel."

Even after Hodges blasted Jim Hannan at Yankee Stadium, he never lost faith in him. After a game in which Hannan hung a slider and gave up a home run, Hodges asked Hannan why, after Hodges had specifically told him to throw low sliders—not fastballs—had he thrown a fastball? Hannan told Hodges he had thrown a slider, but because he was not getting enough pitching practice, the ball had stayed up. The very next day, Rube Walker told Hannan to follow him out onto the field where Hodges was ready to watch Hannan throw sliders and Joe Pignatano was ready to catch them. In mid-delivery, Hodges yelled out for Hannan to stop and told him there was something wrong with the way he was gripping the ball: the thumb on his throwing hand was coming up. Hodges told Hannan that on a slider, to generate the right spin, the thumb had to be down. Hannan adjusted his grip accordingly and his slider improved dramatically.

In 1967 the Senators improved as well.

Beginning on July 9, 1967, they won eight straight games to jump-start a three-week period in which their record (17-6) was the best in the league. As they flirted just below .500, even Hodges admitted his team was playing "very good," but he kept the heat on his players, demanding more improvement. "Once we attain a .500 record," Hodges said, "we're not going to be satisfied." By early August, as the team reached .500, despite Hodges trying to water down expectations ("There is no use talking pennant until we climb five or six games above .500"), the Senators were viewed as contenders. At the time, hope invigorated the fans as well as the reporters, who clustered around the Western Union machine in the press box awaiting scores from other American League pennant contenders like the White Sox, Twins, Tigers, and Red Sox. In mid-August, when the Senators returned from a successful road trip, they were only six games out of first place. That night, four thousand banner-waving fans greeted the team at National Airport, a highlight of a season in which home attendance reached its highest level since 1948. Their banner read, "GO HODGES—WE WANT PENNANT!"

In 1967 Hodges established himself as a master of in-game decisions

34. Jim Hannan returning to the dugout after being removed from a 1969 game after walking the first two Baltimore batters in the ninth inning at RFK Stadium. The Senators' manager (standing in the middle of the dugout) is Ted Williams. Reprinted with permission of the DC Public Library, *Star* Collection, © *Washington Post*.

during extra-inning games. Two memorable Senators victories that season were extra-inning cliff-hangers, such as the come-from-behind win over the Twins in Minnesota on August 10. In that game, the Senators trailed 7–0 after six innings but tied it up and forced extra innings. The Nats held on until a Ken McMullen home run in the top of the twentieth inning gave them a 9–7 victory at 1:30 a.m. after five hours and forty minutes of play, then the second-longest

35. The Senators' lineup on Opening Day 1967. From right, Ed Brinkman, shortstop; Bernie Allen, second base; Fred Valentine, center field; Frank Howard, left field; Jim King, right field, Dick Nen, first base; Ken McMullen, third base; Doug Camilli or Jim French, catcher; and Pete Richert, pitcher. Reprinted with permission of the DC Public Library, *Star* Collection, © *Washington Post.*

night game in history. It was especially sweet for Dave Baldwin; it was the first win of his Major League career. Afterward, with all the "whooping and hollering," Baldwin said, "You would have thought we had won the pennant."

Earlier that summer, the Senators played what was then the longest night game in baseball history (six hours and thirty-eight minutes). The game was against the White Sox at D.C. Stadium. Paul Casanova, who caught all twenty-two innings, won it with a bases-loaded single. When it ended at 2:44 a.m., after using every position player on his roster except his backup catcher, Hodges said, "If you don't get ulcers in a game like that, you never will."

After the Senators' two exciting extra-inning wins, the Baltimore Orioles players started to make jokes—as they would in 1969 regarding the "Miracle Mets"—about the "The Miracle of Washington." But the Senators were no

36. Thousands of fans greet the Senators at the airport, August 13, 1967. Reprinted with permission of the DC Public Library, *Star* Collection, © *Washington Post*.

longer a joke. In 1967, despite having the lowest team batting average in the league (.223), the Senators finished in a sixth-place tie with the then defending champions, the Orioles.

By 1967 Hodges had grown more confident in his in-game decision making, often choosing a more aggressive approach. Hodges usually didn't try to anticipate what an opposing manager would do but instead allowed his moves to flow naturally from the circumstances presented. But not always: in a game against the Yankees at D.C. Stadium on August 26, 1967, the Senators were trailing 3–2 in the bottom of the ninth with a runner on second and the pitcher's spot due up. Hodges sent up left-handed-hitting Dick Nen to hit against righty Jim Bouton. Although Nen was usually put into games as a defensive replacement rather than as a pinch hitter, Ralph Houk, the Yankees' manager, responded by lifting Bouton and replacing him with Steve Hamilton, his best left-handed reliever. Nen never swung the bat. Hodges inserted righty Fred Valentine to pinch-hit for Nen and Hodges had the matchup he wanted, a lefty throwing to a righty. Valentine hit a two-run walk-off homer for a 4–3 Senators win. "After Hodges made a move," Ron Swoboda said, "you would sit there and think about why he did it . . . eventually you'd come around to seeing he was right."

Some of the managerial techniques Hodges experimented with in Washington would be utilized when he took over the Mets. During the 1967 season, Hodges decided to use the recently acquired veteran pitcher Camilo Pascual every fifth day (and not the typical four) in the hope that the additional rest would make him more effective. It worked. Pascual's earned run average was significantly lower (one and a half runs) than the previous season. In addition, because the Senators were still a poor-hitting team, Hodges utilized a righty-lefty platoon at those positions where he felt he had to give up defense for improved hitting. But as he would with the Mets, at the crucial positions of catcher, shortstop, and center field, he didn't sacrifice fielding for hitting. And because of their weak hitting, Hodges sometimes demanded his players hit behind the runner to advance them into scoring position. "If we had a powerful club," he said, "there'd be no worry because, with a bunch of power hitters, the job will get done. But we don't have that kind of team."

In 1967 Eddie Stanky, Leo Durocher's protégé on the Dodgers and Hodges's former teammate, was managing the Chicago White Sox. "Gil can lose a 1–0 ball game and come to the plate the next day with the lineup cards as pleasant as ever with everybody," Stanky said. "But Hodges burns inside. I know him. He keeps it in and it eats him inside." In contrast to Hodges, Stanky didn't know when to shut up. In 1967 the White Sox finished three games behind Boston and their future Hall of Famer, Carl Yastrzemski, who propelled the Red Sox to the pennant. That season, Stanky said that Yastrzemski was "an All-Star from the neck down." The next day, in a doubleheader against the White Sox, Yastrzemski got six hits and tipped his cap to Stanky after each one. Before a subsequent Senators–Red Sox game, reporters tried to bait Hodges into saying something negative about Yastrzemski. "I think," Hodges said, "I'll bake him a cake." Yastrzemski hit two home runs and the Senators lost. Hodges later joked that he should have "put poison in that cake." In response Yastrzemski said, "Comparing Hodges to Stanky is like comparing a Cadillac to a Chevrolet."

But decency and self-effacement—even of a Cadillac—do not preclude a temper. Never was this clearer than after a game in Detroit in 1967 when, with two out and no one on base in the bottom of the eighth inning and Washington leading, 4–1, Darold Knowles allowed a single and then committed what for Hodges was the unconscionable sin of walking the next batter to bring the tying run up to the plate. Bill Freehan then hit a three-run homer to tie the game. In the ninth with two out, the Tigers' Willie Horton singled to drive in the game-winning run.

After the game, Hodges entered the Senators' clubhouse before anyone else. There were wooden stools in front of each locker. Hodges smashed seven of them into kindling. Rube Walker and Joe Pignatano kept the players out of the clubhouse until Hodges calmed down. But even in the hallway, the players could hear the wood cracking. Walker and Pignatano went in first and picked up the pieces of broken wood. Only then were the players allowed into the clubhouse. Dave Baldwin said, "Hodges was very good at controlling his temper ordinarily, but an episode like that makes a big impression on the players. If the stools had broken legs, could that happen to an errant player as well? It works on your imagination."

A deeply religious man who prided himself on keeping his emotions in check, Hodges later wrote that he was "ashamed" by his actions in the locker room after the loss in Detroit. But Hodges's eruptions, in combination with his silence, distanced him from his players. Although he used his pitching coach, "warm country bear" Rube Walker, to do "foolishness all the time" to keep his players loose, some wished he were more communicative. But Hodges wanted to win a pennant, not a popularity contest.

As Bob Broeg, the longtime dean of St. Louis sportswriters, and a man who knew Hodges throughout his playing and managerial career, later wrote, "As a manager, keeping his distance from his players and his counsel from the press, Hodges was neither a saint nor a Satan. But he was admired by many, including me, and respected by even more."

In 1967 the Senators won seventy-six games—the most by any Senators team since 1953, and they had briefly been pennant contenders. The "Miracle of Washington" finished fifteen and a half games out of first—a dramatic improvement since Hodges's first season when they finished forty-eight and a half games out.

The Senators were on the doorstep of becoming a winning team. But success came at a price. Every April as the Senators headed north, Hodges had a chest cold, in part because he couldn't break his smoking habit. "Hodges," Russ White said, "smoked one pack of cigarettes after another. You could just see it coming."

HOME

Queens (1968–72)

20

THE METS GET SERIOUS

I'm no Casey Stengel when it comes to making speeches. I'm not even Wes Westrum.
But the wind was blowing out and it carried my voice, so they heard it well.

Gil Hodges was often asked if he wanted to return to New York to manage
the Mets. In 1965 he replied, "I must be loyal to Washington or I couldn't live
with myself." When asked if she would like her husband back home managing
the Mets, Joan Hodges said, "The answer is yes." In September of 1967, work
appeared to have won out over family. "I have a contract that goes through
1968," Hodges said, "and I have every intention of honoring it."

But Mets chairman M. Donald Grant was convinced Hodges was the man
"that can win us the pennant." Wes Westrum, Stengel's replacement as Mets
manager, never would. He lacked his players' respect. "We rode over him,"
Mets third baseman Ed Charles said, "like he didn't exist."

When Casey Stengel was in charge, *New York Times* writer George Vescey
wondered how an average person would fare leading the Mets as their lovable
losers' act wore thin. Vescey got his answer when he once had breakfast with
Westrum; the Mets' manager smoked ten cigarettes, admitting he couldn't
sleep, and said that the night before, after a tough loss to Houston, he "almost
broke down." As Hodges would learn, "managing the Mets can do very bad
things to a man's health."

Near the end of the 1967 season, Westrum resigned. But the Mets' general manager, Bing Devine, was not convinced Hodges was the man for the
job. Devine would have been more comfortable hiring Harry Walker (Don
Clendenon's least favorite manager), whom he knew from his years as an

executive with the Cardinals. But Devine—who would return to St. Louis to become the Cardinals' general manager that December—followed Grant's wishes and dutifully dispatched Johnny Murphy to badger George Selkirk into allowing the Mets to meet with Hodges.

That was no easy task. "He has it in him to become the game's outstanding manager," said one Senators executive. "He has a forceful personality and he can be tough when it's necessary. When he talks to a player, that player knows he's been talked to. And Gil has so much decency that he commands respect. He always knows what to do and is a patient instructor. He even gets mad at the right times." Selkirk initially accused the Mets of "meddling and tampering," but relented when the Mets agreed to pay financial compensation if Hodges signed with them. "I had to let them talk to Hodges and get it over with," Selkirk said. "Gil was in a terrible sweat. . . . I could see that poor Gil was worried and had been browbeaten. I had to put an end to that and told the Mets they could make a deal."

Hodges flew to St. Louis where he and Devine sat next to each other during the fifth game of the 1967 World Series. Afterward, when he drove Hodges to the airport and the two men spoke at length, Devine realized Hodges was the "ideal choice for the Mets."

But Hodges wondered if he wasn't jumping from the frying pan into the fire. The Senators were on the threshold of the first division; the Mets were back in last place, scoring fewer runs and winning fewer games than any other team in baseball. Home attendance had decreased by four hundred thousand, and unless the Mets showed significant improvement, he would be boarding a sinking ship. Hodges called Buzzie Bavasi for an update on the Mets. Bavasi said, "If you'd be willing to manage a minor league team, then you'll have no problem managing the Mets."

Hodges took the job anyway. "It is a tough decision to make," he said, "but there is more than a normal course of events to this. My home and business are in New York and the family angle plays a big part." But he hedged his bets, signing a three-year contract for $57,000 a season. Even if the Mets were as bad as Bavasi implied, Hodges had a three-year annuity (if he was fired) at a very high salary for a manager who had never had a winning season. By comparison, after the Cardinals defeated the Red Sox in the 1967 World

Series, their manager, Red Schoendienst, received only a one-year contract for $45,000.

At the press conference announcing his signing, Hodges admitted feeling relieved. When asked if he had recommended anyone to succeed him as the Senators' manager, Hodges said, "They didn't ask me, and I didn't volunteer any names." The Hodges-Selkirk divorce was painful, but Selkirk exacted his pound of flesh. In exchange for Hodges, the Mets paid the Senators $100,000 (and pitcher Bill Denehy, who never won another Major League game). Between the $100,000 and their three-year commitment to Hodges, the Mets had invested over a quarter of a million dollars of Mrs. Joan Payson's money to bring Hodges home. Payson was no fool. "I'm glad to read in the papers," she told Hodges, "that your wife was pleased by your return to New York."

The Mets organization was confident they had made the right decision. Johnny Murphy said, "Gil's addition is the biggest thing that has happened to the club since I've been here." Casey Stengel, who knew Hodges well enough to see behind the nice-guy image, said, "The players liked him, but not too much, because they ain't very good if they get too fond of ya."

Hodges would fit in smoothly with Murphy, who would take over the general manager's job when Devine left, again leaving Hodges in a situation where his general manager was new to the job and sought his input. In fact, Hodges became the first Mets manager to select his own coaches, as he brought Pignatano, Walker, and Yost with him from Washington. The lone holdover was Yogi Berra.

Although Berra was as much a part of Yankee Stadium as the center-field monuments, he had been fired as the Yankees' manager in 1964 and hired as a Mets coach. A new manager with less self-confidence than Hodges might have forced Berra out. But, as Berra wrote, "Gil could have told me good-bye. He didn't. I went to see him, to tell him I would leave. I told him I wanted to be where I was wanted. I didn't want a job because I was Yogi Berra. I thought I could help, but it was up to him. I really respected him. He treated everyone the same. Fairly."

The first weekend after Hodges was hired, he was in Florida watching Mets prospects at an Instructional League camp in St. Petersburg. In November, on three consecutive Saturdays, Hodges, along with several Mets players, took a promotional train ride on the Long Island Railroad to Babylon, Cedarhurst, and Huntington, hoping to grow the Mets' fan base. And what better way to do that than roll out Hodges, the former Dodgers slugger, together with Ron Swoboda, the player that management anticipated would become the Mets' top power hitter.

The pairing of Hodges and Swoboda was baseball's version of *The Odd Couple*. Swoboda was gregarious, Hodges a closed book. Hodges required shirts, jackets, and ties on road trips, considered Nehru jackets outside his "scope," and watched sideburns "closely." Swoboda was a product of the 1960s when long hair and "love beads" were cool, so it was understandable when Swoboda later said, "We never came together well." Swoboda had a problem with authority figures and often responded to Hodges "out of pure anger. At times, I bristled at the way Hodges would push his authority around."

Entering the 1968 season, the Mets marketed Swoboda as a future star. In his rookie year Swoboda had hit nineteen home runs, more than Mickey Mantle had in his first season. But those nineteen home runs would be the most he ever hit in one season. When Swoboda signed his 1968 contract, Casey Stengel told him, "You're going to be somebody." Even Hodges got caught up in the sales pitch, saying, "He's the right fielder, period." Only Swoboda, at twenty-three, was realistic about his capabilities saying, "I've never gone to spring training with a job."

Hodges soon learned why. That March, in a spring training game against the Orioles, when it was Swoboda's turn at bat he was not in the on-deck circle or the dugout, and Hodges sent up a pinch hitter. When Swoboda returned, seeing Hodges had removed him from the game, he went into the clubhouse. Hodges sent Yogi Berra to get him: "Tell him, I miss him." Hodges didn't fine Swoboda but "felt sure" he understood the need to stay focused. To emphasize that point to the entire team, the following day's practice began at 1 p.m., a particularly early hour since that day's game would not begin until 7:30 p.m., and players were not usually required to arrive until three hours before game time.

Swoboda gained his focus early in the season, briefly leading the National League in home runs, but that season he struck out over one hundred times.

"I was trying hard to be an everyday ballplayer," he later said, "and I probably wasn't."

That season, a fan asked Hodges, "When are the Mets going to get a constant slugger?"

"A what?"

"A constant slugger. Someone who hits the ball all the time, not Swoboda, who just hits good sometimes."

"Well," Hodges said, "our plans are to make Swoboda a constant slugger."

Hodges hoped to do the same with Tommie Agee. In 1966 Agee, then the Chicago White Sox center fielder, hit twenty-two home runs, stole forty-four bases, and won the American League Rookie of the Year Award. But the following season, he played poorly and lost favor with his manager, Eddie Stanky. Hodges had seen Agee play enough to know he was a gifted fielder and felt he could handle Agee with a lighter touch than Stanky, who was not shy about embarrassing Agee publicly. "The first thing Hodges wanted to do when he became the manager was to acquire Tommie Agee," Johnny Murphy said. "He wanted a guy to bat leadoff with speed and that could hit for power. He also . . . needed a guy in center to run the ball down."

On December 15, 1967, the Mets traded their best hitter, Tommy Davis, and starting pitcher Jack Fisher for the twenty-five-year-old Agee and a utility infielder, Al Weis. Agee's success or failure would go a long way toward determining Hodges's future. But in March of 1968, in his first at bat in a Mets uniform, Agee was hit in the head with a high inside pitch thrown by Bob Gibson. Agee was carried off the field on a stretcher and taken to the hospital for X-rays to see if his skull was fractured. It wasn't, but Gibson's "welcome to the National League" pitch set the tone for Agee's season. He hit .217 with only five home runs and seventeen runs batted in, striking out over one hundred times.

Publicly, Hodges did everything he could to build up Agee's confidence. "He needs to relax a little," Hodges told reporters. "He's not alone. A number of other people around the league are in the slumps, too." Privately, as Agee's close friend Cleon Jones said, Hodges "took Tommie under his wing." Most players dreaded an invitation to Hodges's office, but Agee felt comfortable enough with his new manager to discuss his personal problems. And despite

Hodges's tendency to use his coaches as a buffer between himself and his players, he had a sense of knowing which of his players, like Agee (and Tug McGraw), needed his personal support. "Gil and Agee got very close," Maury Allen wrote. "Agee would go into his office, close the door, and spill his guts with Gil." At the time, Agee was involved with a woman who was having emotional problems, and he was concerned about her mental health. He needed somebody to talk it through with, and "Gil was always willing to listen."

Hodges also had input as to the other player the Mets received from the White Sox. The Mets had been offered either Wayne Causey or Al Weis. Causey was the better hitter, but Hodges lobbied for Weis. From his years managing the Senators, Hodges knew Weis was an excellent middle infielder. Hodges also knew both his starting shortstop, Bud Harrelson, and his second baseman, Ken Boswell, would be required to spend several weeks during the 1968 season fulfilling their Army Reserve duty, and Weis would be the perfect replacement. When Weis arrived for spring training, Hodges told him he was a key component of the trade. But Hodges then "asked" Weis to give up switch-hitting and bat only right-handed, since he would be a platoon player for the Mets and it would be better for the team if he focused on his natural, right-handed swing. Weis had spent years developing the ability to switch-hit but understood the porous line between Hodges asking and Hodges telling, so he began hitting only right-handed. The change proved crucial in 1969. Hodges, in his role as the "winter manager," voiced his opinion on another trade with Chicago, who owed the Mets a player-to-be-named-later from a previous trade. Hodges urged that the player be the veteran left-handed-hitting J. C. Martin, an excellent defensive player who would be platooned with the Mets' right-handed-hitting catcher, Jerry Grote.

A fearless, tough, opinionated Texan, Grote had a strong throwing arm, lighting-quick hands, and a commanding presence. He was the best-fielding catcher of his era. Hall of Fame catcher Johnny Bench paid Grote the ultimate compliment, saying that if they were both on the same team, Bench would be the one asked to play another position. But Grote viewed himself as a power hitter and struggled at the plate; in 1967 Grote batted .195 while swinging for the fences. However good a fielder Grote was, Hodges couldn't have a starting catcher who barely hit his weight, so Hodges studied hours of film and noticed that Grote didn't keep both his hands on the bat as he followed through with his swing. This was news to Grote—and easily correctible. Grote also held the bat very high and away from his body, resulting in a long swing. Hodges told Grote he didn't have to be a home run hitter but merely had to hit the ball consistently. Hodges suggested that Grote hold the bat lower and closer to his body and grip the bat higher on the barrel (resulting in less power but more control). It worked. In 1968 Grote hit .282 and was named to the National League All-Star team for the first time.

In addition to Agee, Weis, and Grote, another player Hodges would rely on for his defensive ability was shortstop Bud Harrelson. Harrelson was slightly built and over the course of the season was prone to losing weight and wearing out. Hodges couldn't change Harrelson's body type, but he tried to change his mind-set.

Under Westrum, when the switch-hitting Harrelson (a natural righty) came to bat from the left side, he admitted to "glancing back towards the bench to see if a pinch-hitter was coming." When Hodges heard this, he told Harrelson, "That was a mistake. Never look back. If the manager wants you out of there, he'll let you know. Don't give him any ideas." In other words, even if you lack confidence, don't let on. That same spring, when the player's weights were taken, Hodges was watching. When Harrelson weighed in, Hodges told him, "You're the strongest 147 pound player I ever saw." Harrelson knew Hodges "was just blowing my horn," but it helped Harrelson's self-esteem. "He made me feel like a tiger," Harrelson said.

Hodges officially began managing the Mets on the morning of February 21, 1968, when he walked out onto Huggins-Stengel Field in St. Petersburg and addressed his players. "My name is Hodges," he said, "I don't know how things were before, but if I say we start at 10 o'clock, we start at 10. That's the way I do things. If that's a change, okay."

Hodges then briefed his players on his training camp rules, from curfew time (midnight) to which card games were acceptable (hearts, gin, and bridge) and which weren't (poker), even telling them how much to tip the chambermaids ($1 per week) and that the hotel bar was off-limits. Hodges closed by saying, "I don't believe in petty fines . . . for trivial things," but "I do believe in minimum fines of say, $25."

All fines Hodges collected were donated to charity. And Hodges fined his players with specificity. During a road trip, Hodges once saw outfielder Art Shamsky late one night in the hotel lobby. Shamsky had been hungry, room service was closed, and he'd come downstairs to get burgers from a twenty-four-hour place across the street. Those were expensive burgers. Hodges fined Shamsky $100 for breaking curfew and another $50 for not having a tie and jacket on.

As he did in Pompano Beach, stopwatch and walkie-talkie in hand, Hodges commanded over the Mets practices in a precise, no-time-to-waste style. His coaches walked around with notebooks in their back pockets so they could refer to Rube Walker's instructions as to how long each pitcher was to throw that day to gradually build up arm strength to avoid injury. Pitchers also took fielding practice, and pity the poor pitcher Hodges saw standing in the outfield not paying attention. Hodges would come out from behind the cage, take a ball out of his pocket, pick up a bat, and yell, "You guys want a lounge chair out there?" A fungo shot at the lackadaisical player immediately followed. "He hit me in the chest on one hop more than once," said Mets pitcher Jon Matlack.

By March, Ed Charles appreciated the pride Hodges instilled in the Mets: no one was riding over Gil Hodges "like he didn't exist." As a young boy growing up in Florida, Charles once chased the Brooklyn Dodgers' train with Jackie Robinson on board as it passed through his town. For Charles, seeing Robinson "was like the Messiah had come." In the 1950s, because of quotas that limited the number of black players on Major League rosters, Charles spent six years in the Minors despite being an All-Star in the South Atlantic League. Charles didn't get a chance to play in the Majors until he was twenty-nine, when he finished second in the American League Rookie of the Year vote. For Charles, playing for Hodges was a pleasure. "If you settle for that Sad Sack image," Charles said, "you can get into a rut. People are always excusing defeats for you. This is the most strenuous training camp I've ever been in. We're working harder than ever . . . and I love it."

"Pitching," Hodges once said, "can stop the best hitters." And that spring, after evaluating his pitchers, he decided to go with youth. After his ace, Tom Seaver (age twenty-four), Hodges settled on a starting rotation with only one veteran, thirty-two-year-old Don Cardwell, who had pitched well against

Hodges back in the 1950s, and three rookies: Nolan Ryan (twenty-one), Les Rohr (twenty-two), and Jerry Koosman (twenty-four). Rohr was soon injured, leaving Ryan as the rookie with the greatest potential. That spring, after watching Ryan pitch four shutout innings against the world champion Cardinals while striking out five of the first six batters he faced, Hodges said, "There are . . . three categories of velocity for pitchers. Ryan is in the first one with Sandy Koufax and Bob Gibson."

Despite the ability to overwhelm hitters—at one point in the Minors, Ryan had amassed 422 strikeouts in only 280 innings—entering the 1968 season Ryan had pitched only three innings in the Majors, and Mets fans referred to him as "the myth" because they had heard so much about, but seen so little of, him. Looking for sensationalistic headlines, the New York writers played up Ryan's injuries with headlines like "Mets' Man of Hour Can Be Headache Most Any Minute." Ryan, a quiet, shy young man who grew up in a small town in Texas, wasn't comfortable in New York with its insatiable press. Knowing firsthand how Koufax had struggled early in his career, Hodges tried to downplay expectations regarding Ryan. In an era when pitchers often threw complete games, Hodges said, "I just want him to give me six or seven good innings."

Unlike Ryan, Jerry Koosman was not highly rated. The only reason the Mets even scouted him was because of a tip from the son of a Shea Stadium usher. That spring, Rube Walker told Koosman to stop throwing his slider because it took away from the effectiveness of his curve, and with that change Koosman went from struggling to dominant.

Despite his reliance on inexperienced pitchers, Hodges predicted the Mets would win seventy games, which would be the highest win total of their brief existence. But Hodges was confident in his defense (anchored by Grote, Harrelson, and Agee) and believed that at least one of his rookie pitchers would surprise him on the upside.

On April 17, 1968, before 52,079 fans (the largest Opening Day crowd that season), the Mets won the first home opener in their history as Jerry Koosman shut out the Giants. It was his second shutout in one week. His first, against the Dodgers, was Hodges's first win as Mets manager. Not only was Koosman the first pitcher in Mets history to throw two consecutive shutouts, but earlier in the week Nolan Ryan had combined with reliever Danny Frisella to shut out

Houston. Ryan had given Hodges what he wanted, six and two-thirds solid innings, before he was forced to leave the game with a blister on his pitching hand. In 1968, between the blisters and his military service, Ryan was unable to put together a solid stretch of quality pitching.

In their first six games of the season, Mets' pitchers had thrown three shutouts. But those were the only three games the Mets had won. A lack of consistent hitting limited them. For example, in the final game of their opening road trip, the Mets played twenty-four innings without scoring a run and lost to the Astros, 1–0. Yet, two months into the season, coming into a home game against the Giants on June 15, the Mets had won four in a row, and with a record of 28-29, if they won, it would represent the latest point in any season that the Mets were playing .500 baseball. More than forty thousand fans were in attendance to watch one future Hall of Famer, Juan Marichal, oppose another, Tom Seaver.

In New York, Hodges established a five-man rotation, ensuring pitchers four days' rest between games. At the time most teams utilized a four-man rotation. Seaver, used to pitching on three days' rest, initially resisted the change. But Rube Walker concluded that based upon his analysis of Seaver's pitching in 1967, even though he would be pitching fewer games, he'd benefit from the extra rest, and that proved true.

Seaver and Hodges shared three commonalities. As young men, both learned the meaning of hard work doing manual labor at companies where their fathers worked, both were former marines, and both knew success as a ballplayer required more than physical ability. "You can line up every pitcher in camp and categorize them by the stuff they throw," Seaver said. "There'd not be much difference. The real difference is mental concentration."

Despite these shared values, in the four seasons they were both with the Mets, Seaver and Hodges spoke at length only a handful of times. The first time was after the Giants game on June 15, and although the conversation was one-sided, it would be a pivotal moment in Seaver's career. He had pitched at least six innings in every one of his starts that season. But going into the top of the fifth with a comfortable 4–1 lead, Seaver lost focus and gave up three successive singles followed by a Willie McCovey home run. The Mets went on to lose, 9–5. That was the closest the Mets would came to .500 all season.

Hodges was upset at how Seaver had lost: anticipating a win, he had relaxed. A Seaver-pitched game usually followed the same pattern: if you didn't get to him early, the game was over. But that was the case only when Seaver stayed focused. Rarely can a pitcher turn it on and off at will; the only pitcher Hodges had ever seen who had that ability was Robin Roberts. Hodges decided it was time to give Seaver his "how-to-be-a-professional speech."

Seaver had never been called into Hodges office before. "He shut the door," Seaver recalled, "and I thought I was dead. He said, 'You were very unprofessional yesterday. I don't care what the score is, how many people are in the ballpark, you let the game get away from you. From now on you go about your business this way,' and he outlined how I should do it, A, B, C. Then he said, 'That's all.' I never said a word. I was glad to get out of there alive." In his next start, Seaver pitched in a professional manner throughout and defeated the Astros, 5–3.

In addition to their focus, Hodges kept track of his pitchers' emotions. A week after Hodges's talk with Seaver, Don Cardwell was pitching and the Mets were leading 4–2 in the sixth in Atlanta. But after an error, a single, and another poor fielding play, the bases were loaded with no outs, and Hodges saw that Cardwell was upset and unable to think clearly about how to pitch to the next batter. Hodges went out to the mound and told Cardwell with respect to his teammates' poor fielding plays, "Don't let it upset you. You can't pitch when you're upset." Cardwell pulled himself together, struck out the next batter, and then induced a ground-ball double play to end the inning. Cardwell didn't allow another base runner, throwing a five-hitter for the win.

In New York, Hodges set an example for his players, rarely losing his temper. But when he did, the results were terrifying. During the 1968 season, Hodges benched Jerry Grote during a brief batting slump. Grote's subsequent comments were exaggerated by the press, making it sound as if he had criticized his manager. Hodges was usually scrupulous in avoiding public criticism of his players—and he expected that same discretion from them when talking about him.

The day after Grote's comments were published, Hodges came to the ballpark in a "rage" and verbally ripped into Grote in front of the entire team. "When he was like that," Tom Seaver said, "we all just sank way back in our lockers." Ed Charles needed only one word to describe what Hodges sounded like in those moments—"Thunder."

When the roaring subsided, Ron Swoboda spoke up in Grote's defense. "We all gasped," Seaver said, "Hodges just stood there, his eyes getting wider and wider and that vein in his neck that always stuck out swelling." Hodges kicked a laundry basket, which sailed over Swoboda's head, and then "went after him, was going to kill him, really, when Rube Walker stepped between 'em. Rube told him to go to his office and cool down and he did." After that, Grote said, "I vowed then and there I wouldn't have anything to do with sportswriters."

Although a peacemaker during his playing career, Hodges supported a combative spirit among his players—when appropriate. During a series in early August of 1968, three days of brushback pitches in Houston culminated in Hodges taking the leash off his players. Going for a triple, the Astros' Denis Menke, known as the "Red Rooster" for his aggressive play, slid into third base and hit the Mets' third baseman, Kevin Collins, with an elbow to the face that knocked him unconscious. Collins had to be taken to the hospital. As soon as Collins was off the field, several Mets knocked Menke to the ground. "Everything was going along all right," Hodges said, "until Harry Walker [the Astros' new manager] ran up and said, 'he didn't do it on purpose.' Everybody in the park saw him do it on purpose."

A few days later, the Mets were in San Francisco and Juan Marichal hit both Agee and Harrelson with pitches, after which home-plate umpire Doug Harvey told Marichal if he hit another Mets batter he would be thrown out of the game. The Mets' pitcher responded by hitting Marichal with a pitch. But that wasn't enough for Hodges. "If Marichal hits another one of our batters, we'll get him," he said. When someone pointed out that the Mets had already "got" Marichal, Hodges replied, "We'll get him twice."

Hodges's competitive nature ran side-by-side with an unwavering moral sense. During the first week of June, New York senator Robert Kennedy was shot and killed. Only two months after the murder of Reverend Martin Luther King, it was an emotionally challenging time for all Americans. On the day of King's funeral, all games had been postponed. But for the day of Kennedy's funeral, baseball commissioner William Eckert ordered no games be played in New York and Washington, but all other games could be played as long as their starting time was after the funeral ended, allowing owners to shift day games to that night so they did not lose revenue.

In Houston, two Astros players, Bob Aspromonte and Rusty Staub, refused to play and were fined. In Pittsburgh, Maury Wills did the same. In Cincinnati, the Reds' player representative, Milt Pappas, refused to play and less than a week later was traded. Arthur Daley cited these events as an example of the adage, "Baseball must be a great game, otherwise it could never survive the men who run it."

The Mets were scheduled to play in San Francisco, and a Bat Day crowd of at least thirty thousand was expected. Out of respect for Senator Kennedy, the Mets' players unanimously voted not to play. But the Giants' owners were unhappy, and there was talk that if the Mets didn't take the field, they would be deemed to have forfeited the game. Considering Hodges was trying everything he could to improve the Mets' record, it was not in his best interest to forfeit the game. Yet, Hodges not only promised his players his full support, but voted with them not to take the field. No forfeit was declared. Hodges told his players that out of respect for Kennedy, he would likely go to church the morning of the funeral and "suggested" they "avoid carousing in public places."

National League President Warren Giles suggested the Mets dock their players a day's pay. Not on Hodges's watch. "I can't imagine . . . fining them for not playing," he said. Hodges's stand instilled the team with "a closeness . . . that had never been present before." Kennedy's widow, Ethel, sent Hodges a note thanking him for ensuring that on the day of her husband's funeral, the Mets-Giants game was not played.

In 1968 the Mets had their best season yet, winning seventy-three games. Thanks to Hodges's leadership and the rapid development of Seaver and Koosman, the Mets became respectable. Hodges was correct in predicting that one of his three rookie pitchers would excel. Koosman became the first National League rookie since Grover Cleveland Alexander (in 1911) to throw seven shutouts in a season. Thirteen of Koosman's first fourteen wins came after Mets losses, and Hodges dubbed him my "bounce-back boy."

Despite an outstanding pitching staff, the Mets were still among the worst-hitting teams in the league, and after the 1968 season Leonard Koppett of the *New York Times* expressed the view of most fans when he wrote that "pennant contention is still years away." But Hodges knew major progress had been made. "The way we've been going," Hodges said, "could ignite the whole operation. I'm very encouraged and can realistically say that when it comes to 1969 and 1970 we could be on our way." But with Hodges's optimism came his characteristic modesty: "It not me that's doing it," he added. "That's for sure."

Hodges's seriousness of purpose had set an example, not just for his players and coaches, but even for the team's broadcasters. On road trips, a bus always took the Mets from their hotel to the opposing team's stadium. In every city, Hodges "would tell the bus driver, 'If the bus is supposed to leave at 2, leave at 2, even if I am not on it. I don't care if it is empty, leave.' One time the bus left [without] Eddie Yost, Rube Walker, and Ralph Kiner."

In Washington that seriousness of purpose was sorely missed. Hodges's replacement, Jim Lemon, was a disaster. Bob Humphreys knew it was "going to be a long year" when Lemon was hired and announced, "I'm going to treat guys like I want to be treated."

"As a manager, you must be firm and have discipline," Humphreys said, "Lemon didn't." And the players lost focus. Near the end of the season, Nellie Fox, Eddie Yost's replacement as third base coach, told Humphreys that as a team the Senators missed over three hundred signs in 1968. Mental mistakes like that wouldn't have been tolerated under Hodges. Lemon also undid all of Hodges's efforts building up Paul Casanova's confidence, and his play suffered. As a result, the same nucleus of players as under Hodges finished with the worst record in baseball, and Lemon was fired after the season. "After Gil left," Dave Baldwin wrote, "we found out what we had lost in the way of positive atmosphere. In 1968, we lacked it entirely."

As the 1968 season was winding down, Hodges's stress level reached a high point as he struggled to keep the Mets out of last place. The Mets had improved tremendously, and moving the team up to ninth place would be symbolic of that improvement. (The Mets would finish the season one game ahead of the last-place Astros.) On September 24 the Mets had a night game against the Braves. At around four in the afternoon, after arriving at Atlanta–Fulton County Stadium, Hodges began to experience dull chest pains. After he threw fifteen minutes of batting practice, the pain worsened. When he came out to home plate with the lineup card, umpire Paul Pryor noticed that Hodges failed to make "his usual wisecrack." By the second inning the pain began to radiate throughout Hodges's upper body. Hodges told Rube Walker to take over and went into the clubhouse. Gus Mauch, the Mets' trainer, called Dr. Harry Rogers, the Braves' team physician. Mauch had suffered a heart attack a few years before and thought Hodges was having one. But Rogers told Hodges to lie down and if the pains continued, he should go to the hospital. Hodges insisted on listening to the game on the radio and spent the next six innings resting on the training table in the clubhouse. After the eighth inning, Hodges was taken by cab to Long Hospital and was placed in the intensive care unit and given oxygen.

At the hospital, Hodges's cardiologist was Dr. Linton H. Bishop Jr., who told Hodges that he had suffered a "small coronary thrombosis." "The lowest point," the then forty-four-year-old Hodges said, "is when the man says you've had a heart attack. That really hits you."

Joan Hodges arrived in Atlanta early the next morning and remained by her husband's side all day, every day, for the duration of his hospital stay. At the time, the technology had not yet been developed, as Dr. Bishop told me, "to fix his vessels," which might have helped prevent a subsequent heart attack. Hodges was a good patient, according to Bishop, and his condition gradually improved. The issue then became, would Hodges be able to again manage the Mets? Hodges wanted to return. "We have two very good pitchers," Hodges told Dr. Bishop, "and have a chance of winning the pennant." But Hodges wanted to be sure that he was not putting his health at further risk by managing. Bishop assured him that as long as he "got back to basics" he would be able to resume his job. Hodges had to stop smoking and lose twenty pounds. "If I felt for one minute that I couldn't do my job as well as before," Hodges said, "or if I felt it might hurt me—I wouldn't attempt it. I'd pull in the strings right now."

During his hospital stay, Hodges received a visit from Brooklyn native Joe Torre, who was then playing for the Atlanta Braves. Torre was familiar with Hodges. During the 1957 World Series between the Yankees and Braves, Torre's mother, Margaret, had appeared on the *Today Show* and was asked who her favorite player was. Everyone thought she would say Frank Torre, her oldest son, who was then playing first base for the Braves. But Margaret said, "Gil Hodges."

In the fall of 1968, Joe Torre had been feuding with Braves general manager Paul Richards and wanted to be traded to New York. "I tried to talk Hodges into trading for me," Torre said decades later. Torre ended up being traded to St. Louis. The Mets did okay anyway. As Torre later said, "They got Donn Clendenon instead."

In his first press conference after his heart attack, when asked what he would do if his doctor told him he could no longer manage, Hodges joked, "I'd change doctors, that's all." But the reality was that despite assurances that Hodges would be able to resume "full duties," the press conference was done over the phone with Hodges at home in Brooklyn and the press at Shea Stadium. In early November, Hodges had not even walked two blocks since his heart attack.

Hodges's smoking had increased from one pack a day in the early 1960s to three packs a day that August. But smoking was only one of two critical risk factors. Hodges's genes guaranteed that from a cardiac perspective it wasn't a question of if he would fall—only when. The men in his family were genetically predisposed to cardiac problems. Charlie had died from a pulmonary embolism at fifty-six, and Hodges's brother, Bob, would die following triple-bypass surgery at age fifty-five. Although Hodges had both of the primary risk factors, stress played a role. Despite Hodges's claim that he did not bottle up his emotions, those who knew him best thought otherwise. Don Drysdale wrote, "Gil kept a lot inside . . . and I've always wondered whether he kept too much inside. . . . It would have been better for his health had he let go more often." Hodges assumed that his own mental strength would keep him off the cigarettes and help him stay with the "basics." But signs soon surfaced that quitting would be difficult. "I didn't miss the cigarettes at first," Hodges said, "but I do miss them now after meals."

The day after his heart attack, Dr. Bishop denied Hodges permission to listen to the Mets-Atlanta game. Bishop knew his patient. A few days later, when Hodges was reading the paper and learned the Mets had lost the opening game of their final series of the season, he still felt the frustration that was so much a part of his job. "Those damn 11-inning games again," he said.

When the Cardinals played the Tigers in the World Series that October, Bishop allowed Hodges to watch the Series on television, but only after he assured Bishop he had no "emotional involvement." During that Series, Cardinals shortstop Dal Maxvill failed to get a hit (0 for 22) and Hodges's 1952 debacle once again made the rounds. Even Vice President Humphrey said, speaking of Maxvill, "Just like Gil Hodges."

That fall, several synagogues and religious schools in New York City were damaged by arson. One was in the East Flatbush section of Brooklyn. Through intermediaries, Rabbi Silber, the school's principal, got word to Hodges that they needed publicity to raise funds to rebuild. Shortly thereafter, Hodges, still recovering from his heart attack, paid Rabbi Silber a visit and handed him an envelope with $500 in cash. "The boys," Hodges said, "put a little something together."

That winter, after "prodding" from his friend (and lawyer) Sid Loberfeld, Hodges wrote a book, *The Game of Baseball*. Hodges refused to use the more marketable title "How to Be a Winning Manager" not only because he had never managed a winning team but because such a book, Hodges wrote, would be limited to four words: "Have the right players." There are chapters on managing, pitching, hitting, defense, umpiring, even Little League ball; not surprisingly, there's no chapter about the press. Hodges's what's-said-in-the-locker-room-stays-in-the-locker-room approach produced a work of plain vanilla that would never be confused with Jim Bouton's ribald classic of that same era, *Ball Four*.

The Game of Baseball was destined to go out of print, but it does end on an upbeat note: "Even managers who win the pennant have some bad days along the way. . . . I don't really know, but I'd sure like to find out."

In 1969, he did.

21

CONTENDERS

Look in that mirror and tell me if Cleon Jones is giving me 100 percent.

Hodges was back in uniform for the opening of training camp. During one of his first press conferences, when asked how many games the Mets would win in 1969, he said, "Eighty-five." In response, finding it hard to imagine the Mets as anything other than a losing team, many of the writers laughed out loud. Visibly upset, Hodges left the room to compose himself. A few minutes later, he returned.

"Gentlemen," he said, "losing is no laughing matter."

There were no more questions.

Hodges sensed that the Mets would be a winning team in 1969. He knew that a baseball team's fortunes tended to even out from one season to the next, and luck had not been on the Mets' side in 1968: they had lost thirteen of fifteen extra-inning games, and pitcher Jim McAndrew set a Major League record losing four consecutive games all by shutout. Hoping to quantify the win total he anticipated in a way his players could easily embrace, he told them eighty-five wins was only a dozen over their 1968 total and could be reached if each pitcher on the roster won just one more game than they had the previous season. The pitchers, bolstered by rookie Gary Gentry, a college star at Arizona State, viewed that as readily attainable. Much depended on either Gentry or Nolan Ryan stepping up as a reliable third starter behind Tom Seaver and Jerry Koosman. Hoping to add to his endurance, Ryan had gained twenty pounds, and that spring the Mets players hated trying to hit his fastball during batting practice. Hodges's take on Ryan was unchanged—he still had to prove himself.

That spring, with Hodges's encouragement, the Mets negotiated with Atlanta's GM, Paul Richards, to obtain Joe Torre. But the Mets frustrated Richards, presenting him with a list of players they refused to trade (Seaver, Koosman, Ron Swoboda, Cleon Jones, Jerry Grote, Bud Harrelson, and Amos Otis). "They have given me seven untouchables," Richards said. "If they had so many untouchables, how come they don't win a pennant?"

Hodges made concessions to his recovery. He still hit fungoes, but no longer pitched batting practice; he stopped smoking (temporarily), but still favored an occasional scotch; he still arrived four hours before game time, but if the Mets ended a series with a night game, the team slept over rather than take a late-night plane flight; and he kept his weight down despite an "occasional bout with lasagna."

Like Hodges, baseball was in no laughing mood that spring. Professional football was threatening baseball's reign as the nation's favorite team sport. The lords of baseball viewed the upcoming season as a marketing opportunity in need of a celebration. Conveniently, the 1869 Cincinnati Red Stockings were baseball's first professional team, and 1969 was proclaimed baseball's centennial season with a myriad of promotions following suit, and each league was split into two divisions, creating baseball's first League Championship Series. Yet more than anything else, it would be the unexpected and dramatic rise of the Mets that rekindled fan interest as they battled the Cubs, a gifted team with four future Hall of Famers (infielders Ernie Banks and Ron Santo, outfielder Billy Williams, and pitcher Ferguson Jenkins) for the Eastern Division title.

During spring training, Art Shamsky, one of the few legitimate long-ball threats the Mets had, injured his back. As the Mets' roster had to be cut down to twenty-five players, the Mets ultimately decided to send the bed-ridden Shamsky down to the Minors to get back into playing shape. Shamsky was upset: no veteran player likes being sent down to the Minors. But Hodges promised Shamsky he would recall him as soon as he was physically able to play. "Unlike a lot of other managers I played for," Shamsky told me, "Hodges looked at you and told you exactly what was on his mind." Hodges kept his promise. Shamsky returned to the Mets and hit fourteen home runs and was the only Met (other than Jones) to bat .300 or higher that season.

Bob Mandt, one of the Mets' first employees back in 1962, started as the team's mailroom clerk. By 1969, having moved up in the ranks to ticket department manager, one of his duties was to make sure the Mets' manager received two sets (four seats to a set) of A and B club boxes on the first base side of the dugout for every home game. But by 1969 ticket demand was up and Mandt received orders from his boss, Mets vice president for business operations, Jim Thomson, to give Hodges only one set of club boxes behind first base and a second set in the less desirable area behind home plate. A tough, broad-chested Irishman, Thomson was not the kind of guy you bothered with a lot of questions. But Mandt knew Hodges would be displeased. It was a well-established policy which seats the Mets' manager received. Mandt asked if anyone had told Hodges. Thomson replied, "Don't worry about it."

On Opening Day, April 8, a few hours before game time, thirty-three-year-old Bob Mandt sat in his office at Shea taking care of last-minute details. Opening Days were always hectic, but this one was particularly crazed. The Mets' opponent was the Montreal Expos, one of two new National League expansion teams, and there were last-minute arrangements to be made for Jean Drapeau, the Montreal mayor, and other Canadian dignitaries. Mandt's phone rang. "Bob," Hodges said, "I only received one set of club boxes." Mandt hemmed and hawed. "Bob," Hodges said, "could you please come to my office?"

Mandt had been to parties listening to Casey Stengel talk for hours and gone out for beers with Wes Westrum, but to Mandt, Hodges was a mysterious and "awesome figure." Mandt made a beeline for Hodges's office, which didn't even have a private entrance, so anyone coming in or out had to pass through the Mets' clubhouse. When he arrived, Hodges's door was open and he was talking with one of his coaches. Dick Young was waiting just outside the office to see Hodges. Upon spotting Mandt, Hodges dismissed the coach, bypassed Young, and invited Mandt in. Hodges's office was spare: a gray metal desk, a Charlie Brown statue, a leather-armed swivel desk chair, a couch, a couple of guest chairs, a "'*Something good*' is going to happen to us" sign, and a large illuminated wall clock. The desk was neat and tidy with a few family photos. The eighteen-inch-tall, stuffed white rabbit (a gift from a fan who was convinced a mere rabbit's foot would never bring the Mets enough luck) would not arrive until that September. Already in uniform, Hodges sat in his swivel chair and leaned forward, his massive hands folded in front of him on the desk. Hodges starred into Mandt's hazel peepers. "Bob, who made the decision to give me only one set of club seats?" Mandt said he didn't know. Hodges stared and said nothing. In his shirt and tie and horn-rimmed glasses, Mandt held his ground. In later years Joe Torre (then the Mets manager) would call Mandt, Clark Kent. The tension was unbearable. Mandt thought this is what it must feel like to die. Finally, Hodges relented and rephrased: "Who told you to give me only one set?"

"Thomson."

"Thanks, Bob," Hodges said being both polite and dismissive. Fifteen minutes later, Mandt's phone rang. It was Thomson. "Did you see Gil?" he asked. Thomson didn't wait for a reply; but before he slammed down the phone, he said, "Send him the other four seats."

That day, despite the presence of Drapeau, New York City mayor John Lindsay was not in attendance. This was in stark contrast to the end of the season—after the Mets had captured the hearts of the entire city—when Lindsay would be in front of the cameras cavorting with Mets players at every opportunity. As Robert Lipsyte wrote, "Lindsay came to baseball late, but often."

But to show his appreciation for Hodges, Rabbi Silber was at Shea on Opening Day to give a special invocation before the game. The Mets lost to the Expos, 11–10. Despite the loss, Gene Mauch, the former Phillies manager then leading Montreal, knew these were not the same old Mets. "In the old days," Mauch said, "we'd come in here for nine games. We'd win four, the Mets would give us three and the others we'd scramble for. It won't happen this year."

Despite that assessment, the first month of the season, the Mets had a losing record and a crucial personnel change wasn't going well. Hodges had hoped that Amos Otis, a rookie center fielder, would relish the chance to play third base in place of the thirty-six-year-old Ed Charles, whose career appeared over. But Otis, a generation removed from Hodges's if-I-can-help-us-win-I'll-play-anywhere philosophy, didn't want to play third. He had good reason. Otis had not only been an All-Star outfielder in the International League, but he was the fastest player on the Mets and his speed was of little utility at third. As a result, Otis was a work-in-progress unwilling to progress. The Mets' director of player personnel, Whitey Herzog, was adamant that Agee should be moved to right and Otis be given the center-field job. But Hodges, with a solid dose of Irene's moral rigidity, expected his players to do whatever was best for the team—even if it meant playing in an unfamiliar position—and would not change his mind. Jim McAndrew recalled that was the only time he ever saw Hodges and Herzog argue. Otis was soon back in the Minors and the left-handed rookie Wayne Garrett settled into a platoon with Charles.

As of May 30 the Mets were in fourth place, nine games behind the first-place Cubs. Other than Cleon Jones, their hitting was mediocre. Tommie Agee was batting .190 and Hodges benched him.

A game that typified both the Mets' early-season play in 1969 and Nolan Ryan's career with the Mets took place on May 3 in Chicago. Injuries to Jerry Koosman and Jim McAndrew gave Ryan his first start of the season. He out-pitched Ferguson Jenkins through six innings, and the Mets led 2–0. In the seventh, with no outs, Chicago had runners on first and second. A time out was called and Ryan was told to be ready for a bunt, in which case he was instructed to throw to third base to get the lead runner, thirty-eight-year-old Ernie Banks. As expected, the batter bunted and Ryan fielded the ball but "then flung it into left field." Banks scored. Hodges then came out to the mound to get Ryan "refocused." Ryan struck out the next batter and Jenkins was due up. Leo Durocher pinch-hit for Jenkins, and Ryan blew two fastballs for strikes past the pinch hitter. But after the second pitch, Ryan "turned his back to home plate, looked gloomily toward the outfield, then limped into the clubhouse" with a strained groin muscle. The Mets lost, 3–2.

By early May the Cubs had the best record in baseball. In addition to Jenkins, they had two other excellent pitchers, Bill Hands and Ken Holtzman, as well as the best infield in the National League: Ernie Banks at first, Glenn Beckert at second, Don Kessinger at short, Ron Santo at third, and Randy Hundley behind the plate, each an All-Star that season. But the Cubs had an Achilles' heel in center field, where Adolfo Phillips had been their starter the past two seasons. Phillips had slipped considerably at bat but was still an asset with his glove at a crucial position. In 1969 Phillips broke a bone in his right hand during spring training and took a few weeks to return to the starting lineup; Durocher complained that Phillips "doesn't want to play."

By May, Durocher had benched Phillips and made rookie Don Young his starting center fielder. Young had played Single A ball the previous season, making his promotion to the Majors a huge jump. That June, around the time the Mets were acquiring first baseman Donn Clendenon from the Expos, the Cubs traded Phillips. Durocher deemed him expendable. At the time of the trade, the Cubs were twenty games over .500, 38-18. After the trade, they were 54-52. Before the acquisition of Clendenon, the Mets were 30-25; after, 70-36. From a managerial perspective, the turning point of the season was Durocher's knee-jerk reaction to Phillips' slow return from injury juxtaposed with the Donn Clendenon trade.

Beginning on May 28, the Mets won eleven straight games, moving into second place. Not only was the winning streak the longest in Mets history, it was the first time the Mets were in second place in June. That streak, soon followed by the acquisition of Clendenon, solidified the Mets. In each of Clendenon's first sixteen games, he drove in either the lead or the winning run. Before losing a couple of games to the Phillies at the end of June, the Mets won twenty of twenty-five games, the best stretch in their history.

In early July, the Mets won five in a row on the road and returned home to play three games against the Cubs in the first crucial series in Mets history. Four days later, the Mets would travel to Chicago to play three games. Hodges then offered a quote bordering—for him—on the hyperbolic. "There's no question about it," Hodges said, "the two series with the Cubs are bigger than any others. . . . We need to take two out of three each time." They did, leaving the Mets only three and a half games behind the Cubs and revealing much about Durocher and Hodges's divergent approaches.

The first game, on July 8 before fifty-five thousand fans, had a World Series intensity, and journalists from all over the country were in attendance. The game even brought out one of the more famous broadcasters of the era, Howard Cosell. As Cosell did his pregame interview with Hodges, in the stands behind them kids were screaming for Hodges to sign autographs. After the interview, wise-guy Cosell turned toward the stands and yelled in a voice that could be heard in the upper deck, "Listen, kids . . . Hodges told me to tell you that right after the game he'll be outside with a ball for each one of you."

Jerry Koosman started against Ferguson Jenkins. Going into the bottom of the ninth, Jenkins had allowed just one hit and the Cubs led 3–1. Koosman was the Mets' lead-off batter, but Hodges sent Ken Boswell up to pinch-hit. Boswell hit a ball to shallow center field. Don Young misjudged the ball and it fell in for a double. After Tommie Agee fouled out, Hodges sent Donn Clendenon up to pinch-hit. Clendenon hit a drive to deep left-center. Young caught it but crashed into the outfield wall and dropped the ball. Runners were on second and third, one out, and Cleon Jones tied the game with a double. After a walk and a ground out, runners were on second and third with two outs and Ed Kranepool was up. Rather than walk Kranepool to set up a force play at any base, Durocher had Jenkins pitch to him. Kranepool hit a soft liner over the shortstop's head, giving the Mets a memorable come-from-behind victory. The win, in combination with the spontaneous outpouring of emotions on the field and in the stands, prompted the *New York Times*—for the first time since 1962—to run a front-page story about a Mets' triumph. Up in the television booth, Mets announcer Lindsay Nelson was screaming, "It's absolute bedlam! You could not believe it! It's absolute bedlam!"

Managers pride themselves on maintaining a lead in the late innings. Nothing is more of a morale booster for a team than a come-from-behind win in the ninth. The Cubs, on the other hand, lost the game and their composure. And it started with their manager. In the Cubs' locker room after the game, in front of his players and the press, Durocher laced into Don Young: "It's tough to win when your centerfielder can't catch a fucking fly ball." Durocher said, "Jenkins pitched his heart out. But when one man can't catch a fly ball, it's a disgrace. He stands there watching one, and then gives up on the other. . . . My fucking three-year-old could have caught those balls!"

The Mets won the second game of the series as Tom Seaver retired the first twenty-five Cubs batters in succession. But the Cubs' new center fielder, Jimmy Qualls (playing in place of Young), ended Seaver's bid for a perfect game with a single with one out in the ninth.

The next day, the Mets lost the final game of the series. The Cubs broke it open in the fifth when Al Weis dropped a low throw during a rundown and Ken Boswell gracefully tagged a runner without the ball in his glove. After the game, Hodges didn't blame either player for the loss. Hodges was not one to belittle a player for a physical (as opposed to a mental) error. "Errors," Hodges wrote, "are part of the game." In fact, he didn't say much of anything, other than, "It was a good series anytime you take two out of three. I'm happy about it. Not satisfied, but happy."

Hodges sat and ate his new postgame low-calorie meal, a cup of yogurt, as reporters surrounded his desk. Jack Lang fiddled with Hodges's Charlie Brown statue. Lang had a relationship with Hodges going back to Ebbets Field and was not intimidated by the silence. But even Lang hedged. "You don't have to answer this question if you don't want to," Lang asked, "but did you notice any mistakes out on the field, besides the mechanical ones?" Hodges said, "No," and he didn't say anything more.

The questions kept coming, but the only thing Hodges admitted was that he didn't like raspberry yogurt, "but it's all they've got." Finally, one reporter had enough and headed for the door saying, "I can't take the quiet."

"I can't stand the quiet, either," Hodges said, "but I can't leave."

Hodges's responses—at least those longer than the question—were often bathed in a subtleness that would be best appreciated in the *New Yorker*, not the back page of the *Daily News*. When Hodges was asked about a play at first base in which Ron Santo was called safe because Ed Kranepool had taken his foot off the base, Lang told Hodges, "If anyone should know about taking his foot off the base, it's you." Hodges smiled. "I wish you'd told me that before I went out to argue the play," he said, "I could have used that line."

In the other clubhouse, Leo Durocher was asked if the fans had finally seen "the real Cubs."

"No," the Lip snarled, "but those are the real Mets."

That same month, in a slick marketing campaign—in contrast to Hodges's book, *The Game of Baseball*, which had been published in March with little promotion—Ken "Hawk" Harrelson's *Hawk* was excerpted in *Sports Illustrated*. Not surprisingly, when asked about Harrelson's negative comments about Hodges, Tom Seaver, Jerry Koosman, and Ed Charles circled the wagons around their manager. "Gil handles players like men, not babies," said Charles, "If someone wants to be petted, that's different. But if Gil hounds anyone, it's like a man. All I can say is he's done a wonderful job with me." Surprisingly, the player with the most realistic approach was Ron Swoboda. "Those are stock comments that could be made about most managers," he said. "I've heard that 'holier-than-thou' description of a dozen managers. Once you become a manager, you get blamed for all the mistakes made on the field. It's a lousy job."

When asked about Harrelson's book, Hodges said, "I've got no comment." But Hodges must have spoken about the book with his family's priest back in Petersburg, because in Father Vieck's papers, I found a copy of an article, "Harrelson Slams Ex-Manager," with a handwritten note attached that read, "He was deeply hurt." But Hodges rebuffed the hurt with humor: a few days after his "no comment," when asked if he would make a statement regarding *Hawk*, Hodges said, "Probably. But we could all be old then."

During the 1969 season, after a Cubs victory, Ron Santo began a routine of jumping up as high as he could and clicking his heels together. The fans loved it, but it was considered unprofessional under baseball's unwritten code that you should never show up the opposition with gestures. That July, after the Cubs' victory in the opening game of the three-game series with the Mets at Wrigley Field, Santo did his jump-and-click routine. The next day, before the second game of the series, Santo and Hodges brought their team's lineup cards out to the umpires. Santo, well aware that he was breaking one of baseball's unwritten rules, turned to Hodges and said, "The only reason I click my heels is because the fans will boo me if I don't."

Hodges replied, "You remind me of Tug McGraw. When he was young and immature and nervous, he used to jump up and down, too. He doesn't do it anymore."

By then, Hodges had spent a lot of time watching Tug McGraw. In 1965, when the left-handed McGraw was only twenty, he had shown tremendous potential when he became the first Mets pitcher to defeat Sandy Koufax. But during spring training in 1968, Hodges wouldn't let McGraw practice his most effective pitch, a screwball, hoping he would work more on his curve. As a result, McGraw pitched terribly and Hodges sent him down to the Minors. But in the spring of 1969, Hodges needed an effective lefty in the bullpen to complement the veteran right-hander Ron Taylor. Hodges decided McGraw was his man. In this regard Hodges was in lockstep with the colorful Whitey Herzog. "If you don't have outstanding relief pitching," Herzog once said, "you might as well piss on the fire, and call the dogs."

Hodges had three criteria for a reliever: strength ("so he can work frequently"), guts ("because when you send for him, you're in trouble"), and "a guy who's . . . got the overpowering fast ball for the strikeout." McGraw was strong and fearless and had honed his screwball into a devastating strikeout pitch during his season in the Minors. On the next to last day of spring training, Hodges called McGraw into his office and told him he would always be an average starter, but could be outstanding as a reliever. Hodges then gave McGraw a choice: did he want to be a starter in Jacksonville or a reliever for the Mets? McGraw gave Hodges the answer he anticipated.

In the second game of the season, McGraw pitched six and a third innings in relief, allowing just one run. Hodges knew McGraw was ready to take on more responsibility and again called McGraw into his office. As McGraw recalled, "He . . . complimented me on the job I had done . . . as a long relief man. 'I need a stopper. I am giving you the job.' I walked out without much emotion. My confidence had been high. Now it was just a bit higher." In 1969 McGraw finished with a record of 9-3 and saved several crucial games.

But if McGraw could bring order to chaos on the field, off it he was, in the baseball jargon of that era, a flake. But he was an entertaining flake. When asked the difference between playing on grass and Astroturf, McGraw said, "I don't know, I never smoked Astroturf." Once, a few seasons later on Camera Day, McGraw blackened his face, put on Willie Mays's uniform (Mays was then playing for the Mets), and went onto the field before a game to sign autographs. "No problem," Mays said, "McGraw is McGraw." Hodges dealt with McGraw, as he would any other player, with one set of rules. When McGraw showed up at spring training with a mustache and General Custer hairdo, Hodges had him "shave the former and clip the latter."

Yet, like Tommie Agee, for McGraw, "Gil's door was always open." McGraw respected his old-school manager. Along with his mother, father, and brother, he included Hodges in a small group of people who meant the most to him. "When Gil was running the club," McGraw said, "you always felt sane, even if you were kind of insane."

But Hodges was not immune from his own emotional moments. One took place on July 30, 1969, in the second game of a doubleheader against the Astros at Shea Stadium. Houston won the first game, 16-3. The loss was particularly frustrating. The Mets had trailed by only two runs entering the ninth, but the Astros then scored eleven runs as they became the first team in National League history to hit two grand slam home runs in the same inning. In the second game, the Astros jumped out to a 7–0 lead in the third inning. To a chorus of boos, Hodges removed Gary Gentry and replaced him with Nolan Ryan. The first batter Ryan faced hit a ball to left field that Cleon Jones went after in a "nonchalant" way, and his throw back to the infield was described as a "balloon."

Hodges called time out. To more boos he started to walk toward the pitcher's mound. It is doubtful that Hodges intended to take Ryan out of the game; he had pitched to only one batter and the Astros pitcher was due up next. More likely, Hodges, who believed that necessity sometimes requires "a blast that wakes a player up," was intending to blow reveille for Cleon Jones. Hodges was superstitious. During the Mets' eleven-game winning streak, he hit infield practice for twelve straight games until the Mets lost. He also never stepped on the foul lines when walking over them. But this time when Hodges walked onto the field, he barely missed stepping on the first-base foul line. "When he was like that," Bud Harrelson said, "you just said, 'Holy Shit.'"

Hodges walked past Ryan. After making eye contact with Hodges, Harrelson made a face that said, "Me?" Hodges shook his head no and rolled his eyes toward left field as if saying, "The other guy."

It made no difference to Hodges that Cleon Jones was leading the National League with a .346 average, no difference that he had been the starting left fielder in the All-Star Game, no difference that the New York Catholic Youth Organization had recently voted him the "Most Popular Met." Jones had broken rule one of Hodges's ten commandments. As Hodges wrote, "It's not whether . . . a teammate caught the ball, it's 'Did he give it a try?' That's very important, because from Little League to the major leagues, that try is the one thing that each player owes to his teammates."

Hodges and Jones stood alone in left field. The record differs as to what was said. Jones's version: "What's wrong?" "What do you mean what's wrong?" "I don't like the way you went after that last ball." "Gil, we talked about this in Montreal. You know I have a bad ankle and as long as I wasn't going to hurt the team I would continue to play. Look down." Hodges's feet were in a puddle. "It is bad out here. I didn't know it was that bad. You probably need to come out of the game." "Fine."

Hodges's version: "Are you hurt?" "No." "Come with me."

No matter what was said, Hodges turned and started back to the dugout with Jones sloshing along a few steps behind him. Hodges had acted totally out of character. The man who usually reprimanded his players in private had pulled a player out of a game in the middle of an inning in direct violation of one of baseball's unwritten rules—never show a player up publicly. But to Hodges, that rule was valid only if a player gave it "that try." The incident became baseball folklore. Four decades later while discussing the poor fielding habits of the Washington Nationals players, and what their manager should do about it, writer John Feinstein suggested, "Pull a Gil Hodges."

Up in the press box, Matt Winick, the Mets' assistant director of public relations, waited for the phone to ring. During a game his job was to notify the press on the severity of injuries. But Winick couldn't call the Mets' dugout to find out about Cleon Jones. Hodges had a firm rule: No one was allowed to call the Mets' dugout during a game. Hodges wanted to make sure he made all in-game decisions without any interference. Due to Hodges's rule, Winick usually received a call from the Mets' trainer regarding injuries. But this time it was Hodges's voice at the other end: "He has a bad leg." Winick repeated that to the reporters, who began shouting questions. *Which leg? What's wrong? Will he miss any games?* Hodges offered nothing more, and as Winick later said, "I certainly wasn't going to say another word."

"You look into the mirror after something doesn't work out," Hodges once said, "and you ask yourself, 'Would I do the same thing again?' If you can say *yes*, that's fine. But when you start getting *no* back from the mirror, then you're in trouble."

The next day, behind the closed door of his office, Hodges asked Jones one loud and pointed question: "Look in that mirror and tell me if Cleon Jones is giving me 100 percent." Hodges benched Jones for two games and then gradually worked him back into the lineup. Not one to hold a grudge, Hodges put the incident behind him. Later in the season, with Jones in contention for the batting title, Hodges moved him from third to first in the batting order.

"It may help him," Hodges said, "pick up the points he needs to catch up. All of us . . . want him to win it."

Jones had a harder time recovering. "It's over with," Cleon Jones said a few years later while Hodges was still his manager, "and I don't like to talk about it. Maybe he was making a point. Anyway I know I'll never forget it."

Legend has it that the Mets suddenly improved after the Jones incident. But the Mets played losing baseball (seven wins, eight losses) in the subsequent two-week period ending on August 13 when the Mets, then in Houston, lost their third straight game to the Astros, 8–2. At that point, the Mets had fallen nine and a half games behind the Cubs. In the *Daily News*, "Basement Bertha," Bill Gallo's iconic cartoon character that symbolized the frustrations of all Mets fans, said, "Hey, Gillie—Don't tell me that kid on Apollo '69 is comin' back to earth!"

That night, Hodges shut the door to the visitor's clubhouse in the Astrodome. Timed so his players would have something to think about on the long flight back to New York, Hodges gave the Mets "a real ass-chewing," wrote Donn Clendenon. The "thunder" lasted twenty minutes. "He didn't holler much, [but] when he did . . . it shook the whole team up. . . . Gil told us . . . some of the guys wouldn't be back . . . next year if we didn't shape up. Gil's ass-chewing was the real turning point for the season."

After the "ass-chewing," the Mets returned to New York for a ten-game home stand beginning on August 15 against the San Diego Padres. Tom Seaver, who had recently been bothered by muscle strain in his pitching arm, was scheduled to start, but minutes before the game was going to begin after a thirty-minute rain delay, Hodges replaced Seaver with Gary Gentry as his starter. Hodges was concerned that if Seaver started the game and it was again delayed, it would add to the stress on his arm. In addition, if the game began and was then called due to rain, Seaver would have been utilized in a no-decision and unavailable for the rest of the series. The game was stopped in the bottom of the first inning and was called off about an hour later. A doubleheader was then scheduled for the next day and a well-rested Tom Seaver started the first game. Hodges appeared a "supreme prophet" as Seaver shut out San Diego and the Mets swept four games from the Padres.

The Mets' next game was against San Francisco. Juan Marichal pitched for the Giants; Gary Gentry for the Mets. Gentry threw ten innings of shutout ball and was replaced by Tug McGraw. In the thirteenth, with two out and Willie McCovey at bat, Hodges called for a four-outfielder alignment, moving his third baseman, Bobby Pfeil, to the left-field corner and shifting Cleon Jones to left-center. McCovey hit what appeared to be a home run, but Jones, perfectly placed, jumped up, bounced off the fence at the 371-foot sign, and caught the ball for the final out of the inning to maintain the tie. Without the defensive change, Jones would not have been in position to catch the ball. In the fourteenth, Tommie Agee hit a home run for a 1–0 Mets win. The Mets won nine of ten on the home stand.

After the Mets returned home from their final West Coast road trip, they won three of four games against the Phillies and were just two games behind the Cubs. By then, the story of the Mets' metamorphosis was spreading. Commercial pilots flying into Kennedy Airport began announcing that day's Mets score. In San Francisco a tavern on Mission and Sixth hung a large sign on its front wall reading, "This is the Year. Go, Go, Go, Mets." The crew of the aircraft carrier *America* sent Hodges a telegram, "Down the Cubs. Full speed ahead." Joe Durso wrote, "The Mets had become . . . a national institution."

The Cubs arrived at Shea to play a two-game set in early September. If the Mets could win both, they would be in a first-place tie. In the first game, Jerry Koosman faced Bill Hands. Hoping to intimidate the Mets, Leo Durocher ordered Hands to throw his first pitch of the game at Tommie Agee's head. Agee hit the dirt, barely avoiding being knocked senseless. With his first pitch in the next inning, Koosman hit Ron Santo on the arm. But Durocher's strategy didn't produce the intended results. In Agee's next at bat, he hit a two-run homer, and the Cubs were the ones who were intimidated and backing away from the plate. Koosman struck out thirteen for a 3–2 win. "Nobody told me to throw at Santo. Hodges didn't say a word," Koosman said. "It's just something you learn. It's how the game is played."

The next day, desperate to make sure the Cubs' losing streak did not reach six games, Durocher decided to pitch Ferguson Jenkins on two days' rest. But before Jenkins took the mound, during the top of the first with the Cubs at bat, a black cat appeared on the field near home plate. The cat walked toward the Cubs' dugout, stopped directly in front of Durocher, stared at him, and then disappeared beneath the stands. Santo said, "It freaked me out a little." Jenkins found it "a little eerie."

How did the cat get on the field? The grounds crew at Shea denied any involvement. "We knew that Durocher was one of the most superstitious men in baseball," Donn Clendenon later wrote. "Leo always sat in the same spot . . . on the right-hand side of the Cubs' dugout, near the bat-rack. So three days before . . . we went out and got a black cat and fed the cat sardines from Durocher's favorite spot in the visitor's dugout."

Whether it was the cat or the short rest, lacking his usual control, Jenkins walked two batters in the first. Both scored and the Mets were on their way to a 7–1 win. After the game, a policeman was sent to Hodges's office to let him know Joan Payson would be making an appearance in the Mets' locker room to congratulate her team. Hodges quickly instructed his players to get their pants on. When Mrs. Payson arrived, wrote Robert Lipsyte, "She looked even more excited than she had in 1968 when one of her horses won the Belmont Stakes."

The day after the cat outstared the Lip, Chicago lost to Philadelphia, and the Mets swept the Expos in a doubleheader and moved into first place. The Mets then flew to Pittsburgh for a four-game series with the Pirates beginning with a doubleheader on September 12. The Pirates started right-handed pitchers for both games; Art Shamsky, part of Hodges's left-handed-hitting platoon, expected to be in the starting lineup. But the games coincided with the Jewish holiday of Rosh Hashanah and Shamsky had to make a decision whether or not to take the day off due to his religious beliefs. Shamsky decided to get his manager's opinion. Consistent with his usual methodology, Hodges put the question back on his player. "Follow your conscience," Hodges said, "and I will support that." Shamsky later wrote, "I walked out of his office with more respect for him than ever before."

Shamsky sat out both games but the Mets swept the doubleheader by 1–0 scores with Jerry Koosman and Don Cardwell not only shutting out the Pirates, but both driving in the only run. After victories in St. Louis and Montreal, the Mets returned to Shea in first place with a record of 91-58. But they lost their next three games by a combined score of 20 to 2 to Pittsburgh. Yet, despite losing three straight, Hodges decided upon a calm approach. "We've played badly," Hodges said, "for three games. It's not good to lose this way. We have to hit better, play better. But it's only three games. We'll be all right. Did the Cubs lose?"

They had; the Mets were still in first place. The Mets wouldn't lose another game until the last day of the regular season as their pitchers threw forty-two consecutive scoreless innings over five games. In contrast, the Cubs lost eighteen out of their final twenty-seven games, including eight in a row from September 3 through 11, their longest losing streak in over two years.

The Mets clinched the Eastern Division title on September 24 as Gary Gentry shut out the St. Louis Cardinals, 6–0. The Mets gained the lead when Donn Clendenon hit a three-run home run. His teammates ran out onto the field to congratulate him. But it was only the first inning; the game's outcome was still in doubt. One person in the Mets' dugout never moved. Hodges, wrote Tom Seaver, "never allowed himself even a grin . . . . His eyes remained on the field, studying Steve Carleton, the St. Louis pitcher, studying the game."

After the game, Seaver poured a bottle of champagne over Hodges's head signifying how sweet the win was for Hodges; it came one year to the day since his heart attack. A telegram from Atlanta read, "Happy to see you're No. 1. Hope your team does as well as your heart. Linton H. Bishop, Jr., M.D."

Hodges's prediction that the Mets could win 85 games proved low. The Mets won 100 games as Hodges consistently outmanaged Leo Durocher. In July, about the same time Hodges was giving Cleon Jones his wake-up call, Durocher was missing-in-action. On the Saturday of a weekend series at Wrigley Field against the Dodgers, Durocher complained he was ill and left the ballpark before the game was over. That game went into extra innings and the Cubs lost. The next day, Durocher, again claiming he was ill, failed to even show up. The press later learned that Durocher was not sick, but had left the game early on Saturday to fly with his new wife (his third) on a chartered plane to Wisconsin for visiting day at the sleep-away camp of his twelve-year-old stepson. Yet, despite taking days off for himself, Durocher insisted on playing his key players without rest throughout the brutally hot Chicago summer when Wrigley Field had no lights and every home game was played in the afternoon. "If a man had a slight injury or was just plain-tired, Leo didn't want to hear about it," Ferguson Jenkins said. "He just rubbed a man's nose in the dirt and sent him back out there. You played until you dropped."

Durocher had set a poor example. Late in the season when the Cubs were just three games out of first place, thirteen players missed bed check in Montreal. When he learned over half his team had broken curfew, Durocher admitted, "It was my job to motivate them, and I had failed."

After the "ass-chewing," the Mets played their best baseball of the season, winning thirty-eight of their final forty-nine games. Johnny Murphy, who had played for Hall of Fame manager Joe McCarthy on pennant-winning teams, was not a man prone to hyperbole. Of Hodges's 1969 performance, Murphy said, "I never saw a better job of managing."

As a senior partner in a brokerage firm, M. Donald Grant understood finances. And like Branch Rickey, who felt it was better to win a pennant than a World Series because players on a championship team cost more to re-sign, Grant knew the same was true for managers. So a few days after the Mets clinched the Eastern Division title—but before the playoffs began—Grant sent his chauffeured limo to pick Hodges up and bring him to his Wall Street office.

Ted Williams had recently signed a contract to manage the Senators for $200,000 a year. In 1969 the Senators had their best season since 1945, but finished in fourth place. If the Mets won the World Series, it wouldn't be unreasonable for Hodges to expect a six-figure contract. Grant nipped that one early, offering Hodges a new three-year contract for $70,000 a year.

On Wall Street, as a warning against excess amid the bulls and bears, people like to say, "The pigs get slaughtered."

Gil Hodges was no pig.

In response to Grant's offer, he simply said, "Give me a pen."

22

MIRACLE

These young men showed that you can realize the most impossible dream of all.

The Atlanta Braves, the Mets' opponent in the inaugural National League divisional playoff series, won seventeen of their final twenty-one games to win the NL West. They had two great power hitters, Henry Aaron and Orlando Cepeda, and a third future Hall of Famer, pitcher Phil Niekro. But the Mets had defeated the Braves eight times in their twelve meetings that season and Hodges was optimistic. "Their strength is their hitting," he said. "But I think our pitchers should be able to take care of that." When a reporter suggested to Lum Harris, the Braves' manager, that the Mets would sweep his team, Harris visibly flinched. "Nobody's going to beat us three straight," Harris shot back, "nobody." Harris and Hodges were both in for an awakening.

The best three out of five series opened in Atlanta. Game one starter Tom Seaver lacked his usual control and the game was tied 4–4 in the seventh. On a full count, Seaver threw Aaron a curve ball. "I was guessing curve," Aaron said after the game. "If he'd thrown me a fast ball I probably would've struck out." Instead, Aaron hit a home run to give Atlanta the lead as Hodges noticed "the whole [Mets] bench sagged." But in the eighth, the Mets scored two runs to retake the lead, 6–5. With two outs and the bases loaded, Seaver was due to bat. Hodges could let Seaver bat or send up a pinch hitter hoping to break the game open and entrust reliever Ron Taylor (who was already throwing in the bullpen) to get the last six outs of the game. Hodges sent left-handed-hitting J. C. Martin—a .209 hitter in 1969—up to pinch hit against Niekro, a righty with a terrific knuckleball. Martin hit one sharply to center field, driving in three runs, and Taylor held the Braves scoreless to secure the win. Afterward,

Hodges made no mention of his crucial decision. Instead, he only spoke about his team. "Our kids never gave up," he said, "just as they never gave up all year. They bounced back."

A reporter unused to Hodges's humor asked him if winning the first game of the playoff series was especially gratifying. Hodges looked the interviewer over in a way that "could be considered interested or deadly, depending on the beholder's mood." Then, very slowly, Hodges said, "It is most gratifying to win the first game of the playoff series, and it is gratifying and important, to win the second and the third." The intimidated reporter was gone by the time Hodges reached his punch line, adding, "I talked to Casey right before the game."

Regular season or playoffs, Hodges was unchanged. What to him was a silly question received a polite but cutting response. And if a player reported to the clubhouse late, he got fined, it didn't matter who the player was or what the effect might be on an already pressure-packed playoff series. During the Atlanta series, Tommie Agee was putting on his uniform in the clubhouse at 11:00 a.m.; his teammates were already out on the field. When Hodges spotted Agee, he said, "Congratulations." Someone asked Agee why Hodges had congratulated him. "We were supposed to be on the field at ten minutes to eleven." Agee said, "That cost me $25." When it was suggested that Hodges would return the money if he had a good game, Agee said, "No. Everybody on this club knows the rules."

Faced with more right-handed starting pitching in games two and three, Hodges continued to use used his left-handed platoon: Ed Kranepool at first, Ken Boswell at second, Wayne Garrett at third, and Art Shamsky in right. They came through to offset poor pitching performances by Jerry Koosman and Gary Gentry. In the second game, after Martin Luther King's widow, Coretta, threw out the ceremonial first pitch, the Mets jumped out to a 9–1 lead. But Koosman gave up six runs and the bullpen, first Ron Taylor and then Tug McGraw, secured the win.

Hodges saved his boldest move for game three back in New York. Atlanta scored two runs off Gentry in the first inning (Aaron hit a two-run homer that hit the flag pole in center field 410 feet from home plate), and by the third inning they had Gentry on the ropes. With runners on second and third, and no outs, Braves slugger Rico Carty drove a long foul ball to left field that missed being a home run by only a few feet. With the count 1-2 on Carty, Hodges made the highly unorthodox move of pulling Gentry out mid-batter. But Hodges had seen enough at bats where a good hitter like Carty, after getting a read on a pitcher, follows up a hard-hit foul ball by straightening it out for a base hit. Hodges figured he needed just one more strike to retire Carty and had the luxury of first base being open in case Carty drew a walk. It was a perfect situation for Nolan Ryan to finish off Carty, who had never faced Ryan before. The Braves' bench told Carty what to expect. "Heck," said Aaron after the game, "we knew what he threw."

Hodges hoped the speed of Ryan's pitches would surprise Carty. With his first pitch, a fastball, Ryan struck Carty out and got the Mets out of the inning without yielding a run. Nolan Ryan pitched seven innings, allowing three hits and two runs as the Mets came from behind to win on a home run by Wayne Garrett.

Afterward, Johnny Murphy noted that the "seven untouchables" that Braves general manager Paul Richards had belittled had won a pennant. Richards replied, "They ought to send the Mets to Vietnam. They'll end the war in three days."

In the midst of a challenging reelection campaign he wasn't expected to win, Mayor John Lindsay had made the mistake of having his name announced before the third game. The fans booed him louder, and longer, than they booed the Braves. But after the game, cameras captured Lindsay laughing as Jerry Grote doused him with champagne. Leaving nothing to chance, Lindsay made sure to hug Hodges. "Gil," Lindsay said, "you're the most wonderful man I've ever seen." In the Braves' locker room, Lum Harris sat in a state of disbelief. "I admire Gil Hodges," Harris said. "To me, there's no question he's manager of the year. But I still believe if we played 'em three more games, we'd beat 'em three straight."

Before the World Series began, Hodges felt relaxed. He was playing with house money; even the Mets' head of scouting, Bob Scheffing, told Hodges that the Orioles were the best team he had seen all year and the Mets couldn't beat them. "Sometimes," Robert Lipsyte wrote, "in the post-game crush, the subtlety of Hodges is lost," but not on October 8, a rainy day in New York when team practice had been canceled and reporters were looking for an angle to fill up column space. With all other options washed away, they tried to get Hodges to give them a headline-worthy quote about the Orioles. At worst, with the New York City mayoral election only a few weeks away, perhaps a political quote; after all, Lindsay had attached himself to Hodges like a barnacle to a sturdy dock. The writers had no chance to get Hodges to say anything controversial, but they tried.

"Gil, have you been asked to endorse a candidate in New York's mayoralty election?"

"Yes, I have."

At this point, Hodges closed his mouth, Lipsyte wrote, "as if it were a trunk lid."

"And?"

"And I won't."

"Why?"

"It's not my place to become involved in politics. I was asked to come out for Kennedy, but I don't think I should become involved. I'd give the same advice to my players."

"Do you think people would vote for a candidate you endorsed?"

"I consider that a political question. Let's talk baseball."

"Who were the most important managers in your career?"

"All five of them—Leo Durocher, Charles Dressen, Burt Shotton, Walter Alston, and Casey."

"Which one had the most impact on your own managing style?"

"Each in his own particular way. You've got to be yourself."

"Some people think of you as a Walt Alston type."

"I see myself as Gil Hodges."

Hodges was an even greater challenge for Karl Ehrhardt, the Sign Man. Beginning in 1964, Ehrhardt, a commercial artist who grew up in Brooklyn rooting for the Dodgers and adopted the Mets in 1962, would come to Shea with dozens of signs he had created, sit in one of the box seats behind third base, and, depending upon what was taking place in the game, would hold up one of his 20-by-26-inch black placards with white-block lettering, and the television cameras would cut to him. In his black derby, Ehrhardt was an integral part of the team's persona. But out of the 1,200 Mets signs Ehrhardt eventually created, only one was specifically for Hodges. It featured a large hook and read "NOW GIL?" and was useless unless the Mets' pitcher was in trouble and Hodges was slow to bring in a reliever. In the four years Hodges managed the Mets, Ehrhardt used the sign only once. "Hodges," Ehrhardt told me, "was on top of things right away."

In Baltimore, Earl Weaver spent September hoping the Mets would beat out the Cubs. "[The Mets] had a bigger ballpark," Weaver said, "so we figured the World Series share would be bigger."

Weaver had reason to be confident. The Baltimore position players were superior to those on the Mets and they not only had two pitchers, Mike Cuellar and Dave McNally (each won at least twenty games that season) who could go head to head with Tom Seaver and Jerry Koosman, but a third starting pitcher, a future Hall of Famer, Jim Palmer, who was 16-4 with an ERA of 2.34. Like Leo Durocher, Weaver's demeanor set the tone for his team. "I don't believe in that team of destiny business," Brooks Robinson said before the Series began. "We're better than the Mets." And then, referring to the 1966 World Series when Baltimore swept a Dodgers team that relied on Sandy Koufax and Don Drysdale, Robinson added, "We beat those two guys and these guys can't be as good as them."

In Washington, Russell Baker, the Pulitzer Prize–winning writer, summed up the feeling in the nation's capital when he wrote, "I can't cheer [for the Mets]. Two years ago my team, the Senators, another expansion club, had also reached the takeoff point, thanks in part to a good manager, Gil Hodges. . . . Somehow Gil taught those kids who had never done anything before but muddle around in the cellar to play baseball. . . . Baseball was what Gil had the Senators playing by the end of the 1967 season. Next year, we figured. Wait until next year. Next year belongs to us. Then, one night . . . the Mets sneaked into town and stole Gil. No . . . I can't cheer."

But two others did. On October 9 at the Marine Air Terminal at La Guardia, as the Mets boarded a chartered United Airlines Caravelle bound for Baltimore, Ralph Kiner—who for the first time in his baseball career (as either a player or a broadcaster) was participating in a World Series—was happily interviewing them. A second, New York mayor John Lindsay, was also at the airport for a bit of shameless pandering as he read his poem "Ode to the New York Mets," a parody of "Casey at the Bat." Prior to boarding, but only after the photographers asked him to do so, Hodges raised his right hand and gave the "V for victory" sign. Some younger fans, born after World War II but all too familiar with the Vietnam War, thought Hodges had flashed the peace sign.

Hodges believed that if the Mets could get a split of the first two games in Baltimore, they would be in a much better position in New York for Games Three through Five. But Tom Seaver pitched poorly in Game One and Brooks Robinson ended the Mets' best threat of the day with one of his bare-handed, all-in-one-motion, overhand-scoop-and-throws to get Rod Gaspar for the final out of the seventh with two men on base. The Mets lost, 4-1.

After the game, the Orioles rubbed it in. Brooks Robinson said, "We are here to prove there is no Santa Claus." Earl Weaver upped the ante saying, "The Mets have desire. . . . [We] have just as much desire—and a lot more talent." Even as the Orioles' Don Buford circled the bases after hitting a home run on the second pitch of the game, he told Bud Harrelson, "You ain't seen nothing yet."

In Game Two Jerry Koosman pitched magnificently. He held the Orioles hitless for the first six innings, and Donn Clendenon gave the Mets a one-run lead with a fourth-inning home run. The lead held until the seventh when the Orioles tied the game. In the top of the ninth, with the game still tied, 1-1, and two outs, Ed Charles hit a bouncer just past Brooks Robinson for a single. Then on a 2-2 count to Jerry Grote, Hodges had a base running decision to make regarding Charles, who at thirty-six was no longer a fast runner. But as the visiting team, Hodges played for the win (not a tie) and signaled for Charles to run on the pitch. "Strictly speaking, it's not a hit-and-run play," Hodges said after the game, "it's a run-and-hit. The runner goes and takes his chances."

Grote came through with a ground ball single and Charles made it to third, which he wouldn't have been able to do had Hodges not ordered the run-and-hit. Al Weis was due up next. For Hodges the question was, should he let the weak-hitting Weis bat, or send up a pinch hitter? Hodges had faith in Weis and let him bat. Now the ball was in Earl Weaver's court. Should he order an intentional walk to Weis, a move likely to force Hodges to pinch-hit for Koosman? Weaver chose to pitch to Weis. "I didn't want Koosman out of there,"

Weaver said after the game. "He'd pitched eight hard innings and I'd rather have my big hitters face a tired Koosman in the ninth than a fresh arm."

Weis hit Dave McNally's first pitch for a single to shallow left field and Charles scored to put the Mets up 2–1. Based on how shallow Weis's hit was, had Charles been on second, he probably wouldn't have scored what turned out to be the game's winning run. In the bottom of the ninth, Koosman got the first two outs and Frank Robinson was the batter. Hodges wanted to prevent an extra-base hit, so he moved Weis from second to the left-field corner as a fourth outfielder. Hodges had used this technique against Robinson when he managed in the American League. But this time, the strategy ended up a wash as Robinson walked. The next batter, Boog Powell, also walked and with two on and two out, Brooks Robinson, one of the best clutch hitters in baseball, came to bat.

After the two walks (both on 3-2 pitches), Rube Walker noted, "Koosman had thrown 103 pitches, 22 of them in the ninth inning alone. He was cutting it a little too fine. You can start aiming the ball too much at that stage of things." Hodges brought Ron Taylor in to pitch.

"I would have liked to stay," Koosman said after the game, "but nobody questions Gil. . . . He came out and asked for the ball and said I had done a real fine job."

Taylor had pitched the last two innings the day before, but he was right-handed (Brooks Robinson hit right-handed) and Hodges's only pitcher with prior World Series experience. (Taylor had pitched in the 1964 World Series for the Cardinals.) Hodges gave Taylor no advice as to how to pitch to Robinson. All he said was, "You've got to get one man out." Robinson grounded one to Ed Charles, who fielded the ball cleanly, but his throw was low and it bounced in front of Donn Clendenon, who scooped it up out of the dirt. Robinson was out; the Mets had won; Hodges had his split; and Al Weis had hit the game-winner.

Ted Williams attended the first two games, sitting in a field box carefully studying the interactions between Hodges in the dugout and third base coach Eddie Yost. Williams concluded, "Hodges doesn't do anything. Once the game starts, Yost runs the club. He gives all the signs. Hodges just sits there."

"I never made my own decisions," Yost told me.

But you have to understand Williams's perspective. He was the first manager in baseball history to employ a bench coach. Williams was a genius at hitting, but strategy was not his thing; so he hired Joe Camacho, a grammar school principal who ran a summer baseball camp for Williams, to be his bench coach and handle all in-game strategy.

Hodges appeared to be just sitting there, but that was intentional. Since, as a player, Hodges had been so good at stealing other teams' signs, he went to extraordinary lengths to make sure his signs were not.

"Gil was so quick," Yost said, "the other team really didn't know where the signs were coming from, or when. He gave them, all right. But he gave them far ahead of time. Say there's a man on first, and the batter hits one of those first-to-third singles. As the runner is sliding into third, Gil is giving me the squeeze sign. I glance into the dugout and I see it. The other people in the park are watching the play, they don't see it." Some signals between Yost and Hodges were "discreet little things: a smile [perhaps explaining why Hodges rarely smiled during games], a wink of the eye, a certain slight move of the head."

It was, as Dick Young wrote, "the distraction of magicians, the distraction that makes the hand quicker than the eye. At all games involving a ball, 99.99% of the people watch the ball." Hodges used this to his advantage, making his signs pilfer-proof.

And game strategy was sacrosanct to Hodges. After Game Two, a reporter asked Hodges if he had originated the concept of using a four-man outfield. "Heavens no," said Hodges, "Branch Rickey invented it. He and John McGraw had the most brilliant minds baseball ever produced. They introduced almost every strategic concept."

In the Orioles' clubhouse, after losing just one game, arrogance turned to anger. Frank Robinson noted this was the first World Series game he had ever lost with the Orioles and he made a negative comment about the Mets. "I thought it was very strange that they didn't show any enthusiasm when they loaded the bases in the seventh inning," Robinson said, referring to Game One, adding that he saw no change in Game Two. Robinson's comments were relayed to Hodges.

"I'm glad to see that Frank is watching our bench," Hodges replied, "but I'm not concerned with what he says."

At Shea, the Orioles' third game starter, the right-handed Jim Palmer, brought Hodges's left-handed platoon off the bench after eight days off. Other managers might have continued to play their right-handed platoon based upon their success in the first two games in which the Mets batted .308. But the platoon system had worked well all summer and there was no reason to think otherwise in October. Gary Gentry held the Orioles scoreless through six and two-thirds innings, Nolan Ryan did the same for the balance of the game, and Tommie Agee almost single-handedly outplayed the Orioles in the field and at bat. Leading off the game, Agee hit Palmer's fourth pitch 400 feet for a home run. In the second inning, with two men on and Gentry at bat, Paul Blair, the Orioles' Gold Glove–winning outfielder, moved into shallow center field, since Gentry had only one run batted in all season and had not gotten a hit since August 3. But Gentry hit a fly over Blair's head for a two-run double. After throwing the ball back into the infield, Blair stood in center field in total disbelief. The Mets led 3–0. In the fourth, after hits by Frank Robinson and Boog Powell, the Orioles had runners at the corners with two outs when Orioles catcher Elrod Hendricks hit a long drive to the fence in deep left-center that looked like a sure extra-base hit that would score two runs. But Agee, who had been playing Hendricks (a left-handed batter) toward right, sprinted over to catch the ball—backhanded—and then banged into the fence. Agee held on, the ball perched precariously at the top of his mitt like an extra-large scoop of vanilla ice cream on a sugar cone.

In the seventh, after two long fly outs to Agee in center field, Gentry walked three successive batters. Hodges came out to the mound. Gentry reluctantly handed the ball over to Hodges as Nolan Ryan made his way in from the bullpen. Paul Blair was the next batter. After two fastballs, the count was 0-2, when Blair hit Ryan's next pitch to deep right-center field. It looked like a certain extra-base hit that would bring in at least three runs. But Agee dove for the ball and made a one-handed catch as he skidded on his stomach, coming to a halt with his legs extending up behind him like landing flaps. When Agee caught the ball, Blair was a step away from second and felt he might have had an inside-the-park home run had Agee missed it, which would have tied the game up. Instead, the Mets still led, 4–0. Watching film of Agee's second catch, you can see Art Shamsky, the right fielder, hustling in behind Agee. In *The Game of Baseball*, Hodges gives an example that sounds eerily like Agee's second catch: "Let's take a sinking line drive, hit to the left of the center fielder. He may not be sure . . . he can catch it, but he can . . . give it a better try if he knows the right fielder is coming over to back him up."

In the ninth, with two outs and a 5–0 lead, Ryan sandwiched two walks around an infield single to load the bases. With Blair at bat, Hodges went out to the mound but chose to leave Ryan in, and he struck out Blair. The Mets had a 2–1 series lead.

Game Four was a rematch of Game One with Mike Cuellar pitching for the Orioles against Tom Seaver. It was also Moratorium Day, and there were antiwar protests all over the country. Despite Mayor Lindsay's request that flags at all city facilities be flown at half-staff in keeping with the spirit of the day, the flag at Shea, a city-owned facility, was not lowered. Outside Shea, antiwar protesters distributed pamphlets that amplified antiwar sentiments Seaver had expressed, and a controversy loomed. But when Seaver walked into the Mets' clubhouse, Donn Clendenon filled another role Hodges had envisioned for him: tension reducer. "Look who's here," Clendenon said, "It's the chubby right-hander, smiling and ready to go."

Cuellar pitched well, but Seaver was outstanding. The Mets held a 1–0 lead in the ninth. With one out, after singles by Frank Robinson and Boog Powell, Hodges walked out to the mound for a conference with Seaver and Jerry Grote. Ron Taylor and Tug McGraw were already up and throwing in the Mets bullpen. But Hodges left Seaver in the game. The next batter was Brooks Robinson. Seaver wanted to either jam Robinson inside or throw him a breaking ball down. Whatever he threw, it didn't work. Robinson hit a line drive to right that appeared to be a sure base hit. There was no way Ron Swoboda was going to even reach the ball, let alone catch it. But Swoboda, who would later say he wanted the ball to be hit to him, was ready. The conservative play would have been to concede that the runner on third would score and cut the ball off on one or two hops to prevent an extra-base hit. But Swoboda was no conservative. He ran to his right, dove head first, stretching out the full length of his body while extending his gloved left hand as far as he could, and caught the ball—backhanded—inches off the ground. Hundreds of hours of fielding practice with Eddie Yost had paid off. Robinson tagged up on the catch to tie the game at 1–1.

In the bottom of the tenth, Jerry Grote hit a fly ball to left that fell in for a double. Hodges sent Rod Gaspar in to run for Grote. The next batter, Al Weis, who would finish the World Series with the highest batting average on either team (.455), was walked intentionally. Hodges sent J. C. Martin out to hit for Seaver. Billy Hunter, managing the Orioles because Weaver had been tossed for arguing a called strike, replaced righty Dick Hall with lefty reliever Pete Richert. Hodges, looking to advance the runners, had J. C. Martin put down a sacrifice bunt toward first. The bunt was perfect. The ball stopped rolling about ten feet in front of home plate. On a bunt, a catcher moving forward toward first base is in the best position to pick up the ball and throw the runner out. But the crowd was so loud that Richert didn't hear catcher Elrod Hendricks calling for the ball. Instead Richert, Hodges's former Senators pitcher, picked the ball up just as Hendricks reached for it. Richert's throw hit Martin in his left wrist and bounced away as Gaspar scored the game-winning run. Martin was running inside the baseline when the ball hit him and should have been called out for interference, but Hunter didn't protest the call.

After the game, with his team up three games to one, Hodges was asked about his team's chances. "Better than yesterday," he said. Hodges's "straight-faced, deliberately understated pronouncements of the obvious" had become his trademark response. And Hodges was straightforward even at his own expense. When asked if J. C. Martin was a particularly good bunter, Hodges said, "I really don't know."

To this, there was snickering from the press.

In the Baltimore clubhouse, Paul Blair, echoing the very words used by the Cubs and Braves, said, "I know they're not a better ball club than we are." But pitching had prevailed. Until Robinson had scored in the ninth inning, the Orioles, a team that had been shut out only eight times in 162 games that season, had been held scoreless for nineteen straight innings over the course of three consecutive games.

Pearl Bailey sang the national anthem before Game Five. A dedicated Mets fan, Bailey referred to Hodges as a "cool cat." But in the sixth, with her team down, 3–0, Bailey nervously watched as Hodges walked the shoe-polished ball out to DiMuro. The idea of taking a ball that had rolled into the dugout and using it as evidence to present to the umpire was not a new experience for Hodges. Earlier that season, against the Giants' Gaylord Perry, a highly successful grease-ball pitcher who used Vaseline to doctor baseballs, Hodges held on to any balls Perry threw that ended up being fouled into the Mets' dugout. Following successive strikeouts by Cleon Jones and Ed Kranepool, Hodges marched a ball with a jelly-like substance on it out to the umpire. In that game, the umpire did not give any weight to Hodges's evidence. But persistence was Hodges's strong suit, and the same technique worked against the Orioles.

After Al Weis's game-tying home run, the Orioles lost their edge. In the eighth, reliever Eddie Watt fell behind Cleon Jones in the count and Jones then hit one off the center-field fence for a double. Ron Swoboda then doubled to left to score Jones. With two outs, Jerry Grote hit a line drive to first baseman Boog Powell, who misplayed the ball and then tossed it to Watt, who dropped the ball while covering first. One play, two errors, another run scored, and the Mets had a two-run lead heading into the ninth. Cleon Jones would soon be taking a knee to give thanks that the Mets were the first expansion team in baseball history to win a championship, Karl Ehrhardt was raising his final sign of the game, "THERE ARE NO WORDS," Jerry Koosman was leaping into Jerry Grote's arms, and in the timeless image that captured the moment for posterity, as Grote held Koosman aloft, in the background, Ed Charles was jumping for joy. "This," Charles said later that day, "is the summit."

Thousands of fans swarmed the field, "like extras in a Genghis Khan movie," wrote George Vescey, "all hot-eyed and eager for plunder." They ripped out the bases (even home plate) and hundreds of pieces of turf as if Shea had been transformed into the surface of the moon and everyone wanted a souvenir for the folks back home. Orange flares flashed, firecrackers exploded, and the outfield fence became a canvas for graffiti. The Mets' clubhouse was a madhouse, "as dense as the subway at peak rush hour." Ron Swoboda said, "I'm going to celebrate for two days and then commit myself to Roosevelt Hospital."

In the chaos, Mets announcer Lindsay Nelson got Hodges up on a small platform in the middle of the clubhouse to accept the World Series trophy. Admiring the trophy, Hodges said, "Beautiful, beautiful." He then thanked

"Johnny Murphy, Mrs. Payson, Mr. Grant, the board, the players, and the fans." But his final words were not of elation, but relief. "Thank God it's over," he said. As Hodges stepped off the platform, Nelson told Hodges to be careful, using words that would prove prophetic: "It's a big step down."

Hodges's *Thank God it's over* comment is revealing. He usually gave his players the sense that he was calm and under control, but inside, Hodges was a small-town guy who was never comfortable in the limelight. He worried a lot more than he would ever admit; and for Major League managers as well as players, there is much to be concerned about. Some deal with it better than others. Hodges's teammate Johnny Podres, with his laid-back, gambler's attitude—*just give me one run, boys, and we'll win*—could relax under pressure. Hodges, like Hall of Fame pitcher Stan Coveleski, who was inducted into Cooperstown in 1969, felt the stress deeply. In a book Tom Seaver wrote about that season, he even quotes Coveleski. "The pressure never lets up," Coveleski said, "Doesn't matter what you did yesterday. That's history. It's tomorrow that counts. So you worry all the time. It never ends. Lord, baseball is a worrying thing."

Russ White was among the first to enter Hodges's office to congratulate him; Casey Stengel immediately followed and stuck his craggy face into Hodges's chest as Hodges tilted his head back and laughed. White looked on in the background as photographers captured the moment for posterity. A short time later, Mrs. Joan Payson was in Hodges's office—"an oasis of order," compared to the madness in the clubhouse—and when Hodges's phone rang. Payson answered. It was President Nixon offering congratulations. "Half laughing and half crying," Payson said, "Here's Gil, here's Gil." Nixon reminded Hodges that he had made the final put-out of the 1955 World Series. Hodges told Nixon just what he wanted to hear, that "he was known as a great sports fan." A torrent of reporters followed. Hodges "was calm, speaking softly, but distinctly, mopping his face, listening attentively, answering carefully, smiling quickly—working in a way," Leonard Koppett noted, "harder than during a game."

A few hours later, Hodges went upstairs to the Diamond Club at Shea for the Mets' team party. When the Mets' director of Minor League player development, Whitey Herzog, walked into the party intending to congratulate Hodges, Herzog was surprised that it was Hodges who "jump[ed] out of his chair" and came to him to say, "No Whitey, I want to congratulate you. I really appreciate all the things you've done since I got here. Everything you've told me about a ballplayer has been true, and you've never been wrong on an evaluation. You're more of the reason we're the champions than anyone else."

"I was a nobody," Herzog told me decades later, referring back to his status in 1969 as a former journeyman player and midlevel baseball executive. "It was one of the finest compliments I ever received in baseball."

The next day, the Associated Press named Hodges Manager of the Year, and sportswriters wanted a quote from him. But Hodges was home in Brooklyn. The Mets' publicity director, Harold Weissman, told the media, "He's exhausted. You can understand that. He went through a very tough day yesterday." On a day dedicated to his family—in a move that today, in our era of texts and tweets, seems unfathomable—Hodges took his phone off the hook. Actions like that did not endear him to the press. But Hodges had his priorities—and limitations. Managing his team was stress he forced himself to handle, but there were times when dealing with incessant questions from the press was beyond the call of duty. Unlike Casey Stengel, who was almost always willing to talk baseball, Hodges was not. But his players knew they would not have won without his setting the tone for the team. As J. C. Martin said, "He'd come out to the mound in a tight situation when one run's going to beat you and a kid's out there pitching, and he'd have his hands in his hip pockets and he'd be talking so low you could hardly hear him. Never once did I see Gil Hodges react in a way to cause panic. Never once! I don't care what happened. We could pull the dumbest play in the world, but he'd never show panic. And he instilled that in his players. You got the feeling, 'Just do what Gil says and don't panic.'"

J. C. Martin, who was traded to the Cubs after the 1969 season and finished his career playing for Leo Durocher, tellingly added, "Leo was the type of manager to cause panic and confusion among his players. . . . Gil would have won with the Cubs in '69. . . . It was the manager that made the difference."

The Monday following the World Series, the city gave the Mets the honor of a motorized parade up Broadway from Battery Park to City Hall and then uptown to Bryant Park. As the Mets headed toward City Hall, out of the windows along Broadway came a deluge of tons of IBM punch cards, stationery,

37. Ticker-tape parade down Broadway with Joan, October 20, 1969. AP Photo/Harry Harris.

38. Visiting with members of the St. Joseph's baseball team and their athletic director, Richard Scharf (*on right*), and George Post (*on left*), 1969. Courtesy of Mike Campbell.

confetti, and ticker tape. Hodges and Joan were in the lead convertible. The crowds were even larger than those that had celebrated the Apollo 11 astronauts that past August, and the police allowed the crowds to flow beyond the sidewalks and into the street where, at one point, the fans totally blocked Broadway and had to be moved back so the motorcade could proceed. In a speech at City Hall, Mayor John Lindsay thanked all the Mets for giving New Yorkers "a summer of joy." For the day, Lindsay renamed the 2400 block on Bedford Avenue where Hodges lived and presented him with the new street sign, "Gil Hodges Place." Hodges gave a brief speech saying he was "happy and proud to be the manager of the Mets," adding—in hopes of maintaining some semblance of privacy at home—that just because his street had been renamed didn't mean everyone had to visit. Later that day, at a party at Gracie Mansion, for the first and only time in his life, Karl Ehrhardt spoke with Hodges. Ehrhardt was impressed because Hodges not only recognized him but took the trouble to introduce himself. "Karl, I want to thank you," Hodges said, "for all you have contributed to our success."

When Donn Clendenon was presented with a new Dodge Challenger as the Series' MVP, taking a page out of Hodges's handbook, Clendenon said, "I don't think any one man could take credit for the Mets' victory. It was a team effort. In fact, I wish I could divide these prizes 32 ways."

That winter, the cover of a New York magazine showed a re-creation of the well-known painting *George Washington Crossing the Delaware*, with Mets players at the oars, newly reelected Mayor Lindsay "scanning the horizon . . . for TV cameras on shore," and at the bow, standing tall and proud, was Gil Hodges.

23

STRUGGLES IN THE
SPOTLIGHT

I just hope I don't spoil things for the future by getting so far ahead of schedule.

When Hodges returned to New York, he envisioned gradual, season-by-season improvement as he had experienced in Washington. But after 1969, slow-and-steady was no longer an option. In a city spoiled by decades of Yankee dominance, expectations were unrealistically high for a team built on pitching and defense that squeezed out runs like toothpaste from a well-rolled tube.

The championship left Hodges unduly focused on the short term. After Agee's tremendous season, recalcitrant third baseman Amos Otis was off the untouchables list. On December 3, 1969—with Hodges's urging—the Mets traded Otis to Kansas City for third baseman Joe Foy. In the American League, Hodges had seen Foy hit with a modicum of power and play a solid third base for the Red Sox. After Ed Charles's release, the trade made sense. But Foy, who had grown up in the Bronx, fell in with the wrong crowd back in New York and developed what was then referred to as a recreational drug problem that left him a shell of the player Hodges once knew.

That trade would be Johnny Murphy's last. That winter, after suffering a heart attack, Murphy died, and Bob Scheffing was promoted to the general manager's position. M. Donald Grant picked Scheffing to serve as a rubber stamp for his decisions. The better choice would have been Whitey Herzog, the Mets' head of Minor League development. But Herzog often embarrassed Grant by telling him—to his face—how little he knew about baseball players. Scheffing's $50,000 salary was less than Hodges's, indicating that Murphy's passing wouldn't diminish Hodges's input on personnel moves.

On March 5, 1970, after the entire Mets squad had arrived in St. Petersburg for spring training, the town held a dinner in their honor. Hodges didn't attend due to a bad reaction to an influenza shot, but his reaction may have been political as well as physical. After seeing Mayor Lindsay's arrow turn north thanks to the magnetic Mets, the Republican governor of Florida, Claude Kirk, made sure he was center-stage at the dinner, where he called antiwar protestors "hecklers in the uniform of the day, disheveled filth and long hair; by golly they looked like hell and talked like hell." By way of contrast, Kirk then pointed to the Mets seated behind him and said, "Just look at their haircuts and the way they're dressed. By God, they are America the beautiful. Stand up, Mets." The players all stood up (some very slowly), unhappy being props for a stump speech. Then M. Donald Grant reiterated Kirk's words, saying, "The hippies will have us, we must fight. . . . These men are representatives of New York and of our country. Real he-men." Concerned about their jobs—Grant was pompous but powerful—none of the players said anything in response. But when Tug McGraw's name was called, he raised his hand shoulder-high and flashed the peace sign. McGraw later said, "I was ashamed. If I really had the guts, I would have held my hand way up high."

With politics behind them, the Mets began the 1970 season on a high note. For the first time in their history, they won their opening game, defeating the Pirates 5–3 in extra innings; Donn Clendenon, Hodges's Mr. Reliable, won it with a two-run pinch-hit single. But a week later, after Mrs. Joan Payson raised the 1969 Championship banner prior to the Mets' home opener, the results were more indicative of how the season would go. The Mets had a one-run lead in the ninth, but the Pirates tied the game on a home run, and in the tenth McGraw threw a wild pitch that led to a 6–4 Pirates victory. Afterward, Hodges remained upbeat. "It's a long season," he said. "We'll be back Thursday."

But by the end of April, the three everyday players Hodges hoped would be his best hitters, Tommie Agee, Cleon Jones, and Joe Foy, were in batting slumps, forcing him to open his bag of managerial tricks. First, he benched all three. "That's what 25 men are for; maybe a day or two of rest will help," Hodges said after a game in which their replacements Mike Jorgenson, Dave Marshall, and Wayne Garrett started and the Mets defeated the Dodgers. When that didn't help, Agee, Jones, and Foy miraculously all showed up at

Shea on their day off. "They asked if they could take batting practice," Hodges said, no doubt straight-faced. "It was a day off for the team so we didn't have any pitchers to throw to them. But they took turns pitching to each other. The important thing was that they were willing to come out on their own." Agee improved: in June he set a Mets record for most home runs in a month with eleven. But Cleon Jones was still batting .167, so Hodges moved him from his usual spot in the order to bat lead-off. But no matter what he did to motivate Jones, 1970 would be his poorest season playing for Hodges. Before one game, Hodges noticed that Jones was not on the field for batting practice and found him in the clubhouse. "That'll cost you $1,000," Hodges said.

"That doesn't bother me," Jones replied.

"Now it's $2,000," Hodges answered. "Let me know when I get to a number that bothers you."

Joe Foy was another case altogether. In batting practice before a double-header, Foy was falling down in the batting cage, "high as a kite." Hodges didn't play him in the first game; but Foy, unable to sit still, walked up and down in the dugout and committed the cardinal sin of crossing in front of Hodges's line of sight while the game was on. To make matters worse, Foy held his hand out to Hodges and said, "Slap me five, Gil." Foy was clearly impaired, but Hodges played him in the second game. The results were no different from Hodges handing his bat to Jack Barron and saying, "Show me."

"That," Ron Swoboda said, "was the end of Foy."

In 1970 motivational problems were a natural consequence of the Mets having won a championship. It didn't help that opponents were gunning for them, and no amount of maneuvering on Hodges's part could change that. In one early-season game, following a ninth-inning loss to San Diego (a team the Mets had defeated 11 out of 12 in 1969), it was a bad sign that the Mets' clubhouse "emptied about 30 minutes after the game." As Leonard Koppett wrote later that season, "The Mets don't have the emotional fire, the constant alertness, the perfect blend of relaxed enthusiasm and team unity they had a year ago. It's complicated to describe but easy enough to see."

In June of 1970, the Mets requested waivers on Ed Kranepool. At the time he was batting .114 and no other team claimed him, so the Mets optioned him to the Minors and brought up a twenty-three-year-old switch hitter, Ken

Singleton. Singleton, whose father was a Brooklyn Dodgers fan, was then leading the International League with seventeen home runs and a .388 batting average. "Singleton has a chance to become like Mantle," Hodges said, "even though it's doubtful he has the same all-out power."

"I was in awe," Singleton said with respect to being in the Majors and playing for Hodges, whom he had often watched on television with his dad. But sending down a veteran midseason and bringing up a rookie was unusual for Hodges. The following season, Ron Swoboda said, "It wasn't the same as last year. Gil wasn't the same. He shifted people more than he did before. He seemed uncertain. He was as much responsible for us losing as we were. Maybe he didn't play the right guys at the right time." In response, Hodges said, "Ronnie is immature. When he gains maturity he will probably be a better player."

Veteran Ron Taylor understood that if you do well, you play; if you don't, you won't. After the season, Taylor said, "I don't think I was that bad, I wasn't used that much towards the end [of the 1970 season] and that affects a relief pitcher's confidence. I think Hodges is a great manager. I respect his judgment, and that makes it even worse."

Hodges's response to players who thought they should be playing full-time was rarely expressed but always implied: when I want you to play, I'll pencil your name into the lineup; if not, don't complain, pull for your teammates, and stay alert because I could call you in to pinch-hit or pinch-run if I think it's the right move. "That's where I think he's wrong," Swoboda said after he was traded to Montreal. "A ball player has to be talked to. When you're going good you don't need it. Hell, that's when you're riding the top of the crest. It's when you're going bad that you need a little comfort."

"Hodges just isn't built that way," Maury Allen wrote.

Despite Jerry Koosman being injured for much of the season and pitching nowhere near as effectively as he had in 1969, Cleon Jones batting .277 (a huge drop from his .340 average in 1969), and Tug McGraw giving up over a run more per game than he had in 1969 (deadly for a relief pitcher), Hodges had the Mets in a first-place tie with the Pirates on September 9. But in the final two weeks of the season, the two teams played each other seven times and the Mets lost six of those games to finish the season in third place with a record of 83-79. Five of those six losses were by just one run. After one of those brutal defeats, Hodges, sitting alone in the clubhouse at Three Rivers Stadium in Pittsburgh, admitted, "It's been a long, long, long season." He had started smoking cigarettes "quite openly" again. When asked if he had given his team a pep talk, Hodges said, "No, I didn't call any team meetings . . . to urge them on. I don't make speeches like Knute Rockne. I'm not the type."

The most fun Hodges had that season was managing the National League in the 1970 All-Star Game, and his signature was all over the final play of the game. That play, one of the most famous in All-Star Game history, involved a twelfth-inning home plate collision between Pete Rose and the American League catcher, Ray Fosse. The play inspired the title of a book by James Reston Jr., *Collision at Home Plate*, the collision symbolizing the bitter conflict between Rose and the commissioner of baseball, Bart Giamatti, that resulted in Rose's lifetime suspension from baseball. On the play, Rose scored the game-winning run in front of his hometown Cincinnati fans as he sent Fosse sprawling with a flying body block that looked more likely to have occurred in a football rather than a baseball game. The play would never have occurred if Hodges, in a controversial move, had not selected his old teammate on the 1962 Mets, Jim Hickman, as a reserve (ahead of Cubs outfielder Billy Williams). Hickman hit the single to center field that drove Rose home with the winning run. And Amos Otis, then a Kansas City Royal after leaving the Mets and playing in his first All-Star Game, made the throw from center field that caused Rose to turn himself into a human projectile. Hodges had even wished Otis good luck before the game started. "That," Otis said, "was half as much as he talked to me during my whole time with the Mets."

Earl Weaver, the American League manager whose player was the one knocked over, didn't defend Fosse. "I thought Rose got there a little ahead of the ball, and Fosse was trying to block the plate," Weaver said. "They did what they had to do." Hodges made one of his classic ambiguous comments that could be interpreted as meaning it was either a hustling play or a dirty play depending on your perspective on Rose. "It took a fellow like Rose," Hodges said, "to do something like that."

What is clear from that game is how strategically effective a manager Hodges was and how he again got the better of Weaver. Hodges had the upper hand

39. With Earl Weaver prior to the 1970 All-Star Game in Cincinnati. Bettman/Corbis Images.

before the game even began. When the managers came out to exchange line-ups, Weaver asked the umpires many questions regarding the special All-Star Game rules (such as the number of innings starting position players had to remain in the game), since he never played in the Majors, let alone in an All-Star Game. When the umpires turned to Hodges—who had played in six All-Star Games—and asked him if he had any questions, he just shook his head no.

Hodges had previously looked over the field to be familiar with the specifics of a brand-new Riverfront Stadium in the first All-Star Game ever played on Astroturf. When Hodges had then stepped onto the field, he was wearing a Cincinnati uniform with a No. 46 jersey that read "Maloney," a starting pitcher for the Reds. Apparently, someone had forgotten to ship Hodges's Mets jersey to Cincinnati and photographers gathered to capture the rare sight. But Joe Pignatano soon arrived with Hodges's uniform and a few minutes later, Hodges was back on the field wearing his familiar No. 14. His first words were, "Has anyone seen Maloney around here?"

Hodges made wise use of his pitchers. Seaver started, followed by Jim Merritt (fourth inning), Gaylord Perry (sixth), and Bob Gibson (eighth). In the seventh, with the National League trailing by one run, Hodges told Claude Osteen, then an All-Star pitcher for the Dodgers, to go to the bullpen to warm up and to make sure one of the coaches called him in the dugout as soon as he was ready to pitch.

"I was amazed," Osteen later said. Gibson was already set to enter the game in the eighth, and nobody was tougher in a big spot than Gibson. Why, Osteen wondered, would Hodges ever send him into a game to relieve Gibson? In addition, not only did Osteen rarely pitch in relief, but Hodges had Hoyt Wilhelm, a future Hall of Fame reliever, available. But Hodges selected Osteen, who headed off to the bullpen keeping his questions to himself. The American League scored two runs in the eighth—off Gibson—to take a 4-1 lead.

During a ninth-inning National League rally, having anticipated the possibility that the game could go into extra innings, and not wanting to waste a player, Hodges sent Osteen in to pinch-run for Willie McCovey, who had singled. The National League tied the game up and Osteen went in to pitch the tenth, taking McCovey's place in the lineup, which meant that when the pitcher's normal ninth spot in the batting order came up, Hodges could send in a pinch hitter without removing Osteen from the game. Osteen pitched the final three innings of the game and didn't allow a run. Contrast Hodges's use of his pitchers with Weaver's. After using veterans Jim Palmer, Jim Perry, Catfish Hunter, Fritz Peterson, and Mel Stottlemyre, in the crucial extra innings of the game, with his own veteran Baltimore pitchers Mike Cuellar and Dave McNally available, Weaver chose Clyde Wright (who was appearing in his first and only All-Star Game) to pitch. In the twelfth, with two out, Wright yielded three consecutive singles to Pete Rose, Bill Grabarkewitz, and the game winner to Jim Hickman. Anyone who attended the game, including President Nixon, never forgot the collision, but few recall that it was Hodges who left Riverfront Stadium with a thrilling come-from-behind win in his one and only appearance as an All-Star Game manager.

In 1970, as the oddsmakers had predicted (despite the Mets being the defending champions), the Pirates, led by their two superstars Roberto Clemente and Willie Stargell, won the division. Cincinnati defeated the Pirates in the playoffs to win the National League pennant, but lost to Baltimore in the World Series in five games. Reds manager Sparky Anderson told Hodges, "I don't know what your magic was, but I can't find it."

In 1970 Hodges couldn't find it either, but he tried to be positive. "The satisfaction of this year," Hodges said that October, "is that it shows last year was no fluke and indicates we'll be contenders for years to come." But third place was a huge comedown for Mets fans, who supported their team in extraordinary fashion. In 1970 the Mets drew 2,697,479 fans for their home games, then the second-highest total in baseball history. Only the 1962 Los Angeles Dodgers, playing in their brand-new stadium at Chavez Ravine, had drawn more. Home and away, the Mets played before 4,366,390 people in 1970. For Hodges, who believed it was "sound advice" to be seen but not heard, there was nowhere to hide. And Hodges was also not equipped for the deluge of the fourth estate. In *The Game of Baseball*, Hodges lists opposing managers and players, fans, and umpires as those you "always" have to deal with, but only "sometimes the press."

After 1969, for Hodges, the press was no longer a "sometimes" thing. In his own inimitable style, legendary college basketball coach Al McGuire knew all too well the character flaw in coaches like Hodges. "Look," McGuire said, "if you're into coaching heavy . . . if you're gonna charge up the hill into the machine guns, then you might as well stay at St. Ann's in the fifth grade; because coaching up here is something else. You're gonna have to deal with the fifth column, the memos and pipes." McGuire's reference to staying at St. Ann's and charging into machine gun fire is appropriate for Hodges, the devout Catholic and former marine. As a player, surrounded by teammates like Jackie Robinson and Pee Wee Reese, Hodges could easily stay out of the spotlight. But as the manager of the best baseball team in New York, he frustrated even veteran writers. During spring training in 1971, when there was talk of a possible trade between the Mets and the Dodgers, Joe Durso tried to get a scoop from Hodges, who was still close with Dodgers executives. Durso quoted Hodges as saying only, "It is a known fact that they [the Dodgers] are looking for pitching." That, Durso wrote, was "one of his longest speeches of the spring."

As a manager, Hodges viewed reporters as a necessary evil. In this respect he would have been more comfortable back in Indiana coaching a high school baseball team. Perhaps hoping to simulate the coaching life he never enjoyed, Hodges often tried to find the time on the way to Shea to stop in at Gil Hodges Field and watch a Little League game. Hodges would have had less stress coaching a high school team, but ever since he first stepped onto Ebbets Field, professional baseball held him in its grip, and "no matter how tough the criticism gets," Hodges wrote, "the job has to be done the way you think it should be done." But during spring training in 1971, Hodges smoked a pipe, telling reporters, "If things get rough, I might go back to cigarettes."

As is always the case, when a team doesn't live up to expectations, the buck stops with the manager. Before the 1970 season started, when Tom Seaver was asked what will keep the Mets from growing "fat and complacent," Seaver said, "No. 14. There's one set of rules around here—his. We do it his way or he gets somebody else." At the end of the 1970 season, Hodges mandated a reporting weight for each of his players for the following spring and set a fine for each pound a player was over. In the off-season following the Mets' championship, his players had spent a lot of time celebrating on the dinner circuit and many had reported to spring training overweight. Hodges didn't want that happening again. "Gil suggested I come in at 200, so I did," Jerry Koosman said, adding, "It was just a suggestion of course." Tug McGraw showed up to spring training eight pounds overweight. Hodges fined him $400. "It was supposed to be a hundred dollars a pound," McGraw later said, "but I got a discount."

Entering the 1971 season, other than replacing Joe Foy, Hodges didn't think any major personnel changes were in order: improved seasons from

Jerry Koosman and Cleon Jones would be enough to get the Mets back into first place. The only significant trade the Mets made was for thirty-two-year-old third baseman Bob Aspromonte, who had briefly played for the Brooklyn Dodgers and was popular in New York. But Aspromonte was no longer an everyday player and 1971 would be his final season. Cleon Jones did return to form; he batted over .300 and even stood up for Hodges, saying, "Criticism of the manager is a lot of bull. He can't win games for you. He can give the team a winning spirit, and does." But Donn Clendenon hit only eleven home runs and the offense sputtered. The Mets' hitting was so poor that season that when Hodges was taking batting practice before a game in San Francisco and hit one on a line drive that bounced over the outfield fence, Aspromonte said, "He hasn't played in eight years and he hits like that. He embarrasses us." Because of a torn muscle behind his left shoulder, Koosman couldn't throw as hard as he once had and his performance grew worse, not better. In 1971 the Mets didn't even play meaningful games in September and again finished in third place, fourteen games behind Pittsburgh, who were not just the best team in the National League that season, but defeated the Orioles in the World Series.

In 1971 Hodges tried whatever he could to shake things up: he sometimes played Ed Kranepool (back up after a season in the Minors) in right field, eventually tried Nolan Ryan in the bullpen, even pitched Tom Seaver on short rest. Nothing helped. One night in Montreal, after writing his own name in the manager's slot on the lineup card, Hodges joked, "It's the only name I'm sure of." A few weeks later, Karl Ehrhardt held up his final placard of the season: "THE PARTY'S OVER."

The 1971 season was a turning point for Nolan Ryan. "I just wanted a year where I pitched in turn," he said. "I want to find out if I can do it—here or someplace else. I've talked to Gil every season since I joined the club. I've never gotten any satisfaction. He says I'll pitch in turn when my control improves, but I say my control will improve when I pitch in turn."

Hodges and Ryan were two strong-willed men. In a game in which Ryan was pitching beautifully but later admitted he was losing speed on his fastball as the game went on, Hodges took Ryan out in the seventh with the Mets leading, 3–0. A reporter later asked Hodges, when did Ryan realize he was tiring? Hodges replied, "When I told him."

Previously, with limited opportunities to pitch regularly due to his required military service (during the 1970 season Ryan had to spend one weekend a month in the army plus two weeks of summer military duty), Ryan never had a full, uninterrupted season. But in 1971 Ryan arranged to serve his military duty locally, and this enabled him to start every fifth day. Until the end of June, Ryan was outstanding. He had an 8-4 record and seemed on his way to twenty wins; but then, for no apparent reason, he lost control of his pitches and won just one game over the next eight weeks. Ryan admitted, "I couldn't ask for a better break. They've given me every opportunity. I always wanted to start every fourth or fifth day and I have. I'm as puzzled as everyone else."

Although Ryan started twenty-six games that season, he finished with a 10-14 record and gave up nearly four runs a game. But Ryan also continued to strike out almost a batter an inning and display jaw-dropping potential. Red Schoendienst, who had seen Sandy Koufax pitch in his prime, said of Ryan, "There is a man who throws the fastest ball I've ever seen." But 1971 would be Ryan's last season with the Mets. Hodges's view was different from Schoendienst's. For Hodges, who was fond of saying that a pitcher can win a game without striking out a single batter, control mattered much more than strikeouts. Even so, a year before, Hodges had continued to tout Ryan, denying the Mets would ever trade him. "He's on the threshold of not only being a good pitcher," Hodges said, "but a great one."

But after the Mets finished as the worst-hitting team in the National League in 1971, Hodges stopped thinking long-term. From that perspective, Nolan Ryan's 1971 season could be best summarized based upon two consecutive late-season games he started, one against the Cardinals, the other against the Phillies. Against the Cardinals, Ryan struck out twelve batters in only six innings, allowing just one run on four hits, and gave up only one walk. Although the Mets lost the game, 2-1, Ryan appeared to get stronger as the game went on. In Ryan's very next start, he could not control his pitches; in just over two innings, Ryan allowed five walks and three hits, hit a batter, and cost the Mets four runs. The latter game was the one that stuck with Hodges and ultimately decided Ryan's fate. With other young pitchers like Jon Matlack in the Mets' Minor League system ready for the Majors, Hodges was willing to take the risk of trading Ryan. "Whether or if or how he's going to do it, I don't know," said Hodges of Ryan, "but he's got ability."

Ryan was traded to the California Angels for third baseman Jim Fregosi. Hodges called Fregosi "a professional hitter . . . a bear-down type of guy . . . a hustling ballplayer. At least he was when I was over in that league." It was a clear sign that Hodges had still not mastered Rickey's ability to evaluate a player, not for what he had done in the past, but for what he could still do in the future.

During the 1971 season, writer Leonard Koppett noticed that the one area in which the normally self-effacing Hodges was "just a trifle smug" was his understanding of the rule book. In a game on June 6 against the Dodgers, slugger Richie Allen was written into the lineup card, but when Allen couldn't be found when the Dodgers took the field in the first inning—without notifying the umpires—Alston sent Bill Russell out to play left field instead of Allen. After the game, Koppett wondered if Alston could have still used Allen as a pinch hitter since the umpires had never announced that Russell had replaced him. With great certainty, Hodges said, "No sir. Allen might just as well leave the ballpark at that point. He had been substituted for. He was out of the game for good." Koppett thought that Hodges's conclusion didn't sound right and got out a rule book to challenge him. With great specificity, Hodges directed Koppett through the general rules on player substitutions (Rules 3.06 and 3.07) to the applicable exception, Rule 3.08 (a) (3), which applies to cases where a fielder reaching his position usually occupied by the fielder he has replaced, even if unannounced, is a legal substitution. Hodges told Koppett that the same situation had once occurred when he was managing in Washington: in the ninth, with the Senators leading the game, the opposing manager illegally sent up a player (who was out of the game) as a pinch hitter. The Senators won that game, and since Hodges didn't want to embarrass the opposing manager, he never registered a protest with the umpires. In the 1971 game, Alston never attempted to play Allen. The Mets lost to the Dodgers, 4–3.

After 1969 Hodges would rely more heavily on Tug McGraw. But in 1970 the results were mixed. In the second game of a doubleheader in San Francisco on July 19, 1970, Hodges called McGraw in to pitch in the bottom of the eighth with the bases loaded, one out, and the Mets up by two runs. The Mets had lost six of their last seven games and were in desperate need of holding on to the lead.

The first thing McGraw did when he came in was to try and ad-lib a pick-off play with his shortstop, Teddy Martinez. Hodges immediately noticed and bolted out of the dugout. He asked McGraw what he was talking about with Martinez. Generally, when Hodges came to the mound, even in a close game with the bases loaded, he was, as McGraw wrote, "all Hodges: calm, relaxed, no sign of emotion."

This time Hodges was not so calm. He knew something was amiss. Teddy Martinez was in his rookie season as the Mets' third-string shortstop and he would play in only three other games that season. (The only reason he was playing in that game was because Bud Harrelson had played in the first game of the doubleheader and Hodges was giving him a rest; Al Weis had started the second game but had been lifted for a pinch hitter.) Most significantly, Martinez was from the Dominican Republic and spoke little English. McGraw admitted he was trying to set up a "trick play" with Martinez for a pick-off attempt at second base. As McGraw later wrote, "Hodges really flipped his lid." With "real quiet heat," Hodges told McGraw, "Trick play my foot. You've got a rookie shortstop who doesn't speak English, you're trying to set up a play we didn't practice, it's a close game, and you're not even worried about getting the hitter out yet. How . . . are you to going to get this hitter out?" Without waiting for an answer, Hodges said, "If we don't win this game, it's [your] ass."

McGraw pitched out of the jam and the Mets won. Afterward, McGraw admitted, "I was so shook up that I was crying and laughing and trembling all at once. They even gave me sedation and sent me back to the hotel with a coach. And the next day, Gil had a long talk with me. He knew I had . . . problems. I couldn't relax . . . I couldn't concentrate on pitching. I was all mixed up. He helped straighten me out."

Asked to comment on how he "straightened" McGraw out, Hodges said, "McGraw just had to find himself, all over again."

Earlier that season, on May 4, on the campus of Kent State University, the Ohio National Guard shot and killed four students protesting the Vietnam War. A photograph of a female student bending over a slain student, her face a mix of shock and disbelief, became one of the defining images of the era.

The Mets played a home game the next day and one sensitive former marine had sought out a stoic one looking for answers. "When Gil was running the ball club," Tug McGraw wrote of that visit, "you always felt things were sane, even if you were kind of insane. I couldn't function, . . . I was blown out of my mind . . . I went to Gil, not so much because he was the real strength of the outfit, physically and morally sort of immovable. And that was one of those times when he opened up and did a lot of talking."

"Listen," Hodges told McGraw behind the closed door of his office, "I was in the service, too. It was a different situation, a lot more clear-cut. Now the only thing I can tell you, or tell myself, is that life can be bitter, the way it is today. Adversity comes and goes, bitterness comes and goes. But the thing that stays is your commitment to what's right. Think of where it all starts— your family and your sense of right and wrong. . . . If you let the worst in us ruin the best in us, you'll never find the answer. We'll look for it together." McGraw noticed that Hodges was also affected by the shootings. "He was sweet to me, gentle and . . . fatherly," McGraw wrote, "and I could see that he didn't know exactly what to say either."

As Hodges struggled to duplicate the Mets' 1969 lightning-in-a-bottle success, even a consummate professional like Donn Clendenon could give him grief. Before one game, Clendenon reported to Shea late. Hodges asked him why.

Clendenon, who had spent the afternoon looking at artwork in Manhattan and had gotten caught up in rush hour traffic, said, "I spent too much time at the museum."

"He looked at me in utter disbelief," Clendenon later wrote. "Didn't say another word. He just turned and walked away."

24

EASTER SUNDAY

That's right, kid. You made it.

As training camp opened in the spring of 1972, Gil Hodges appeared relaxed. Gil Jr. had been married the month before and thoughts of watching his grandchildren playing baseball at Gil Hodges Field must have crossed his mind.

That winter, in addition to his son's wedding, Hodges received more publicity than usual. Despite the fact that he was smoking again, Hodges, along with another heart attack survivor, Dave Stallworth, a forward on the 1970 New York Knicks championship team, appeared in a public-service commercial for the Heart Fund. And with strong prodding from Father Vieck, the Indiana General Assembly unanimously voted to name a new bridge to span the White River just north of Petersburg in honor of Hodges. Over the years, a number of drivers (including several marines home on leave) had been killed in accidents on the single-lane bridge. The new bridge would have two lanes and be wide enough to easily accommodate cars crossing it in either direction simultaneously. Hodges had no interest in attending the ceremonies that would take place when the bridge opened, and he would be asked to say a few words. Yet during construction, whenever he spoke to Father Vieck, Hodges would ask, "How are they coming along with my bridge?"

That February, a book about the Brooklyn Dodgers, unusual for its part memoir, part journalistic history, and part where-are-they now structure, was published: Roger Kahn's *The Boys of Summer*. Kahn had covered the Dodgers for the *New York Herald Tribune* and divided the book into two parts: the first described his experiences traveling with the team in 1952 and 1953; the second documented what Kahn saw and heard when he went back almost twenty years later and visited with those same players in their post-baseball lives. The players trusted Kahn and they allowed him access to interview them in depth. In many cases, such as Roy Campanella in his wheelchair and Jackie Robinson worn down by time and illness, they were truly "the boys of summer in their ruin."

Hodges was the only one who was still making his full-time living in baseball; he was also the only one who clearly disliked being interviewed. Hodges, Kahn wrote, "built an outer barrier of calm, but he churned beneath the way a sea churns below a pale, rippled surface." Kahn suggested that Hodges would have been happier back home in Indiana, living a less stressful, less public life like his brother Bob had.

That spring, Hodges was excited about the Mets' prospects: with Jerry Grote catching, Ken Boswell at second, Bud Harrelson at short, and the newly acquired six-time American League All-Star Jim Fregosi at third, an outfield of Cleon Jones, Tommie Agee, and Ken Singleton, and a righty-lefty platoon at first, Hodges was confident the Mets would score more runs. Tom Seaver was old reliable, and the righty-lefty bullpen combination of forkball-throwing Danny Frisella and Tug McGraw was among the best in baseball. Jon Matlack, a twenty-two-year-old lefty with "a long fastball that moves" and a fine curve, appeared ready to make the team and take a regular place in the rotation.

Near the end of spring training, after the final team cuts had been determined but not yet announced, Matlack sat in the Mets' clubhouse trying to figure out if he was going to be on the Major League roster to start the season. He saw his jersey was still hanging by his locker and started to count the number of other jerseys. If there were just twenty-four others, that meant he had made the team. Matlack didn't know it, but at that moment Hodges was watching him from the hallway. As a general rule, Hodges rarely stopped in the players' part of the clubhouse to chat. But Hodges, who was more empathetic than he cared to show, knew exactly what Matlack was doing and feeling. It was no different than Claude Osteen sitting on the Senators bench as his catcher was replaced or Bob Mandt stuck between a rock and a hard place. But Hodges waited. He wanted Matlack to figure it out on his own. Only after

Matlack "sort of smiled" did Hodges reveal himself to the rookie pitcher, who was usually so intimidated by Hodges that if he saw him in a hotel lobby he would walk the other way.

"That's right, kid," Hodges said, "you made it."

But there were concerns that had Hodges churning. First, a number of important players were injured, including Jim Fregosi, who broke his thumb fielding a grounder hit by Hodges during fielding practice. In addition, the players' association had voted to conduct its first strike. The immediate goal was to increase pension benefits, but there was a sense that far greater changes were coming to baseball, especially regarding the infamous reserve clause. The strike was sure to delay the opening of the season, creating another layer of uncertainty in the final year of Hodges's three-year contract. After two consecutive third-place finishes, Hodges knew a renewal of his contract was no certainty unless his team returned to playing meaningful games in September.

And Hodges was being criticized by a soon to be famous former player. Early in the year, the California Angels' newest pitcher, Nolan Ryan, said, "There just wasn't much communication from Hodges and Walker and it's my feeling that one of the reasons I never achieved anything with the Mets was because I never received any instruction."

When asked if he was uncommunicative, Hodges laughed and said, "No comment."

One person Hodges was highly communicative with that spring was Vic Colvin, who used to post Hodges's batting average in his store window on Main Street in Petersburg. Colvin was in Florida and had come to pay Hodges a visit in St. Petersburg. On a sunny day near the end of March, after he had spent some time reminiscing with the Mets' manager, Colvin got back in his car, but before he drove away, Hodges, recalling Colvin's affection for numbers, came clopping across the parking lot in his spikes to give Colvin a copy of that season's statistic-laden Mets media guide. Colvin took a photo of Hodges leaning into the car window. It would be one of the last photos ever taken of Hodges.

Near the end of spring training, Hodges looked more drawn and pale than usual to Bob Broeg, the longtime dean of St. Louis baseball writers, who had known Hodges for decades. The two men felt close enough to call each other *Cuz* (apparently another writer, Jack Rice, once pointed out that they resembled each other). Broeg warned Hodges about the dangers of smoking. "I know, Cuz," Hodges said, "I shouldn't do it, but . . ."

The strike resulted in the cancellation of one of the Mets' final exhibition games, scheduled for Easter Sunday, April 2, against the Montreal Expos. That morning, Hodges attended mass at St. Ann's Church in West Palm Beach. The day before, despite Whitey Herzog's objections, the Mets had agreed to trade three young players, shortstop Tim Foli, first baseman Mike Jorgenson, and power hitter Ken Singleton, to Montreal for the veteran outfielder Rusty Staub. According to Scheffing, Hodges was "tickled" by the trade. The twenty-eight-year-old Staub had been an All-Star the previous five seasons and was an outstanding hitter. But at that point, no public announcement had been made, and other than Mets management, no one—not even the players involved—knew about the trade. Rusty Staub was also attending services at St. Ann's that morning and, after services ended, he approached Hodges to "pay his respects." The two men had briefly spoken once before when Hodges had selected Staub to play on the 1970 National League All-Star team. That morning, although he was well aware of the trade, Hodges made no mention of it to Staub. Hodges, along with Joe Pignatano, Rube Walker, Eddie Yost, and Mets trainer Tom McKenna, made small talk for a good five minutes with Staub. Well aware of Hodges's reputation for silence, Staub "was totally astonished by the amount of conversation."

After services, using a golf cart, Hodges, along with Pignatano, Walker, and Yost, played twenty-seven holes. Hodges was in good spirits; and, as usual, he outdistanced everyone with his tee shots. Umpire Tom Gorman, who was also in West Palm Beach when the strike began, had seen Hodges the day before when Hodges had asked him if he wanted to play golf the next day. Gorman turned him down. And in an indication of the admiration he had for Hodges, Gorman later wondered if he had joined Hodges's foursome, perhaps they would have only played eighteen holes, not twenty-seven, and "Maybe it would have been different . . ."

At about 5:15 p.m., the four men walked off the Palm Beach Lakes golf course toward their hotel rooms at the adjacent Ramada Inn. Pignatano asked

Hodges what time they would gather for dinner. Hodges then spoke his final words, "Seven-thirty."

"He went over," said Yost, who was walking next to Hodges, "like a tree." As Hodges fell backward, his head hit the curb. Pignatano and Walker attended to Hodges as best they could while Yost ran inside to call emergency services. Mets statistician Arthur Friedman heard the commotion and went outside to see Hodges motionless on the ground, his head in a pool of blood, and ran to a nearby room for a pillow and blanket. A few minutes later, Hodges was taken by fire truck to Good Samaritan Hospital, a five-minute drive. He was admitted at 5:25 p.m. Despite a tube inserted in his throat and a needle directly into his heart, it was too little, too late. Hodges was unresponsive, the pupils of his eyes dilated. Twenty minutes later, two days short of his forty-eighth birthday, Hodges was pronounced dead due to a heart attack. It was twenty-seven years (almost to the day) since Hodges first stepped foot on Okinawa, where he started smoking.

Of the moment he saw the news of Hodges's death flash across the bottom of his television screen, Father Herbert Redmond said, "I felt very bad and immediately said the Catholic prayer for the dead." Nineteen years after he had asked his congregation to pray for Hodges, Redmond recalled that had been "the only time I said anything [from the pulpit] without preparation."

The news left Don Drysdale, in his own words, "absolutely shattered." He was then working as a broadcaster for the Texas Rangers and was at his Ft. Worth home due to the strike. Drysdale "flew apart," unable to even pull himself together to attend Hodges's funeral. He spent the next three days in his apartment unable to speak to anyone. "It was," Drysdale wrote, "like I lost part of my family."

John Drof, the former editor of the *Petersburg Press*, was working in Washington when Hodges died. Drof had his hand on the pulse of the nation's capital where Hodges had toiled for five long, hot summers trying to make the Senators relevant. "It was," Drof said, "nothing like a celebrity death." Instead, in verbiage almost identical to Drysdale's, Drof said, "It felt like a member of the family had died."

Bob Addie of the *Washington Post* similarly wrote, "It was more, to me, than the loss of a great baseball figure. Gil often was pictured as 'aloof' and 'cold.'

He was neither. He was reserved, but he was as warm and as loyal a friend as I have ever known. He was unfailingly courteous to all people and, in this era of iconoclasts, he was the nice guy . . . who stood the test of corrosive time."

"Oh, no. Oh, no. Oh, no," Leo Durocher cried out when he learned of Hodges's passing. "It's hard to find words to describe a guy as fine as he was," Durocher said, "they don't come any finer, both on or off the field."

Baseball commissioner Bowie Kuhn praised Hodges as "a thorough champion as a player, manager, and friend to baseball. His unique decency and class inspired us all."

Campaigning in Wisconsin for the Democratic nomination for president, Mayor Lindsay said Hodges's dedication and leadership "will stand as a lesson for all of us."

After comparing Hodges to Hal Chase, the most graceful first baseman he said he had ever seen, Casey Stengel said, "It's a personal loss to me, the club and to baseball. I was very close to him. . . . He had a terrific respect for standing up for the rights of . . . others."

Walter Alston spoke of 1954, the year he started managing in the Majors, and how Hodges, as one of the more experienced players on the Dodgers, made his job easier. Alston was moved to add, "Gil . . . never gave anyone any trouble; he was a great man on the field and off. . . . We were quite close, and all I can say is that there was never a finer man in baseball than this gentleman."

"I'm sick," said Johnny Podres. "This ruins everything for me. We . . . shared so many wonderful experiences. I've never known a finer man."

"It's a saddening experience, losing a great man like Gil," said Jackie Robinson, adding, "He was the core of the Brooklyn Dodgers."

Hodges's opponents were moved as well. "He was a wonderful man and he's done a wonderful job in baseball," said Hank Bauer, the former Yankee outfielder who fiercely competed against Hodges in many World Series. "His death will be felt by everyone in the sport."

Even those who sometimes clashed with Hodges tempered their comments. Ed Kranepool said, "He was more than just a baseball manager to the players. He took a personal interest in his players on and off the field. If any of us had family problems, Gil was always there to help out. He's not only going to be a loss to baseball but especially to us, the Met players."

"To me," Tom Seaver said, "he was the leader. We always knew that if things went bad, Gil wasn't going to bend. He was the backbone of the ball club and everybody else stemmed off him. He gave every player on the club a living example of a true professional. He made every sacrifice to maintain that status himself."

Tug McGraw said, "As long as I'm a ballplayer, no matter who my manager is, there'll be one man I'll be playing for—Gil Hodges."

But not all the words spoken about Hodges were positive. You can't take a team that lost 101 games the season before your arrival to 100 wins in your second season without paying a price. In this regard, writer Joe Durso well understood the man who took the clown out of the Mets. "He was reverent, friendly, strong, and silent," Durso wrote. "To most of his players his style added up to a 'lack of communication.' But after he suffered his first heart attack . . . they closed ranks around him and charged to their 1969 pennant while denying that any 'conspiracy of silence' had been formed in the clubhouse to protect him."

Seaver even admitted that the communication gap between Hodges and his players "was real [but] only for those players who didn't approach the game in the same professional manner he did."

Ironically, Hodges's body was flown back to New York on an airplane the Yankees had chartered for their players, and on board was their outfielder, Ron Swoboda. When the 727 landed at the West Palm Beach airport to pick up the Mets contingent heading back to New York, Swoboda got off the plane and stood alone on the tarmac and watched Hodges's body being placed on board. Swoboda, who had been acquired by the Yankees the prior season, had gone through, in his own words, some "insane shit" with Hodges; but at that moment he felt "a tremendous baseball guy had gone too soon."

With the man who taught them "responsibility and respect and discipline" gone, Tug McGraw summed up the feeling of the Mets' players when he said, "I felt stranded."

If his players felt "stranded," the loss to his family was far greater. In addition to Joan, his wife of almost a quarter of a century, Hodges left four children: Gil Jr. (twenty-two), Irene (twenty-one), Cynthia (sixteen), and Barbara (eleven). "He's a gentle father," Irene once said. Then, giving a hint that her father was as quiet and strict at home as he was at work, she added, "One word from him, though, can mean an awful lot."

In Brooklyn, the day after Hodges's body landed at La Guardia, morning dawned, gray and misty. Around 9:00 a.m. people began lining up outside the Torregrossa & Sons Funeral Home on Flatbush Avenue to pay their respects. Among them was twelve-year-old Frederick Gentile, wearing a baseball cap with the letters "GH." "We have a parade at the beginning of each season," Gentile, a veteran of the Gil Hodges Little League, said, "and he used to come to it every year." But the day had originally been intended only for family and friends to come inside and pay their respects, since Hodges's body would be available for public viewing the following day at the church where the funeral service would take place. Weeb Ewbank, the coach of the New York Jets, and rare for a manager, two umpires, Tom Gorman and Nick Colosi, came to pay their respects. Around 3:00 p.m. as the line outside stretched around the block and had grown to over a thousand people, Joan Hodges asked that the doors to the funeral home be opened to everyone. "Gil," she said, "would never have wanted all those people standing out in the rain."

One of those on line was a sad, signless Karl Ehrhardt. Inside, he stopped next to the fully open casket. Hodges, wearing both his wedding and Mets World Series ring, was dressed in his favorite navy blue suit. But the image that would remain in Ehrhardt's memory was different. "Hodges was so big," Ehrhardt told me decades later, "his head hit the top of the casket and his feet the bottom."

Terence Cardinal Cooke, archbishop of New York, offered St. Patrick's Cathedral for the funeral service. Although the nuptial mass for Gil Jr. had been celebrated there, the family respectfully declined. Somehow, Gil Hodges and a "big-splash" funeral on Fifth Avenue didn't go together. Instead, the small brick Catholic Church, Our Lady Help of Christians, where he attended mass every Sunday and where his children were baptized, nestled on a Brooklyn block surrounded by modest homes with stoops and tiny lawns, was more fitting. But the church could seat only six hundred and attendance was therefore by invitation only.

Only a few blocks from his home on Bedford Avenue, Hodges lay in state at Our Lady Help on East Twenty-Eighth Street off Avenue M for most of the afternoon and evening on Wednesday, April 5, as a thousand people passed by Hodges's open coffin and policemen kept the line moving. It was an informal Brooklyn crowd: kids in sneakers, jeans, and windbreakers, adults in their work clothes. Flags on all city buildings in Brooklyn were lowered in Hodges's honor.

The funeral service started at 11 a.m. with hundreds of people standing outside the church waiting for one final glimpse of the copper casket. Inside, Bowie Kuhn, National League President Chub Feeney, and American League President Joe Cronin represented the Major Leagues. The Mets hierarchy were there as well: from Joan Payson and her management team, M. Donald Grant and Bob Scheffing, to Hodges' cabinet: Rube Walker, Eddie Yost, Joe Pignatano and Yogi Berra, who all sat together in one row near the front, to his players, from his greatest star, Tom Seaver, to the newest, Jon Matlack. Team President Michael Burke, general manager Lee MacPhail, and manager Ralph Houk represented the Yankees. Mayor Lindsay attended. A contingent flew in from Petersburg: Father Vieck, Bob Harris, and Hodges's mother, Irene. It was her first time on an airplane.

The priests wore white. Most of the flowers, including Easter lilies that decorated the side altars, were white as well for what was deemed not an occasion of mourning, but a "joyous" resurrection of the soul. Most of the organ music played was secular and everyone joined in singing the recessional, "The Battle Hymn of the Republic." Bishop Francis J. Mugavero was the principal concelebrant, but Hodges's longtime pastor, the Reverend Charles E. Curley, preached the homily, giving an example of what endeared Hodges to the people of Brooklyn. Hodges could have left services early each Sunday to avoid the never-ending autograph seekers, Curley said, but he always remained to the very end as to not disturb the services. "Gil was a hero," Curley said, "one to look up to and imitate."

"I repeat that suggestion of long ago," Curley concluded. "Let's all say a prayer for Gil Hodges."

The "Boys of Summer" were there in force, including Sandy Koufax, Jackie Robinson, Pee Wee Reese, Ralph Branca, Carl Furillo, Joe Black, Don Newcombe, and Carl Erskine. But not Roy Campanella. He lay critically ill from an embolism in his lung in a hospital in Valhalla, New York, his doctors withholding the news of Hodges's death from him for fear of the effect it might have.

After the funeral, as the casket was being taken out of the church, the organist played "Back Home in Indiana." In Ebbets Field, their organist, Gladys Goodding, had played that song whenever Hodges hit a home run or fellow Hoosier Carl Erskine was warming up in the bullpen. Considering how many home runs Hodges hit and the number of games Erskine pitched in, Erskine figured that after the National Anthem, Goodding played "Back Home in Indiana" more than any other song. So when Erskine heard it again as he watched the casket being carried out, he was so overcome that when Howard Cosell stuck a microphone in his face, Erskine waved him off, the only time he ever refused an interview.

Despite Hodges's purchase of his own burial plot in Indiana, Joan buried her husband in Holy Cross Cemetery in Brooklyn. There was little space left there, though; Holy Cross Cemetery, which dated back to 1849, was one of the oldest in Brooklyn, so the archdiocese allowed a tree to be removed so Hodges could join an eclectic mix buried there that ranged from the famous (Diamond Jim Brady) to the infamous (Willie Sutton, bank robber extraordinaire) to the familiar (Edward McKeever, a former owner of the Brooklyn Dodgers). Hodges may have wanted to be buried in Indiana, but his grave site, less than two miles from where Ebbets Field once stood, seemed right. But before Hodges was even laid to rest, M. Donald Grant began behaving badly in what Joe Durso called, "a ... series of tasteless actions ... [and a loss of] the chief values they had long treasured in Gil Hodges—dignity, clarity and poise."

First, despite publically expressing a false sense of piety when the topic of Hodges replacement was mentioned ("Our hearts go out to his family, which is our only concern at the moment," Grant said), within hours of Hodges's death, Grant had decided to offer Yogi Berra the managerial job. The next day, Berra arrived in Hobe Sound, an affluent enclave on Florida's East Coast where Grant had a winter home, and they worked out an agreement. Unaware of Berra's hiring, the press speculated that the leading candidate to replace Hodges was the Mets' director of player personnel, Whitey Herzog.

A former player and coach, Herzog, who had helped create one of the deepest Minor League systems in baseball, was a rising star within the Mets organization and the press loved him. But Herzog was no star to the man that mattered most, M. Donald Grant. Herzog had won no points with Grant, telling him how little he knew about baseball. Grant made Herzog pay. To avoid speculation that Herzog would be named the new manager, Grant ordered him to stay away from Hodges's funeral. That deeply pained Herzog. Years later, in his autobiography, Herzog wrote, "I've never forgiven them for that."

Considering Hodges's stand when Senator Robert Kennedy died, Grant's second flub was a whopper. Hodges's funeral was set for Thursday, April 6, the day the Yankees and Mets were both scheduled to open their seasons. Michael Burke said, "Gil has long been a good friend of many people in the Yankees organization. As a great player, manager and person he has meant much to baseball in our city. It would be inappropriate for us to open the new season on the day set aside for services in his memory." Even if the strike were settled by Thursday, the Yankees were going to delay their Opening Day game against the Orioles at Yankee Stadium to Friday.

Grant claimed the Yankees were trying to upstage the Mets. He said his team had to play their opener in Pittsburgh in order to avoid a forfeit—after all 45,000 tickets had already been sold. The Mets players, led by Bud Harrelson, said that Grant could do as he pleased, they'd all be in Brooklyn for Hodges's funeral. The players' strike continued and the issue became moot.

Lastly, in a move that makes you understand how Hodges's death, and Grant's now unrestrained leadership of the Mets, was the beginning of the team's decade-long decline, word was passed around at Hodges's funeral that immediately after the burial, the Mets would hold a press conference at Shea. At 4 p.m., standing in the Mets' locker room, only a couple of hours after Hodges was laid to rest, M. Donald Grant announced that Yogi Berra was the new manager and Rusty Staub the new right fielder. "They hated to transact business on such an emotional day, but they were worried that the strike might end suddenly and the news would leak out," wrote a perturbed Joe Durso, "but have subtracted . . . the grace they valued in Hodges."

Jack Lang and Dick Young expressed the same sentiment. Even staid Arthur Daley punched out a pungent bit of prose titled "What Was the Hurry?" with words like *appalling, disgraceful,* and *tactless.*

In the end there was no need; the strike lasted another week. But Grant forced Berra to walk an emotional tightrope on the day he had to both attend Hodges's funeral and be named his successor. "We left a good man today,"

Berra said with great dignity immediately following Grant's poorly timed announcement. "I hope I can fill his shoes."

Before the Mets' home opener on April 15, with the American flag fluttering at half-mast and his players wearing black armbands, a lone marine stood at home plate and blew taps. Metropolitan Opera star Robert Merrill, a friend of Hodges, sang the national anthem. Tom Seaver, with relief help from Tug McGraw, defeated the defending champion Pirates, 4–0. On that damp, bitter day, the Mets officially retired Hodges's No. 14, but no public announcement was made before or during the game. All management did was issue a press release stating that Hodges's number was being retired.

"We didn't want to make it something maudlin," said Jim Thomson, the man who once tried to deny Hodges his customary two sets of club boxes. "But nobody will ever again wear No. 14 on the Mets."

EPILOGUE

A LIFE

A life is not important except in the
impact it has on other lives.

JACKIE ROBINSON

On September 18, 1972, a bright sunny morning in southern Indiana, the dedication ceremony for the Gil Hodges Bridge took place with over one thousand in attendance, including a bevy of politicians from the governor of Indiana on down, as well as Irene, Bob, Marjorie, Gil Jr., and Carl Erskine, and a stone monument adjacent to the bridge listing Hodges's statistical accomplishments was unveiled. But his greatest legacy remains the impact he had on his friends, family, teammates, players, and fans.

Bob King, Hodges's boyhood friend, became the town barber. Whenever Hodges visited Petersburg, King's shop was one of his first stops. King made the most of Hodges's efforts regarding June, the pretty young lady in Buchanan's Drug Store. They made it well past the requisite three dates—their marriage lasted fifty-three years until Bob's death in 2001.

A photo taken at Sportsman Park in St. Louis prior to a Dodgers-Cardinals game in the late 1950s shows Barbara Vance's young son standing next to a particularly happy looking Dodgers player who had been called over by a contingent from Petersburg shouting, "Hey, Bud." They weren't calling for beer. Barbara Vance died in 2010.

In 1954, after hitting .300 or higher in his five seasons in the Minors, at the age of thirty, Chuck Harmon finally broke through baseball's quota system, becoming the first black man ever to play for the Cincinnati Reds. For the next few years, whenever the Reds played the Dodgers and Harmon was on first base, he and Hodges would exchange brief pleasantries about the old days back home in Indiana.

For many years, Bob Hodges worked as a vice president for Gus Doerner Sporting Goods in Indiana. He later coached the University of Evansville baseball team, and in 1975 and 1976 he was named the Indiana Collegiate Conference Coach of the Year. In 1978, following heart surgery, Bob died and was survived by his wife, Gladys, five sons, and two daughters. He's buried in Walnut Hills Cemetery.

Marjorie Hodges became a nurse and married Hal Maysent, a hospital executive. They had three sons and a daughter. Like her mother, Marjorie experienced the death of two of her adult sons.

Irene Hodges lived in Petersburg the rest of her life. A private woman before the death of her husband and sons, her final years left her appreciative of Carl Erskine, who, in his position with the Indiana Banker's Association—and out of respect for his former teammate—visited her whenever his work brought him to southern Indiana. Irene died in 1988 at eighty-three, survived by fifteen grandchildren and thirteen great-grandchildren. She's buried in Walnut Hills Cemetery beside Charlie.

Joan Hodges still lives on Bedford Avenue.

Gil Jr. continues in his father's footsteps, running a charity dedicated to improving the lives of children through sports.

Unlike many of the teams they competed against in Hodges's day, St. Joseph's College stayed true to its small town roots and—with a nod toward Father Speckbaugh—academics is still the priority. Today, St. Joseph's competes at an NCAA Division II level. Its baseball team plays its home games on a field named for Gil Hodges.

As a Dodgers coach, Jake Pitler engaged in "salty exchanges of insults with players that helped create a warm companionship on the Brooklyn team," much like Hodges had Rube Walker do with the Senators and the Mets. When the Dodgers moved to Los Angeles, Pitler retired to upstate New York, not far from Olean. He died in 1968.

Branch Rickey Jr. never escaped his father's long shadow. But his role in Hodges's signing always remained one of the proudest moments of his professional career. In 1961 Rickey Jr. died due to complications from diabetes; like Hodges, he was only forty-seven.

In Pittsburgh, Hall of Fame executive Branch Rickey never came close to the success he experienced earlier in his career; but his efforts to start a new baseball league (the Continental) indirectly resulted in the creation of the two teams Hodges would manage. Rickey died in 1965.

After leaving Chicago, Leo Durocher managed the Houston Astros and then retired. Near the end of his life, Durocher mellowed but remained self-absorbed, letting it be known that he only wanted to be elected to the Hall of Fame while he was alive. Durocher died in 1991. He was inducted in 1994.

Unlike his more theatrical umpiring partner, Jocko Conlan, there is no plaque in Cooperstown for Hodges's favorite umpire, Larry Goetz. Goetz, a Cincinnati native, loved baseball, and in retirement he rarely missed attending a Reds home game. He died in 1962. His memory lives on in the first-floor art gallery at the Hall of Fame, where he is one of the three umpires depicted in Norman Rockwell's famous painting *Bottom of the Sixth*.

Colonel Robert Merchant spent his entire career in the military serving in Korea and Vietnam. After his death in 1990, his wife, Virginia, donated his papers documenting his twenty-seven years of military service to the Marine Library in Quantico, Virginia. After Okinawa, Hodges and Merchant never met again, but whenever Merchant saw Hodges's name in the sports pages, he would refer to him as my "competent man."

In the 1960s, Chuck Askey lived in San Diego, and whenever the Mets came to town to play the Padres, there were always two tickets waiting for Hodges's old marine buddy and his son.

After the war, Hodges's tent mate Romeo Paulino opened up a barbershop in Manville, New Jersey, and was still cutting hair in 2011, when I paid him a visit and learned that, unlike Hodges, I lack "the bump of knowledge."

After being traded to the Cubs, Chuck Connors played for their Minor League team in Los Angeles. In such proximity to Hollywood, he eventually became the star of *The Rifleman*, one of the most popular early television shows set in the American West. "Having the Dodgers in Los Angeles is wonderful," Connors, who grew up in Brooklyn, once said. "It's just like being home. But the embarrassing thing is that my four sons want to meet only one member of the Dodgers, my old roomie, Gil Hodges, the man who kept me off the team."

"Hodges," former Dodgers batboy Tod Parrott said, "had a huge impact on my existence." He was the kind of person Tod's father called a "stand-up guy," there "when it counts" through "the thick and the thin."

When the Mets officially retired Hodges's No. 14 in a public ceremony at Shea in 1973, Roy Campanella couldn't attend. But he sent a telegram, which Vin Scully read: "Gil Hodges was the greatest guy I ever had the pleasure to play with." Campanella died in 1993.

In 2012, sixty-two years after he put on Hodges's uniform to shag fly balls and ended up signing a couple of baseballs, Vin Scully said, "I'm embarrassed to say it but if those kids are still living, they think they have Hodges' autograph."

After Walter O'Malley fired Clyde Sukeforth, Rickey hired him as a Pirates coach. Knowing he didn't have the right "temperament for it," Sukeforth later turned down several managerial offers. He died in 2000.

Ralph Kiner wished he had hit a few less home runs in 1951 so Hodges would have won the National League home run title that season. "That way," Kiner told me, "Gil might be in the Hall." Kiner died in 2014.

In the mid-1960s, while managing the Detroit Tigers, Charlie Dressen suffered a heart attack and Hodges was asked about the possibility of his replacing Dressen. In response, Hodges issued a highly supportive statement about the managerial abilities of the man who wanted him to bunt more. Dressen died in 1966.

Dick Williams, Hodges's feisty train bunk mate, was a mediocre player but a HOF manager, winning pennants in Boston, Oakland, and San Diego. He died in 2011.

Walter Alston managed the Dodgers for twenty-three years (always on one-year contracts). In his autobiography he named Hodges among his "favorite people." Alston was inducted into the Hall of Fame in 1983. He died the following year.

Don Drysdale was voted into the Hall of Fame in 1984. In his autobiography, *Once a Bum, Always a Dodger*, the only teammate he spends an entire chapter writing about is Gil Hodges. "Will I ever know a better human being," Drysdale wrote, "or have a better friend?" Drysdale died in 1993.

Tampa batboy Steve Garvey became an All-Star first baseman for the Los Angeles Dodgers.

Wes Parker won six Gold Gloves as the Dodgers' first baseman.

Doris, the little girl who gave Hodges her St. Christopher's medal, was so broken-hearted when the Dodgers moved to Los Angeles she didn't follow baseball again until she lived in Boston and fell in love with the Red Sox. As an adult, Pulitzer Prize winner Doris Kearns Goodwin developed an ability to write as clearly as she spoke to Hodges on that spring day in 1951.

In 1972, just a few months before Hodges's death, Sandy Koufax became the youngest person ever elected to the Hall of Fame.

When the Gil Hodges Bridge was dedicated in 1972, Walter O'Malley wrote, "There is something symbolic about a bridge being named in memory of Gil Hodges. When the Dodgers played in Brooklyn there was no more popular player. When we moved to Los Angeles, Gil built a bridge of his own in winning millions of new fans on the West Coast. . . . His life span was short but few achieved more than Gil in important works for his family, his fellow man and God." O'Malley died in 1979 and was inducted in the Hall of Fame in 2008.

When former Dodgers batboy Charlie DiGiovanna died of a heart attack three days after Christmas in 1958, he left a wife and three young children. Hodges was one of several Dodgers players who helped raise over $5,000 for his family.

Senators outfielder Tom Brown could never forget about football. He became a defensive back for Vince Lombardi's Green Bay Packers and played in the first two Super Bowls.

After a difficult post-baseball life, Tom Cheney died of Alzheimer's in 2001.

Dave Stenhouse became the baseball coach at Brown University, where he utilized many of Hodges's managerial techniques.

Ryne Duren overcame his demons, stopped drinking, and worked to help other athletes with their addictions. He died in 2011.

Ken "Hawk" Harrelson is a broadcaster for the White Sox.

After Hodges sent him to Hawaii, Alan Koch never played in the Majors again. When Koch contemplated quitting baseball and going to law school, he even discussed it with Hodges, who admitted that he regretted never having finished his college degree. "Alan, you have something to fall back on that nobody else has on our club," Hodges told Koch. "An education." Like many of Hodges's players, Koch never appreciated what Hodges taught him until years later. "For most players, if you weren't in the major leagues you would be in the lunch-bucket league, a blue-color worker. I thought I was giving 100% effort to baseball; Hodges knew better," Koch recalled. "For me, baseball was an avocation, not a vocation."

After Drysdale and Koufax lost the first two games of the 1965 World Series to the Twins in Minnesota, the Dodgers returned to Los Angeles for the crucial third game. Claude Osteen got the start. Hodges's protégé, "thinking every time" he pitched the ball, shut out the Twins, 4–0. After the Dodgers won the Series in seven games, headlines in Los Angeles read, "Chavez Ravine and Claude Osteen."

After his chat with Hodges, Frank Howard's playing career lasted another half-dozen seasons and he became a four-time All-Star.

Writer Russ White rejoices that baseball has returned to the city where Hodges let him put on a Nats uniform and practice with the team.

Relief pitcher Dave Baldwin believes that were it not for Hodges, his Major League career would have been the proverbial "cup of coffee" and he would have never lasted long enough to qualify for a Major League Baseball pension, which he is still happily collecting.

Near the end of the 1968 season, Al Salerno and another American League umpire, Bill Valentine, attempted to unionize. National League umpires had already unionized and were paid at a higher level than their American League counterparts. Joe Cronin, the American League president, fired Salerno and Valentine a few days after they met with the National League Umpires Association. Salerno never umpired again and spent the rest of his life an angry and bitter man. He died in 2007.

After that first meeting in Pompano Beach, Marvin Miller met with Hodges several times over the years and got to know him well. "I liked the way he conducted himself," Miller told me. Miller died in 2012.

In St. Louis, Joe Torre played for Red Schoendienst, who had "the greatest influence" on his managerial career, teaching him that the key is to learn "how to get respect and be liked." From Hodges he would have learned the former, but not necessarily the latter. Prior to 1996, Torre lost over one hundred more games than he won in his managerial career. But after taking over the Yankees that season, with players like Derek Jeter and Mariano Rivera, Torre won four World Series.

Jon Matlack was voted the National League Rookie of the Year in 1972 and became an All-Star pitcher for the Mets.

Amos Otis became a mainstay of the Kansas City Royals' outfield for fourteen seasons, winning three Gold Gloves.

The Mets traded Tommie Agee after the 1972 season and his career ended a year later. He died of a heart attack in 2001 at fifty-nine.

The 1969 season grew so meaningful to Art Shamsky, he wrote a book about that magical year in New York sports history when the Mets, Jets, and Knicks all won championships.

Nolan Ryan had a remarkably long career that ended with his induction to the Hall of Fame with a higher percentage of votes than anyone else in baseball history (other than Tom Seaver). In his autobiography, Ryan ends the section that describes the years he spent in New York as follows: "I read that Gil Hodges approved the deal, that he wanted Jim Fregosi, and that he thought I was the starting pitcher he would miss the least." Success as president of the Texas Rangers has mellowed Ryan; in 2009 he attended the fortieth anniversary celebration of the 1969 Championship at Citi Field.

Following the 1969 World Series, despite being invited to join several of his teammates and sing in Las Vegas for the then significant sum of $10,000, Ed Charles upheld his prior commitment and departed for a tour of military bases and hospitals in Vietnam. "Background is not the primary concern," Charles once wrote. "But backbone is." Hodges instilled backbone. "Hodges shaped us right up," Charles told me, "and the rest is history."

Eddie Yost always considered Hodges becoming the Senators' manager the biggest break of his career. He died in 2012.

Although the Mets won another pennant in the strike-shortened 1973 season, Yogi Berra was fired in 1975. "Too many players," wrote Joe Durso, "have taken advantage of Yogi Berra's good nature. Hodges was so strict that few dared to take liberties."

After Hodges's death, without any other strong voice to oppose him, M. Donald Grant ran the Mets into the ground. By decade's end, Seaver was playing for the Reds, Koosman for the Twins, Grote for the Dodgers, McGraw for the Phillies, and Matlack for the Rangers. In the late 1970s, when the Mets were hopelessly behind late in games, Shea Stadium could grow eerily quiet. At those moments, Karl Ehrhardt would hold up a sign reading, "WELCOME TO GRANT'S TOMB." Grant died in 1998; Ehrhardt in 2008.

In 1979 the Mets reverted back to a retro version of the 1962 squad and finished with the worst record in the league. They would not improve until the Doubleday family purchased the team (Joan Payson died in 1975) and hired an experienced general manager, Frank Cashen, who had built the Orioles team the Mets defeated in 1969. The Mets won their second (and to date only other) championship in 1986.

Whitey Herzog became both the manager and the general manager of the St. Louis Cardinals, turning them into a championship team. For his unique ability to simultaneously act as both summer and winter manager, Herzog was inducted into the Hall of Fame in 2010.

In a sure sign that time heals all wounds, Cleon Jones told the crowd at Citi Field during the fortieth anniversary celebration of the 1969 Mets, "If it wasn't for Gil Hodges, none of us would be here today."

Ron Swoboda became a broadcaster in New Orleans. He admits, "If I had just kept quiet and done whatever Hodges asked of me, they would have kept me on the team and my baseball career would have continued far longer than it did." Swoboda added, "Not figuring out how to get along with Hodges was my most egregious failure as a professional baseball player. Hodges thought about the team first and foremost. . . . There was no better manager than Gil Hodges."

By 1974 Tug McGraw was the highest-paid relief pitcher in baseball. "Gil Hodges," McGraw said, "made me realize that my enthusiasm was great, but it had to be channeled properly. I developed true concentration—blocking out everything from my mind but the pitch I was about to make."

Several years after being traded from the Mets to the Phillies, with the bases loaded, in the ninth inning of the seventh game of the 1980 World Series, a highly focused McGraw struck out Kansas City's Willie Wilson for the final out of the game, and for the first time in their ninety-seven-year history, the Phillies were World Series champions.

The next season, in the fourth game of the divisional playoffs between the Phillies and the Expos, in the top of the tenth with no outs and the Expos' Gary Carter on first base, Larry Parrish attempted a bunt but hit the ball in the air. McGraw reached for the ball as though he was going to catch it on a fly to keep Carter frozen near first base, but, instead, let the ball drop and fired to first to start a double play that killed the Expos' scoring threat. McGraw was later asked about the play. "It goes back to the late 1960s," McGraw said. "Gil Hodges used to make us practice that play every day in spring training. Ever since then, if a man's on first base with nobody out, whenever a guy bunts, I think of trapping it. It worked this time, thanks to Gil Hodges."

McGraw's appreciation went beyond the playing field. "I loved him," McGraw said, "I loved him more than any man I have ever loved in my life. He understood me, he helped me, he guided me. I was a kid when he came to the Mets. He made me a man. . . . We only had four years together before he died—damn—but I knew he cared about me, not just as a pitcher, as a . . . human being. And it was Gil who straightened me out . . . . He got me to study myself, to believe in myself, to stand up to myself. . . . He made me a better man." McGraw died of cancer in 2004.

Bud Harrelson wore his 1969 World Series ring for one year and then gave it to his father, who wore it for the rest of his life. Today, Harrelson owns an interest in a Minor League Baseball team and still believes that "any day at the ball park is a good day." On those good days, Harrelson can be found sitting at his desk in his office at the Long Island Ducks' ballpark in New York, a framed photograph of Hodges staring down at him from the wall.

In his 1992 Hall of Fame acceptance speech Tom Seaver said, "Gil Hodges was the most important person in my career. Above all, he taught me how to be a professional. I know that God is letting him look down at me now."

Earl Weaver was inducted into the Hall of Fame in 1996 but has never stopped replaying the fifth game of the 1969 World Series. "I've often wondered," Weaver said regarding the shoe-polish-stained ball, "what would have happened if it had been shown . . . not by Hodges, an honest man, but by a sly operator like Weaver." He died in 2013.

Bob Mandt spent over half a century working for the Mets, eventually replacing Jim Thomson as chief of operations. But what gave Mandt his greatest thrill was the greeting he would always get from Tom Seaver, who knew that Mandt had also survived a visit to Hodges's office. "My brother," Seaver would say. Mandt died in 2010. A field-level box at Citi Field is named in his memory.

John Lindsay never won another election. He died in 2000.

Rusty Staub became one of the most popular players in Mets history and was a key component of their 1973 pennant-winning team. Although Staub never won a championship, he told me the greatest disappointment of his career was that "Hodges died before I got there. I would have liked to play for him."

Donn Clendenon became an attorney and had a successful legal career until the 1980s, when he became addicted to cocaine. Clendenon checked himself into a recovery center and eventually became a certified addiction counselor, dedicating the rest of his life to helping others. In his autobiography, published a few years before his death from leukemia in 2005, Clendenon left no doubt about his feelings toward the manager of the 1969 Mets.

"Gil Hodges," Clendenon wrote, "was my idol."

"There must be very few of us," wrote Roger Angell, "who exulted through the Mets' triumphant campaign of 1969 who do not retain some similar permanent portrait of Gil Hodges—enormous hands thrust inside the pockets of his blue windbreaker; his heavy, determinedly expressionless face under the long-billed cap; and his pale intelligent gaze that presided over that turbulent summer and somehow made it come right for his young team and for all of us."

Howie Rose, the Mets' longtime play-by-play announcer, grew up in New York and was one of those who "exulted" in 1969. He captured the if-you-work-hard-and-believe-you-can do-anything mentality that team embodied when he spoke at their fortieth anniversary celebration, calling it "a legacy for generations to come."

In death, Hodges stands out in a way he never did in life. Most headstones in Holy Cross Cemetery turn gray as they age, but not Hodges's. As the decades pass, Hodges's headstone, cut from a slab of pink granite, remains a vibrant shade of brown, and as you walk down Terrace Row from the cemetery entrance toward the St. Catherine section where he's buried, it's the one you notice first.

Hodges is memorialized in several places. In New York, the Marine Parkway–Gil Hodges Bridge spanning the Rockaway Inlet connecting Brooklyn and Queens, a stretch of Bedford Avenue near Hodges's home, and a nearby elementary school, as well as a community garden on Carroll Street in Brooklyn, are all named for him. In Indiana there is a bronze bust of Hodges in the Petersburg municipal building, and on Main Street a huge mural depicts him at numerous points in his baseball career. But there is one particular place where Hodges's legacy lives on in relative anonymity.

When little Nicky Lipariti grew up and had his own family, his son Ciro also played his Little League ball at Gil Hodges Field in Brooklyn. Back then the sign overlooking the ballpark still read "GIL HODGES FIELD." Today, that sign is long gone, replaced with one with the name of the field's current sponsors. But thanks to Hodges, on warm summer days, beneath the roar and clatter of the elevated subway line on McDonald Avenue, you can still hear the sound of children playing baseball.

And if the wind is blowing just right, you can hear them in Los Angeles and Washington, Petersburg and Princeton, even Okinawa and Tokyo, amidst echoes of long-forgotten laughter.

AFTERWORD

HODGES AND THE HALL

> Voting shall be based upon the individual's record,
> ability, integrity, sportsmanship, character, and
> contributions to the game. . . . Those whose careers
> entailed involvement in multiple categories [e.g.,
> player and manager] will be considered for their
> *overall contribution* to the game of Baseball.
>
> HALL OF FAME ELECTION RULES

To answer Moose Skowron's question about why Gil Hodges isn't in the Baseball Hall of Fame (HOF) requires an understanding of the rules for election,
Hodges's unique credentials, and the election process itself.

After a player has been retired for five years, the Baseball Writers' Association of America (BBWAA) can vote on his candidacy. Induction requires
an affirmative vote of at least 75 percent. For those not elected during their
fifteen (changed to ten in 2014) years of eligibility with the writers, their case
then comes before a veterans committee. The committee size has varied over
the years (it's currently set at sixteen) and a 75 percent vote is again required.
Historically, the veterans committee has usually been composed of a mix of
HOF members, veteran broadcasters, and/or baseball executives who meet
to discuss the candidates and then vote. Currently, the veterans committee
votes on eligible players, managers, umpires, and executives according to the
era in which they were active. There are three eras: pre-integration (pre-1947),
golden (1947–72), and expansion (post-1972). For each era, voting takes place
once every three years.

It's difficult to get a diverse group of hundreds of writers from across the country to agree on anything let alone the HOF worthiness of all but the greatest players. Hodges's playing career coincided with some of the all-time greats such as Henry Aaron, Willie Mays, Mickey Mantle, Stan Musial, and Ted Williams—all of whom were elected in their first year of eligibility. By all objective standards (e.g., career home runs, lifetime batting average, or wins above replacement) Hodges was simply not as good as these players. But that doesn't mean he is unworthy of induction, since only a small percentage of players are elected in their first year of eligibility. Quite the contrary, despite a career batting average of .273, Hodges's statistical record in the context of the era he played in (before pitching mounds were lowered from fifteen to ten inches in 1969 and before steroids and HGH have more recently inflated the career totals of countless players) merits induction.

After the 1962 season, Hodges's last full season as a player, his 370 home runs placed him tenth on the career home run list. At that point, only Babe Ruth (714), Jimmy Foxx (534), Ted Williams (521), Mel Ott (511), Lou Gehrig (493), Stan Musial (463), Mickey Mantle (404), Eddie Mathews (399), and Duke Snider (389) had hit more home runs than Hodges. The only other players then with at least 300 career home runs were Ralph Kiner (369), Willie Mays (368), Joe DiMaggio (361), Johnny Mize (359), Yogi Berra (350), Ernie Banks (335), Hank Greenberg (331), Al Simmons (307), Rogers Hornsby (301), and Chuck Klein (300)—and all are in the HOF.

Hodges's seven consecutive seasons (1949–55) of driving in at least 100 runs left him just one season short of tying Mel Ott's then existing National League record. He hit at least 22 home runs eleven seasons in a row, tying him with Mel Ott for the National League record for the most consecutive seasons with at least 20 home runs. Hodges still holds the record for hitting the most sacrifice flies in a season with 19. When Hodges retired, he held the National League career grand slam home run record with 14. His home run and RBI totals for the decade of the 1950s are higher than all other players with the exception of Duke Snider. Gil Hodges and Lou Gehrig are still the only two players to ever hit four home runs in one nine-inning game and hit for the cycle in another.

In addition to his outstanding power hitting, Hodges won three Gold Gloves at first base (1957–59) and would have certainly won more had the award been established prior to his last three seasons as an everyday player. His footwork at first base was so renowned that in 1957 he was the subject of a *Look* magazine article that compared photographs of his fielding steps to those of a dancer. Yet had Hodges remained a catcher, a position rarely played by a hitter with his power, his HOF candidacy might have been perceived more favorably. Although there is no guarantee he would have been as productive in the more physically demanding catcher's position, Hodges's career hitting totals are remarkably close to those of HOF catcher Johnny Bench. Overall, Hodges made a significant contribution to Dodger teams that won six pennants and two World Series in the eleven-year period in which he was their starting first baseman (1949–59).

If Hodges's statistical legacy merits his being voted in (but just not on the first ballot), why didn't the writers do so over his subsequent fourteen years of eligibility? The short answer is Hodges came very close, but poor timing, his early death (out of sight, out of mind), overly aggressive campaigning by others after his death, his personality, and his dual career as a player and a manager didn't work in his favor. HOF voters prefer that a candidate be outstanding in one particular category, whether it be home run hitting or fielding, as opposed to a jack-of-all-trades like Hodges.

The first time Hodges was on the ballot was 1969. He received 82 votes (24 percent), a solid start indicative of a player who would most likely muster the required 75 percent vote before his fifteen years of eligibility ended. Hodges's vote total jumped to 145 votes (48 percent) in 1970, placing him third in the voting ahead of Early Wynn, Enos Slaughter, Johnny Mize, Pee Wee Reese, Red Schoendienst, and George Kell—all of whom were later elected either by the writers or the veterans committee. At some point during his time on the ballot, Hodges would also finish ahead of the following players, all of whom were later enshrined: Bob Lemon, Robin Roberts, Eddie Mathews, Duke Snider, Phil Rizzuto, Don Drysdale, Jim Bunning, Richie Ashburn, Hoyt Wilhelm, Nellie Fox, Harmon Killebrew, Juan Marichal, Hal Newhouser, Luis Aparicio, and Billy Williams.

Poor timing played a role in Hodges's never receiving the required 75 percent vote. Beginning in 1972, Hodges had the misfortune of competing with ten first-ballot Hall of Famers: Sandy Koufax (1972), Warren Spahn (1973), Mickey Mantle (1974), Ernie Banks (1977), Willie Mays (1979), Al Kaline (1980), Bob Gibson (1981), Hank Aaron and Frank Robinson (1982), and Brooks Robinson (1983).

Unlike most, Hodges took a low profile regarding his own candidacy; I couldn't find a single quote from Hodges regarding his chances for induction. Based on comments he made when Mickey Mantle retired, Hodges viewed Cooperstown as a place for the game's all-time greats (such as Ruth, Gehrig, and Mantle) and didn't view himself on that level. But after Hodges's death in 1972, strident lobbying on his behalf backfired. In 1978 Red Smith wrote, "There has been an aggressive campaign for Gil Hodges going on for several years now, insistent, hard-sell electioneering that may have turned off a good many voters who might otherwise have included Gil on their ballots."

Red Smith began a 1979 piece titled "Five Men Worthy for Cooperstown," this way: "'Voting,' says a rule governing election to the Baseball Hall of Fame, 'shall be based upon the player's record, playing ability, integrity, sportsmanship, character, contribution to the team(s) on which the player played . . .' Translated, this means that all my baseball friends are or should be enshrined in Cooperstown and any player who gives me a short answer is obviously deficient in character and must languish in outer darkness."

In this regard, Hodges's tight-lipped approach with the press likely cost him votes. At a minimum, it intimidated some of the younger writers. "He always looked dispassionate," Marty Noble recalled decades later, comparing Hodges's eyes in a well-known George Kalinsky photo to those of a shark, "disarming—no emotion."

Yet Hodges still received at least 50 percent of the vote in eleven of the fifteen years he was on the ballot. Three times he received at least 60 percent of the vote, with a high of 63 percent in 1983, his final year of eligibility where he missed election by just forty-four votes. Historically, those who finish with at least a 60 percent vote are eventually enshrined. But so far not Hodges: his cumulative vote total over his fifteen years on the ballot is higher than any other player not subsequently elected.

Since there is a great deal of subjectivity involved in determining who belongs in the HOF, the players on the veterans committee have a natural inclination to favor their former teammates. This preference begins even before one's plaque is affixed to the walls of the HOF: in Bert Blyleven's 2011 acceptance speech at Cooperstown, he specifically mentioned the HOF worthiness of two of his former Minnesota Twins teammates, Jim Kaat and Tony Oliva.

In this regard, Hodges's poor luck continued when his candidacy reached the veterans committee in 1985. The very next year was Ted Williams's first year on the committee. It wasn't coincidental that that year (1986), the veterans committee selected Bobby Doerr, Williams's longtime teammate on the Boston Red Sox. Williams also hoped to get Dom DiMaggio, another Red Sox teammate, into Cooperstown. Williams never succeeded with respect to DiMaggio, but Williams was an intimidating figure and had a clear preference for American League players such as Phil Rizzuto, who was inducted in 1994. A member of the committee, HOF outfielder Monte Irvin, told me Williams didn't support Hodges's candidacy, responding with a dismissive, "Oh, you National League guys."

According to the longtime Detroit Tigers broadcaster Ernie Harwell, who was on the committee from 1988 to 1991, Williams, as well as all other members of the veterans committee, never gave any consideration to which players had come closest to being elected by the writers. If they had, Hodges would have been an obvious choice. Harwell told me that one of the key criteria he would use in deciding how to vote was what the players on the committee who played against the potential HOF candidate thought of him. "They had," Harwell said, "the insider's view." Harwell voted for Hodges giving consideration to both his playing and managerial record in what he referred to as a "subliminal melding."

There has been conjecture that Williams held a grudge against Hodges. People who knew Williams well, like Joe Camacho (his bench coach on the Washington Senators), his former teammates Johnny Pesky and Bobby Doerr, as well as Williams's close friend, the writer John Underwood, all told me they never heard Williams mention Hodges. However, the comments I found Williams made regarding Hodges, such as his saying Yost—and not Hodges—makes all the Mets in-game decisions were not only incorrect but unfavorable. "I feel I'm a little bit the enthusiastic type of manager," Williams once said. "I might put a little extra zing into the guys. But then, there are managers who've been successful who don't do that. Gil Hodges doesn't." Williams didn't know Hodges well; if there was ever any manager who could put an "extra zing" in his players, it was Hodges.

Williams died in 2002. By then over four decades had passed since Hodges's last full season as an everyday player (1959), and many of the stars on the Brooklyn Dodgers who might have had both the will and the cachet to effectively lobby for him on the veterans committee (Robinson, Campanella, Reese, and Drysdale) had died. In 2011 Tommy Lasorda valiantly argued on Hodges's behalf, but Billy Williams made a passionate, and ultimately winning, plea for his Cubs teammate Ron Santo. In their fifteen years on the writers' ballot, Santo received a cumulative total of 1,749 votes; Hodges, 3,010.

Unfortunately, today, when Hodges's name is mentioned, the reference invariably focuses on him as an icon with a halo over his head, his nice-guy image masking his baseball accomplishments. For example, few know Hodges recovered from his 1952 World Series debacle and tied a record for the most World Series (three) in which a player led his team in batting average (1953, 1956, and 1959).

Hodges was even pushed out of the limelight shortly after his death, as two of baseball's most legendary players died later that same year. When Jackie Robinson died on October 24, 1972, the news made headlines far beyond the sports pages. And Roberto Clemente died on December 31, 1972, when a cargo plane he had chartered to bring humanitarian aid to earthquake-ravaged Nicaragua crashed shortly after taking off. Clemente was only thirty-eight and had just gotten his three thousandth and final career hit that fall. The five-year waiting period for induction into Cooperstown was waived and Clemente was enshrined in 1973.

Hodges's case for the HOF is unique because star players rarely become successful managers, and no player in baseball history has so successfully combined the disparate roles of manager and power hitter as well as Hodges. But I spoke to one HOF player who places limited weight on a person's "overall contribution to the game of baseball."

In 2008, a few days before the final All-Star Game ever played at the old Yankee Stadium, I was walking down Madison Avenue on a beautiful July afternoon when I heard a commotion and there in front of me was Reggie

Jackson. When I spotted Jackson, a reporter from the *New York Post* was interviewing him. I waited for that interview to end and then asked Jackson if he would answer a question. He agreed.

"Which World Series–winning manager," I asked, "hit the most home runs in his playing career?"

"Yogi," Jackson replied more as a question than an answer.

"No. Yogi Berra never won a World Series as a manager."

"Who?"

"Gil Hodges."

"That's a trick question."

I thought it was a great question synthesizing the two things baseball fans admire most—championships and home runs. But there still appears to be a tendency by some HOF members (such as Jackson and the late Earl Weaver) to view a candidate as either a player or a manager, not both.

Another argument against Hodges's election is that the Dodgers teams of the 1950s are already well represented with six HOF players: Campanella, Drysdale, Koufax, Reese, Robinson, and Snider. But there is no limit on how many players can be in the HOF from one team. The 1932 Yankees have nine players in the HOF: Bill Dickey, Lou Gehrig, Tony Lazzeri, Joe Sewell, Babe Ruth, Earl Combs, Lefty Grove, Herb Pennock, and Red Ruffing.

Lastly, although a perceived lack of character and integrity stemming from the use of steroids or HGH is used to exclude a player from the HOF, possessing those same qualities doesn't enter the analysis to include a player in the HOF. Roy Sievers, an estimable home run hitter in the 1950s with the Washington Senators, summed it up best in a letter he wrote me about Hodges: "He was a great human being and great ballplayer. Can't understand why he is not in the HOF."

ACKNOWLEDGMENTS

It is always wise, when you hear something about a
man, to remember who told you and why he told you.
RED BARBER

In 2006 when I called Mrs. Joan Hodges and told her I was writing a biography of her late husband, she said, "You're the first person who ever called me to talk about Gil that I'm not speaking with."

What I did to earn that honor I'm still not sure. But a biographer can only play the cards he's been dealt, and Mrs. Hodges's decision proved a formidable impediment to my illuminating Hodges's family life. As a result, my primary focus is Hodges's professional career and his interactions with his teammates and players. You can imagine my feelings when I learned that Mrs. Hodges subsequently cooperated with two other writers on their joint biography of her husband. To add insult to injury, one of them is a Yankees fan.

But I had far more supporters than detractors. First and foremost among them was Gil Hodges's sole surviving sibling, Marjorie Maysent, whose help was both invaluable and heartfelt. I will always be grateful for the faith she showed in me.

In most ways this project has been a labor of love. In this regard I came across the following dialogue between Gil Hodges and longtime *Sports Illustrated* photographer Herb Scharfman, which took place in Hodges's office at Shea Stadium on July 9, 1969, while Scharfman was taking photo after photo of Hodges.

"Herbie," said Hodges, "I don't believe there's any film in there."

"Aw, Gil," said Scharfman, "I like to take your picture."

George Vecsey, who was also in Hodges's office, said, "Herbie, you've been spending your whole life taking pictures of Gil Hodges."

In his thick Brooklyn accent, Scharfman replied, "I'll tell you something. It's been a pleasure."

Thanks to all the writers who gave of their time: the late Maury Allen, Tom Adelman, Rob Edelman, Frank Graham Jr., Arnold Hano, Bob Hertzel, Steve Jacobson, the late Jack Lang, Jane Leavy, Robert Lipsyte, Lee Lowenfish, Bob McGee, Marty Noble, Danny Peary, Phil Pepe, Josh Prager, Michael Shapiro, John Thorn, John Underwood, George Vescey, Russ White, and Dave Anderson, who told me, "You must sometimes be a pest to get an interview, but be a pleasant pest."

Thanks to all those I interviewed regarding Hodges's formative years in Indiana, especially Randy Harris, the former mayor of Petersburg who helped me locate many of the following: the late Kae Adkerson, the late Charles Anderson, Howard Briscoe, the late Charles Browning, Susan Dellinger (email), the late John Drof, Jerry Hargus, Bob and Sondra Harris, the late George Harris, Chuck Harmon, Vance Hays, the late Mildred Hisgen, Donald Hume, the late Jim Kelley, June King, the late Jack Kinman, the late Wayne Malotte, Art Miley, Wyatt Rauch, the late Robert Smith, Clark Teuscher, the late Bill Thomas, the late Barbara Vance, and Rosemary Weathers.

Thanks to those who spoke to me about Hodges's military service and/or what it was like be in a AAA unit on Okinawa: Chuck Askey, Neil Fiala (email), Lester Foster, George Howe (correspondence only), Virginia Merchant, Romeo Paulino, James Powers, and Vincent Powers; and the late Walter Loeb for his recollections of conditions on Okinawa during the typhoon. Thanks to Annette Amerman of the Marine Corps History Division for helping me understand rifle scores and the significance of various codes used in the 1945 Military Occupation Specialty Manual. Thanks to Barry Zerby at the National Archives; Alisa Johnson and Kristen Yarmey at the Marine Corps Archives in Qantico; and the editor of *Leatherneck* magazine, Colonel Walter Ford. Thanks to Gil Hodges Jr. for assisting me in acquiring a copy of his father's war records and granting me a brief phone interview.

Thanks to those who shared their recollections of Hodges's playing career: Herman Alevy, Bob Aspromonte, Yogi Berra (by email through Dave Kaplan),

Wayne Block, Bob Borkowski, Ralph Branca, the late Jim Brosnan, Roger Craig, Tommy Davis, Don Demeter, Jim Desmond, Bobby Doerr, Carl Erskine, Jim Gentile, the late Ernie Harwell, the late Gene Hermanski, Jim Hickman, Bob Howell, Monte Irvin, Ransom Jackson, the late Clyde King, Fred Kipp, Sandy Koufax, the late Clem Labine, Rene Lachemann, Alvin Miller, the late Andy Pafko, Wes Parker, the late Johnny Pesky, the late Johnny Podres, Tod, Lynn, and Brian Parrott, the late Robin Roberts, Rachel Robinson, Ed Roebuck, Norm Sherry, Tom Simpson, the late Bobby Thomson, the late Frank Torre, and the late Dick Walsh.

And those who spoke of Hodges's managerial years in Washington: Dave Baldwin, Charlie Brotman, Tom Brown, Joe Camacho, Casey Cox, Mike Epstein, Jim Hannan, Frank Howard, Bob Humphreys, Alan Koch, Darold Knowles, Dick Lines, Jim Lonborg, Mike McCormick, Ken McMullen, the late Marvin Miller, Cal Neeman, Claude Osteen, Bob Priddy, Ken Retzer, the late Al Salerno, Bob Saverine, Roy Sievers (correspondence only), the late Moose Skowron, Dave Stenhouse, and Fred Valentine.

And in New York managing the Mets: the late Sparky Anderson, Dr. Linton H. Bishop Jr., Ed Charles, Mike DiMuro (email), the late Karl Ehrhardt, the late Jim Fregosi, Joe Guidice, Doug Harvey, Bud Harrelson, Whitey Herzog, Reggie Jackson, Cleon Jones, the late Ralph Kiner, Jerry Koosman, Nick Lipariti, the late Bob Mandt, Jon Matlack, Jim McAndrew, Joe McDonald Jr., Joe Pignatano, Danny Reilly, Tom Seaver (correspondence), Art Shamsky, Ken Singleton (email), Bill Slocum, Rusty Staub, Lewis Sweedler, Ron Swoboda, Joe Torre (through Phil Hochberg), the late Earl Weaver, Al Weis, Matt Winick, and the late Ed Yost. Thanks to Tony Hodges for speaking with me about his father, Bob Hodges.

Thanks to the following for their encouragement and guidance: Janet Beneda, Dennis Bunker, Andrew Costin, the late Ron Gabriel, Phil Hochberg, Alan Okun, and John Saccoman.

Thanks to Sandy McBeth for her photographs of Hodges's high school years. Thanks to Jay Horowitz and David Newman of the Mets for their help in putting me in contact with some of Hodges's Mets players.

Thanks to those who assisted me at various libraries: Betty Ahlemann and Shirley Bahme of the Princeton (Indiana) Public Library; Gregg Grunow of the Martha Woodroof Hiden Collection of the Newport News Public Library System; Yasuko Makino of the Princeton University Library (East Asian Division); Faye Haskins and Jason Moore of the Washingtoniana Division DC Public Library; and Judith Walsh, Joy Holland, and Olivia Norales Geaghan of the Brooklyn Collection, Brooklyn Public Library.

Thanks to Ken Meifert, Craig Muder, and John Horne at the National Baseball Hall of Fame and Museum in Cooperstown for assisting me regarding the statistical details of Hodges's HOF candidacy and tracking down photos.

Thanks to Howard Alter, David Anderson, Keith Costa, Steve Frakt, Dan Frishwasser, Jim Hockenberry, Cecil Marshall, and Anne Neumann for reading my manuscript and offering invaluable feedback.

Lastly, thanks to my very patient editor, Rob Taylor, his assistant, Courtney Ochsner, and the entire staff at the University of Nebraska Press.

NOTES

EPIGRAPHS

vi   **What you leave behind**: www.brainyquote.com.

vi   **Gil Hodges was not**: Phone interview with Sandy Koufax, October 14, 2010.

PREFACE

xiii   **There is a fundamental**: *New York Times*, April 4, 1972, 49.

xiii   **more than one million**: Thorn, *Total Baseball*, 2422–24.

xiii   **a few brief shining seasons**: Leonard Koppett wrote, "The Mets struck it big in 1969: It was a truly national event . . . in no sense at all a Brooklyn-Queens victory. . . . The locality just didn't count. Then the Mets became ordinary, and the world forgot them, and their hard-core, considerable following again became the metropolitan middle class": *New York Times*, April 2, 1972, A1.

xiii   **"not colorful, not what"**: *The Sporting News*, April 15, 1972.

xiv   **"It looked"**: *Washington Post*, April 27, 1967, C4.

xiv   **"Can you tell me why"**: Phone interview with Bill "Moose" Skowron, January 4, 2007.

xiv   **"He was a first baseman of rare"**: Red Smith, *New York Times*, December 28, 1979.

xiv   **"I don't know anything bad"**: Phone interview with Don Demeter, January 4, 2007.

xiv   **"Hodges was just here"**: Interview with Lewis Sweedler, August 15, 2008.

PROLOGUE

1   *No man lives his image*: Hodges as quoted in the *Evansville Press*, March 30, 1970. Unless otherwise stated, the quotes that begin each chapter were all either said, or written, by Gil Hodges.

1   **"perhaps the most"**: Angell, *Summer Game*, 37.

2   **"When everyone else got"**: Seaver, *Perfect Game*, 62.

2   **"He had cold water"**: Cohen, *Magic Summer*, 246.

2   **driven to Shea**: Tulley, "Brother Bob Returns from Shea Stadium," article from October 1969 that was clipped into Father Vieck's Gil Hodges scrapbook. The name of the newspaper the article appeared in was cut away.

2   **very long car ride**: Interview with Marjorie Maysent, August 14, 2006.

3   **"The leadership of Hodges"**: *New York Times*, September 26, 1969, 61.

4   **over fifty feet**: Lowry, *Green Cathedrals*, 165.

5   **"Whatever happened"**: Phone interview with Ron Swoboda, May 24, 2006.

5   **"They had time"**: Phone interview with Earl Weaver, July 30, 2009.

5   **"Gil Hodges [was] as good"**: Gorman, *Three and Two*, 96.

5   **"Lou, the ball hit"**: Vescey, *Joy in Mudville*, 245.

5   **"a certain menace"**: Phone interview with George Vescey, May 11, 2006.

6   **"a product of his white"**: Clendenon, *Miracle in New York*, 2.

6   **and supposedly unaware of how**: There was an important motivation behind Major League Baseball's wanting Clendenon to sign a new contract. On the surface, they didn't want Clendenon to retire because the trade would have to be rescinded. That would present a problem for the Expos because they had already started a marketing campaign around the key player they had acquired in the trade, Rusty Staub. Baseball commissioner Bowie Kuhn used his authority to act "in the best interests of baseball" to allow Staub to remain in Montreal, but forced Houston to accept Jack Billingham, Skip Guinn, and $100,000 as compensation for Clendenon. But the lords of baseball had other motivations. The long-held belief was that the reserve clause in the standard player's contract automatically bound a player to his team in perpetuity. But if a player didn't sign a new contract by March 1, a literal reading of the infamous Section 10A of the standard player's contract gave the owners only a one-year renewal option. The lords knew their power over the players—and therefore their ability to keep salaries artificially below fair market value—rested on the legal interpretation of this very shaky clause. Since he had not signed a contract, and the March 1 deadline had passed, if Clendenon decided to return to baseball he could provide a viable reserve-clause test case for the player's union. And that was exactly what would occur after the 1969 season when Curt Flood refused to sign a contract after being traded. According to his autobiography, Clendenon didn't know of the threat he posed to the reserve clause before signing his three-year contract; however, after the 1969 season, Clendenon, an exceptionally bright man, referred to the reserve clause as "unconstitutional": Joe Durso, *New York Times*, October 22, 1969, 37.

7   **"You're damn right"**: Clendenon, *Miracle in New York*, 97.

8   **In the eighth inning**: *New York Times*, October 17, 1969, 1. In an ironic twist, Davey Johnson, the Orioles' second baseman who hit the final out of the 1969

Series, would be the manager of the Mets in 1986, when they won their second World Series.

8 "It's the first one": *New York Times*, October 17, 1969, 58.

9 threw it at Weaver: Shamsky, *Magnificent Seasons*, 170.

9 "The ball came to me": Jerry Koosman at the question-and-answer session at the fortieth anniversary celebration of the 1969 Mets, August 22, 2009, at Citi Field prior to that day's game. I attended the session and asked the question, since I felt there was more to the story than what Koosman had previously told me. I take Koosman's version with a grain of salt. If Stengel kept a few shoe-polish-stained balls in the dugout, it's likely that Hodges, who played for Stengel in 1962 and never missed a trick, did as well.

9 "You know how magicians": Phone interview with Jerry Koosman, December 5, 2007. In September of 2010, when New York Yankee shortstop Derek Jeter feigned being hit by a pitch in a game against the Tampa Bay Rays and was awarded first base despite the fact that the ball hit the knob of his bat and not him, Bruce Weber addressed the issue of cheating in baseball ("Week in Review," *New York Times*, September 19, 2010, 2). Weber wrote, "I would describe the dividing line this way: If a player's ruse is spontaneous, if it occurs in response to the action on the field, then it's legit. Deviousness plotted in advance or off the field, however, is a problem, the sporting equivalent of malice aforethought. That's why a base runner's decoding an opposing catcher's signs and flashing them to the batter is good baseball, but hiding a sign-stealing coach inside the centerfield scoreboard with a pair of binoculars is not." When Nippy Jones convinced umpire Augie Donatelli to change his call during the 1957 World Series, the ball never left the field of play: Isaacs, *Innocence & Wonder*, 55.

I. COAL MINER'S SON

13 *My dad*: Hodges talking about his father, *The Sporting News*, June 15, 1963, 5.

13 on January 3, 1901: Obituary, *Petersburg Press*, November 29, 1957.

13 When Charlie was still: Phone interview with Marjorie Maysent, February 24, 2007. Although a sealed and certified copy of Gilbert Ray Hodges's birth certificate issued to me by Gibson County shows the family name as Hodges, there remains a difference of opinion. Some insist the family name was Hodge. In an early version of the White Pages called the Caron Directory for Princeton, Indiana, for the years 1925-26, a "Chas Hodge (miner)" with a wife named Irene resided at 218 Ford Street, but by 1930-31 the name had metamorphosed into "Hiram P. Hodges, miner" residing at 806 N West. In 1939 Bud and Bob were referred to as Hodge in a box score and related article that appeared in the *Petersburg Press*. A photo of the high school basketball team that Hodges played on has each player's

name written across his torso, and his name is show as "G. Hodge." As late as April 17, 1945, the *Petersburg Press*, in a front-page article, referred to two local brothers as "Bob and Bud Hodge." When I interviewed Charles Browning, a classmate of Gil Hodges at Saint Joseph's College, by phone on February 9, 2007, he said Irene was "always disappointed he [Gil Hodges] didn't carry the name, Hodge." But Hodges's sister, Marjorie, is certain the family name was always Hodges. "Hodge," she told me, "was just a nickname. When people saw dad they would say, 'Here comes old Hodge.'" An article that appeared in the *Petersburg Press Dispatch*, June 15, 2005, B-12, titled, "Gilbert Ray (Bud) Hodges" by former mayor and longtime resident Jack Kinman, a 1938 graduate of Petersburg High School and a man whom I met and interviewed and found highly credible, confirmed that Charlie Hodges's nickname was Hodge.

13   **German-Irish descent:** Amoruso, *Quiet Man*, 184.

13   **died of whooping cough:** Roeder, *Artful Dodgers*, 69. This book, first published in 1954 and edited by Tom Meany, is a collection of essays written by numerous sportswriters (Meany, Bill Roeder, Roscoe McGowen, Mike Gaven, and Harold Rosenthal) who covered the Dodgers either in Brooklyn or, in a version published in 1963, Los Angeles. Roeder covered the Brooklyn Dodgers for the *New York World-Telegram* and wrote the chapter "The Strong Man: Gil Hodges," where I found a treasure trove of material.

14   **nurse had to be sent down:** Earlier versions of Hodges's life report this accident as occurring in 1932. I verified the date in the December 10, 1926, *Princeton Clarion*. Francisco No. 2 was reopened in 1927 and was not abandoned until 1935: Indiana Geological Study, Open File Study 98-5.

14   **Thirty-seven:** McConn, *Frisco II Mine Explosion*, 6.

14   **lost his right eye:** Roeder, *Artful Dodgers*, 70.

14   **hear him coming:** Amoruso, *Quiet Man*, 178.

14   **"Not to worry":** Kinman, "Gilbert Ray (Bud) Hodges," undated article from Father Vieck's scrapbook.

14   **windy:** Phone interview with George Harris, April 20, 2006.

14   **"a competitor":** Charles Anderson, group interview, Petersburg IN, April 2006.

14   **St. Joseph's Parochial:** Miley, *Pike County History*, 416.

15   **"Bob knew he was good":** Wayne Malotte, group interview, Petersburg IN, April 2006.

15   **"stabilizing influence":** Bob King quoted in Amoruso, *Quiet Man*, 178.

15   **Amber, navy bean soup,** and **framed photo:** Interview with Marjorie Maysent, August 14, 2006.

15   **moved his family:** The family spent a few months living a dozen miles south of Petersburg in Oakland City, home of Edd Roush, a Hall of Fame outfielder with

the Cincinnati Reds, but Hodges never met Roush: 2010 email from Susan Dellinger, granddaughter of Edd Roush.

15 **Adams Pharmacy and Howard's Café:** From a photograph of Main Street circa 1931.

16 **he once challenged:** Wayne Malotte, group interview, April 2006.

16 **didn't have a baseball team:** Roeder, *Artful Dodgers*, 69.

16 **broad jump** and **shot put record:** Roeder, *Artful Dodgers*, 71.

16 **played halfback:** Roeder, *Artful Dodgers*, 71.

16 **six feet, weighed a solid 175:** Roeder, *Artful Dodgers*, 71.

16 **palm a basketball:** Wayne Malotte, group interview, Petersburg, April, 2006.

17 **"could sure move bodies":** Wendell Trogdon, "Gil Hodges: A Miracle Man," *Indiana Basketball History*, Fall 1997, 17.

18 **routed Petersburg:** Petersburg High School, *Senior Finale*, 1941.

18 **semifinals of the National Invitational:** Jacobson, *Carrying Jackie's Torch*, 107.

18 **baseball games against Gil:** Phone interview with Chuck Harmon, April 27, 2006.

18 **American Legion circuit:** Roeder, *Artful Dodgers*, 71. Hodges played for the Princeton (managed by Eldon Sisson) and Petersburg American Legion teams: *Princeton Clarion*, June 29, 1940.

19 **grades were average:** In a letter Hodges wrote to his sister when he was in college, he notes that his grades in high school were usually in the B to C range.

19 **"neither absent nor tardy":** *Petersburg Press*, May 13, 1941.

19 **couldn't recall:** Interview with Mildred Hisgen, April 2006, Petersburg IN.

20 **"Bud was an excellent dancer":** Phone interview with Barbara Vance Hays, May 18, 2006. Music played at Jimmy's: Trogdon, "Gil Hodges," 17. When I spoke to Barbara's son Vance on May 23, 2006, he said that in that era, "Catholics didn't date outside the faith" and that Irene and Charlie also wouldn't have wanted the relationship to get serious.

21 **"very strong":** Phone interview with George Harris, April 20, 2006. Many miners' sons were not as fortunate as Hodges to work only up top. In 1937 a young man who shared the same first name as Hodges, Gil Carpenter, who excelled playing baseball for the Martinsville, Virginia, team in the Bi-State League, received a letter from Branch Rickey, then the general manager of the St. Louis Cardinals, advising him that he would be given a tryout the following spring. That winter, Carpenter was crushed to death working in a coal mine in Pittston, Pennsylvania: email from Ivy Carpenter, and an October 22, 1937, letter from Branch Rickey to Gilbert Carpenter.

21 **Tigers, who were impressed:** Roeder, *Artful Dodgers*, 67.

21 **Staucet, who later played:** Roeder, *Artful Dodgers*, 72.

21 **Indiana Collegiate Conference title:** Email from Clark Teuscher, sports information director, Saint Joseph's College, March 12, 2007.

21 **much larger universities:** Bill Robertson, "Gil Was Grid Hero, Too . . . for One Day," undated article from Father Vieck's scrapbook.

22 **enjoyed the physical aspect:** Robertson, "Gil Was Grid Hero," Father Vieck's scrapbook.

22 **tin-roofed house:** Amoruso, *Quiet Man*, 184. It would not be until 1943 that Charlie could afford to buy his own home: a two-story house at the corner of Fourteenth and Main.

22 **home-baked cookies:** Interview with Marjorie Maysent, August 14, 2006.

23 **with his forearm:** Robertson, "Gil Was Grid Hero," Father Vieck's scrapbook.

23 **industrial league:** Roeder, *Artful Dodgers*, 72.

23 **Stanley Feezle:** Roeder, *Artful Dodgers*, 72.

2. THE TWIG, THE BRANCH, AND THE LIP

25 *Though I was with him:* Hodges, *Game of Baseball*, 21.

25 **"straight out of Andy Hardy":** Harford, *Merton & Friends*, 7.

26 **"Hodges hits one":** Herb Goren, "Hodges Is in the Picture Now," *Baseball Digest*, February 1951, 96.

28 **"He'll apply himself":** Minot, *Washington Post*, January 15, 1967, D4.

28 **Hodges's tryout:** *Brooklyn Eagle*, September 1, 1943.

28 **"an incredible combination":** Roeder, *Artful Dodgers*, 86.

28 **percentage of the team's net profits:** The worksheets Rickey used to compute the Dodgers' annual profit are in the Branch Rickey Papers, Library of Congress.

29 **"Well, your home run":** Honig, *Baseball When the Grass Was Real*, 100–106.

29 **"The only way":** Lyle and Everett, *Brainstorm in Brooklyn*, 1943, Rickey Papers, Library of Congress, Box 33, Folder 14.

29 **signing bonus of $1,250:** Wolf, *Los Angeles Times* (hereafter *LA Times*), January 25, 1958, A2. Duke Snider received $750; Roy Campanella, $2,000; and Jackie Robinson, $3,600. Rickey made mistakes. In 1946, after watching a Penn State graduate named Joe Tepsic work out at Ebbets Field, Rickey gave him a $17,500 bonus. Tepsic's Major League career totals: five at bats, no hits.

30 **"Nice guys finish last":** William Safire, "On Language," *New York Times Magazine*, October 16, 2005.

30 **"What are you crying":** Jimmy Powers, *New York Daily News*, April 21, 1947, 50.

30 **Durocher was paid:** Durocher, *Nice Guys Finish Last*, 188. At the end of the 1940s, managers were paid in a range from $30,000 to $60,000. Durocher was at the high end of that range: *New York Times Sunday Magazine*, June 26, 1949, 19.

30 **"Kid, when you pick one":** Golenbock, *Bums*, 17.

31   **"short, indelicate words"**: Smith, *On Baseball*, 4.

31   **"if there weren't"**: Durocher, *Nice Guys Finish Last*, 3.

31   **"squawk loud enough"**: Harvey Breit, *New York Times Sunday Magazine*, June 26, 1949, 19.

31   **shots off the outfield fence**: *Brooklyn Eagle*, September 1, 1943.

32   **first Major League game**: Roeder, *Artful Dodgers*, 75.

33   **most double plays**: McGowen, *New York Times*, September 28, 1950, 51.

33   **"you never forgot"**: Hodges, *Game of Baseball*, 120.

3. OKINAWA

37   *Sitting around in*: Harold Rosenthal, "The Dodgers' Home-Run Kid," *Saturday Evening Post*, September 8, 1951, 141.

37   **never discussed**: Interview with Marjorie Maysent, February 24, 2007.

37   **stated only his itinerary**: Roscoe McGowen, "Gil's Capable Hands Make Any Job Easier," *The Sporting News*, March 13, 1957, 4.

37   **Hiroshima and Nagasaki**: Rottman, *Okinawa 1945*, 84–85.

37   **"Anybody who wants"**: McGowen, "Gil's Capable Hands," 4.

37   **"slugged it out"**: Herb Goren, "Hodges Is in the Picture Now," *Baseball Digest*, February 1951, 15.

38   **"We kept hearing stories"**: *New York Times*, October 12, 1967, 61, and *New York Times*, October 7, 1969, 54. Hodges's comment to Goren that he had it "pretty good" and his reluctance to discuss his war experiences indicates Hodges may have felt guilty about not serving in a combat unit because of his celebrity status, however nominal, having played in one Major League game at that point in his career. For example, Hall of Famer Eddie Mathews, felt guilty because as a Major League ballplayers he received special treatment during his military service: Mathews, *Eddie Mathews*, 45.

38   **"On Okinawa, you were either"**: Phone interview with James Powers, September 11, 2006.

38   **highly unusual**: Phone interview with Vincent H. Powers, USMC, member of the Eighth AAA Battalion on Okinawa, September 9, 2006.

38   **Aboard the *Phoenix***: Phone interview with Virginia Merchant, widow of Robert Merchant, January 26, 2007.

38   **Hodges was his aide-de-camp**: November 30, 2006, letter from Captain George Howe, USMC, member of the Sixteenth AAA Battalion and a twenty-year marine veteran.

39   **He enlisted**: Gil Hodges's Marine Corps serial number, 894196, is not followed by the letters SS. Those letters (which stand for Selective Service) immediately following the serial number indicate a marine had been drafted: Sledge, *With the*

Old Breed, 171. This excellent war memoir was the basis for the HBO series *The Pacific*.

39 **"terrible trip"**: Hodges's letters written to his parents in 1943.

39 **first song**: Editorial, "A Man for All Seasons," *Wall Street Journal*, January 3, 2003.

39 **"Our arms"**: Sledge, *With the Old Breed*, 174.

40 **got a furlough**: *Pike County Democrat*, December 3, 1943, 7.

40 **in Germany**: *Petersburg Press*, cover, April 17, 1945.

40 **no rifles in the house**: Interview with Marjorie Maysent, August 14, 2006.

40 **rifle score of 271**: Hodges's military records; range of scores: May 5, 2010, email from Annette Amerman, Marine Corps Historical Division.

40 **military police**: Hodges's personnel file.

40 **twenty-five dollars a month**: Hodges's discharge papers.

41 **pot walloping**: Chuck Askey email, November 10, 2006.

42 **"The typical staff officer"**: Box 9, Merchant Papers, Marine Library, Quantico VA.

42 **didn't require the use**: 1945 Military Occupation Specialty Manual.

42 **"operate a typewriter"**: Roeder, *Artful Dodgers*, 82. The after-action reports written by Merchant, which I found at the National Archives and utilized in my research, were most likely typed by Hodges.

44 **set up their guns on Mt. Lasso**: Chuck Askey email, November 10, 2006.

45 **marine had been shot and killed**: O'Donnell, *Into the Rising Sun*, 262.

45 **"When they got through"**: Phone interview with Lester G. Foster, December 6, 2006.

45 **That night, two**: Sixteenth AAA War Diary, May 1945.

45 **"the bump of knowledge"**: Interview with Romeo Paulino in his barbershop in Manville NJ, February 2, 2012.

46 **75 percent of the planes**: "An Evaluation of Air Operations Affecting the U.S. Marine Corps in WWII," National Archives. The filter crews were typically placed adjacent to a hill and could only be destroyed by a direct hit: Phone interview with James Powers, USMC, Eighth AAA Battalion, operations and intelligence section, November 17, 2006.

46 **assigned to guard duty**: Interview with Romeo Paulino, February 2, 2012.

46 **"Somebody gimme a cigarette"**: Sledge, *With the Old Breed*, 61.

46 **received a Bronze Battle Star**: Hodges's personal military records.

47 **still a dangerous place**: Interview with Walter Loeb, U.S. Army 282nd Coastal Artillery Battalion, Okinawa, August 21, 2006.

47 **giving the children**: Sledge, *With the Old Breed*, 192–93.

47 **"laughing and running"**: Sledge, *With the Old Breed*, 179.

47 **"Moose"**: Phone interview with Romeo Paulino, December 7, 2006.

47   **threw with his left arm**: Phone interview with Lester G. Foster, corporal, USMC, who served with Hodges in the Sixteenth AAA Battalion, December 6, 2006.

47   **Bill Dickey flew in**: Roeder, *Artful Dodgers*, 76.

47   **result of his slipping**: *New York Times*, April 25 and 26, 1946; also *New York Times*, June 11, 1945. Durocher paid nearly $7,000 to settle the related civil suit.

47   **typhoon**: Interview with Walter Loeb, August 21, 2006.

47   **"intangible air"**: Sledge, *With the Old Breed*, 226.

47   **"I remember seeing"**: Simon, *Mansfield News Journal*, February 18, 2008.

48   **"Amen"**: Lang and Simon, *New York Mets: 25 Years*, 67.

4. NEWPORT NEWS

49   *Fitz was our*: Hodges, *Game of Baseball*, 20.

49   **dehydrated potatoes**: Sledge, *With the Old Breed*, 23 and 32. Having survived the war in Europe, Bob Hodges was also safely home.

49   **"He partied more"**: Interview with Marjorie Maysent, August 14, 2006.

49   **"I was in Evansville"**: *The Sporting News*, June 15, 1963, 16.

50   **"God Almighty!"**: Drysdale, *Once a Bum*, 94.

50   **Harris could still recall**: Interview with Bob Harris, Petersburg IN, April 2006.

50   **"What kind of glove"**: Devaney, *Gil Hodges, Baseball Miracle Man*, 29.

50   **"Nice guy"**: *Sport Magazine*, October 1956, 62.

50   **three roommates**: Roeder, *Artful Dodgers*, 76.

50   **Killefer was impressed**: *The Sporting News*, August 4, 1948, 2.

51   **one of Tod's favorite players**: Phone interview with Tod Parrott, February 13, 2007.

51   **"No," replied Tod**: *The Sporting News*, April 18, 1946, 4.

51   **he was optioned**: *New York Times*, April 14, 1946, 87.

52   **"When the ball"**: Roeder, *Artful Dodgers*, 77.

52   **missing several games**: *Newport News Daily Press*, June 26, 1946, and August 16, 1946.

52   **"pretty good"**: *The Sporting News*, March 13, 1957, 3–4.

53   **"the only one on the team"**: Phone interview with Clem Labine, January 2006.

54   **Hodges beat out a hit**: *Newport News Daily Press*, September 27, 1946.

54   **several All-Star players**: *Newport News Daily Press*, September 1, 1946.

54   **assists (90) and fielding percentage**: John Ross, "Homers by Hodges," *Sport Magazine*, September 1951, 70.

54   **steal of home**: *Newport News Daily Press*, July 12, 1946.

54   **three-run homer**: *Norfolk News Daily Press*, July 21, 1946, section B.

54   **walk-off home run** and **three for four**: *Newport News Daily Press*, August 29 and 30, 1946.

55   **"Is good receiver"**: *Sport Magazine*, October 1956, 62.

55   **"Hodges left the outside"**: Phone interview with Clem Labine, January 2006.

55   **"the most popular"**: *Newport News Daily Press*, September 2, 1946.

56   **risk losing him on waivers**: Roeder, *Artful Dodgers*, 79.

5. HANGING ON

61   *In 1947, I had a great seat*: Hodges, *Game of Baseball*, 14.

61   **petition**: I only listed Walker, Bragan, and Higbe as signing the petition based on their subsequent admissions. There were other petitioners, but none of the sources that document them come from first-person accounts.

61   **Hodges refused to sign**: Peterson, *Only the Ball Was White*, 198.

61   **"liked and admired Hodges"**: Rampersad, *Jackie Robinson*, 290.

61   **"He's going to"**: Durocher, *Nice Guys Finish Last*, 179.

62   **"the most complete"**: Hodges, *Game of Baseball*, 87.

62   **"I listened to Gil"**: Robinson, *Jackie Robinson: An Autobiography*, 119.

62   **"A lot of the players"**: Parrott, *Lords of Baseball*, 248.

62   **went their separate ways**: Halberstam, *Summer of '49*, 276: "The gap between white and black was very large then, and when the game was over they went their separate ways."

62   **"Gil was one of the first"**: Phone interview with Rachel Robinson, July 22, 2010; confirming Robinson, *Jackie Robinson: An Intimate Portrait*, 90, 118: "Though we shared a few fun evenings with Joan and Gil Hodges, whom we especially liked, there was little socializing with team members except at Dodger parties. In his own quiet way, Gil was a mainstay of the team: a slugger, an outstanding fielder, and a man of strong character. Jack counted on him."

62   **"All your friends in on passes"**: Parrott, *Lords of Baseball*, 257. Like Hodges, Reese felt comfortable enough with Robinson to use humor to help him through. Once, in Cincinnati, a letter sent to the Reds' offices threatened Robinson if he took the field. During pregame warmups, Robinson stood near Reese, who said, "You mind moving over a little Jack? This guy may be a bad shot": *New York Times*, April 16, 2007, D2.

62   **white Dodgers teammates**: Rampersad, *Jackie Robinson*, 260: Ralph Branca was on that barnstorming team, but he was then no longer on the Dodgers.

63   **"in the toilet"**: *Baltimore Afro American*, September 17, 1949, 9.

63   **"I don't care"**: Parrott, *Lords of Baseball*, 260.

65   **"made the trek"**: *Press Dispatch*, June 22, 2005.

65   **"the boy could use a few lessons"**: *New York Daily News*, May 12, 1947, 37.

65   **"Without anyone"**: *The Sporting News*, August 4, 1948, 2.

66   **"If we're so good, how come"**: Snider, *Duke of Flatbush*, 20–21. Hodges was on the bench because Bruce Edwards was batting .295 with nine home runs and eighty RBIs.

66   "watching your mother-in-law": Durocher, *Nice Guys Finish Last*, 236.

66   "knew how to reach": Hodges, *Game of Baseball*, 21.

66   smiling from ear to ear: Photo, *New York Times*, September 27, 1947, 18.

67   "the guts of a burglar": Smith, *To Absent Friends*, 272.

67   only slider: Eig, *Opening Day*, 260.

67   shotgun: *Press Dispatch*, June 22, 2005.

67   played on the college's basketball: Phone interview with Art Miley, November 9, 2006, and an email from Ed Collins, alumni director of Oakland City College, November 29, 2006.

67   "pretty sharp": Interview with Donald Hume, Petersburg IN, April 2006.

68   "to forget about": Parrott, *Lords of Baseball*, 328.

68   0 for 32: *The Sporting News*, August 4, 1948, 2.

68   nine hits: *The Sporting News*, July 14, 1948, 5.

68   "wouldn't trade Hodges": *The Sporting News*, April 7, 1948, 28.

68   "one of the greatest": *The Sporting News*, May 19, 1948, 8.

68   "That was it": Hodges, *Game of Baseball*, 15.

69   "Preston Ward can run": *New York Times*, April 4, 1972, 49. That spring, with Hodges still a catcher, "the Dodgers . . . opened first base as if it had been a land grant for homesteaders, and everyone rushed for a crack at it": Roeder, *Artful Dodgers*, 80.

69   "Whoever says this is an easy position": Falkner, *Nine Sides of the Diamond*, 40.

69   "the best first-baseman I'd seen": Durocher, *Nice Guys Finish Last*, 245.

69   "just like he'd been": *The Sporting News*, July 21, 1948, 7.

70   "My feet didn't know": *The Sporting News*, July 21, 1948, 7.

70   "there were plenty of": *The Sporting News*, July 21, 1948, 7.

70   "One is the ground ball": Roeder, *Artful Dodgers*, 81.

70   seventeen at bats: *The Sporting News*, July 14, 1948, 18.

70   "Gil's play at first base": *New York Times*, July 18, 1948, 61.

70   "laid his hands": *The Sporting News*, July 28, 1948, 10.

71   "stand there with the ball": Barney, *Rex Barney's Thank Youuuu*, 115.

71   more home runs than any other pair: *New York Times*, January 26, 1964, S82.

71   "If someone will tell me": Gaven, *Artful Dodgers*, 169.

72   booed at Ebbets: *Sport Magazine*, August 1960, 61, and *New York Times*, June 17, 1948.

72   "football block": *The Sporting News*, June 23, 1948, 29.

72   twisted right knee: *The Sporting News*, June 23, 1948, 29.

72   "I deserved it": *Sport Magazine*, August 1960, 61.

72   no fractures: *New York Times*, June 18, 1948.

72   visited the Reds' clubhouse: *New York Times*, June 17, 1948.

73   **her nightly prayers:** Allen, *Brooklyn Remembered*, 85–87.

73   **"the only reason he wears a glove":** *The Sporting News*, August 4, 1948, 2.

73   **"I'll take her home":** Allen, *Brooklyn Remembered*, 87. Snider had been Hodges's roommate in Peggy and Ben Chase's home in 1947, Miksis in 1948.

73   **there to serve as best man:** Interview with Marjorie Maysent, August 14, 2006. Her parents didn't attend because "it was a long trip back then."

73   **a dead arm:** Harold Rosenthal, "The Dodgers' Home-Run Kid," *Saturday Evening Post*, September 8, 1951, 29.

6. BREAKING THROUGH

75   *Hitting is a physical act:* Hodges, *Game of Baseball*, 85.

75   **twenty-seven Minor League:** Hirsch, *Willie Mays*, 71. By 1990 the equivalent ratio was six to one.

75   **said he couldn't go:** Roeder, *Artful Dodgers*, 83.

75   **left-handed pinch hitter:** *The Sporting News*, October 13, 1948, 17.

75   **"They say all men have":** *New York Times*, July 3, 1958, 28.

75   **Rickey considered trading:** *The Sporting News*, April 14, 1949, 2.

76   **"I felt pretty low":** *New York Daily News*, September 2, 1950, 31.

76   **"first base insurance":** *The Sporting News*, November 3, 1948, 6, and November 17, 1948, 16.

76   **work with Hodges:** Huhn, *Sizzler*, 261.

76   **"I'm anxious to work":** *The Sporting News*, December 1, 1948, 4.

76   **"Do you know what":** Roeder, *Artful Dodgers*, 83.

76   **grand slam home run:** *New York Times*, April 18, 1949, 21.

77   **.321 batting average:** *The Sporting News*, May 18, 1949, 38.

77   **nineteen-game hitting streak:** *The Sporting News*, June 1, 1949, 17. That season, Eddie Stanky also had a nineteen-game hitting streak. Although both Hodges and Stanky batted .285 for the season, Stanky hit only one home run, Hodges twenty-three.

77   **On June 1 in the ninth inning:** *New York Times*, June 1, 1949, 44.

77   **walk-off home run:** *New York Times*, August 31, 1949, 29.

77   **"miraculous catch":** *New York Times*, May 9, 1949, 28. After the 1949 season, the two Major Leagues created a seventeen-minute educational film on how to play first base and third base. Hodges and his American League counterpart, Ferris Fein of the Philadelphia Athletics, were selected for the first base instruction. They demonstrated the "mechanical and impulsive" requirements of fielding first. The film was included on a tape of the 1949 World Series and distributed throughout the United States: *New York Times*, December 20, 1949, 42.

77   **hitting for the cycle:** *New York Times*, June 26, 1949. In this particular game, Hodges not only hit for the cycle but also had two home runs, finishing with five

hits in six at bats. The game was also unusual in that two of Hodges's extra-base hits were to right field; normally, Hodges was a dead pull-hitter. Years later, when Hodges and Branca were participating in an old-timer's game and a reporter asked about this game, Hodges yelled out to Branca, "Hey Ralph, why don't you tell us about that masterpiece you threw in Pittsburgh." To which Branca replied, "I only gave up one touchdown, an extra point, and a field goal": Phone interview with Ralph Branca, September 24, 2010.

78   "How does a man": *The Sporting News*, October 12, 1949, 7.

78   **Hodges and Robinson played in every game**: *The Sporting News*, December 21, 1949, 19. The others were Stan Musial, Bobby Thomson, Del Ennis, Richie Ashburn, and Granny Hamner.

78   **seven players**: *New York Times*, July 10, 1949, S4. The only other team to send as many players as Brooklyn was St. Louis. The Yankees sent five players that year.

79   "very little use of strategy": Hodges, *Game of Baseball*, 87.

79   "freak hit": *New York Times*, July 13, 1949, 33.

79   "the luckiest hit": *The Sporting News*, July 20, 1949, 8.

79   "That thing Eddie Joost hit": *New York Times*, July 13, 1949, 33.

80   "too close to headquarters": *New York Times*, October 13, 1949, 36.

80   "malicious attempt": *The Sporting News*, October 5, 1949, 2, and October 12, 1949, 4.

80   **The first time Hodges acted**: Phone interview with Jack Lang, July 2, 2006.

81   "He was the biggest": Amoruso, *Quiet Man*, 33.

81   **breaking Reynolds's jaw**: Armour, *Joe Cronin*, 48.

81   "Boy, oh, boy": Harold Rosenthal, "The Dodgers' Home-Run Kid," *Saturday Evening Post*, September 8, 1951, 140.

81   **out of first place**: *The Sporting News*, October 5, 1949, 2.

81   **final day of the season**: *New York Times*, October 3, 1949, 22.

82   "hit a new crescendo": *New York Times*, October 3, 1949, 1.

82   **Hodges ran these meetings**: Interview with Carl Erskine, Anderson IN, April 21, 2006.

83   **119 stolen bases**: *New York Times*, October 3, 1949, 22.

83   **opening game**: *New York Times*, October 6, 1949, 1.

83   "slight" car accident: *New York Times*, October 7, 1949, 37.

83   **first time the Yankees**: *New York Times*, October 7, 1949, 1.

84   "He beat me more than Hodges": Halberstam, *Summer of '49*, 282.

84   **Game Three**: *New York Times*, October 8, 1949, pg. 1.

84   **Game Four**: *New York Times*, October 9, 1949, S1. Newcombe started, but he was not at his best. A triple by the Yankees' Bobby Brown was the game's crucial hit.

84   "We're still in there": *New York Times*, October 9, 1949, S3.

84   "never had a chance": *The Sporting News*, October 19, 1949, 9.

84   Game Five: *New York Times*, October 10, 1949, 1.

84   a Brooklyn department store: *The Sporting News*, October 26, 1949, 8.

85   playing basketball: Barney, *Rex Barney's Thank Youuu*, 144, also *The Sporting News*, December 14, 1949, 1, and *New York Times*, December 14, 1949, 46.

85   visit Petersburg: Interview with Bob Harris, April 20, 2006.

85   beautiful brown boxer: Interview with Marjorie Maysent, August 14, 2006.

7. FOUR IN ONE, ONE FOR FOUR

87   *For that fourth homer*: *Baseball Digest*, February 1951, 18.

87   contract for $13,000: *New York Times*, January 27, 1950, 37.

87   Furillo signed for $18,500: *New York Times*, February 17, 1950, 37.

87   Hodges was not on board: *New York Times*, February 28, 1950, 35.

88   it was highly unusual: Phone interview with Ralph Branca, September 24, 2010.

88   didn't fine Hodges: Interview with Carl Erskine, April 21, 2006.

88   Cox would begin practicing: *New York Times*, March 3, 1950, 28.

88   But Joan had fallen down: *Sport*, August 1960, 58.

88   "We wanted Gil to wait": *New York Times*, March 7, 1950, 30.

88   "They didn't have a uniform": *LA Times*, posted on website, April 8, 2012.

90   born on March 12, 1950: *New York Times*, March 13, 1950, 28.

90   "I realized that he wouldn't leave": Harold Rosenthal, "The Dodgers' Home-Run Kid," *Saturday Evening Post*, September 8, 1951, 142.

91   "I'll be in tomorrow": *New York Times*, March 16, 1950, 52.

91   missing seventeen days: *New York Times*, March 17, 1950, 37.

91   "cut loose": *New York Times*, March 10, 1951, 9.

91   two singles and a walk: *New York Times*, March 22, 1950, 44.

91   "a neat pick-up": *New York Times*, March 24, 1950, 33.

92   opened their season: *New York Times*, April 19, 1950, 39.

92   second game: *New York Times*, April 20, 1950, 39.

93   Shotton benched Hodges: *New York Times*, July 10, 1950, 25. Red Schoendienst had come into the game as a defensive replacement for Jackie Robinson, who had been removed for a left-handed pinch hitter. To give Shotton the benefit of the doubt, before the game he said, "Not only will I start the eight players named by the fans, but if we are out in front, I may go all the way with them. I don't intend to make this an exhibition parade of players. We want to win this game": *New York Times*, July 11, 1950.

93   "You've been away so long": Joan Hodges, "The Day I Was Proudest of My Husband," *Parade*, August 1, 1954.

93   Wilson's Pool Hall: Group interview in Petersburg IN, April 2006.

94   **Palace Pool Room:** *Seattle Times*, February 20, 2008.

94   **a rare start:** Hodges, *Game of Baseball*, 53.

95   **"As far as I see it":** *New York Times*, April 4, 1972, 49. Details of the four-homer game are from Retrosheet and the *Evansville Courier*, January 29, 1956, 5E.

95   **only one other player:** Hodges was the first National League player since 1900 to hit four home runs in a nine-inning game. Another National League player, the Phillies' Hall of Fame outfielder Chuck Klein, hit four in 1936 but needed ten innings to complete the feat. Before 1900, Bobby Lowe of the Boston Nationals did it in nine innings in 1894, and Ed Delehanty hit four inside-the-park homers for the Phillies in 1896: *New York Times*, September 1, 1950, 31. Hitting four home runs in a game is still a rare event; as of 2010, only fifteen players have done it: *New York Times*, June 13, 2010, S2.

95   **"I'm not in the record books":** *Washington Post*, June 11, 1964, K3.

96   **"I hope it brings":** Dick Young, "Hodges Hits 4 in 1 Tilt, Asks 1 for 4," *New York Daily News*, September 2, 1950, 28.

96   **"I'd say that confidence":** *New York Daily News*, September 2, 1950, 28.

96   **"barring a miracle":** *New York Daily News*, September 1, 1950.

96   **strength of their pitching:** *New York Times*, March 1, 1951, 36.

96   **final two weeks of the season:** *New York Times*, October 2, 1950, 37.

96   **On September 23:** *New York Times*, September 24, 1950, S1.

97   **three-run homer (his thirty-second of the season):** *New York Times*, September 28, 1950, 51.

97   **last day of the season:** Stout, *Dodgers: 120 Years*, 162–64; *New York Times*, October 2, 1950, 1; and *New York Times*, October 1, 1950, 159.

98   **"fastballs, low and away":** Phone interview with Robin Roberts, February 5, 2008.

98   **"you're strong enough":** Phone interview with Ralph Branca, September 24, 2010.

98   **"Milt played it right":** *New York Times*, October 2, 1950, 36.

98   **"he never saw me":** *Baseball Digest*, February 1951, 14.

98   **thirteen home runs and drove in forty runs:** I subtracted Hodges's hitting totals as posted in the *Daily News* on September 1, 1950, from his year-end totals.

99   **jubilant fans:** *New York Daily News*, October 1, 1950, 6.

100   **"I just forgot the last time":** *Baseball Digest*, February 1951, 13.

8. GREAT EXPECTATIONS

101   *The ability to hit*: *New York Times Sunday Magazine*, June 16, 1968, 12.

101   **Rickey sold his 25 percent interest:** Heylar, *Lords of the Realm*, 40.

101   **"From that evening on":** Smith, *To Absent Friends*, 404.

101   "had more explanations": Kahn, *Great Baseball Writing*, 439.

102   "not a holdout": *New York Times*, January 25, 1951, 33.

102   Hodges finished eighth: *New York Times*, November 3, 1950, 34. Hodges's HR and
       RBI rankings: *New York Times*, February 6, 1951, 44. Half his homers off curve balls:
       New York Times, June 10, 1951, S2.

102   .994 fielding mark: *New York Daily News*, December 21, 1950, C20.

102   But Hodges charged the plate: *Baseball Digest*, February, 1951, 17.

102   "So he flicked": *New York Times*, June 10, 1951, S2. That play was also discussed by
       Bill Roeder, who wrote that Newcombe "resisted the urge to punt": *Artful Dodgers*,
       82.

102   better grip: Interview with Carl Erskine, April 21, 2006. The pine tar was espe-
       cially helpful when Erskine threw a curve ball. Before batting gloves became
       common, hitters used pine tar to get a better grip on the bat.

103   "used more pine tar": Phone interview with Rene Lacheman, October 26, 2010.
       Soap and water do not remove pine tar, so Hodges always kept a jar of mechanic's
       compound in his locker for this purpose: Erskine, *Tales from the Dodgers*, 187.

103   "If you had 25 Gil Hodges": *New York Times*, June 10, 1951, S2.

103   "to give his pitchers": Phone interview with Clyde King, August 7, 2007.

103   "The team was taking a train": Phone interview with Roger Craig, December
       4, 2006. On road trips, Hodges would, on occasion, put his arm around a married
       teammate he knew was not getting his rest (not to mention engaging in activities
       Hodges felt were inappropriate) and say something to the effect of, "Why don't
       you come have dinner and a few drinks with me and some of the other fellows and
       afterwards we can all get a good night sleep."

103   "Pee Wee was the captain": *Union-Tribune*, January 11, 2005, posted online at
       SignonSandiego.com.

103   "Guys like Pee Wee and Snider": Williams, *No More Mr. Nice Guy*, 48. Williams,
       who should have been playing in the Minors, was resented by his veteran team-
       mates, who knew that even the twenty-fifth player on the roster would eventually
       find his way onto the field during the long season where one poor play could be the
       difference between receiving—or not receiving—a World Series check.

103   regulars slept on the lower berths: Ritter, *Glory of Their Times*, 82.

104   "How did you do?": Kahn, *Boys of Summer*, 344. Williams was not Hodges's kind
       of guy, and this may explain why he reacted so strongly. Dressen assigned Wil-
       liams the role of "the Dodgers' DSA: designated smartass." Dressen had Williams
       sit on the bench and scream at the opposition. "From Dressen," Williams wrote,
       "I learned more about . . . needling than hitting": Williams, *No More Mr. Nice Guy*,
       48–49.

104   "When I came up": *New York Daily News*, June, 1973.

104 **"I wish we had better hitting coaches"**: Phone interview with Clem Labine, January 2006. Labine was implying that more could have been done to school Hodges in overcoming his blind spot on the outside corner of the plate and have him hitting for a higher average. The reality is Hodges felt he could best help his team hitting home runs and was willing to sacrifice his batting average to do so.

104 **$20,000 salary**: *New York Times*, February 6, 1951, 44. Robinson's pay: *New York Times*, February 4, 1951, 134.

104 **"definitely will report in time"**: *New York Times*, March 4, 1951, 148.

104 **"The Dodgers . . . put it to me"**: *Sport*, May 1959, 76.

104 **a reluctant Hodges flew**: *New York Times*, March 8, 1951, 39.

105 **Hodges didn't feel pressure**: *New York Times*, March 10, 1951, 9.

105 **Hodges didn't play**: *New York Times*, March 18, 1951, S1.

105 **"Joan cried"**: *Sport*, May 1959, 76.

105 **National Children's Cardiac Home**: *New York Times*, March 19, 1951, 39.

105 **an eight-pound girl**: *New York Times*, March 21, 1951, 55.

105 **On the evening of March 24**: *New York Times*, March 25, 1951, 129.

105 **opened the 1951 campaign**: *New York Times*, April 18, 1951, 52.

105 **five in the first ten games**: *New York Times*, April 28, 1951, 23.

105 **National League record**: *New York Times*, July 6, 1969, S3. Hodges's mark was not broken until Willie McCovey hit twenty-six in 1969.

105 **On July 6 he hit his twenty-eighth**: *New York Times*, July 7, 1951, 21.

106 **crossword puzzle**: *New York Times*, September 4, 1951, 25.

106 **"How about Gil Hodges"**: *New York Times*, May 28, 1951, 37. A decade later, Roger Maris broke Ruth's home run record and suffered greatly at the hands of the press, who unfavorably compared him to Babe Ruth and Mickey Mantle.

107 **"out of focus"**: John Ross, "Homers by Hodges," *Sport*, September 1951, 24.

107 **"I never saw Ruth play"**: Ross, "Homers by Hodges," 71.

107 **"Ruth Jr., eh"**: *New York Times*, June 7, 1951, 49.

107 **"Maybe I'll change"**: *New York Times*, June 10, 1951, 52.

107 **Before the All-Star Game**: *Complete Baseball*, September 1952, 14, 62. On August 29 Hodges went 3 for 5 with two home runs and seven RBIs in a 13-1 rout of the Reds at Ebbets Field. Hodges's second home run, his thirty-sixth of the season, broke the Dodgers' single-season home run record: *New York Times*, August 14, 1951, 27. That same month, on August 11, 1951, the Dodgers defeated the Boston Braves 8-1 in the opening game of a doubleheader, which extended the Dodgers' winning streak to six games, giving them a record of 70-35, and marked their largest lead of the season over the Giants at thirteen and a half games. That game was the first color broadcast in baseball history. Ten thousand viewers received color wheels allowing them to convert the images on their screens. Red Smith found the "reproduction . . .

excellent, striking, and only faintly phony," writing that Hodges's well-muscled arms "were encased in a pelt of somewhat lovelier tone—about the shade of medium roast beef—that Gil wears in real life."

107 **"almost painfully silent"**: *Complete Baseball*, September 1952, 62.

108 **largest margin in franchise history**: Stout, *Dodgers*, 172, 174.

108 **"Eat your heart out"**: As recalled by Don Newcombe on the television show *The Way It Was: The 1951 National League Baseball Pennant Race*, hosted by Curt Gowdy and broadcast in 1974; I viewed the show at the Museum of Television and Radio, New York City.

109 **children's autograph requests**: Interview with Carl Erskine, April 21, 2006.

109 **"For a man who was generally described"**: Father Vieck, "Gil Hodges . . . An Inspiration to Youth," from Father Vieck's scrapbook. The article was published in September of 1972, most likely in the *Petersburg Press-Dispatch*. Vieck noted the positive impact Hodges had the children: "As he held his giant hand on some kid's shoulder you could just see the youngster's mind and eyes beaming . . . 'he acknowledges me' . . . 'He, imagine it! Respects me.' There is no way to describe his way with kids." The legend of Hodges's need to meet children's autograph requests dates back to an often-recounted incident that took place in 1947 or 1948 at Ebbets Field when Charlie and Bob Hodges had come to Brooklyn. They were on the field before a game when a boy approached another Dodgers player for an autograph. "The player swung his hand around at the youngster and said, 'Beat it kid.'" Charlie saw this and told his son, "Bud, I don't know if you will ever achieve any fame in baseball or not, but if you do, and if I ever see or hear of you doing anything like that to any kid . . ."

109 **"He accepted the medal with great solemnity"**: Goodwin, *Wait Till Next Year*, 137-39. The month after his encounter with Doris Goodwin, on June 14 in the final game of a three-game set in St. Louis, in the top of the ninth, with two outs, a runner on base, and his team trailing 1-0, Hodges stepped to the plate. Cardinals manager Marty Marion came out to the mound and told his pitcher, Joe Presko, to keep the ball low and away. He did, but Hodges hit a two-run home run anyway. The ball traveled over four hundred feet, and the come-from-behind win gave the Dodgers a three-game sweep: *New York Times*, June 15, 1951, 28.

109 **"I didn't have a chance"**: *New York Times*, July 11, 1951, 36.

110 **"Some people have street smarts"**: Phone interview with Clyde King, August 7, 2007.

110 **hit in the face by a pitch**: *New York Times*, July 16, 1951, 28.

110 **"stiff," Hodges "insisted"**: *New York Times*, July 17, 1951, 22.

110 **Hodges was only player**: Phone interview with Bobby Thomson, November 26, 2006.

110 **Hodges's fortieth:** *The Sporting News*, October 10, 1951, 8.

111 **Never before—or since:** Prager, *Echoing Green*, 206.

111 **"It's Like a Wake":** *New York Times*, October 4, 1951, 1. Negative perceptions, even if untrue, can stick with a person for the rest of his life, even beyond the grave. When I discussed Hodges's fielding abilities with longtime *New York Daily News* sports reporter Phil Pepe, he told me it was unfortunate that Hodges decided to hold Alvin Dark on (phone interview with Phil Pepe, August 31, 2010).

111 **barnstorming teams:** *The Sporting News*, October 10, 1951, 27.

111 **American Baseball Academy:** *New York Times*, November 6, 1951.

112 **"We're very careful in picking":** *New York Times*, December 7, 1952, 44.

112 **Petersburg city council:** *Petersburg Press*, November 9, 1951.

9. A BITTER UNIQUENESS

113 **A Bitter Uniqueness:** Spoken by Red Barber during the 1952 World Series to describe Hodges setting a Series record for futility, going without a hit in twenty-one times at bat. I viewed a video of the sixth and seventh games of the Series at the Museum of Television and Radio.

113 *I'm an authority on slumps:* "Gil Hodges: The Most Nice Guy in Baseball," *Look Magazine*, July 14, 1964, 98A.

113 **ninety-nine (forty-six on called third strikes):** *New York Times*, March 8, 1952, 16. Yet Hodges was one of only a handful of players who drove in over 100 runs. He was third in the National League in runs scored (118) as well as total bases (307) and received a $23,000 salary for 1952: *New York Times*, February 10, 1952, 155. Although Hodges only finished fourth among National League first basemen in fielding percentage in 1951, "as a first sacker, Gil had no peer": *New York Times*, February 10, 1952, 155. Ted Kluszewski led National League first basemen in fielding percentage in 1951 at .997, but this is not a very effective statistic for judging a player's true fielding ability. Players with range can reach many hit balls, while a less mobile player, like Kluszewski, could not. For six seasons beginning in 1950, Kluszewski led the National League in fielding percentage: Ira Smith, *Famous First Basemen*, 303. But even though Hodges made more errors, his peers considered him to be the best-fielding first baseman in the National League: April 11, 2010, phone interview with Frank Torre, who played first base in the 1950s for the Milwaukee Braves. In 1951 Hodges led the league in assists with 126: *New York Times*, December 20, 1951, 53.

113 **"If we can get Gil":** Harold Rosenthal, "Will Hodges Do It?" *Complete Baseball*, September 1951. Of Hodges's 40 home runs in 1951, 24 came with no one on base, a ratio not unlike that of Ralph Kiner, who hit 25 of his 42 home runs with no one on base that season; but no one was trying to change Kiner's swing.

113　**"No one"**: *New York Times*, March 16, 1952, S2.

113　**"how everyone jeered"**: Red Smith, "Views of Sport," *New York Herald Tribune*, September 12, 1953, HOF clipping file. The Dodgers had been altering Hodges's hitting stance as far back as May 1948 when Arky Vaughan, "a spread-stance hitter with a short, sharp swing (and no stride), talked Hodges into a spread stance . . . [but] all that new style did for [Hodges] was to move the swivel—or pivot-point— above the waist, forcing him to get his power from shoulder and arm movement alone": *New York Times*, May 27, 1953, 39.

113　**"hit to right field"**: *New York Times*, February 23, 1952, 16.

114　**"holding his bat like a torcher"**: *New York Times*, May 27, 1953, 39.

114　**"I see poor Gil"**: *New York Times*, May 27, 1953, 39.

114　**Yet Hodges defended Dressen**: Red Smith, "Views of Sport," *New York Herald Tribune*, September 12, 1953, HOF clipping file. Dressen's methodology was fixed during his playing career in the 1920s when no hitter was considered great unless he batted over .300.

114　**In 1951 his 93 walks**: *New York Times*, February 10, 1952, 155.

114　**"the runner on first"**: Rickey, *American Diamond*, 173.

114　**"scratching, diving, hungry ballplayers"**: Durocher, *Nice Guys Finish Last*, 6.

114　**not usually better**: Hodges, *Game of Baseball*, 86.

115　**Dressen offered him fifty dollars**: Hodges, *Game of Baseball*, 115–17.

116　**"but better it"**: *LA Times*, April 5, 1959, E2.

116　**"couldn't care less"**: Hodges, *Game of Baseball*, 120. For an umpire and a player, Goetz and Hodges had a close friendship. When Hodges won the Jack Singer Good Sportsmanship Award, Goetz was the person selected to present the award to Hodges: *New York Times*, September 24, 1951, 32.

116　**"And although he was genuinely"**: Smith, *To Absent Friends*, 276. Goetz worked on the same three-man crew as Beans Reardon and Jocko Conlan, the Hall of Fame umpire.

116　**the old hidden ball trick**: Erskine, *Tales*, 37–39.

116　***See It Now***: I watched the episode at the Museum of Television and Radio, New York City.

117　**From May 29 to June 1**: *New York Times*, June 2, 1952, 26.

117　**into the All-Star Game**: After only five innings of play, that year's All-Star Game became the first in history to end early because of rain. Durocher said he had intended to have Hodges replace the left-handed-hitting Lockman (playing in the only All-Star Game of his career) to open the fifth inning against Bobby Shantz, a lefty pitcher in the midst of an MVP season in which he led the American League in wins. As a starter, Lockman had already played the required three-inning minimum, and with Hodges at bat, the hitting matchup would favor the National

League. But Durocher later claimed he had "forgotten about it." Shantz struck out Lockman: *New York Times*, July 9, 1952, 30. Hodges was named a reserve on the 1953, 1954, 1955, and 1957 National League All-Star teams and had one at bat in each of those games, but only managed one hit (in the 1955 game).

117 **On August 31**: *New York Times*, September 1, 1952, 12.

117 **hard—but legal—slide**: *New York Times*, September 8, 1952. Hodges's quotes on Williams and Rigney: Arnold Hano, "Gil Hodges, Best-Loved Dodger," *Sport*, August 1960, 62. As a result of Hodges's slide, Rigney was forced to leave the game with a three-inch gash that required five stitches, and he was replaced by third-string second baseman Bobby Hofman. But Gil Hodges's memory was only partially correct. Rigney did replace Williams in the September 7 game, but Hodges spiked Rigney the next day, September 8, in the top of the fifth inning of the opening game of a day-night doubleheader. What Hodges neglected to mention was that he had reached first base after being hit by a pitch thrown by the Giants' Hoyt Wilhelm. Could Hodges have cut Rigney in retaliation for Wilhelm's intentionally hitting him with a pitch? By the fifth inning, the Dodgers had a 5-2 lead, and Wilhelm might have "wasted one" to drill Hodges for knocking Williams out of the prior day's game. In the bottom of the fifth inning, Dodgers pitcher Joe Black forced the Giants' George Wilson to duck on one pitch. In the seventh inning, Giants pitcher Montia Kennedy had Hodges hitting the dirt during his at bat, and narrowly missed hitting Joe Black in his at bat. At that point, umpire Lee Ballanfant warned both Durocher and Dressen: the next pitcher to throw a beanball would be tossed out of the game. In the ninth inning, the Giants' fourth pitcher of the day, Larry Jansen, was tossed after hitting Dodgers third baseman Billy Cox in the hip: *New York Times*, September 9, 1952, 24. This type of escalation was not unusual when the Dodgers played the Giants, since both Durocher and Dressen used the two-for-one rule: if you hit one of our players with a pitched ball, we will hit two of your players. That summer, on August 5, the NL had issued a directive to try to reduce the frequency of the beanball wars between the two teams, requiring that after a warning, if the offense is repeated the pitcher will be thrown out of the game and the manager fined "a substantial amount and suspended." Hodges's hard slide into Williams didn't end Williams's career but added to his preexisting back problems. Williams returned to play again in 1952, made the 1953 National League All-Star team, and was a key member on the Giants' 1954 World Championship team. But Williams was eventually forced to retire because of recurrent back problems. Red Smith wrote Hodges "runs the bases like Ty Cobb": "Views of Sport," *New York Herald Tribune*, September 12, 1953, HOF clipping file.

118 **Robinson knocked down Davey Williams**: *New York Times*, October 25, 1972, 97.

118 **"never felt sharper"**: *LA Times*, September 29, 1957, K8.

118 **0 for 10 slump:** Red Smith, "Views of Sport," *New York Herald Tribune,* September 12, 1953, HOF clipping file.

118 **In Game One:** *New York Times,* October 2, 1952, 1.

118 **In Game Two:** *New York Times,* October 3, 1952, 1, and *New York Times,* October 3, 1952, 27.

119 **fallaway slide:** Photo in *New York Times,* October 3, 1952.

119 **The Dodgers won Game Three:** *New York Times,* October 4, 1952, 20.

119 **"I'll get one tomorrow":** *New York Times,* October 4, 1952, 20.

119 **The Dodgers lost the fourth game:** *New York Times,* October 5, 1952, S1.

119 **Martin read the sign:** Deindorfer, *Fireside Book of Baseball,* 72.

120 **For the fifth game:** *New York Times,* October 6, 1952, 28.

120 **"first Republican to be jeered":** Smith, *Red Smith on Baseball,* 150–51.

120 **"and the vote of the witnesses":** Smith, *To Absent Friends,* 277.

120 ***Jack Benny Program:*** Originally aired on October 5, 1952. I viewed it on October 18, 2007, at the Museum of Television and Radio in New York. Hodges also did print advertisements for Chesterfield Cigarettes—"Gil Hodges says they give you good pitch. Stick with it": from the Andy Fogel collection, as seen at the Museum of the City of New York during the "Glory Days" exhibit in 2007.

121 **"a big ovation":** Mel Allen on the television broadcast of the game, Museum of Television and Radio in New York.

121 **even when he was hitting poorly:** Hodges, *Game of Baseball,* 16–17.

121 **"rarely . . . rivaled in modern baseball"** and **"seemed to endear":** *New York Times,* April 3, 1972, 1.

122 **Goetz hadn't slept:** Hodges, *Game of Baseball,* 120.

122 **For the final game:** *New York Times,* October 8, 1952, 1. During Hodges's final at bat of the seventh game, following a questionable strike call, the Dodgers' bench started jawing at the home plate umpire, Larry Goetz, who tossed the perceived culprit, Ralph Branca, out of the game. It was the first time in Series history a player who was not in the game was tossed.

122 **"his name was lost":** Phone interview with Frank Graham Jr., March 27, 2011. In 1952, when a left-hander started against the Dodgers (as Lopat did in Game Seven), Snider usually batted in the second half of the order. But Snider was then setting Series records for most total bases and extra-base hits, and Dressen batted him third against Lopat.

123 **"That proves":** *New York Times,* October 8, 1952, 39. The previous record had been set, in six games, by Billy Sullivan of the White Sox and James Sheckard of the Cubs, both during the 1906 Series and later matched, in 1911, by the Giants' Johnny Murray: *New York Daily News,* October 8, 1952; according to *World Series Records* (The Sporting News), 351, James Sheckard of the Cubs also went 0 for 21

in the 1906 World Series. In the 1968 World Series, the Cardinals' Dal Maxvill failed to get a hit in twenty-two at bats. Maxvill was a light-hitting shortstop (.217 career batting average), and the lasting image of Series futility still belonged to Hodges.

123   **"The agonized face"**: *LA Times*, July 28, 1957, G10.

124   **"1952? . . . I don't remember"**: Hodges, *Game of Baseball*, 16.

124   **"poor Gil Hodges"**: *New York Times*, October 7, 1957, 30.

124   **Despite his World Series debacle**: *New York Times*, November 13, 1952, 40. Hodges was the only player in the NL to drive in one hundred or more runs each season from 1949 to 1952.

124   **"the loftier intelligences"**: Red Smith, "Views of Sport," *New York Herald Tribune*, September 12, 1953, HOF clipping file.

124   **the Dodgers offered Hodges and Furillo**: *New York Times*, December 7, 1952, S5.

124   **"We are not parting"**: *New York Times*, December 9, 1952, 46.

124   **"At least $600,000"**: Daley, *Kings of the Home Run*, 150.

124   **"This ain't no free country"**: *New York Times*, October 8, 1952, 39.

125   **"Everywhere I went"**: Tom Meany, "When Gil Hodges Slumped, All of Brooklyn Went to Bat for Him," *Collier's*, August 21, 1953.

IO. SAY A PRAYER

127   *I would appreciate*: Undated letter written by Hodges to Ty Cobb, spring of 1953, Jerry Stern Collection, displayed in "The Glory Days: New York Baseball, 1947–1957" exhibit, Museum of the City of New York, 2007.

127   **"laughed along with the other"**: Meany, *Collier's*, August 21, 1953.

127   **"Hodges is still a pretty good"**: Red Smith, "Views of Sport," *New York Herald Tribune*, September 12, 1953, HOF clipping file.

127   **Jimmy Cannon**: Phone Interview with Frank Graham Jr., March 27, 2011; the column ran in the *New York Post* on December 4, 1952, 58.

127   **salary was reduced**: *New York Times*, January 7, 1953, 27.

128   **Furillo had eye surgery**: McGowen, *Artful Dodgers*, 131–33.

128   **"as pale as a ghost"**: *New York Times*, March 2, 1953, 27.

128   **"nothing of note"**: Red Smith, "Views of Sport," September 12, 1953, *New York Herald Tribune*, September 12, 1953, HOF clipping file.

128   **By March 23**: *New York Times*, March 24, 1953, 38.

128   **"The main thing about hitting"**: *The Sporting News*, April 8, 1953, 7.

130   **"And I'll remember you"**: Meany, *Collier's*, August 21, 1953, 25.

130   **painful growth**: Meany, *Collier's* August 21, 1953, 25.

130   **"mysterious ailment"**: *New York Times*, March 30, 1953, 16.

130   **"rest indefinitely"**: *New York Times*, April 2, 1953, 36.

130 **allergic reaction:** *Brooklyn Eagle*, April 2 and 3, 1953, photos. Considering Hodges's severe reaction to the shots he received in 1943, the diagnosis made sense.

130 **"They had me scared":** *New York Times*, April 3, 1953, 29; relationship between Dr. Fett and Harry Hickey: *New York Times*, March 16, 1999. Despite Fett's astute diagnosis, Walter O'Malley's later treatment of Harry Hickey (see chapter 12) shows O'Malley as a what-have-you-done-for-me-later type.

130 **"reflects the genuinely":** Red Smith, "Views of Sport," *New York Herald Tribune*, September 12, 1953, HOF clipping file.

131 **On May 5:** *New York Times*, May 6, 1953, 41; May 6, 1953, game: *New York Times*, May 7, 1953, 40. Wes Parker, a Gold Glove–winning first baseman with the Los Angeles Dodgers, who often threw batting practice for the Dodgers as a youngster in the late 1950s, told me, "Hodges owned the inside half of the plate": Phone interview with Wes Parker, February 9, 2007. Hodges's weakness was the outside pitch, and he found right-handed pitchers who threw sharply breaking curve balls baffling. Sal Maglie, a righty, who spent most of his career pitching for the New York Giants, would pitch Hodges inside to drive him off the plate, and then come back with a low outside curve ball that Hodges found unhittable: Neyer and James, *Guide to Pitchers*, 288.

131 **"A slump like mine":** Meany, *Collier's*, August 21, 1953, 26.

132 **"The way Brooklyn fans":** *New York Times*, August 26, 1955, 13.

133 **"a boy who could hit":** Meany, *Collier's*, 27.

134 **"I've had slumps":** Meany, *Collier's*, 26.

134 **"would call constantly to the clubhouse"; "bring home a quart of milk"; and "a distraction":** Phone interview with Frank Graham Jr., March 27, 2011.

134 **benching:** *New York Times*, May 17, 1953, S1.

134 **"Such is the magnificence":** *New York Daily News*, May 17, 1953, 90.

134 **"I might put Gil":** *New York Times*, May 17, 1953, S1.

135 **Hodges's first at bat:** *New York Times*, May 22, 1953, 20.

135 **On May 29:** *New York Times*, May 30, 1953, 9.

136 **"It is too warm":** Meany, *Collier's*, August 21, 1953, 24. Hodges entered the 1953 All-Star team as a pinch runner and defensive replacement for Ted Kluszewski. Hodges's only at bat of the game came against Satchel Paige. Hodges hit a line drive to left center that Larry Doby hauled in near the scoreboard. The National League won 5–1.

136 **On August 17:** *New York Times*, August 18, 1953.

136 **Hodges crashed into:** *New York Times*, September 12, 1953, 20. The Dodgers lost, 9–8.

136 **"impaled himself":** *New York Times*, September 28, 1953, 29.

136 **"It won't hurt me to swing unless I try":** *New York Times*, September 13, 1953, S1.

137   **"If it is a fissure fracture"**: *New York Times*, September 20, 1953, S1.

137   **September 25 in Philadelphia**: *New York Times*, September 26, 1953, 10.

137   **"'quite determined'"**: *New York Times*, September 30, 1953, 39. In 1953 Hodges was the only active Major Leaguer with five consecutive seasons of one hundred or more RBIs, which was also a Dodgers record: *Cincinnati Times-Star*, August 19, 1953, 19.

137   **In Game One**: *New York Times*, October 1, 1953, 1.

138   **"but we're two down"**: *New York Times*, October 2, 1953, 25.

138   **For the third game**: *New York Times*, October 3, 1953, 1.

138   **In Game Four**: *New York Times*, October 4, 1953, S1.

138   **"scorcher"**: *New York Times*, March 17, 1955, 81.

138   **"the big wink"**: *New York Times*, October 5, 1953, 36.

139   **starting pitcher for Game Six**: *New York Times*, October 6, 1953, 1.

139   **"I'm going to my mother-in-law's"**: *New York Times*, October 5, 1953, 35.

139   **Dressen would not return**: Meany, *Artful Dodgers*, 27–29.

139   **"broke daring new ground"**: Rampersad, *Jackie Robinson*, 260; also *New York Times*, October 11, 1953, S7, *New York Times*, October 12, 1953, 33, *New York Times*, November 2, 1953, 31.

139   **"opposition to interracial play"**: Rampersad, *Jackie Robinson*, 260.

139   **Walter Alston**: Meany, *Artful Dodgers*, 29–40.

139   **"an island of silence"**: *New York Times*, November 5, 1954, S2.

139   **"so unnatural as to be uncomfortable"**: *New York Times*, November 24, 1954, 29.

140   **"Let's settle this outside"**: Phone interview with Tom Simpson, August 29, 2006. Simpson briefly pitched in the Majors in 1953.

140   **"I realize that if I don't"**: Meany, *Artful Dodgers*, 33.

140   **"He knew exactly"**: Koppett, *Man in the Dugout*, 335.

141   **Opening Day**: *New York Times*, April 14, 1954, 36. Early in the season, the Dodgers, Phillies, and Braves briefly spent time in first place, but by summer the Giants had gained a comfortable lead atop the National League standings. The Dodgers pulled to within a half game of first place in mid-August but fell four games back shortly after Labor Day. The Giants clinched the pennant on September 20 as Sal Maglie defeated the Dodgers, 7–1.

141   **Tommy Lasorda**: *New York Times*, September 5, 1954, S2.

141   **Hodges played in every game**: *New York Times*, February 21, 1954, S1. For the 1954 season, Hodges had negotiated a raise of "about 3,500" to an "estimated $26,000."

141   **200th home run**: *New York Times*, August 16, 1954, 20; career home run totals: *New York Times*, January 23, 1955, S1. Among active National League players, only Musial (292) and Hank Sauer (232) had more career home runs than Hodges (212).

That season, Ted Kluszewski was the only player in either league to hit more home runs or drive in more runs than Hodges.

141 **sacrifice flies**: Beginning with the 1954 season, Major League Baseball's Rules Committee reinstated the pre-1926 sacrifice fly rule. Official scorers were instructed to credit batters with a sacrifice fly when "with less than two outs, the batter hits a fair fly ball which is caught and a runner scores after the catch, or is dropped and the runner scores, if [in] the scorer's judgment, the runner could have scored after the catch had the ball been caught." A batter was not charged with a time at bat when hitting a sacrifice fly, and this helped lift Hodges's batting average: *New York Times*, October 20, 1955, 46. In 1954 the next-highest sacrifice fly total was eleven. Before 1926, sacrifice flies counted on scoring fair flies. From 1927 to 1930, they were also awarded for advancing a runner to second or third. From 1931 to 1953, there were no sacrifice flies (except for 1939). From 1954 to 2006, there were sacrifice flies on scoring fair flies. From 2007 to 2009, on scoring flies, both fair and foul. An October 2010 email from John Thorn helped clarify the history of the sacrifice fly rule.

141 **Hodges finished tenth**: *New York Times*, December 17, 1954, 41. Pee Wee Reese (ninth) and Duke Snider (fourth) both finished ahead of Hodges in the voting; Ted Kluszewski finished second.

141 **"home plate much too late"**: *New York Times*, July 13, 1954, 25. Ironically, considering his driving skills, that off-season Hodges worked as a car salesman for a Chrysler-Plymouth dealership on Flatbush Avenue: *Brooklyn Eagle*, December 24, 1954.

141 **Robert Gray**: Photo and caption in *Brooklyn Eagle*, January 10, 1955.

142 **"Gil is no platform spellbinder"**: *New York Times*, August 26, 1955, 13.

143 **Irving Rudd**: Golenbock, *Bums*, 344. Rudd couldn't convince Hodges to change his mind, and he was prepared to give Rudd $1,000; Rudd declined. Rudd described Hodges as "the all-American boy—trustworthy, loyal, helpful, courteous, kind, obedient, cheerful, thrifty, brave, clean, and reverent": Rudd, *Sporting Life*, 79.

II. THE DAY NEXT YEAR ARRIVED

145 *Jack, don't say anything else*: Spoken by Hodges to Jackie Robinson on April 5, 1955: Robinson, *I Never Had It Made*, 119.

145 **"I've never seen"**: *New York Times*, March 16, 1955, 47.

145 **"We are proud men"**: *New York Times*, March 16, 1955, 47.

145 **"We have an excellent chance"**: *New York Times*, March 16, 1955, 47.

145 **"a pretty good idea"**: *New York Times*, April 3, 1955, 51.

146 **"We will win"**: Phone interview with Johnny Podres, February 7, 2006.

147   **Alston and Robinson started screaming**: Robinson, *I Never Had It Made*, 119. In 1963 on a bus ride to the Pittsburgh airport, after his players wouldn't stop complaining about the poor quality of their transportation, Alston ordered the driver to pull over and told his players that if they didn't like the bus, they "could meet him outside." No one took Alston up on his offer. Some of his players thought the incident was that season's turning point: Davis, *Tales from the Dodgers Dugout*, 122–23.

147   **confrontation seemed imminent**: Phone interview with Johnny Podres, February 7, 2006.

148   **"cut down their swings"** and **"more base hits"**: *New York Times*, March 10, 1955, 38.

148   **"to get a good look at Hodges"**: *New York Times*, March 29, 1955, 35.

148   **sixteen games in the outfield**: *New York Times*, January 15, 1956, S1.

148   **several of his hits were game winners**: *New York Times*, September 9, 1955, 28.

148   **On April 9**: *New York Times*, April 10, 1955, S1.

148   **opened their season**: *New York Times*, April 14, 1955, 37.

149   **ninth straight game**: *New York Times*, April 21, 1955, 38.

149   **tenth win in a row**: *New York Times*, April 22, 1955, 29.

149   **bonus over $4,000**: Dickson, *New Dickson Baseball Dictionary*, 77. A "bonus baby" was typically a teenager who received a significant signing bonus.

149   **"with the team, not of it"**: Stout, *Dodgers*, 205.

149   **"So this is what they paid"**: Phone interview with Mike McCormick, January 5, 2011.

149   **"My contact with Gil was negligible"**: Phone interview with Sandy Koufax, October 14, 2010.

150   **Hodges batted. 477**: *New York Times*, January 15, 1956, S1; only twenty players hit over .300 in 1955: *New York Times*, October 20, 1955, 46. Hodges had several memorable games in 1955. On July 3 Hodges's three-run homer against the Pirates gave the Dodgers a win and snapped a three-game losing streak: *New York Times*, July 4, 1955, 7. Hodges hit his eleventh career grand slam of his career on August 3 in Milwaukee to help the Dodgers defeat the Braves, 9–6. Hodges was 3 for 5 in the game and hit a second home run in addition to his grand slam. He drove in six runs: *New York Times*, August 4, 1955, 19.

150   **marched from Ebbets**: *New York Times*, September 17, 1955, 17.

150   **Charley DiGiovanna**: *New York Times*, August 16, 1955, 26. DiGiovanna eventually worked his way up to the position of assistant clubhouse manager. He was a favorite with the Dodgers players who did not like having to sit and sign their names on dozen of baseballs before every game, and DiGiovanna became adept at forging their signatures.

151 **did better in Game Two:** John Drebinger, *New York Times*, September 30, 1955, 1.

151 **not pitched a complete game since June 14:** *New York Times*, October 6, 1955, 35.

151 **In Game Four:** *New York Times*, October 2, 1955, S3.

152 **"look feeble and dispirited":** *New York Times*, October 6, 1955, 35.

152 **first lefty to pitch a complete game:** Golenback, *Bums*, 426.

153 **301-foot distance:** *New York Times*, September 25, 1955, S3.

154 **"Ladies and gentlemen":** *New York Times*, June 25, 2010, B9.

155 **"more reverential":** *New York Times*, October 5, 2010, B17.

155 **take a knee or bow their heads:** Interview with Carl Erskine, April 2006.

155 **"I looked at Pee Wee":** *New York Times*, October 5, 2010, B17.

155 **Alston was in control:** *New York Times*, September 13, 1955, 35.

155 **"Imagine a grown man crying":** *New York Times*, October 5, 1955.

155 **"but not nuts"** and **"No one realized":** Phone interview with Sandy Koufax, October 14, 2010.

156 **"This, for a Brooklyn":** *New York Times*, October 5, 1955, 44.

156 **"Gee, Daddy":** Hodges, *Game of Baseball*, 149.

156 **"like a swimmer"** and **"Try that again":** Frank Graham Jr., *Farewell to Heroes*, 277.

156 **"Right now the matter":** *New York Times*, October 6, 1955, 34.

12. WHERE IN AMERICA WOULD YOU SEE THAT?

157 *You know me:* Hodges's response after driving in seven runs in the first two games of the 1956 World Series, when asked if he would break Lou Gehrig's record of the most runs batted in during a World Series: *New York Times*, October 6, 1956, 24.

157 **"Those fellows are on their own":** *New York Times*, February 24, 1956, 29.

157 **seven-year-old son, Steve:** Garvey, *Garvey*, 19 and 23.

158 **"He's a good sport":** *New York Times Sunday Magazine*, June 24, 1956, 6.

159 **"What do you do":** *New York Times*, July 5, 1956, 29.

159 **glove exchange:** *New York Times*, September 9, 1956, S1.

160 **"Thanks for that homer":** *New York Times*, September 12, 1956, 44.

160 **"All the hits"** and **"But not him":** *New York Times*, September 13, 1956, 44.

161 **first in nineteen games:** *New York Times*, September 6, 1956, 29.

161 **rain-delayed game:** *New York Times*, September 24, 1956, 30, and *New York Times*, September 25, 1956, 1. At the time, there was a 6 p.m. Sunday curfew in Pittsburgh for baseball games.

161 **"spectacular play":** *New York Times*, September 15, 1956, 24.

161 **"hit a hot grounder":** *New York Times*, September 26, 1956, 37.

161 **doubleheader on September 29:** *New York Times*, September 30, 1956, S1.

162 **"quiet hero"** and **"has been interviewed":** *New York Times*, October 4, 1956, 38.

162   **"I wouldn't say"**: *New York Times*, October 6, 1956, 24. Hodges had broken his regular bat, a Louisville Slugger, in the first game. This forced him for the second game to use a similar-sized bat made of northern white ash from the Adirondack Mountain region manufactured by the McLaughlin-Millard Co. in upstate New York. Although Hodges had signed a contract with McLaughlin (a company that had only been in existence since 1946) for them to use his signature on their bats, he preferred using the more traditional Louisville Sluggers made in Kentucky. Earlier in Hodges's career he used a heavier bat (38 or 39 ounces) but by the mid-1950s was using a 34-ounce bat. It is not uncommon for players to use lighter bats as they age and their swing slows. By way of a comparison, in 1956 Willie Mays also used a 34-ounce bat and Mickey Mantle's bats varied from 32 to 34 ounces: *New York Times*, July 4, 1956, 22, and *New York Times*, April 11, 1955, 32.

162   **"first time a Yankee team had lost the first two games"**: *New York Times*, October 6, 1956, 1.

162   **In the seventh**: *New York Times*, October 7, 1956, 202.

163   **first perfect game**: *New York Times*, October 11, 1956, 65.

163   **"tricky, low liner"**: *New York Times*, October 9, 1956, 1.

163   **Andy Carey**: *New York Times*, January 8, 2012, 26.

163   **"Hodges let me breathe"**: *LA Times*, April 14, 1957, S45.

163   **"the best catch I ever made"**: Mantle, *My Favorite Summer, 1956*, 269.

164   **"That's the way to pull the ball"**: *New York Times*, June 7, 2007, D3. The key to the Series had been pitching. Starting with Game Three, five different Yankee pitchers threw five consecutive complete games that varied from solid (Whitey Ford in Game Three and Tom Sturdivant in Game Four) to outstanding (despite losing, Bob Turley in Game Six and Johnny Kucks in Game Seven) to extraordinary (Larsen's perfect game). All this while the Dodgers badly missed Johnny Podres, who was then fulfilling his military service.

164   **covered all expenses**: Phone interview with Dick Walsh, the Dodgers' traveling secretary on the trip, March 8, 2007. Some players like Furillo, who had served in the Pacific during World War II, refused to make the trip: Shapiro, *Last Good Season*, 306.

164   **"Have you stopped to think"**: Parrott, *Lords of Baseball*, 26.

165   **Dick Walsh**: Phone interview with Walsh, March 8, 2007, and email on March 20, 2007. Walsh had previously been to Japan and spoke some Japanese.

165   **born on August 19**: Photo with caption, *New York Times*, August 21, 1956, 23. Cynthia was born in Lutheran Hospital in Brooklyn; the Dodgers were in Philadelphia. Hodges flew in to see his newborn daughter and then rejoined the team in St. Louis.

165   **"If there is anything"**: Vin Scully, "The Dodgers in Japan," *Sport*, April 1957, 26.

165   **"If you gave some"**: Phone interview with Dick Walsh, March 8, 2007.

166   **landed in Tokyo**: Scully, "Dodgers in Japan," 92, and *New York Times*, October 19, 1956, 30.

166   **"flowers everywhere"** and **"morally strong"**: Phone interview with Fred Kipp, October 26, 2006.

166   **opener of their exhibition series**: *New York Times*, October 20, 1956, 34.

166   **roomed with Reese**: Phone interview with Dick Walsh, March 8, 2007.

167   **"We hope they [the Dodgers]"**: *New York Times*, October 23, 1956, 42.

167   **Kipp threw a two-hit shutout**: *New York Times*, November 1, 1956, 55.

167   **"He would bend down"** and **"uncanny imitation"**: Scully, *Sport*, April 1957. As a boy growing up in Chicago, Dick Walsh had seen another player, Rabbit Maranville, display Hodges's exaggerated movements when the Boston Braves played the Cubs at Wrigley Field. The speedy Maranville was a light-hitting shortstop with a .253 career batting average who was elected to the Hall of Fame in large part for the notoriety in received for his clownish behavior on the field as well as his lengthy career (twenty-three seasons), which enabled him to accumulate 2,605 hits. Unlike Maranville, Hodges would have never dreamed of "putting it on" during a Major League game in America. Yet, on the Japan trip, Hodges enjoyed himself and became demonstrative on the field during games.

167   **"That terrific hitting"**: *New York Times*, November 3, 1956, 30.

168   **In Nagoya**: "Hodges Pantomime a Hit in Japan, *New York Times*, November 8, 1956, 54.

168   **But in a game played November 10**: "Gil Plays It Straight," *New York Times*, November 11, 1956.

168   **final game**: *New York Times*, November 13, 1956, 64.

168   **But Hodges's greatest contribution**: Scully, "Dodgers in Japan," 92–93. The newspaper that sponsored the trip, *Yomiuri Shinbun*, covered the Dodgers' games, yet their reportage makes no mention of Hodges's escapades, or the fans' reaction: March 8, 2007, email from Yasuko Makino, Princeton University Library (East Asian Division), after reviewing the twelve times Hodges's name is mentioned in *Yomiuri Shinbun* from October 18 to November 13, 1956.

169   **"all business in the summer"**: Phone interview with Johnny Podres, February 7, 2006.

169   **"his eyes danced"**: Phone interview with Dick Walsh, March 8, 2007.

13. THE LAST SEASON

171   *No way*: Hodges's response when told by Dick Walsh that 1957 would be the Dodgers' last season in Brooklyn: Phone interview with Dick Walsh, March 8, 2007.

171 "**shaved down a bit**": *New York Times*, December 28, 1956, 31. Hodges was the third-highest-paid player on the team with a salary of $37,000. Only Snider ($44,000) and Campanella ($42,000) were paid more. The Dodgers' next highest salaries were Reese ($36,000) and Jackie Robinson ($31,500): as per a typed sheet headed, "Dodgers' Salaries, 1956, Japanese Trip Squad, Including Numbers," from "The Glory Days: New York Baseball, 1947–1957" exhibit, Museum of the City of New York; $35,000 salary—same as prior season: *New York Times*, January 11, 1957, 37.

171 **home opener**: *New York Times*, April 19, 1957, 25.

171 **.365 batting average**: *LA Times*, June 17, 1957, C1.

172 **Hodges finished seventh in the voting**: *New York Times*, November 15, 1957, 30. The six players who finished ahead of Hodges (Aaron, Musial, Schoendienst, Mays, Spahn, and Banks) and the two who finished after him (Mathews and Frank Robinson) are all in the HOF.

172 **"Hodges Misses Goals"**: *New York Times*, September 30, 1957.

172 **"practically . . . carrying"**: *New York Times*, June 23, 1957, 170.

172 **"special skill"**: *LA Times*, July 8, 1957, C2. Hodges didn't get into the game until the bottom of the ninth inning with two outs and the National League trailing, 6–5, and the tying run on second base. Alston sent Hodges up as a pinch hitter against the right-handed Bob Grim. With the count 1-0, Hodges "ripped a low liner to left that sounded like bad news for the Americans but Minnie Minoso gathered it in for the final out." The National League All-Star team, which in prior years would have included half a dozen Dodgers players, had only three: Hodges, Gino Cimoli, and Clem Labine: *LA Times*, July 10, 1957, C1, and *New York Times*, July 4, 1957, 29.

172 **"wearing a grin"**: *LA Times*, July 15, 1957, C1, and *New York Times*, July 15, 1957, 23.

172 **twelfth grand slam**: *The Sporting News*, July 31, 1957, 23, and *New York Daily News*, July 19, 1957, 44. Six of his grand slams were hit at Ebbets Field, six on the road. By the time the season was over, Hodges had hit at least one grand slam against every National League team. Hodges was also the only player to hit all twelve grand slams playing for one team. Hodges hit the record-breaking thirteenth grand slam less than two weeks later at Wrigley Field in Chicago. Hodges hit one more in his career to give him a total of fourteen, which stood as the National League record until well after he retired.

173 **with his grand slam home run**: *LA Times*, August 2, 1957, C1.

173 **"one I'd like to see"**: *The Sporting News*, April 22, 1972, 8.

173 **Gil Hodges Night**: *The Sporting News*, July 31, 1957, 23, and *New York Daily News*, July 20, 1957, 26. Since it was good PR to have Hodges driving around Brooklyn in your car, eleven local dealerships sent a car to the event. Eleven baseballs, each

bearing a different make of car, were tossed into a container. Gil Hodges Jr. was asked to pull one out. By chance, he selected the Dodge, which had been driven onto the field, along with a Pontiac, Oldsmobile, Buick, Chevrolet, Lincoln, Plymouth, and a VW.

174 **"never talks himself up"**: *New York Times*, July 19, 1957, 37.

176 **"He knew just how to handle me"**: Drysdale, *Once a Bum*, 90. Drysdale's autobiography is the source for much of the information in this chapter regarding the relationship between the two men. Hodges's actions in the Pittsburgh bar were also told to me in my January 2006 phone interview with Clem Labine.

177 **"Don, fill it in for whatever you want"**: Meany, *Artful Dodgers*, 152–53.

177 **"It was funny"**: *New York Times*, March 2, 1957, 50.

178 **"I didn't mind starting fights"**: Courant.com, August 12, 2007.

178 **"I don't exactly look for any trouble"**: *New York Times*, August 16, 1968, 23.

178 **"The next thing I knew"**: Mathews, *Eddie Mathews*, 152.

178 **"most forceful pacifier"** and **"halfway to third base"**: *New York Times*, June 14, 1957, 28.

178 **"Stay right there"**: Drysdale, *Once a Bum*, 89. The National League fined Drysdale $40, Logan $100. The Braves won the game, 8–5: *New York Times*, June 16, 1957, E2.

179 **"to beg off playing"**: *New York Times*, June 15, 1957, 12.

179 **"got the message"**: Hodges, *Game of Baseball*, 66. When I spoke to Robin Roberts in a phone interview on February 5, 2008, he said he "had no recollection of ever hitting Hodges." During the 1956 season, the Dodgers' backup infielder, Don Zimmer, was hit by a pitch and suffered a shattered cheekbone. That year, Hodges predicted that as a result of those types of injuries, "Someday ball players will wear helmets like fighters in training": *New York Times*, June 25, 1956, 40. In the early 1970s, batting helmets became mandatory: Jensen, *Timeline History of Baseball*, under the year 1971.

179 **Brooklyn and baseball**: W. C. Heinz, "The Guy Who Never Left Brooklyn," *Coronet*, June 1960, 150, 153.

180 **"It was a cross"**: Phone interview with Dick Walsh, March 8, 2007. Walsh was right about Minneapolis. Three years later, the original Washington Senators moved there and became the Twins. Walsh later became the Dodgers' director of stadium operations at Chavez Ravine and the general manager of the LA Convention Center.

180 **last Dodger to ever come to bat**: Sprechman and Shannon, *This Day in New York Sports*, 268.

181 **luncheon**: *LA Times*, October 29, 1957, C1, and *New York Times*, October 29, 1957, 38.

181 **just along for the ride:** *LA Times*, October 30, 1957, C1.

181 **"shuddered" and "I'm a Brooklyn resident":** *LA Times*, October 31, 1957, C3.

181 **while working at Ditney Hill:** Interview with Donald Hume in Petersburg, April 2006.

181 **Charlie Hodges suddenly died:** *New York Times*, November 24, 1957, 87, and *Petersburg Press*, November 29, 1957, 1; also Charlie Hodges's certificate of death issued by the Pike County Health Department.

181 **"I want to congratulate you":** Interview with Sonny Harris, April 20, 2006.

181 **eight funeral plots:** Interview with Bob and Sonny Harris, April 20, 2006.

182 **writing thank-you cards:** John Drof, group interview in Petersburg, April 2006.

14. THE WORST PLACE EVER

185 *If I hit one ball*: Hano, "Gil Hodges," 59.

185 **Gold Glove:** Thorn, *Total Baseball*, 727–30; 1957 was the first and only season one award was given out at each position. Vic Power won the AL Gold Glove every season from 1958 through 1964.

185 **not to throw over:** Interview with Carl Erskine, April 16, 2006. Erskine told me that Hodges never shared his knowledge of the opponent's signs with other team members. He was concerned that if the signs were changed, one of his teammates might be injured.

185 **"revolutionized bunt defense" and "go for the long ball":** Musial, *"The Man's" Own Story*, 126.

186 **advantages over a righty:** Holding runners on first base (the left-hander's glove is the one closest to the runner, allowing him to make a quicker tag on pick-off throws) and how a left-handed first baseman can release from holding a runner on base more quickly than a right-hander and be able to move further from first base to be in a better fielding position. The left-hander's quicker release has to do with less cumbersome footwork needed to begin moving to the right, since a lefty first baseman faces home plate as he holds a runner on, but a righty will be facing more toward second base: Falkner, *Nine Sides of the Diamond*, 51 and 53; as for throws: see Hernandez, *Pure Baseball*, 80.

186 **"it's a pretty tough position right-handed":** Keegan, *First Baseman*, 36.

186 **"I don't want to interfere, son":** *New York Times*, October 17, 1971, S2, and confirmed by Danny Murtaugh, *New York Times*, March 29, 1970, 160.

186 **"will beat you just as often":** Hodges, *Game of Baseball*, 93.

186 **attempting a bunt:** Hodges, *Game of Baseball*, 114.

187 **"made everything look easy":** Phone interview with Dave Anderson, September 20, 2010.

187 **"a master at this deception":** *New York Times*, October 10, 1971, 22.

187   **"the best-fielding right-handed first baseman"**: Phone interview with Jack Lang, February 2, 2006. Lang saw almost every game Hodges played in Brooklyn from 1948 until 1957. For several years, Lang was the official scorer at Ebbets Field and was compensated with a weekly case of Schaeffer beer. When Lang indicated a hit, the H in the Schaeffer Score Board lit up; on errors, the E was illuminated. When the beer stopped, he refused to continue as official scorer. They gave the job to someone else.

187   **"was in a class by himself"**: Phone interview with Frank Torre, April 11, 2010.

188   **the best player on the Dodgers**: *LA Times*, January 19, 1958, C2. After a couple of seasons as a Dodgers coach, Dressen later managed in Milwaukee and then Detroit.

189   **"in the neighborhood of $35,000"**: Hodges was one of the most valuable Dodgers. Only Duke Snider ($42,000) was paid more: *LA Times*, December 16, 1958, C1. The other Dodger players attending the baseball clinic were Gino Cimoli, Junior Gilliam, George (Sparky) Anderson, Ed Roebuck, Bob Lillis, and Roger Craig.

189   **she often flew back**: Allen, *Brooklyn Remembered*, 90. In his memoir of his years as the Dodgers' travel secretary and ticket sales manager, Harold Parrott wrote, "Joan Hodges, Gil's fussy wife, saw a cockroach in the apartment she got [in LA] and fled all the way back to Brooklyn, never to return that season. The beast she saw must have been larger and nastier than a Brooklyn cockroach, for Joan took the pains to tell all the other wives, before she took off in a huff, about the perils of living in Los Angeles": Parrott, *Lords of Baseball*, 302.

189   **"This country estate living"**: *LA Times*, February 23, 1958, F5.

189   **"I felt unmistakable pangs"**: Hodges, "To Dad: A Silent Promise," *Guideposts*, September 1960, 2–3.

190   **"Be smooth"**: Phone interview with Wes Parker, February 9, 2007.

190   **"had great hands and never"**: Falkner, *Nine Sides of the Diamond*, 42.

190   **in the Los Angeles Coliseum**: *New York Times*, March 26, 2008, D2.

191   **"You couldn't reach it"**: Parker, *Win or Go Home*, 103.

191   **"as a bowling alley is for tennis"**: *New York Times*, October 10, 1959.

191   **"let O'Malley pitch on opening day"**: *LA Times*, January 21, 1958, C1.

191   **would lead the Majors in home runs**: *LA Times*, March 8, 1958, A1.

191   **Ebbets Field was the easiest**: *LA Times*, February 9, 1958, C5.

191   **"The only record I'll break"**: *New York Times*, April 19, 1958, 16.

191   **Alston told Hodges to forget**: *New York Times*, January 12, 1959, 64.

192   **300th home run**: *New York Times*, April 24, 1958, 40.

192   **On Opening Day**: Stout, *Dodgers*, 246.

192   **"in the history of major league baseball"**: *LA Times*, May 29, 1958, C2.

192   **"not in the bars much"**: Phone interview with Johnny Podres, February 7, 2006.

193   **extra batting practice:** *LA Times*, June 12, 1958, C1.

193   **"I didn't feel too comfortable":** Frank Finch, *LA Times*, June 13, 1958, C3.

193   **"I'm just not hitting":** *LA Times*, July 19, 1958, A1.

193   **"two dollars down on a horse":** Phone interview with Johnny Podres, February 7, 2006.

193   **"Gil has been having such a tough time":** *LA Times*, June 14, 1958, A2.

193   **"has become more offensive minded":** *LA Times*, June 15, 1958, C3.

194   **"Gil is having such a rough time with the bat":** *LA Times*, June 16, 1958, C3.

194   **"I got in the wrong":** *LA Times*, March 25, 1958, C2. Larker played in ninety-nine games in 1958, batting .277. After seeing Hodges's hitting struggles, Larker astutely said, "That ball park was particularly tough on Gil Hodges because he pulled everything anyway. Pitchers pitched him differently there. They threw him a lot of breaking balls out of the strike zone; when they got ahead of him, they'd break it outside about six inches and he'd swing at it": Parker, *Win or Go Home*, 106.

194   **"Gil agreed that a rest might help him":** *LA Times*, June 20, 1958, C2.

194   **"That Cincinnati thing":** *New York Times*, July 9, 1958, 30.

195   **"generally raised Cain":** *LA Times*, July 16, 1958, C2.

195   **"eating his heart out":** *LA Times*, July 27, 1958, C1.

195   **"Hodges can play anywhere"** *LA Times*, August 18, 1958, C5. In 1958 Hodges played 122 at first base, fifteen at third base, five in right, four in left, and one at catcher: *LA Times*, February 1, 1959, C5. Despite his slump, Hodges could occasionally dominate a game with his bat: in a July 26 win over the Phillies, Hodges went 4 for 5, with five runs batted in, and on September 7 he hit two home runs (his twenty-first and twenty-second of the season) and drove in three runs in a 7–5 win over the Cardinals.

195   **no longer the player:** *LA Times*, August 22, 1957, C2. Much to his credit, Walter O'Malley made sure that Campanella was paid his full salary for the 1958 season and kept the future Hall of Famer employed in various capacities for the rest of his life: *LA Times*, December 16, 1958, C1, and Stout, *Dodgers*, 247.

196   **more than three million fans:** *LA Times*, September 28, 1958, C1. The Dodgers drew 817,010 fans in their final year in Brooklyn.

196   **"Next year"** and **"I can't believe Gil is over the hill":** *LA Times*, September 26, 1959, A2.

196   **"I'd want Hodges on first base":** *LA Times*, August 24, 1958, C1.

196   **"management had mistakenly":** *LA Times*, September 29, 1958, C1.

196   **"As soon as the season ends":** *LA Times*, September 9, 1958, C2.

196   **"the great needle":** Interview with Carl Erskine, April, 2006.

196   **Jack Barron:** Phone interview with Don Demeter on March 4, 2008, and follow-up call on March 8, 2008. In 1958 Demeter was an outfielder with the Dodgers. He

later became the pastor of Grace Community Baptist Church in Oklahoma City. In 1958 a comic strip, *Gil Thorp*, was created by Jack Berrill: The name is a combination of Gil Hodges's first name and the last name of the great Olympic athlete Jim Thorpe. Both men were heroes to Berrill. *Gil Thorp* tells the story of the athletic director of fictional Milford High School who, in addition to coaching the baseball, basketball, and football teams, helps his teenage students deal with their personal challenges: Jack Berrill obituary, *Seattle Times*, March 16, 1996.

15. WORLD CHAMPIONS

199   *This is more gratifying*: Hodges after the Dodgers forced a three-game playoff with the Braves to determine the NL pennant winner: *LA Times*, September 28, 1959, C1.

199   "I'd spoil": *LA Times*, December 16, 1958, C1. At the time of Hodges's salary reduction, he was third (behind Stan Musial and Del Ennis) among active National League players in career runs batted in. In addition, his 320 career home runs put him fifth in NL history. But his 934 career strikeouts were the most in NL history. Duke Snider was next with 933: *LA Times*, February 1, 1959, C5, and *LA Times*, January 23, 1959, C2.

199   "You need a man": *LA Times*, February 19, 1959, C1.

199   "Hodges commands": *LA Times*, September 2, 1961, A2.

199   "Sleep is very important": *New York Times*, July 8, 1962, 127.

200   in bed by 9:30: *LA Times*, April 11, 1959, A2.

200   numerous game-winning hits: In the thirteenth inning of a game at the Coliseum on May 22, his drive off the screen in left field scored the winning run to give Drysdale a 2–1 victory over the Giants. A week later, Hodges hit a walk-off home run into the center-field seats in the bottom of the ninth against the Cardinals for a 7–6 come-from-behind win and the fans gave him a "resounding ovation"; in San Francisco, in the ninth inning of a game on July 21, Hodges's double scored the game's only run to give the Dodgers a 1–0 victory: *LA Times*, May 23, 1959, A1; *LA Times* May 31, 1959, C1; and *LA Times*, July 22, 1959, C1.

200   injuring his right ankle: *New York Times*, July 24, 1959, 1, 16.

200   "heard something pop": *LA Times*, July 25, 1959, A1.

200   turned his right ankle: *LA Times*, July 31, 1959, C2.

200   "I don't know, maybe I'll never": *LA Times*, August 13, 1959, C2.

200   "fairly spry": *LA Times*, August 14, 1959, C2.

201   No matter which town we visit: *LA Times*, August 21, 1959, C2.

201   pinch-hit single: *LA Times*, August 22, 1959, 1.

201   Hodges returned to the starting: *LA Times*, August 24, 1959, C2.

201   twentieth home run: *LA Times*, August 25, 1959, 1.

201 homered off his old nemesis: *New York Times*, August 26, 1959, 33.

201 And on August 30: *New York Times*, August 31, 1959, 26.

201 three-game sweep: *New York Times*, September 22, 1959, 47.

201 Although it was a day off: *LA Times*, September 22, 1959, C1.

201 lost, 11-10: *New York Times*, September 23, 1959, 47, and *The Sporting News*, September 30, 1959, 23.

202 "Any prolonged absence": *LA Times*, September 24, 1959, 1.

202 deemed him fit to play: *LA Times*, September 25, 1959, C1.

202 "Guess I haven't got an alibi": *LA Times*, September 26, 1959, 1, and *New York Times*, September 26, 1959, 17. At then lightless Wrigley Field, the game would have been stopped due to darkness after the eleventh inning had Hodges not won it.

202 "brilliant": *LA Times*, September 26, 1959, A2.

203 Game One: *New York Times*, September 29, 1959, 47.

203 Game Two: *New York Times*, September 30, 1959, 1, and Parker, *Win or Go Home*, 128-30.

203 first seventh-place team to come back to win: *LA Times*, September 22, 1959, C1.

203 "defense was far more important": *LA Times*, July 28, 1959, C1.

203 fewest errors: *New York Times*, December 17, 1959, 56.

203 National League Manager of the Year: *LA Times*, October 13, 1959, C1.

204 Series proceeds: *LA Times*, September 28, 1959, C1; thirty-five full World Series shares were voted: *LA Times*, October 9, 1959, C7. As player representative, Hodges was the team's leader when it came to deciding how to split up either their World Series share or any additional payment they received for finishing in second or third place. In this regard Hodges decided to delay as long as possible the team meeting to determine how the money would be divided. "If we finish first, I would imagine that we would divide the money differently than if we finish second or third": *LA Times*, September 21, 1959, C3.

204 "You hate to take": *LA Times*, October 2, 1959, C1.

204 In Game Three: *LA Times*, October 5, 1959, 38.

205 White Sox manager Al Lopez: *New York Times*, October 6, 1959, 47.

205 "rarely if ever uses": *New York Times*, October 6, 1959, 46.

206 "easily one of the nicest human beings": *LA Times*, October 12, 1961, C1.

206 *Steve Allen Show*: Originally broadcast on Monday, October 5, 1959, viewed at the Museum of Television and Radio in New York City, June 12, 2007.

206 Koufax allowed: *LA Times*, October 7, 1959, C1. After the first five games of the series, Hodges had eight hits in eighteen at bats. At that point, in his last twenty-five World Series games (since his 1952 debacle), Hodges was batting .345: *LA Times*, October 8, 1959, C3.

207 "It may affect my throwing" and "I want to play": *LA Times*, October 8, 1959, 1.

207   **"throwing rather than pitching"**: *LA Times*, October 9, 1959, 1.

207   **"greatest team"** and **"What more can you ask?"**: *LA Times*, October 9, 1959, C1.

207   **weakest championship team**: James, *Guide to Baseball Managers*, 205. At the time, the Dodgers' eighty-six-game win total was the lowest for any World Series winning team; they didn't have a player in the National League's top five in home runs, runs batted in, runs scored, or hits: Parker, *Win or Go Home*, 130.

208   **"without Gene Snyder's"** and **"feel important"**: Hodges, *Game of Baseball*, 145.

208   **Larry Sherry**: "Sherry Pitches with Confidence," *New York Times*, October 6, 1959, 46.

208   **Lou Gehrig Memorial Award**: *LA Times*, January 10, 1960, C4. Wally Moon, who won the National League Comeback Player of the Year Award in 1959 and finished fourth in the MVP voting, hit .302 in 145 games with 19 home runs and 74 runs batted in after batting just .238 in 1958. Twelve of Moon's 19 home runs went over the left-field screen: *LA Times*, October 23, 1959, C1, and *New York Times*, November 9, 1959, 42. Hodges finished the season with 25 home runs, 80 runs batted in, and a batting average of .276. Hodges led the Dodgers in home runs, the seventh time in his career (1949, 1950, 1951, 1952, 1954, 1958, and 1959) he'd done so. In 1949 he was tied with Snider, and in 1958 with Charlie Neal.

208   **contract for $39,000**: *LA Times*, February 10, 1960, C1.

208   **"Please don't step on my toes"**: Phone interview with Norm Sherry, October 15, 2010. Norm and Larry Sherry were brothers.

208   **"They don't come no better than Gil"**: *New York Times*, March 23, 1960, 44.

209   **"Anything Skip wants"**: *LA Times*, May 5, 1960, C3, and *LA Times*, February 24, 1961, C1.

209   **Hodges asked Walter Alston**: *New York Times*, January 13, 1983. Carl Erskine told me the Dodgers' pitchers did not like pitching batting practice.

209   **"Any questions?"**: *Home Run Derby* dialogue is supplied from watching the videotapes of these episodes of the program.

210   **Hodges told Koufax he had to pitch seven innings**: Leavy, *Sandy Koufax*, 102, and Felser, *Baseball's Ten Greatest Pitchers*, 87–88. Alston remained at Vero Beach that day and managed the Dodgers' A team.

210   **expansion draft**: *LA Times*, March 28, 1961, C3.

210   **started to use a 31-ounce bat**: *LA Times*, June 30, 1961, C3.

210   **baseball smarts**: *LA Times*, July 16, 1961, G3. That season, Joan was pregnant and again remained in Brooklyn. With his family growing, Hodges put his six-room home at 1120 E. Thirty-Second Street (off Avenue K) up for sale. The real estate advertisement listed features like oil heat, an enclosed porch, a birch kitchen, and a knotty pine basement. But the key selling point, in bold capital letters, was the fact that the house was "GIL HODGES' HOME": *LA Times*, April 16, 1961, G6, and

New York Times, July 7, 1961, 46. After selling the home on Thirty-Second Street, the Hodges family moved about half a mile away to a split-level home with four bedrooms on Bedford Avenue off Avenue M, where Gil Hodges would live for the rest of his life: *New York Times*, December 17, 1967, 189.

211 **"A second game"**: *LA Times*, July 17, 1960, G4, and *LA Times*, June 7, 1961, C2. The second All-Star Game had been added to help raise additional funds for the players' pension fund.

211 **"Back at Ebbets Field"**: *LA Times*, June 7, 1961, C2.

211 **forty-eight lanes**: *New York Times*, February 7, 1961, 44.

211 **Brooklyn Cancer Fund**: *New York Times*, December 5, 1961, 58.

211 **"Gil, I bowled 182"**: *New York Times*, December 12, 1967, 189.

16. CASEY

215 *A lot of Stengel's influence*: *New York Times*, March 10, 1966, 37.

215 **Joan Payson Whitney**: *New York Times Sunday Magazine*, June 23, 1968, 28.

216 **predicted Stengel would manage**: *LA Times*, October 3, 1961, C2.

216 **"because he is a devoted"** and **"It's wonderful to be back"**: *New York Times*, October 13, 1961, 43.

217 **"I talked to George Weiss"**: January 11, 1962, letter from Bavasi to Hodges that appears in the appendix to Amoruso, *Quiet Man*.

217 **"I don't think this club hasn't"**: *New York Times*, January 31, 1962, 24.

217 **highest single-season total since 1900**: *New York Times*, September 26, 2010, S11. In 1899 the NL's Cleveland Exiles finished 20-134: *Baseball Digest*, February 1951, 5.

217 **"Those guys were not happy"**: Burke and Fornatale, *Change-Up*, 20. To get an idea of how bad the Mets were in 1962, the three other expansion teams of the era, Houston, California, and Washington, each won at least sixty games, 50 percent more games than the Mets.

217 **"You never heard"**: Berra, *Yogi: It Ain't Over*, 34.

217 **"Casey did a lot"**: Creamer, *Stengel*, 89.

218 **"I don't mind"**: Creamer, *Babe*, 278.

218 **"No one," Stengel said**: *New York Times*, January 20, 1962, 16.

218 **"particularly admired"**: Creamer, *Stengel*, 13.

218 **came to knowing baseball rules**: Conlan, *Jocko*, 117.

218 **"couldn't wait to get rid"; "despite knowing that Hodges was"; and "ear-brows"**: Phone interview with George Vescey, May 11, 2006. Another New York writer of that era, Robert Lipsyte, recalls that Casey said "tear," not "squeeze": Lipsyte, *SportsWorld*, 43, confirmed in an email from Lipsyte on December 13, 2007.

218 **In 1950 Stengel knew**: Creamer, *Stengel*, 237.

218 **"As an older player"**: Hodges, *Game of Baseball*, 26.

219 **"Don't ask me, Norm"**: Phone interview with Norm Sherry, October 15, 2010.

219 **"Every spring it gets harder"**: *New York Times*, February 27, 1962, 39.

219 **"But not too bad for the first day"**: Shecter, *Once upon A Time*, 36.

219 **"stance and his mannerisms"**: Angell, *Summer Game*, 13–14.

219 **362nd of his career**: *New York Times*, April 12, 1962, 44.

220 **Merrill Lynch**: *New York Times*, April 13, 1962, 52.

220 **"Quality men"**: *New York Times*, January 14, 1971, 46, and also Lipsyte, *Sports World*, 43.

220 **"he could hardly light the cigarette"**: Snider, *Duke of Flatbush*, 59. Hodges was not the only star player to smoke during games. Joe DiMaggio did as well.

220 **asked out of the lineup**: Shecter, *Once upon A Time*, 62.

220 **"perhaps, and this is no"**: Cosell as spoken on his *Clubhouse Journal* show prior to the Mets' first spring training game, March 10, 1962: audio tape courtesy of Marc Gold.

220 **"The boos are still ringing in my ears"**: *New York Times*, March 26, 1966, 20.

220 **Hodges's error**: *New York Times*, May 5, 1962.

220 **twelfth-inning, two-run single**: *New York Times*, May 7, 1962, 41.

220 **ninth-inning home run**: *New York Times*, May 13, 1962, S1.

221 **Suddenly, Stengel jumped**: Reilly, *Baseball and American Culture*, 212. Don Demeter told me in a phone interview on March 8, 2008, that in one game when he was playing for the Phillies he saw Hodges, sitting next to Stengel in the dugout, tap Stengel to wake him up.

221 **"obligingly hit the ball"**: *New York Times*, June 20, 1962, 27.

221 **"That has to be Leo"**: *New York Times*, May 31, 1962, 26.

221 **"That wasn't a game"**: Phone interview with Sandy Koufax, October 14, 2010.

221 **.316 with eight home runs**: *New York Times*, May 31, 1962, 26.

222 **"First base is serious"**: *New York Times*, June 5, 1962, 51.

222 **"Marvelous" Marv Throneberry**: Hodges, *Game of Baseball*, 26.

222 **In a June 17 game**: Angell, *Summer Game*, 44; *New York Times*, September 26, 2010, S11.

222 **"was satisfactory"**: *New York Times*, October 19, 1962, 35.

222 **"Hey, Stan" and "enormous and strong"**: Phone interview with Wayne D. Block, May 17, 2010. The homer placed Hodges tenth on the career home run list. (See afterword, "Hodges and the Hall.") Hodges didn't last long in the top ten. Willie Mays passed Hodges as the leading right-handed home run hitter in National League history on April 19, 1963, with his 371st home run: Adell and Samelson, *Amazing Mets Trivia*, 55.

223 **"Don't you think"**: Golenbock, *Amazin'*, 131–32.

224   **the Mets signed Ed Kranepool:** *New York Times*, June 29, 1962, 17.

224   **"Gil polished me":** Burke and Fornatale, *An Oral History*, 21–22.

224   **On September 22, 1962:** *New York Times*, September 23, 1962, 199.

224   **riddles:** Shecter, *Once upon A Time*, 129–30.

224   **"Gil Hodges Night":** *New York Times*, August 25, 1962, 13.

224   **"Could it be":** *New York Times*, September 17, 1962, 55.

225   **"Gil Hodges will never be a manager":** Shecter, *Once upon A Time*, 136–37.

225   **Alvin Miller:** In-person interview with Judith and Alvin Miller, East Windsor NJ, January 15, 2008. Miller could not recall exactly what year the incident took place but thought it was sometime in the early 1960s. Hodges taking time out of his busy schedule to do-the-right-thing was a common event in Brooklyn. A few years later, when Gil Hodges Jr. was playing baseball for Midwood High School, Hodges attended the team's final game of the season. And after Midwood defeated Erasmus, Hodges didn't go straight home. He took the time to go into the losing team's locker room to shake the hand of all the Erasmus players and to compliment them on *playing a good game*. One never forgot how it felt to shake Hodges's hand. "It was," Joe Guicie said, "like shaking stone": Phone interview with Joe Guidice, March 2, 2007.

225   **knee problems:** *New York Times*, April 14, 1963, 167.

225   **"Last year, I predicted":** Shecter, *Once upon A Time*, 102.

226   **"I'm grateful":** *New York Times*, May 10, 1963, 23.

17. IN THE CELLAR

229   *I appreciate this nice-guy routine*: *Look Magazine*, July 14, 1964, 98A.

229   **"nothing," he wrote:** Hodges, *Game of Baseball*, 130–31.

229   **Nicky Lipariti:** Photo, *New York Times*, May 5, 1963, 207.

230   **"You've got to have the right":** Honig, *When the Grass Was Real*, 181.

230   **"He can have a job":** *Washington Post*, July 11, 1963, C2.

230   **"Sloppy ball players":** *Washington Post*, December 22, 1966, B1. Selkirk had been named the Senators' general manager less than a year before he hired Hodges. The Senators job was the first (and last) time he was hired as a general manager.

230   **"I'll tell you about Hodges":** *Washington Post*, May 24, 1963, B1. Hodges signed a contract with the Senators for $34,500, the same amount as his Mets contract: *The Sporting News*, June 1, 1963, 9. The day after the Senators signed Hodges, they sold outfielder Jimmy Piersall to the Mets. The Mets denied the two moves were related, but it appears they were.

231   **"a complete stranger":** *Washington Post*, May 23, 1963, A1.

231   **"I asked baseball people":** *Washington Post*, May 24, 1963, B1. The Senators had a history dating back to Bucky Harris in 1924 (and Joe Cronin in 1933) of

hiring managers with no previous managerial experience. In 1963 Hodges would take batting and infield practice to keep in shape. Since Harris and Cronin were player-managers, the writers would interpret his taking batting practice as Hodges preparing to pencil himself into the lineup, especially before the Senators acquired Don Zimmer from the Dodgers as a right-handed pinch hitter. Although Hodges was often motivated by the Senators' poor hitting, and by his own admission that "it is a long time before a man loses his desire to play this game," once Hodges started managing, he never played again: *Washington Post*, April 21, 1964, A18. But in Washington, Hodges would pitch and catch during batting practice. In 1965, while catching batting practice, Hodges required five stitches to close a gash in the back of his head from a player's swing. Earlier that season, Hodges was hit in the head by a line drive while he was pitching batting practice and ended up spending a night in the hospital for observation: *Washington Post*, September 24, 1965, D3, and *Washington Post*, June 13, 1965, C1.

231   **Johnny Murphy**: Smith, *To Absent Friends*, 195.

231   **Selkirk and Murphy**: *New York Times*, October 7, 1967, 18.

231   **outstanding relief pitcher**: *New York Times*, December 28, 1967, 51. When George Weiss took over the Mets as general manager, Murphy was his first hire. He started as chief scout, was promoted to vice president in 1964, and would eventually become the Mets' general manager. Most important, although he was an introverted type (his nickname was "Grandma"), he was one of the few executives in the front office who was not afraid to disagree with Mets chairman M. Donald Grant: Smith, *To Absent Friends*, 195; also *New York Times*, January 15, 1970, 45.

231   **"He'd get mad"**: Peary, *We Played the Game*, 148. Walker and Selkirk's comments indicate there were instances when Hodges lost his cool during his playing days. For example, on September 7, 1951, as the Dodgers were battling the Giants for the pennant, the *New York Times* addressed rumors that tensions created by the pennant race had led to fisticuffs in the Dodgers' clubhouse. The article implies that Hodges had flattened Newcombe, and Reese, "caught in the middle," suffered bumps and bruises. But the piece concludes, "Hale, hearty, and as friendly as ever, Hodges, Newcombe and Reese laughed loudest yesterday. 'Ridiculous!' is the word with which they dismissed the rumors": "Dodgers Get Big Laugh over Dissension Rumors," *New York Times*, September 7, 1951, 40. I was unable to confirm the story. Newcombe, the only surviving member of the three players mentioned, never responded to interview requests.

231   **"best agitator"**: Phone interview with Johnny Podres, February 7, 2006.

231   **"I believe in fitting"**: *Washington Post*, May 23, 1963, A1.

231   **Eddie Yost**: *Washington Post*, May 26, 1963, C1. Like Hodges, Yost was once honored by the Queens County Catholic War veterans with their Sports Award:

New York Times, August 30, 1952, 7. Yost didn't hit for a high average (.254 for his career), but he had a great batting eye. He often had an on base percentage over .400 by drawing so many base on balls and was referred to as "The Walking Man." In the decade of the 1950s, only three men led the American League in walks: Ted Williams, Mickey Mantle, and Yost. Had Yost played today with the game's emphasis on statistics like on base percentage, combined with his ability to produce high pitch counts that wear out pitchers, Yost would be viewed as an invaluable player: "Eddie Yost, 86, Baseball's 'Walking Man,'" *New York Times*, October 12, 2012, B19. Yost managed the Senators for one game in the brief period after Vernon was fired but before Hodges began managing: "White Sox Victors over Senators, 9–3," *New York Times*, May 23, 1963, 59.

232 **"There's not much you can say"**: *New York Times*, May 24, 1963, 47.

232 ***What's My Line?***: Show no. 665, originally aired on May 26, 1963, viewed at the Museum of Television and Radio in New York City.

232 **four-hour drill**: *Washington Post*, March 11, 1965, D1. Hodges would shake up his own game patterns if he thought it would help the team. On July 19, 1964, Hodges managed the opening game of a doubleheader in Fenway Park against the Red Sox from the third base coach's box, "just to change the luck." Despite sixteen hits, the Senators lost 11–10 and Eddie Yost was out at his regular coaching spot for the second game: *Washington Post*, July 20, 1964, A19.

232 **"D.I."**: *Look Magazine*, July 14, 1964, 99.

232 **"He doesn't demand respect"** and **"Ain't nobody"**: *Look Magazine*, July 14, 1964, 99.

232 **"rooted in a sort of fear"**: *Washington Post*, March 31, 1964, B4.

233 **"I don't see"** and **"I refuse to answer"**: *Washington Post*, June 4, 1963, A20.

233 **"It's going to start costing"**: *Washington Post*, June 13, 1963, A20.

233 **seven players left**: Maury Allen, "Gil Hodges Is a Tyrant!" *Sports Today*, August 1971, 23.

234 **can be taught** and **lowest point since 1908**: *New York Times*, June 16, 1968, SM12.

235 **"There goes my catcher"**: Phone interview with Claude Osteen, December 21, 2006. It should be noted that Osteen thought Hobbie Landrith (not Retzer) was the catcher who was replaced by Mike Brumley (not Cal Needham). But I looked up the facts of the game Osteen was referring to which took place on September 4, 1963. Based on the box score, I have used the correct names. For other details of the Yankees 5–4 win: Addie, "Clout by Maris Beats Nats, 5–4," *Washington Post*, September 5, 1963, B1.

235 **Maris hit a game-winning, two-run homer**: *New York Times*, September 5, 1963, 36. In a phone interview with Cal Neeman on December 22, 2006, he said he signaled for a fastball outside, but "we should have been inside."

236   **"never missed a trick"**: Phone interview with Claude Osteen, December 21, 2006; "He [Hodges] doesn't miss a thing," wrote Bob Addie, "and he isn't shy about taking a player aside and telling him his mistake": *Washington Post*, June 16, 1963, C3.

236   **"He has the right mental attitude now"**: *Washington Post*, November 13, 1963, C1.

236   **"He would call me"**: *New York Times*, February 26, 1978, S3.

236   **holding a 2-1 lead**: *Washington Post*, July 24, 1964, B1; also Baseball Reference. com.

237   **Chuck Hinton**: *Washington Post*, June 9, 1964, A23.

237   **Charles ran back to second**: *Washington Post*, April 20, 1964, A1.

237   **fined him $100**: *Washington Post*, May 10, 1964, C1.

237   **"We all know what a fine"**: *Washington Post*, April 21, 1964, A18.

237   **highest-paid player**: *Washington Post*, December 20, 1964, C1.

237   **"shake up" Hinton**: *Washington Post*, November 3, 1963, C1; "Hodges is remarkable," Hinton said before the 1964 season. "I sincerely believe he's going to be one of the really great managers in the game. I never saw a first year manager with as much control of things as Gil": *Washington Post*, January 3, 1964, A17. Hinton did not respond to my interview request.

237   **"I doubt if he"**: *Washington Post*, January 1, 1964, A21.

237   **Hodges was "instrumental"**: Phone interview with Fred Valentine, December 4, 2006.

238   **Tom Cheney**: *Washington Post*, June 22, 2008, W16.

238   **"in his groove"**: *Washington Post*, February 28, 1964, D1.

238   **"the sharp edge"**: *The Sporting News*, June 1, 1963, 9. Cheney had an awkward delivery and frequently pitched winter ball, which added to the cumulative strain on his arm.

238   **at least 15**: *Washington Post*, July 11, 1963, C1.

239   **"Cheney was throwing half-speed"**: *Washington Post*, July 15, 1963, A16.

239   **shut him down for the season**: *Washington Post*, August 31, 1963, A17. Details of how Hodges used Cheney after he hurt his arm on July 11: On July 25 Cheney started against the Orioles. In the first inning he gave up a single and a walk, but no runs. To start the second, with the score 0–0, Hodges removed Cheney for a relief pitcher. From the circumstances, it appears Hodges pulled Cheney out of the game after he complained of pain. Hodges didn't use Cheney again until August 7 when he inserted him as a reliever for mop-up duty in the sixth inning of a 9–1 Yankees blowout of the Senators. Cheney pitched well; in three innings he allowed two hits and no runs and struck out three. Four days later, on August 11, encouraged by Cheney's three innings of solid pitching, Hodges started Cheney against

the Orioles. Cheney held the Orioles scoreless in the first two innings, allowed a two-run home run in the third, but stayed in the game for the fourth inning. Then, after getting Boog Powell to ground out, Hodges replaced Cheney with reliever Ed Roebuck. Again, the facts (early inning, no one on base, one out) indicate that Hodges would have kept Cheney in the game, unless Cheney said he was hurt and needed to come out. Hodges again gave Cheney almost two weeks' rest. On August 22 Hodges put Cheney into a low-pressure relief appearance with Kansas City ahead of the Senators, 6–1. Cheney pitched one inning and set down the Athletics, 1-2-3. Hodges again waited four days to start Cheney, but he didn't even make it out of the first inning in a game against the Minnesota Twins before being pulled after allowing only two hits and a walk.

239   **"I wouldn't say I could do that"**: Addie, "Tom Cheney 'Ready to Cut Loose,' Scoffs at Rumor His Arm Is Dead," *Washington Post*, March 25, 1964, C1. Prior to the season, Resta pronounced Cheney fit to pitch: *Washington Post*, February 28, 1964, D1.

239   **"Tom Cheney has come along much faster"**: *Washington Post*, April 7, 1964, A19.

239   **"Ah, go out there, you can do it"**: *Washington Post*, June 22, 2008, W16.

239   **"Yeah, you son of a bitch"**: Peary, *We Played the Game*, 614.

240   **Mayo Clinic**: *Washington Post*, June 24, 1964, C1.

240   **"thorough examination"**: *Washington Post*, June 22, 1964, A20. In the spring of 1966, Cheney returned as a non-roster free agent. Despite taking the entire 1965 season off, his arm still ached. Even then, Cheney still didn't listen to Hodges. "Cheney is eager to make a comeback." Hodges said that spring. "He has started to throw well and is putting more and more on the ball. He even tried to change up and threw a screwball. Considering that Cheney is recovering from a 'tender' arm, those pitches will hurt you because you must twist the arm. Cheney also tried to throw a knuckler which could tear your arm up unless you're used to it. I told him to stick to the fast ball and a few curves": *Washington Post*, February 28, 1966, D1.

240   **"I think I'm done"**: *Washington Post*, July 19, 1963, D1.

240   **"Hodges was very patient"** and **"You couldn't count"**: Phone interview with Dave Stenhouse, December 11, 2006. A few years later, Hodges faulted one of his own pitchers for getting caught bringing his hand to his mouth while on the mound preparing to throw a spitball. Although it resulted in an automatic ball call by the umpire, Hodges had no problem with the rule being enforced against his own pitcher. "He's got 10 acres to walk around out there," Hodges said: *New York Times*, April 13, 1968, 34. In 1967 Hodges sent a five-page handwritten letter to AL Commissioner Joe Cronin to protest a game the Senators lost to California, claiming Angels pitcher Jack Hamilton was throwing spitballs: *Washington Post*, June 28, 1967, D1.

241   **"Do I replay the games"**: *Look*, July 14, 1964, 102.

241   **"Now I worry"**: *Washington Post*, August 20, 1963, A1.

241   **"You don't mind if I sit down"**: *Look Magazine*, July 14, 1964, 102.

18. OFF THE FLOOR

243   *In football, when you*: Phone interview with Phil Hochberg, June 17, 2011. Hochberg, the public address announcer for both Washington Redskins football games and Senators baseball games at D.C. Stadium, graduated from law school in 1965. He treated himself and paid his own way to travel with the Senators on one of their road trips. Since Hochberg had only covered home games, he had never traveled on the team bus before, and the first time he walked on to the bus, he went to the back where he got some strange looks from the players. Hochberg then learned there was a seating pecking order: the players sat in the back of the bus and all others, managers, coaches, and writers sat in the front. Hochberg sat next to Hodges on numerous occasions and they once got into a discussion comparing football and baseball. "In football," Hodges told Hochberg, "when you lose you have to wait seven days before you have a chance to win again. But if you lose a baseball game today, you can come back and win tomorrow."

243   **"smooth things out as quietly as possible"**: Phone interview with Russ White, March 10, 2010.

243   **practice fields**: *Washington Post*, March 2, 1964, A18, and March 7, 1964, D1.

243   **"when he took off"**: Phone interview with Mike McCormick, January 5, 2011.

244   **"in deference to the church going"**: *Washington Post*, March 9, 1964, A18.

244   **"Our bunting and base running"**: *Washington Post*, February 29, 1964, A12.

244   **"You better level with him"**: Phone interview with Claude Osteen, December 21, 2006.

244   **change a batter's stance**: *Washington Post*, March 31, 1964, B5.

244   **"disappointed to put it mildly"**: *The Sporting News*, September 24, 1966, 16.

245   **"This camp," Harris said**: Bob Addie, *Washington Post*, March 12, 1964, G3. That spring, in order to restock his starting pitching staff, which had been weakened by injury (Stenhouse and Cheney), Selkirk made the first trade that Hodges didn't agree with. Selkirk purchased a pitcher named Buster Narum from the Baltimore Orioles for cash and a player to be named later. Hodges insisted that a well-regarded outfield prospect was "definitely still . . . Washington property and will remain so." As a general rule, when it came to trades, "Hodges suggests and Selkirk likes to please his manager with the best deal he can bring off." But in this case, Selkirk acted against Hodges's wishes and made that young outfielder, Lou Piniella, the player to be named later. Piniella went on to a productive career, first as a solid-hitting outfielder on several pennant-winning Yankee teams, and later as

a World Series–winning manager in Cincinnati. Narum was out of baseball within a few seasons: *Washington Post*, December 2, 1964, D1, and *Washington Post* June 22, 1964, A20.

245 **"with three diminishing speeds"**: *Washington Post*, April 15, 1964, D1.

245 **"like little boys"**: *Washington Post*, April 14, 1964, D2.

245 **"The wrong Senators"**: *Washington Post*, April 14, 1964, A1. By early June of 1964, one out of every five runs scored against the Senators was unearned: *Washington Post*, June 2, 1964, A15. Although Hodges was old-school, that didn't prevent him from creating new ways to bring parity between the haves and the have-nots in the American League. He suggested that second-division clubs be permitted to carry one player over the twenty-five-player limit and first-division clubs one less. The idea never caught on, but it shows Hodges's creativity and the value he placed on every roster spot.

245 **shoe-polish trick**: *Washington Post*, July 27, 1964, A18.

245 **"I was no gazelle"**: Phone interview with Moose Skowron, January 4, 2007.

246 **"was pressure"**: Phone interview with Ed Roebuck, November 28, 2006.

246 **"my kids would feel a little closer"**: *Washington Post*, September 18, 1964, E1.

246 **two-year contract**: *New York Times*, July 1, 1964, 27.

247 **the largest managerial expense account**: *Washington Post*, October 17, 1965, C1. Hodges received his contract extension shortly before returning to New York to be an AL coach for the 1964 All-Star Game, which was played at the Mets' then brand-new ballpark, Shea Stadium. Selkirk wasn't taking any chances, considering the constant rumors of Hodges being tempted by an offer from the Mets: *New York Times*, July 16, 1964, 49.

247 **"There are only two kinds"**: 1968 New York Mets press guide, 22.

247 **"We need improvement"**: *Washington Post*, July 1, 1964, C1.

247 **Senators were rarely serious**: *Washington Post*, July 1, 1964, C2. The Senators' frugality ended in 1965 with their signing of an eighteen-year-old pitcher, Joe Coleman, in the free-agent draft for $75,000.

247 **"a Gil Hodges deal fully as much"**: *Washington Post*, July 15, 1964, C1.

247 **Cap Peterson**: *Washington Post*, March 10, 1967, D1. Selkirk's reticent to make a major deal stemmed from a trade he made sending relief pitcher Steve Hamilton to New York for the former All-Star pitcher Jim Coates. Hamilton became a fixture in the Yankees' bullpen throughout the 1960s. Coates lasted less than a season in DC.

247 **the general manager's job**: Gaven, *Artful Dodgers*, 169.

248 **"only be as good as my teammates make me"**: *Washington Post*, January 22, 1964, C3.

248 **traded Claude Osteen**: *Washington Post*, February 16, 1965, C1. Hodges knew the Dodgers needed a number three starter to follow Sandy Koufax and Don Drysdale in their rotation. This allowed Hodges to stock the Senators' roster with some of the better young players in the Dodgers organization. In exchange for a starting pitcher who threw every four or five days, the Senators had added depth: two everyday players, McMullen at third and Howard in left, a solid-fielding first baseman in Nen, and two starting pitchers, Richert and Ortega. When Hodges was with the Dodgers, Richert was one of the best pitching prospects in their Minor League system. Like Osteen, Richert was a lefty; he became an All-Star in 1965 and 1966 after Rube Walker helped him develop an effective change-up.

248 **"If I have two pitchers like that"**: *Washington Post*, August 13, 1965, D3. But the Senators needed to score more runs. In 1964, in the sixty-nine games in which their opponent scored five or more runs, the Senators won only eight times: *Washington Post*, April 8, 1965, B1.

248 **wouldn't lose a hundred games**: *Washington Post*, August 10, 1965, C1.

248 **won seventy games**: *Washington Post*, October 1, 1965, C2.

248 **"the most decent, wonderful man"**: Phone interviews with Russ White on March 6 and 10, 2010, and April 7, 2011; also email on March 6, 2010. A shortstop who could hit for power, Don Zimmer, never got a chance to play for the Dodgers, with Pee Wee Reese firmly entrenched as the starter. By the time Hodges was managing in Washington, Zimmer was a backup infielder nearing the end of his career. Because the Senators had Brinkman at shortstop, Hodges gave Zimmer a chance to extend his career by learning how to play the catcher's position, hoping the additional versatility would allow Zimmer a place on the Senators' roster. As for Zimmer, who spent the off-season learning how to catch in the Senators' instructional league, and the better part of spring training working out at second and third base, as well as catcher, he hoped he would become a starter. To Hodges, who had worked out at first base and catcher in 1948, practicing two positions was a necessary evil if it kept you on the team. But Hodges was then a young player on the rise; by 1964 Zimmer was long-in-the-tooth, and practicing at multiple positions was torture. Zimmer saw the handwriting on the wall and extended his professional career playing in Japan. Today, Zimmer is best remembered as Yankee manager Joe Torre's bench coach. I made numerous requests to interview Zimmer, but he never responded.

250 **"I was scared to death"**: Phone interview with Charlie Brotman, January 27, 2010. Brotman did not recall the name of the umpire that challenged him, but another D.C. Stadium announcer in the 1960s, Phil Hochberg, remembers that Al Salerno, whom Hochberg referred to as a "Red Ass," got upset with him for exactly the same reason: Phone interview with Phil Hochberg, June 17, 2011. Could it have

been Salerno that Hodges screamed at in defense of Brotman? In a follow-up call to Brotman on August 13, 2012, Brotman told me, "You may be right."

251 **"jumper's bridge"**: Phone interview with George Sutter of the Washington DC Police and Firefighters Relief Board, October 16, 2006.

251 **"Ryne, you're drunk"**: *New York Times*, May 14, 1978, S2, and Duren, *I Can See Clearly*, 160.

251 **"The decision to put Duren on waivers"**: *Washington Post*, August 21, 1965, D1.

252 **four key elements to being a good manager**: Koppett, *Man in the Dugout*, 334.

252 **"Hodges is one of the genuinely"**: *Washington Post*, April 8, 1964, E2.

252 **"spoons up enough sugar"**: *Washington Post*, January 15, 1967, D4.

252 **no tape recorders**: [AP], "Baseball World Mourns Loss of 'Mr. Nice Guy,'" *Courier Press*, April 3, 1972. In Washington, as he had done in New York during his playing career, despite his dislike of public speaking, when it was for a cause Hodges believed in, he tried to be available. During the same week in May of 1964, Hodges presented an award at the Jelleff Branch Boy's Club's annual awards banquet (*Washington Post*, May 16, 1964, C4) and attended a Peace Corps conference run as part of the "war on poverty" (*Washington Post*, May 19, 1964, A18). Some of the other invitees to the conference (Stan Musial, Johnny Unitas, and Jesse Owens) show the high stature in which Hodges was regarded. In 1965 Hodges received the national award of the Catholic Youth Organization of the Archdiocese of Washington for his contributions to American youth; the previous recipient was President John Kennedy: *Washington Post*, March 24, 1965, C1. Hodges established his own nonprofit foundation to provide college scholarships, and a portion of the proceeds of a Yankees-Senators doubleheader was donated to the foundation: *New York Times*, March 21, 1964, 19. At all these events, Hodges's speaking style was sincere and straightforward and made a positive impression on his audience, as he said "exactly what's on his mind": *Washington Post*, April 18, 1964, D1.

252 **Alan Koch**: Phone interview with Alan Koch, June 21, 2010. I searched through old copies of the *Washington Daily News* in the M. L. King Branch of the DC Public Library but could not find a copy of the article that mentioned the lynching. Based on my follow-up conversation with Russ White on April 7, 2011, most likely at the request of the White House, the piece—which had mentioned President Johnson's name—was pulled from late editions of the paper and that was why I couldn't find it.

254 **signing bonus of $108,000**: *New York Times*, December 13, 1964, S2.

254 **"was not what you would call speedy"**: *Washington Post*, March 3, 1965, F1. Hodges knew about Howard's injured arm when he acquired him: Phone interview with Frank Howard, January 31, 2009. It didn't help that when Howard took cortisone shots to relieve the pain in his arm (Howard had bone chips in his elbow that

required surgery) he would "get violent reactions to them." Howard said, "My arm blows up like a balloon." This in turn affected his swing: *Washington Post*, July 20, 1965, D2, and *New York Times*, March 3, 1966, 38.

254 **"Howard really isn't as bad"**: *Washington Post*, March 20, 1965, E1.

254 **"I am not one to exaggerate"**: *Washington Post*, March 6, 1965, D1.

254 **infield fly rule**: *Washington Post*, April 13, 1965, D1, and April 14, 1965, D1.

255 **"Gil is a patient man"**: *Washington Post*, June 8, 1965, D1.

255 **Hodges advised Howard to move closer**: *Washington Post*, March 5, 1967, C1.

255 **move his hands less**: *Washington Post*, March 17, 1967, D1.

256 **"how much longer"**: Phone interview with Frank Howard, January 31, 2009.

256 **limit strikeouts to ninety a year**: *Washington Post*, February 20, 1964, F2.

256 **"for Washington fans"**: *Washington Post*, September 24, 1965, D1.

257 **"And how is Gil Hodges doing"**: *Washington Post*, October 22, 1963, B1.

19. ON THE DOORSTEP OF RESPECTABILITY

259 *Every time*: *Washington Post*, August 20, 1963, A15.

259 **"an arrow, knee high"**: Phone interview with Marvin Miller, September 10, 2009.

259 **Hodges publicly criticized**: *Washington Post*, September 5, 1966, D2.

260 **Al Salerno**: Bob Addie, *Washington Post*, July 18, 1965, C1. The ball bounced off of Mickey Mantle's glove and bounced on the ground before going into the stands. Had Mantle deflected the ball directly into the stands, it would have been a home run. Word spread. A few days later, when Hodges calmly approached the umpiring crew as he brought out the lineup card before a game in Detroit, umpire Ed Hurley jokingly pretended to "frisk" Hodges: *Washington Post*, July 20, 1965, D1.

260 **"that's the first time"**: *Washington Post*, September 11, 1966, C4. Hodges getting tossed didn't change the game's outcome; the Senators lost anyway: *The Sporting News*, September 24, 1966, 16. Ironically, considering how Hodges often took his time sending up a pinch hitter in the hope that the opposing manager would make a move first, Hodges didn't like rules that he felt unnecessarily delayed the game. After the 1966 season, when the American League revised its rules and allowed a manager to visit the mound at least once an inning—formerly the rule was when a manager came out for the second time in a game, the pitcher was automatically removed—Hodges said, "The rule makers are always talking about speeding up the game, They couldn't have done anything more to slow it up than this one visit per inning rule. Some managers I know will turn a ball game into a Kaffeeklatch": *Washington Post*, December 4, 1966, C2.

260 **"Hodges never cursed"**: Phone interview with Al Salerno, June 7, 2007. The first time Hodges was thrown out in the National League was an automatic call for arguing a ball or strike call: *New York Times*, July 8, 1968, 50.

261 **"I don't believe"**: *Washington Post*, September 11, 1966, C4.

261 **George Susce**: As described in a January 5, 2011, phone interview with Mike McCormick.

261 **"You just run the virgin"**: Phone interview with Al Salerno June 7, 2007.

261 **"horseshit"**: Phone interview with Bob Saverine, March 8, 2011.

261 **"That's 'cursin',' Gil"**: *Washington Post*, September 28, 1966, D1. According to Saverine, Hodges told Kinnamon, "I think it was horseshit too": Phone interview with Saverine, March 8, 2011.

261 **"That Hodges is something"**: *Washington Post*, October 5, 1966, D3.

261 **"You know a lot of the things"**: Phone interview with Sandy Koufax, October 14, 2010.

262 **"If it came from Rube"**: Email from Dave Baldwin, November 2009.

262 **"throw another overhand"**: Dave Baldwin, *Snake Jazz*, 239. That game took place on August 6, 1967. Baldwin had been a college star at the University of Arizona.

262 **Not only did**: Emails from Dave Baldwin, November 2009.

263 **"Hodges," Knowles later said**: Phone interview with Darold Knowles, December 7, 2009.

263 **"I know Sam Mele"**: *Washington Post*, July 16, 1966, D1. In Richert's first start after the All-Star Game, interestingly against Mele's Twins, his arm stiffened after six innings and he had to be taken out of the game, despite holding a 4-2 lead. The Senators lost, 5-4: *New York Times*, July 20, 1966, 64. The Senators traded him to Baltimore in 1967.

263 **"instant sore arms"**: *Washington Post*, July 17, 1966, C2. Hodges and Richert made an interesting pair. Once, when Richert was pitching and Hodges was taking batting practice, Hodges blasted a line drive back to the box, striking Richert with such force it left a red welt on his lower leg. Richert smiled and told Hodges, "You'll have to fine me to make me rub it." At the time, with several other Senators pitchers injured, Hodges replied to no one in particular as he tossed his bat away, "He's our only sound pitcher, that's why I went after him." When Hodges was out of sight, Richert still refused to limp, but pressed an ice bag against his leg: *Washington Post*, April 19, 1966, C1.

263 **"He has been smart"**: *Washington Post*, February 23, 1965, C1.

264 **grabbed Hannan's elbow**: Phone interview with Jim Hannan, November 11, 2010. Mike McCormick recalled a similar story where he once tossed the ball to Hodges when he took him out of the game for a relief pitcher. When McCormick sat down in the dugout near where Hodges was seated, Hodges, not looking at McCormick—but facing straight ahead—said, "Next time you do that it will be $50." McCormick said, "Excuse me." And Hodges replied, "Don't flip it. Hand it to me": Phone interview with Mike McCormick, January 5, 2011.

264 **Ortega's absence**: *Washington Post*, November 14, 1965, C3. "Ortega," Mike McCormick told me, "was the nicest guy but had a drinking problem he couldn't get rid of": Phone interview with Mike McCormick, January 5, 2011. According to Bob Humphreys, Ortega missed room check on Friday night as well as Saturday night: Phone interview with Humphreys, July 13, 2011. I sent Phil Ortega an interview request letter through the Major League Baseball Players Alumni Association but never heard from him.

264 **"What do you think about starting?"**: *New York Times*, July 11, 1966, 50; phone interview with Bob Humphreys, July 13, 2011.

265 **"Hodges pushing Ortega—but just a little"**: Phone interview with Jim Hannan, November 11, 2010. In a phone interview on May 11, 2006, George Vescey had a vague recollection of Hodges once physically throwing a player out of the Senators' clubhouse. Fred Valentine recalled Ortega arriving late but had no recollection of Hodges pushing Ortega: Phone interview with Fred Valentine, March 12, 2007.

265 **"It was good you didn't"**: Phone interview with Jim Hannan, November 10, 2010. That August, Hodges, Hannan, and Casanova would meet to review pitching signs after Hannan had, according to Hodges, "lost his poise": *Washington Post*, August 11, 1966, C1.

265 **Sitting next to Hannan**: Harrelson, *Hawk*, 156. In my phone interview with Hannan, he incorrectly recalled that Bernie Allen and Tim Cullen were sitting next to him; I verified that neither one of them was on the Senators' roster at the time.

265 **Ken "Hawk" Harrelson**: In Kansas City, after almost four full seasons, Harrelson was batting only .229: *Washington Post*, June 24, 1966, D1. On September 4, 1964, when Harrelson was playing for Kansas City, he became the first player to ever wear a batting glove during a game. He apparently had a blister on his hand after playing thirty-six holes of golf earlier that same day, and when the Athletics played the Yankees, Harrelson wore a bright red golf glove when he hit and Mickey Mantle began calling him "Sweetness": *New York Times*, April 1, 2007, BB7.

265 **"a clash of life-styles"**: *New York Times*, October 7, 1969, 54.

265 **only one haircut**: *Washington Post*, July 10, 1966, C4.

266 **"Golfers," Harrelson said**: *Washington Post*, March 24, 1966, C2.

266 **"If I really"**: *Washington Post*, July 10, 1966, C4.

266 **"if he forgets about football"**: *Washington Post*, April 5, 1964, C1.

266 **"Hodges," Harrelson wrote**: Harrelson, *Hawk*, 154. I made several attempts to contact Harrelson through his employer, the Chicago White Sox, but never received a response.

266 **"enjoyed exceptional success against Stottlemyre"**: *Washington Post*, April 10, 1967, A1. According to Dave Baldwin, Hodges's starting the lefty Nen at first

base made sense. Hodges usually went with a lefty-righty platoon at first, and that favored starting Nen against the righty Stottlemyre. In addition, Nen was "the best defensive first baseman" Baldwin ever saw in the Majors, and Harrelson lacked Nen's range or hands and was best suited to play the outfield: Email from Dave Baldwin. Regarding the 1967 home opener, Harrelson wrote, "When Hodges started me the second game of the season and kept me in almost every day after that, I knew he had benched me opening day just to hurt me": Harrelson, *Hawk*, 162. Although it is true that the Senators lost on Opening Day, and won the second game of the season with Harrelson starting at first, in the Senators' first fifteen games, Harrelson started only six times, all against left-handers. During this period, whenever the opposing team started a right-handed pitcher, Hodges started either of his two left-handed-hitting first basemen, Nen (the better fielder) or Bob Chance (the better power hitter). In Harrelson's largely lighthearted book, the only chapter filled with significant venom is titled "Gil Hodges and Me." Harrelson's literary take on Hodges must be viewed within the context of the source. His autobiography, *Hawk*, begins and ends with the line, "You handsome sonofagun, don't you ever die!"

267 **"From the second inning on"**: Phone interview with Mike McCormick, January 5, 2011.

267 **And Hodges gave his catcher**: Phone interview with Russ White, March 10, 2010.

267 **"There are only two outstanding catchers"**: *Washington Post*, November 9, 1967, C3.

267 **"a lot of mileage out of his players"**: *Washington Post*, August 10, 1967, F1.

268 **"a firm hand on the steering wheel"**: Email from Dave Baldwin, November 2009.

268 **Beginning on July 9, 1967**: *Washington Post*, July 31, 1967, D1.

268 **"Once we attain a .500 record"**: *Washington Post*, August 8, 1967, C1.

268 **"There is no use talking"**: *Washington Post*, August 9, 1967, E1.

268 **clustered around the Western Union machine**: *Washington Post*, August 17, 1967, G1.

268 **only six games out of first**: *Washington Post*, August 14, 1967, D1.

268 **home attendance reached its highest level**: *Washington Post*, September 25, 1967, D1.

268 **master of in-game decisions**: *Washington Post*, August 11, 1967, D2.

270 **"If you don't get ulcers"**: *Washington Post*, June 14, 1967, D1.

270 **"Miracle of Washington"**: *Washington Post*, August 11, 1967, D1.

271 **Yankees at D.C. Stadium on August 26, 1967**: *New York Times*, August 27, 1967, S1.

271 **Camilo Pascual every fifth day**: *Washington Post*, January 8, 1967, C2.

272 **"If we had a powerful"**: *Washington Post*, February 26, 1967, C4.

272 **"an All-Star from the neck down"**: *Washington Post*, June 11, 1967, D1.

272 **"Comparing Hodges to Stanky"**: *Washington Post*, June 25, 1967, D4.

273 **"Hodges was very good at controlling"**: Email from Dave Baldwin, November 21, 2009. The stool-breaking incident was not the only example of Hodges losing his temper. After the Senators lost the first game of a doubleheader against the Angels in particularly heartbreaking fashion, Bob Saverine approached a table that had been set up with food for the players to eat between games. Since another player had already started eating Saverine thought it was appropriate for him to do so. "Hodges exploded," Saverine recalled, yelling, "How could you eat after a loss like that?": Phone interview with Bob Saverine, March 8, 2011.

273 **"ashamed"**: Hodges, *Game of Baseball*, 141.

273 **"warm country bear"**: McGraw, *Screwball*, 10.

273 **"foolishness all the time"**: Phone interview with Bob Humphreys, July 13, 2011.

273 **"As a manager, keeping his distance"**: Bob Broeg, *The Sporting News*, April 22, 1972, 8.

273 **"one pack of cigarettes after another"**: Phone interview with Russ White, March 6, 2010.

20. THE METS GET SERIOUS

277 *I'm no Casey*: *New York Times*, February 26, 1970, 63.

277 **"I must be loyal"**: *Washington Post*, September 9, 1965, D5.

277 **"The answer is yes"**: *New York Times*, October 15, 1967, 208.

277 **"I have a contract"**: *Washington Post*, September 3, 1967, D2.

277 **"that can win us the pennant"**: *Washington Post*, September 22, 1967, D2.

277 **"We rode over him"**: Phone interview with Ed Charles, January 18, 2007.

277 **"managing the Mets"**: Vescey, *Joy in Mudville*, 130–31.

277 hiring **Harry Walker**: Lang, *The Sporting News*, December 16, 1967. Walker had both played for and managed the Cardinals, and Devine knew him well.

278 **"He has it in him"**: *New York Times*, October 15, 1967, 208.

278 **"meddling and tampering"**: *Washington Post*, October 10, 1967, D1.

278 **"I had to let them"**: *Washington Post*, October 11, 1967, E1.

278 **"ideal choice"**: *New York Times*, December 10, 1967, 269, and Devine, *Bing Devine*, 43.

278 decreased by four hundred thousand: *Washington Post*, December 20, 1967, D4.

278 **"If you'd be willing"**: As told to me by Hal Maysent, Gil Hodges's brother-in-law, in an interview on August 14, 2006, in Palm Desert, California. Buzzie Bavasi never responded to my interview requests to confirm the conversation.

278 **"It is a tough decision"**: *New York Times*, October 10, 1967, 59.

278   **three-year contract for $57,000**: Joe Durso, *New York Times*, September 27, 1969, 37.

279   **their manager, Red Schoendienst**: *Washington Post*, October 29, 1967, C2. Hodges's existing contract with Washington was not only for more money than Schoendienst but was for two years, not one: *New York Times*, October 12, 1967, 61.

279   **"I'm glad to read"**: *New York Times*, October 18, 1967, 53.

279   **Gil's addition**: Lang, *The Sporting News*, December 16, 1967. That December, James M. Johnson, the controlling owner of the Senators, died setting in motion ownership changes that resulted in Bob Short acquiring the team. A politically savvy man with an eye toward marketing the Senators for a move to Texas, Short became deeply involved in personnel moves and fired Selkirk. Had Hodges remained, he may have met the same fate as Selkirk. When the time came for Short to pick a new manager, he selected a man who was Hodges's polar opposite: Ted Williams, boisterous and brash, and who, unlike Hodges, was never able to lead a team—either as a player or a manager—to a championship: *Washington Post*, December 29, 1967, A1. As a manager, Williams proved to be a mixed bag. One of his players, Darold Knowles—who also played for Hodges—said, "Williams was the worst manager I ever played for": Phone interview with Knowles, December 7, 2009. Mike Epstein thought Williams was the best hitting instructor he ever encountered: Phone interview with Mike Epstein, August 16, 2012.

279   **"liked him, but not too much"**: *Washington Post*, December 28, 1967, F3.

279   **"Gil could have told me good-bye"**: Berra, *Yogi: It Ain't Over*, 137. Berra later wrote, "If I had to name the best manager I ever saw, I guess I would have to say Gil Hodges. Stengel was good, but probably not as good as he thought. The catcher was really outstanding": Berra, *Yogi: It Ain't Over*, 234.

280   **promotional train ride**: *New York Times*, November 3, 1967, 62.

280   **"scope"** and **"closely"**: *New York Times*, April 10, 1968, 60.

280   **"We never came together well"**: Phone interview with Ron Swoboda, May 24, 2006.

280   **"out of pure anger"**: Phone interview with Ron Swoboda, May 24, 2006.

280   **"At times, I bristled at the way"**: Email from Ron Swoboda, January 6, 2010.

280   **"You're going to be somebody"**: *New York Times*, January 23, 1968, 34.

280   **"felt sure"**: *New York Times*, March 26, 1968, 55, and *New York Times*, March 21, 1968, 60.

281   **"I was trying hard"**: Phone interview with Ron Swoboda, May 24, 2006.

281   **"constant slugger"**: *New York Times*, August 1, 1968, 34. Hodges made sure his coaches worked with Swoboda on his fielding. At every practice, Eddie Yost spent a few minutes hitting line drives at Swoboda from 150 feet away. Swoboda wanted to improve his fielding because he disliked it when Hodges would take him out

late in games for a defensive replacement. In time, his ability to see the ball as soon as it came off the bat improved. This paid off with his spectacular fielding play in the 1969 World Series: *New York Times*, October 15, 2009, B19, and phone interview with Ron Swoboda, May 24, 2006.

281 **"The first thing Hodges wanted":** Tommie Agee obituary, *New York Times*, January 23, 2001.

281 **Agee was hit in the head:** *New York Times*, March 10, 1968, S1.

281 **"He needs to relax":** *New York Times*, April 25, 1968, 56.

281 **Agee felt comfortable:** Phone interview with Maury Allen, December 19, 2006.

282 **"spill his guts with Gil":** Allen, *After the Miracle*, 188.

282 **Al Weis:** *New York Times*, February 1, 1968, S2, and *New York Times*, June 9, 1968, S2. Weis was available because in a game against Baltimore on June 27, 1967, he had collided with Frank Robinson and tore the ligaments in his left knee and underwent season-ending surgery. When Hodges had been in Florida for Instructional League play in November of 1967, he had spoken with Weis and learned that he was fully recovered. That knowledge came in handy a few weeks later when the Davis-for-Agee trade came to fruition. Hodges's recommendation turned out to be the right one. Wayne Causey's Major League career ended after the 1968 season, and Weis proved invaluable in the 1969 World Series.

282 **Hodges then "asked" Weis:** Phone interview with Al Weis, October 21, 2011.

283 **"glancing back towards the bench":** *New York Times*, March 24, 1968, S2.

283 **"You're the strongest":** Phone interview with Bud Harrelson, September 15, 2010.

283 **"just blowing my horn":** Anderson, "If Hodges Managed These Mets," *New York Times*, September 27, 1990. When Harrelson was in the Army Reserves and assigned to Fort Totten in Queens, he would wake up at 6 a.m., work all day, and then rush to Shea Stadium at 5 p.m. for a night game. On those nights, Hodges told Harrelson to take a nap in the trainer's room and woke him up in time to play: *New York Times*, February 26, 1978, S3.

283 **"My name is Hodges":** *New York Times*, April 3, 1972, 52.

283 **training camp rules:** *New York Times*, February 22, 1968, 40.

283 **the hotel bar was off-limits:** *New York Times*, April 5, 1970, 213.

283 **minimum fines:** *New York Times*, April 3, 1972, 52.

284 **expensive burgers:** Cohen, *Magic Summer*, 129.

284 **how long each pitcher:** *New York Times*, February 28, 1970, 47, and March 2, 1970, 51.

284 **"He hit me in the chest":** Phone interview with Jon Matlack, November 10, 2011.

284 **"like the Messiah":** Jacobson, *Carrying Jackie's Torch*, 39–41, 50.

284 **"If you settle for that":** *New York Times*, March 4, 1968, 46.

284   **"Pitching," Hodges once said:** *LA Times*, August 20, 1961, G2.

284   **Cardwell, who had pitched well against Hodges:** *LA Times*, September 11, 1959, C2.

285   **"There are . . . three":** *New York Times*, March 28, 1968, 65.

285   **422 strikeouts in only 280 innings:** *New York Times*, April 3, 1968, 56.

285   **"the myth":** *New York Times*, March 28, 1968, 65.

285   **"I just want him":** *New York Times*, April 15, 1968, 58. On May 14 Ryan set a Mets club record with fourteen strikeouts in one game, but lost five of his next seven decisions: *New York Times*, July 4, 1968, 24.

285   **stop throwing his slider:** *New York Times*, July 14, 1968, S2.

285   **won the first home opener:** *New York Times*, April 18, 1968, 59.

285   **first win as Mets manager:** *New York Times*, April 13, 1968, 34.

286   **twenty-four innings:** *New York Times*, April 16, 1968, 1. In the bottom of the sixteenth inning, with the winning run on first base, no outs, and the Houston pitcher, Jim Ray, at bat, Hodges moved Ron Swoboda from right field to first base. And in anticipation of a sacrifice bunt, to intimidate the batter—much as Hodges had done with his charges to the plate—he positioned first baseman Ed Kranepool halfway between first and the plate. Ray struck out fouling off an attempted bunt, the key out of the inning, but the Mets still lost.

286   **established a five-man rotation:** Lang, *The New York Mets*, 113. In addition to utilizing a five-man rotation, Hodges also kept track of pitch counts. The number of pitches thrown each game was recorded and utilized to determine when a pitcher began to lose effectiveness. According to Tom Seaver, "We did have pitch counts. . . . Mine was 135 and I knew it, and Rube knew it": Jerry Crasnick, "Pitch Counts 'Encourage Mediocrity,'" ESPN.com, July 28, 2009. But unlike later generations of managers who utilized pitch counts as an inflexible device for when to remove their starters, under Hodges they were not mandatory. Instead, pitch counts were used to help condition a pitcher's arm strength (especially those returning from injury) and get an understanding for each individual pitcher's fatigue point: Joe Janish, "Do Pitch Counts Protect Pitchers?" ESPN.com, February 17, 2011, and *New York Times*, August 6, 1971, 21. In a summary of a June 1968 game, George Vecsey wrote, "Jerry Koosman, who had started for New York, left after seven innings because he had thrown 129 pitches, his quota for any game": *New York Times*, June 10, 1968, 61; a July 2011 follow-up email from Vescey indicates that although his memory of this game was limited, he believed this info was most likely told to him by Hodges, but Vescey questioned whether "quota" was the appropriate word choice. In Washington, Hodges had also kept track of the number of pitchers thrown during games and even by his relievers in the bullpen when they warmed up. But Hodges only considered pitch counts as one of numerous factors determining when a pitcher

was removed from the game. Hodges put more emphasis on what he saw from his pitcher in that particular game (was the pitcher losing control and walking batters, were the hitters now getting around on the fastball and making solid contact, and what Rube Walker thought): Dave Baldwin email, July 2011.

286 **manual labor**: Seaver, *Perfect Game*, 5-7, 19.

286 **"You can line up"**: *New York Times*, February 23, 1968, 21.

286 **The first time was after**: *New York Times*, June 16, 1968, S1.

287 **he had relaxed** and **Robin Roberts**: Hodges, *Game of Baseball*, 66-68.

287 **"He shut the door"**: Shamsky, *Magnificent Seasons*, 101. The next season, Seaver was pitching in the ninth inning of a game against Cincinnati on July 26, 1969. The Mets led 3-2 and Seaver was pitching with two outs, the bases empty, and the power-hitting first baseman, Lee May, at bat. Since the next two batters were singles hitters, Seaver pitched Lee May off the plate, giving him nothing he could hit for power and deliberately (but not intentionally) walked him. As he had years before, Hodges then educated Seaver in the Claude Osteen rule: Never walk a man in the ninth inning when it will bring the winning run up to bat. Hodges walked out to the mound, looked at May at first base, turned to Seaver, and said, "You look like you wanted to walk him." Without waiting for a reply, Hodges turned and walked back to the dugout. Seaver struck out the next batter (a player named Jimmy Stewart). As soon as the game ended, Seaver went to Hodges's office and said, "You didn't agree with me about walking May." Hodges replied, "If I'd known you were going to strike out Stewart I'd never have walked to the mound": Seaver, *Perfect Game*, 62-63.

287 **"Don't let it upset you"**: *New York Times*, July 23, 1968, 31.

288 **"went after him"**: Bob Hertzel, "Hodges Inspired Fear and Reverence in Seaver," *Baseball Digest*, November 1978, 93. Seaver—who greatly admired Hodges—and who, after reading a copy of Hertzel's article that I sent him, wrote to me about the quotes in the story, "They sound correct to me—if not exact they are surely correct in context": Correspondence from Tom Seaver, March 29, 2010. Ron Swoboda denies the incident ever took place. Jerry Grote never responded to my interview request. Because of the conflicting stories, in February of 2010, I contacted the author of the article, Bob Hertzel, who stood by the accuracy of the story, and I have therefore included it. Swoboda told me he is still embarrassed by some of the things he said to Hodges. I found it fascinating that Swoboda, the player Hodges had such a hard time with, defended the iconic legacy of his former manager while Seaver, who was one of Hodges's favorite players, felt comfortable enough revealing Hodges's humanity.

288 **"I vowed then and there I wouldn't have"**: Allen, *After the Miracle*, 110.

288 **"Everything was going along all right"**: *New York Times*, August 8, 1968, 38.

288   "**We'll get him twice**": *New York Times*, August 11, 1968, S1.

288   **baseball commissioner William Eckert**: *New York Times*, June 7, 1968, 44, and *New York Times*, June 12, 1968, 59.

289   "**avoid carousing in public places**": Vescey, *Joy in Mudville*, 163.

289   "**I can't imagine**": *New York Times*, June 10, 1968, 60.

289   "**a closeness**": Vescey, *Joy in Mudville*, 163.

289   **Ethel, sent Hodges a note thanking**: Oppenheimer, *Other Mrs. Kennedy*, 480. The month after Kennedy's death, Hodges's reputation had grown to such a point that even the far left of America's political spectrum took notice. That July, after Jimmy Breslin wrote an article in the *New York Post* that was critical of the Communist Party, fifteen young members of the Communist Party staged a three-hour protest at the *Post*'s offices. *Post* editor James A. Wechsler, trying to divert the protestors' attention away from Breslin, figured everyone likes to talk baseball and told the protestors there are "more important things in the world, such as Gil Hodges." Wechsler then criticized Hodges's managerial skills, thinking there was no way communists would be supportive of an old-school type of manager like Hodges. "With a pitching staff like that," Wechsler asked, "why are they [the Mets] only four games better than last year?" Much to his dismay, the communists strongly defended Hodges: *New York Times*, July 11, 1968, 20.

289   **first National League rookie**: Elias Sports Bureau.

289   "**bounce-back boy**": *New York Times*, July 27, 1968, 18.

289   "**pennant contention**": *New York Times*, September 1, 1968, S3.

290   "**The way we've been going**" and "**It's not me**": *New York Times*, June 19, 1968, 51.

290   "**would tell the bus driver**": Berra, *Yogi: It Ain't Over*, 137.

290   "**going to be a long year**": Phone interview with Bob Humphreys, July 13, 2011.

290   **Lemon also undid**: Phone interview with Russ White, March 6, 2010. In spring training, Lemon had played every game to win and the Senators finished the exhibition season with the best record in the league, 17-8. But this gave them a false sense of confidence and did not provide enough playing time for the entire twenty-five-man roster. In contrast, Hodges would spend approximately half of each preseason focused on learning his players' current capabilities. Only at that point did he begin playing exhibition games to win. "Spring training is for learning," Hodges said, "I am trying to see what each man can do": Hartley, *Washington's Expansion Senators*, 79, and *New York Times*, March 18, 1968, 62.

290   "**After Gil left**": Email from Dave Baldwin, November 2009.

291   "**his usual wisecrack**": *New York Times*, September 27, 1968, 60.

291   **heart attack**: Hodges, *Game of Baseball*, 151–57; also Lang, *New York Mets*, 77–78. When the Mets were in Philadelphia to play the Phillies that September, Hodges

told his sister Marjorie, who was then living in the area, that he was having arm pain, an early sign of unstable angina. A nurse, Marjorie later regretted not telling her brother to see a cardiologist: Phone interview with Marjorie Maysent, August 5, 2011.

291   **"The lowest point"**: *New York Times*, September 25, 1969, 56.

291   **hospital stay**: *New York Times*, September 25, 1968, 50, and *New York Times*, September 26, 1968, 65.

291   **"to fix his vessels"**: Phone interview with Dr. Linton H. Bishop, June 25, 2009, and *New York Times*, September 28, 1968, 39.

291   **"got back to basics"**: Phone interview with Dr. Linton H. Bishop, June 25, 2009, and *New York Times*, September 28, 1968, 39.

291   **"If I felt for one minute"**: *New York Times*, November 5, 1968, 63.

292   **"I tried to talk Hodges"** and **"They got Donn Clendenon"**: Answers given to questions posed to Joe Torre on my behalf by Phil Hochberg on February 12, 2012, at the Lisner Auditorium in Washington DC during a Smithsonian Institute presentation moderated by Hochberg called "Joe Torre: Managing Major League Baseball."

292   **"I'd change doctors"**: *New York Times*, November 22, 1968, 63.

292   **Charlie had died from**: "Pulmonary embolus due to venous thrombosis": Certificate of Death, Pike County Health Department, confirmed with Marjorie Maysent.

292   **Hodges's brother, Bob**: Phone call with his son, Tony Hodges, August 4, 2011.

292   **"Gil kept a lot"**: Drysdale, *Once A Bum*, 94.

292   **"miss the cigarettes"**: *New York Times*, November 22, 1968, 63.

292   **denied Hodges permission to listen**: *New York Times*, September 26, 1968, 65.

292   **"Those damn 11-inning games again"**: *New York Times*, September 29, 1968, S1.

293   **"emotional involvement"**: *New York Times*, October 2, 1968, 45. Hodges may not have cared who won the World Series, but he must have sympathized with Cardinals shortstop Dal Maxvill, who went 0 for 22. In the 1981 World Series, Dave Winfield came close to duplicating Hodges's "bitter uniqueness," but managed a lone single in twenty-two at bats.

293   **"Just like Gil Hodges"**: *New York Times*, October 7, 1968, 40.

293   **"The boys," Hodges said**: Milton Gross, "Right Guy," *New York Post*, October 10, 1969, and "Israel Presents Four Torahs," *New York Times*, October 4, 1968. Based upon the fact that Hodges would donate the money he raised each season in player fines to charity, that may have been the source of the $500 in the envelope.

293   **"Even managers who win the pennant"**: Hodges, *Game of Baseball*, 159.

21. CONTENDERS

295   *Look in that mirror*: Anderson, "If Hodges Managed These Mets," *New York Times*, September 27, 1990.

295   **writers laughed out loud**: *New York Times*, September 7, 1969, S2.

295   **"losing is no laughing matter"**: Phone interview with Joe Pignatano, March 27, 2006.

296   **"They have given me"**: *New York Daily News*, March 18, 1969, 69, and Vescey, *Joy in Mudville*, 174. Note that neither Nolan Ryan nor Tommie Agee was on the list.

296   **"occasional bout"**: *New York Times*, March 30, 1969, S3.

296   **two divisions**: In 1969 the teams in the NL East were New York, Montreal, Philadelphia, Pittsburgh, Chicago, and St. Louis. The West had Atlanta, Houston, Cincinnati, Los Angeles, San Francisco, and San Diego. Chicago and St. Louis were in the East and Atlanta in the West because the owners in St. Louis and Chicago insisted on being in the same division to maintain their regional rivalry. Since the two divisions had to be balanced (six teams each), Atlanta was deemed west of St. Louis and Chicago.

296   **Art Shamsky**: *New York Times*, April 5, 1969, 38, and *New York Times*, May 9, 1969, 51.

296   **"Unlike a lot of other managers"**: Phone interview with Art Shamsky, December 3, 2007.

297   **Bob Mandt**: Phone interview with Bob Mandt, July 20, 2007.

297   **Hodges's office**: Phone interview with Bob Mandt, July 20, 2007, and August 10, 2007.

297   **"*Something good*"**: *New York Times*, January 13, 1971, 31. The day before the season opener, Hodges had a head cold and a temperature of 102, which makes the patience he showed Mandt rather remarkable: *New York Times*, April 8, 1968, 53. During Hodges's years in Washington, one player—who wisely chose to remain anonymous—spoke of what Mandt and countless others referred to as being *in the brotherhood*. "It's like being bawled out by a computer. It's a bit weird, because he never uses a cuss word and he never raises his voice. But boy, he can really sting you and make you want to crawl under the door": *Washington Post*, February 23, 1966, D1.

297   **stuffed white rabbit**: *New York Times*, September 11, 1969, 56, and *New York Times*, September 7, 1969, S3.

298   **Lindsay was not in attendance**: "Lindsay came to baseball late": *New York Times*, October 20, 1969, 66.

298   **Rabbi Silber was at Shea**: "Highly Respected Eighth Generation Rabbi Dedicated His Life to Helping People with Special Needs," GlobeandMail.com, July 13, 2009.

298   **"In the old days"**: *New York Times*, April 9, 1969, 34.

298   **Hodges had hoped**: Phone interview with Ed Charles, January 18, 2007. One could see why Hodges was frustrated. In Philadelphia on April 15, Otis started his

first regular-season game at third base, and after four consecutive losses, the Mets won. Otis went 1 for 3, scored two runs, and was flawless in the field: *New York Times*, April 16, 1969, 37.

299   **The Mets' director of player personnel**: Phone interview with Jim McAndrew, February 2, 2012. Amos Otis never responded to my interview request.

299   **Agee was batting .190**: *New York Times*, April 19, 1969, 40.

299   **A game that typified**: *New York Times*, May 4, 1969, S1.

299   **Adolfo Phillips**: Stout, *Cubs*, 270. Phillips was batting only .224 at the time of the trade, but his on base percentage was .424.

300   **Clendenon's first sixteen games**: Lang, *New York Mets*, 82.

300   **won twenty of twenty-five**: *New York Times*, June 27, 1969, 26. On June 20 Vladimir Horowitz, the most famous concert pianist of the day, attended his first baseball game to see the *Cardeenahls*, as Horowitz pronounced it, his favorite team, play the Mets at Shea. Before going out on the field to meet the St. Louis players, Horowitz paid Hodges a visit. To Horowitz "surprise and delight," Hodges not only told him that he had attended one of his concerts, but presented him with a gift, a miniature piano. Horowitz then asked to meet Bob Gibson, who was warming up and refused to be interrupted. "He's an artist," Horowitz said. "We shouldn't bother him when he's working." That night, Ryan outpitched Gibson. The Mets won, 4–3: *New York Times*, June 22, 1969, S3 and Taubman, *The Pleasure of Their Company: A Reminiscence*, 100–102.

300   **"There's no question"**: *New York Times*, July 6, 1969, S1.

300   **"Listen, kids"**: Zimmerman, *Year the Mets Lost*, 20.

301   **"It's tough to win"**: Feldmann, *Miracle Collapse*, 164, and Zimmerman, *Year the Mets Lost*, 38–39. After Durocher publicly crucified him, Don Young never played in the Majors again. He ended up cleaning golf clubs at the Camelback Country Club in Scottsdale, Arizona, which was frequented by his former teammates: Talley, *Cubs of '69*, 91. Ron Santo also criticized Young publicly but later apologized.

301   **final game of the series**: Zimmerman, *Year the Mets Lost*, 91, 94, and *New York Times*, July 11, 1969, 24.

301   **"Errors," Hodges wrote**: Hodges, *Game of Baseball*, 101.

302   **"I can't stand the quiet"**: Zimmerman, *Year the Mets Lost*, 117.

302   **"No," the Lip snarled**: Vescey, *Joy in Mudville*, 189–90.

302   **"Gil handles players like men"**: Zimmerman, *Year the Mets Lost*, 105.

303   **"I've got no comment"**: Zimmerman, *Year the Mets Lost*, 106.

303   **"You remind me of Tug"**: Zimmerman, *Year the Mets Lost*, 181.

303   **Tug McGraw**: McGraw, *Screwball*, 136. It didn't help McGraw's case that during spring training in 1968, his dog, Pucci, "left a load right in front of Joe Pignatano's room." Pignatano, whom McGraw referred to as the "Chico Marx of the bullpen,"

"stepped in it—barefooted—and responded with "a frightening Italian clamor"": McGraw, *Screwball*, 132-33, and *New York Times*, February 28, 1968, 40.

304 **Hodges had three criteria for a reliever:** Hodges, *Game of Baseball*, 18. A screwball is a reverse curve. When throw by a left-hander, the ball breaks down and away from right-handed batters. It's a difficult pitch to master because it places an excessive amount of strain on a pitcher's arm: Neyer and James, *Guide to Pitchers*, 52.

304 **Hodges called McGraw into his office:** Allen, *After the Miracle*, 37-38.

304 **Willie Mays's uniform:** McGraw, *Screwball*, 11. McGraw liked to go to the trainer's room an hour before each game and take what he referred to as "my power nap." Although Hodges gave Bud Harrelson slack in this regard due to his military duty, Hodges didn't believe in "power naps." "I thought it was important," McGraw later said. "He thought it meant you were out too late the night before. We had our disagreements."

304 **"shave the former":** McGraw, *Screwball*, 4.

304 **"Gil's door was always open":** Allen, *After the Miracle*, 38.

304 **"When Gil was running":** McGraw, *Screwball*, 144.

305 **"nonchalant" way:** *New York Daily News*, July 31, 1969, 80.

305 **"balloon":** Vic Ziegel as quoted in Vescey, *Joy in Mudville*, 200.

305 **Hodges was superstitious:** Zimmerman, *Year the Mets Lost*, 56.

305 **"When he was like that":** Phone interview with Bud Harrelson, September 15, 2010.

305 **"Me?" and "The other guy":** Phone interview with Bud Harrelson, September 15, 2010.

305 **leading the National League:** *New York Times*, August 3, 1969, S1.

305 **"It's not whether":** Hodges, *Game of Baseball*, 101.

305 **Jones's version:** Shamsky, *Magnificent Seasons*, 116, and confirmed in my phone interview with Cleon Jones on April 15, 2008. In fact, there had been a lot of rain and Shea Stadium was notorious for its poor drainage.

306 **Hodges's version:** As told by Frank Slocum to Dave Anderson, "If Hodges Managed These Mets," *New York Times*, September 27, 1990. I spoke to Anderson on September 9, 2011, to confirm that Slocum, who was then deceased, was a credible source. According to Joan Hodges, Gil Hodges left the dugout intending to take Ryan out of the game, but he was walking with his head down and found himself almost to third base and "didn't want to turn back to the mound, so he kept walking." See YouTube video made during "A Tribute to Gil Hodges," Key Span Park, Brooklyn, April 27, 2003, and Tubow and Duca, *Baseball Codes*, 70. But it's doubtful Hodges was going to pull Nolan Ryan out of the game, since the Astros' pitcher, Larry Dierker, was due up next, and even after Dierker hit a two-run home run to make the score 10-0, Hodges still left Ryan in the game.

306   **"I certainly wasn't going"**: Phone interview with Matt Winick, August 20, 2007.

306   **"You look into the mirror"**: *New York Times*, September 3, 1967, D2. Hodges's rule that under no circumstances could anyone call the Mets' dugout during a game, as a way to ensure that he made all decisions regarding in-game moves without interference, may have its origin in stories of how Brooklyn Dodgers general manager Larry MacPhail would try to direct Durocher to make specific moves during a game. There is a famous story, most likely apocryphal, that Hilda Chester (the lady that rang the cow bell during Brooklyn Dodgers games) once gave a note to center fielder Pete Reiser suggesting that Durocher change pitchers. When Reiser handed the note to Durocher, he assumed it was from MacPhail and Durocher made the change. The Dodgers lost the game. In the early 1970s, once, when a bat flew into the Mets' dugout and struck Tom Seaver in the chest, everyone from M. Donald Grant to the announcers to the fans who saw it on television all wanted to know if Seaver was okay. But no one dared call the Mets' dugout because it would have been contrary to Hodges's rule. Jack Lang complained to Grant, asking, "It seems everyone is afraid of Gil. Can't you do something about it?" Grant smiled and said, "I'm afraid of him, too": Lang, *New York Mets*, 106.

307   **"It may help him"**: *New York Times*, September 28, 1969, S1. On August 2 Hodges sent Jones up to pinch hit in the seventh inning of a scoreless game against Atlanta with two out and a runner on third. Jones singled and drove in the game's only run to give the Mets a 1–0 win. After Jones's hit, Hodges took him out of the game and replaced him with a pinch runner. Jones pinch-hit again the next day during a crucial Mets rally as they tried to overcome a five-run Atlanta Braves lead. Jones came through with a two-run single and the Mets won in extra innings. In that game, after Jones's single, Hodges called Jones to the dugout for a brief talk and decided to let Jones run for himself. Trainer Gus Mauch then reported that Jones's hamstring pull was better: *New York Times*, August 4, 1969, 42. The next day, Jones was back in the starting lineup against the Reds. After the lineup card was posted, reporters attempting to discuss Jones's return to health with Hodges were "met with cold rebuff." To further the point, Hodges spent most of the pregame practice standing in shallow center field, far away from inquisitive reporters in the Mets dugout. George Vescey wrote, "Hodges was managing a team during a pennant race. He was not looking for good-guy awards or a lot of quotes in the newspapers": Vescey, *Joy in Mudville*, 203, and *New York Times*, August 4, 1969, 42.

307   **"It's over with"**: Maury Allen, "Gil Hodges Is a Tyrant!" *Sports Today*, August 1971, 22.

307   **"Hey, Gillie"**: *New York Daily News*, July 31, 1969, 80. The Mets' coaches referred to Hodges as *Gillie*.

307 **"a real ass-chewing"**: Clendenon, *Miracle in New York*, 118. In addition to Hodges, the schedule maker helped the Mets. That season, Houston owned them. The two teams played twelve times and the Astros won ten of those games. In 1969 Houston was the only team the Mets had a losing record against. But after the "ass chewing," the Mets didn't play the Astros again for the rest of the season.

307 **"supreme prophet"**: *New York Times*, August 16, 1969, 18.

308 **four-outfielder alignment**: *New York Times*, August 20, 1969, 53. After the home stand featuring Hodges game saving outfield alignment, the Mets flew to San Diego and swept the Padres three straight. The Mets lost only one of the twelve games they played against San Diego that season; in the thirteen games following the "ass-chewing," the Mets played the Padres seven times, winning all seven.

308 **"This is the Year"** and **"the Mets had become"**: *New York Times*, August 29, 1969, 32.

308 **"Down the Cubs"**: *New York Times*, September 12, 1969, 51.

308 **"Nobody told me to throw at Santo"**: Golenbock, *Amazin'*, 234.

309 **Mrs. Payson arrived**: *New York Times*, September 11, 1969, 56.

309 **"Follow your conscience"**: Phone interview with Art Shamsky, December 3, 2007.

309 **"I walked out"**: Shamsky, *Magnificent Seasons*, 124–25. Shamsky did not play in the first three games of the Pittsburgh series: *New York Times*, September 12, 1969, 51.

309 **"We've played badly"**: *New York Times*, September 21, 1969, S3. From August 9 until the end of the regular season, Tom Seaver won ten games in a row in which he got the decision, Jerry Koosman eight of nine: Lang, *New York Mets*, 93. In 1969, for most of the season, Hodges remained true to his five-man rotation. However, at two crucial periods in the season, Hodges decided to pitch Seaver and Koosman on only three days' rest. The first was during the second week of August, as the Mets were struggling (they had lost 14 of 25 games) culminating with the Houston "ass-chewing." To avoid falling out of contention, Koosman pitched on three days' rest twice, Seaver once; the Mets won two out of those three games. The second time was during the middle of September when the Mets were in a virtual tie with the Cubs on September 9 and ending when they clinched the division. During this period, Koosman pitched on three days rest twice, Seaver three times. The Mets won all five games. Hodges generally avoided pitching Seaver and Koosman on only three days rest in back to back starts. Before pitching Koosman and Seaver on short rest down the stretch, Hodges and Walker asked them if they were okay with that decision. It appears this was asked not as the classic Hodges device of making an order sound like a request. Tom Seaver later noted, "If we'd objected, if we'd felt the change would've hurt us, Gil and Rube would have gone along with our opinions": Seaver, *Perfect Game*, 85–86. The Cubs' big three of Ferguson Jenkins,

Bill Hands, and Ken Holtzman withered down the stretch. "The Cubs' pitchers have been working an awful lot," Jerry Koosman said, "When you pitch over 300 innings, you're a lot more tired in September than a guy who's pitched 200." As of right before Labor Day, the same week that Ferguson Jenkins was asking for an extra day's rest, Koosman had pitched 184 innings, Tom Seaver, 210 innings, and Gary Gentry, 175 innings.

310   **"never allowed himself even a grin"**: Seaver, *Perfect Game*, 66–67.

310   **telegram from Atlanta**: *New York Times*, September 23, 1969, 38.

310   **sleep-away camp**: *New York Daily News*, July 30, 1969, 78.

310   **"If a man had a slight injury"**: Feldman, *Miracle Collapse*, 15. Catcher Randy Hundley played in 151 games that season; shortstop Don Kessinger, 158; and left fielder Billy Williams, 163.

311   **"It was my job to motivate"**: Durocher, *Nice Guys Finish Last*, 321. In August of 1969, when the Mets had a rare day off during their final West Coast road trip, Hodges spent his day off at Candlestick Park watching a Giants–Phillies game to see if he could learn anything that might help his team defeat the Giants in the four-game series that was starting the next day: *New York Times*, August 29, 1969, 32.

311   **Ted Williams had recently signed**: Montville, *Ted Williams: An American Hero*, 270.

311   **"Give me a pen"**: *New York Times*, September 27, 1969, 37.

22. MIRACLE

313   *These young men*: *New York Times*, April 3, 1972, 52.

313   **"Their strength"** and **"Nobody's"**: *New York Times*, October 4, 1969, 43. The twenty runs the Mets scored in the first two playoff games was (with the exception of a July 4, 1969, doubleheader that year against the Pirates), the most runs they had scored in two consecutive games during Hodges's two seasons as manager: *New York Times*, October 6, 1969, 1.

313   **"I was guessing curve"**: Seaver, *Perfect Game*, 16.

313   **But in the eighth**: Cohen, *Magic Summer*, 242.

314   **"Our kids never gave up"**: *New York Times*, October 5, 1969, 83.

314   **"I talked to Casey"**: *New York Times*, October 9, 1969, 59.

314   **"Congratulations"**: Vescey, *Joy in Mudville*, 225.

315   **"Heck," said Aaron after the game**: *New York Times*, October 7, 1969, 55.

315   **"They'll end the war"**: Lang, *New York Mets*, 95.

315   **"you're the most wonderful man"**: *New York Times*, October 7, 1969, 1.

315   **"To me, there's no question"**: *New York Times*, October 7, 1969, 55.

315   **Mets' head of scouting, Bob Scheffing**: *New York Times*, January 25, 1970, 165. The Orioles finished the 1969 season with a team batting average of .265 and 175

home runs; by comparison, the Mets had batted only .241 with 109 home runs: *New York Times*, October 8, 1969, 38.

316 **"I see myself as"**: *New York Times*, October 9, 1969, 5.

316 **Karl Ehrhardt**: *New York Times*, June 18, 2006, S10, and "Karl Ehrhardt, 83, Sign Man and Shea Stadium Fixture, Is Dead," obituary, *New York Times*, February 9, 2008.

317 **"was on top of things"**: Phone interview with Karl Ehrhardt, August 21, 2007.

317 **"[The Mets] had a bigger ballpark"**: McCarver, *Diamond Gems*, 3. Contrast Weaver's approach to Hodges: before the Mets' opponent in the National League championship round had been determined, when asked who he would prefer playing, San Francisco or Atlanta, Hodges said he had no preference.

317 **"I don't believe"**: *New York Times*, October 9, 1969, 59.

317 **"I can't cheer"**: *New York Times*, September 26, 1969, 74.

317 **Mets boarded a chartered**: *New York Times*, October 10, 1969, 59.

318 **Seaver pitched poorly in Game One**: *New York Times*, October 12, 1969, pg. S1.

318 **"We are here to prove"** and **"a lot more talent"**: *New York Times*, October 12, 1969, S2.

318 **"You ain't seen nothing yet"**: Phone interview with Bud Harrelson, September 15, 2010.

318 **In Game Two**: *New York Times*, October 13, 1969, 1, and *New York Times*, October 13, 1969, 60. Asked if he would have been disappointed if he had been removed by Hodges for a pinch hitter, Weis said, "If Gil decided to hit for me, I wouldn't have been in the least disappointed. I've been a utility man long enough to understand these things": *New York Times*, October 13, 1969, 60.

318 **"I didn't want"**: *New York Times*, October 14, 1969, 53.

319 **fourth outfielder**: In the fifteenth and eighteenth innings of a game between the Orioles and the Washington Senators in Baltimore on June 4, 1967, Hodges had repositioned his second baseman, Tim Cullen, to give him four outfielders against Frank Robinson in another crucial situation in a close game: *Washington Post*, June 5, 1967, D1.

319 **"Koosman had thrown 103 pitches"**: *New York Times*, October 13, 1969, 60.

319 **"I would have liked to"**: *New York Times*, October 13, 1969, 60.

319 **"Hodges doesn't do anything"**: Dick Young, "Hodges' Hands Quicker than Ted's Eyes," *New York Daily News*, April 1972, from Father Vieck's scrapbook.

319 **"I never made my own decisions"**: Interview with Eddie Yost at Citi Field, August 22, 2009. Yost explained that one of the reasons Hodges never smiled in the dugout during a game was because in certain instances, a smile was a signal from Hodges to Yost.

320 **Joe Camacho**: Montville, *Ted Williams*, 273–74. In 1969 a combination of Williams's hitting instruction and the pitching mound being lowered from 15 to 10

inches, led to a remarkable improvement in the Senators' hitting (e.g., shortstop Ed Brinkman's batting average increased from .187 in 1968 to .266, the highest of his fifteen-year Major League career). The Senators finished 86-76 for fourth place in the AL Eastern Division and Williams was named Manager of the Year in the AL. But under Williams, the Senators got worse each season. By 1972, after the team moved to Texas, they finished 54-100 and Williams gave up managing.

320 **"Heavens no"**: *New York Times*, October 22, 1969, 36.

320 **"I'm glad to see"**: *New York Times*, October 13, 1969, 61.

321 **Blair stood in center field**: *New York Times*, October 15, 1969, 51.

322 **"Let's take"**: Hodges, *Game of Baseball*, 101.

322 **"Look who's here"**: Seaver, *Perfect Game*, 33, 47; also *New York Times*, October 18, 1969, 40.

323 **"Better than yesterday"**: *New York Times*, October 16, 1969, 58.

323 **"I know they're not"**: *New York Times*, October 16, 1969, 59; also *New York Times*, October 16, 1969, 1.

324 **Hodges marched a ball with a jelly-like**: *New York Times*, June 1, 1969, S1.

324 **"like extras in"**: Vescey, *Joy in Mudville*, 11 and 248.

324 **They ripped out the bases**: *New York Times*, October 17, 1969, 1.

325 **"Thank God it's over"** and **"It's a big step"**: From videotape of the 1969 World Series.

325 **"The pressure never lets up"**: Seaver, *Perfect Game*, 7; the original quote comes from Ritter, *Glory of Their Times*, 123.

325 **Casey Stengel immediately followed**: Phone interview with Russ White, March 6, 2010.

325 **Nixon reminded**: *New York Times*, October 17, 1969, 68.

326 **"jump[ed] out of his chair"**: Herzog, "White Rat," 83.

326 **"I was a nobody"**: Phone interview with Whitey Herzog, January 29, 2010.

326 **"He's exhausted"**: *New York Times*, October 18, 1969, 40.

326 **"He'd come out to the mound"**: Cohen, *Magic Summer*, 246. The Mets' opponents even saw the change: Curt Flood, then a Cardinals outfielder, said, "The . . . Mets were the worst team in the league during the days of Casey Stengel; their players were bitterly, hopelessly humiliated. When . . . Gil Hodges was named manager . . . the Mets became serious": Kahn, *Boys of Summer*, 342.

326 **parade up Broadway**: *New York Times*, October 17, 1969, 1; October 21, 1969, 55.

328 **"a summer of joy"**: *New York Times*, October 21, 1969, 1; Hodges's speech: news footage.

328 **"Karl, I want to thank you"**: Phone interview with Karl Ehrhardt, August 21, 2007.

329 **"I don't think any one man"**: *New York Times*, October 22, 1969, 37.

329 **"scanning the horizon"**: Cannato, "Ungovernable City," 658.

23. STRUGGLES IN THE SPOTLIGHT

331   *I just hope I don't spoil things*: Lang, *New York Mets*, 92.

331   **with Hodges's urging**: Lang, *New York Mets*, 105. Should Hodges have known about Foy's addictive type personality prior to *urging* his acquisition? According to Lang (writing years later), "Hodges knew, or should have known threw the grapevine" that "Foy was having personal difficulties." Jim Lonborg disagrees. The 1967 American League Cy Young Award winner, Lonborg was Foy's teammate in Boston. He told me that aside from "one alcohol-related incident" that was "kept in house," Foy was a "good teammate" and there had been no indication that he would subsequently develop a drug problem: Phone interview with Jim Lonborg, February 17, 2012.

331   **Joe Foy**: New York Mets 1970 press guide. In their eight years of existence, the Mets had tried forty-one players at third base. Ed Charles had been released following the 1969 season, and Hodges was not convinced Wayne Garrett (.218 average with only one home run in 400 regular season at bats in 1969) was an everyday third baseman. Hodges anticipated Foy would be an everyday player, which Hodges preferred over a platoon: *New York Times*, December 3, 1969, 67, and *New York Times*, December 4, 1969, 73. Foy had been acquired by Kansas City from Boston prior to the 1968 season.

331   **Bob Scheffing**: *New York Times*, January 20, 1970, 36.

332   **Hodges didn't attend**: *New York Times*, March 6, 1970, 48. Kirk lost his reelection bid.

332   **"hecklers in the uniform"**: *New York Times*, March 7, 1970, 55. If Hodges did not mandate a dress code, the players wouldn't have appeared so well groomed in their jackets and ties.

332   **"I was ashamed"**: *New York Times*, March 7, 1970, 55, and McGraw, *Screwball*, 145–47.

332   **first time in their history**: *New York Times*, April 8, 1970, 70.

332   **"It's a long season"**: *New York Times*, April 15, 1970, 72.

332   **"That's what 25 men"**: *New York Times*, April 27, 1970, 45.

333   **"They asked if"**: *New York Times*, May 22, 1970, 20.

333   **Hodges moved him from his usual**: *New York Times*, May 28, 1970, 45. In 1970 he still applied a platoon at first base where Shamsky and Clendenon combined for All-Star-like numbers at midseason: a .316 batting average, 16 home runs, and 62 runs batted in: *The Sporting News*, July 18, 1970, 35. To generate more runs, Hodges had the Mets stealing more bases than ever before; by July 4 they had stolen more bases (77) than they had in any previous full season (72).

333   **"That'll cost you $1,000"**: Dave Anderson, "If Hodges Managed These Mets," *New York Times*, September 27, 1990. Hodges's frustrations were further revealed

during the 1970 season when for only the second and third time in his Mets managerial career, he was thrown out of a game. The first time that season was on June 28 in a one-run loss in Montreal to the Expos, after Shamsky was called out for tagging up from third base before a fly ball was caught in left field. Hodges "argued vehemently" and was thrown out. On his way back to the dugout, in a highly uncharacteristic public display of his emotions, Hodges "kicked the dirt violently": *New York Times*, June 29, 1970, 50. Hodges was thrown out of another game a month later after arguing a called strike: *New York Times*, July 27, 1970, 31, and *New York Times*, June 20, 1971, S3.

333   **"high as a kite"**: Phone interview with Ron Swoboda on May 24, 2006. Jerry Koosman made similar statements about that game: Golenbock, *Amazin'*, 269–70. Joe Durso, in an approach consistent with those times, could not write the truth about Foy, but was clearly aware of the situation, writing, "The Mets' disenchantment with Foy stemmed chiefly from his performance off the field. He was considered a likeable member of the team, and a spirited one, but he was occasionally late for work and fell out of favor": *New York Times*, December 1, 1970, 79.

333   **"the end of Foy"**: Phone interview with Ron Swoboda on May 24, 2006.

333   **the Mets' clubhouse**: *New York Times*, April 22, 1970, 76.

333   **"The Mets don't have the emotional fire"**: *New York Times*, August 23, 1970, S2.

333   **At the time he was batting .114**: *New York Times*, June 24, 1970, 56.

334   **"Singleton has a chance"**: *New York Times*, July 25, 1970, 25.

334   **"I was in awe"**: Email from Ken Singleton, December 19, 2011.

334   **"I don't think I was that bad"**: *New York Times*, October 3, 1970, 20.

334   **"That's where I think"**: Maury Allen, "Gil Hodges Is a Tyrant!" *Sports Today*, August 1971, 22.

334   **"Hodges just isn't built that way"**: Allen, "Hodges Is a Tyrant," 25. The Mets traded Swoboda to Montreal for a journeyman outfielder who had never hit a home run in the Majors, Mets fans would sarcastically refer to him as "the immortal" Don Hahn: *New York Times*, April 1, 1971, 53. After being traded, Swoboda offered a comparison of his new manager, Gene Mauch, and his former manager. "Ball players are insecure. They need someone to pump them up. Mauch's got no secrets. He's happy to let everybody know why he does certain things. He gets teed off a lot and shows it. When things happen that he doesn't like, he yells about it. That's how ballplayers are when they're angry. Not like Gil. When he got teed off he kept it hidden, inside, restrained. That's not how ballplayers are when they're angry. Gene's a human being. If he's got something to say, he says it. I've heard more good things about Gene in three days [it was Swoboda's third day with Montreal] that I heard about Hodges in three years": Swoboda, "Seaver, the Mets & Me," *Sport Magazine*, July 1971, 44, 88.

334 **Hodges had the Mets in a first-place tie**: *New York Times*, September 10, 1970, 64.

335 **"It's been a long, long"** and **"No, I didn't"**: *New York Times*, September 27, 1970, S2.

335 **"quite openly"**: *New York Times*, October 3, 1970, 20.

335 **1970 All-Star Game**: *New York Times*, July 15, 1970, 42.

335 **That play, one of the most famous**: Reston, *Collision at Home Plate*, 63–68.

335 **"That," Otis said**: *New York Times*, August 28, 1970, 47. The selection of Hickman was controversial. It required Hodges to omit the Cubs left fielder (and future Hall of Famer) Billy Williams and give his spot to a journeyman player who was then in the midst of his career season. Hodges figured Williams had already played in several All-Star Games, and Hickman, who would finish the season with a .315 average, 32 home runs, and 115 runs batted in, might never get another chance. "Hickman's having a great year and it's a big thing for him," Hodges said, "We're real proud of him": *The Sporting News*, July 25, 1970, 5.

335 **"I thought Rose got"**: *New York Times*, July 16, 1970, 25.

335 **"It took a fellow like Rose"**: *Eugene Register*, July 15, 1970, 3E.

336 **Weaver asked the umpires**: Phone interview with Joe Pignatano, December 6, 2006.

337 **"Has anyone seen Maloney"**: *New York Times*, July 14, 1970, 42.

337 **"I was amazed"**: Phone interview with Claude Osteen, December 21, 2006.

338 **In 1970, as the oddsmakers had predicted**: *New York Times*, April 1, 1970, 77.

338 **"I don't know what your magic was"**: *New York Times*, October 15, 1970, 64.

338 **"The satisfaction of this year"**: *New York Times*, October 1, 1970, 66.

338 **In 1970 the Mets drew**: *New York Times*, October 2, 1970, 54.

338 **"sound advice"**: Hodges, *Game of Baseball*, 97.

338 **"Look," McGuire said**: Frank Deford, "The Depression Baby," in Blauner, *Coach*, 137.

339 **"one of his longest speeches"**: *New York Times*, March 14, 1971, S1.

339 **"no matter how tough"**: Hodges, *Game of Baseball*, 25.

339 **"If things get rough"**: *New York Times*, February 22, 1971, 39.

339 **"fat and complacent"** and **"No. 14"**: *New York Times*, February 20, 1970, 57.

339 **"It was supposed to be"**: Allen, "Hodges Is a Tyrant," 23.

340 **"Criticism of the manager is a lot of bull"**: *New York Times*, November 24, 1970, 51.

340 **"He hasn't played in eight years"**: *New York Times*, August 16, 1971, 19.

340 **Because of a torn muscle**: *New York Times*, February 18, 1972, 31.

340 **In 1971 the Mets didn't even**: In 1971 the Mets were only in contention until June 30 with a record of 45-29, two games behind the first-place Pirates. Over the next six weeks the Mets went 13-31, the worst record in the National League over that

period (including six losses in a row, their longest losing streak since 1968). Going into the All-Star break, the Mets were ten games behind the Pirates: *New York Times*, July 12, 1971, 35.

340   **he sometimes played Ed Kranepool**: *New York Times*, July 21, 1971, 23.

340   **"It's the only name"**: *New York Times*, September 7, 1971, 49.

340   **Karl Ehrhardt held up his final placard**: *New York Times*, October 3, 1970, 20.

340   **"I just wanted a year"**: Allen, "Hodges Is a Tyrant," 24.

340   **"When I told him"**: *New York Times*, July 1, 1971, 65.

341   **during the 1970 season**: *New York Times*, February 23, 1970, 48.

341   **"I couldn't ask for a better"**: "Nolan Ryan: From Alvin to Cooperstown," 23–25.

341   **"There is a man who throws"**: *New York Times*, March 11, 1970, 79.

341   **"He's on the threshold"**: *New York Times*, March 11, 1970, 79.

341   **Nolan Ryan's 1971 season**: *New York Times*, September 1, 1971, 27, and September 6, 1971, 13.

342   **"Whether or if or how"**: "Nolan Ryan," 25.

342   **"a professional hitter"**: Lang, "Mets Regard Fregosi as Cure," *The Sporting News*, December 25, 1971. In 1965, when Hodges was managing the Senators, he said, "We've got to find a way to handle that Jim Fregosi. . . . He's been killing us all year": *Washington Post*, July 8, 1965, F1. Fregosi then had a lifetime .340 batting average against the Senators—but that was six years before the Mets acquired him. To Hodges's credit, in 1970 Fregosi had (for a shortstop in that era) a great season with the Angels hitting .278 with 22 home runs and 82 runs batted in. But Fregosi was injured in 1971, he would be past thirty when the 1972 season began, and it remained to be seen how he would fare switching from short to third.

342   **"just a trifle smug"**: *New York Times*, June 13, 1971, S3.

343   **"all Hodges: calm"**: McGraw, *Screwball*, 140.

343   **"Hodges really flipped"**: McGraw, *Screwball*, 148–49.

343   **"I was so shook up"**: *New York Times*, September 9, 1970, 58.

344   **"When Gil was running the ball club"**: McGraw, *Screwball*, 144, 153–55.

344   **"He looked at me in utter disbelief"**: Clendenon, *Miracle*, 158.

24. EASTER SUNDAY

345   *That's right, kid*: Golenbock, *Amazin'*, 284.

345   **Gil Jr. had married**: *New York Times*, February 13, 1972, 67.

345   **"How are they coming along with my bridge?"**: Kinman, "Gilbert Ray (Bud) Hodges," undated article from Father Vieck's scrapbook.

346   **"a long fastball that moves"**: James and Neyer, *Guide to Pitchers*, 296.

347   **usually so intimidated by Hodges**: Phone interview with Jon Matlack, November 10, 2011.

347   **a number of important players were injured**: *New York Times*, March 7, 1972, 47.

347   **"There just wasn't much"**: *New York Times*, February 29, 1972, 43.

347   **"No comment"**: *New York Times*, March 1, 1972, 30.

347   **Colvin took a photo**: Interview with Kae Adkerson in Petersburg, April 2006.

348   **"I know, Cuz"**: *The Sporting News*, April 22, 1972, 8.

348   **despite Whitey Herzog's objections**: Phone interview with Whitey Herzog, January 29, 2010.

348   **"tickled"**: *New York Times*, April 7, 1972, 1.

348   **"was totally astonished"**: Phone interview with Rusty Staub, March 8, 2012.

348   **"Maybe it would have been"**: Gorman, *Three and Two!*, 103.

348   **At about 5:15 p.m.**: *New York Post*, April 3, 1972, back page.

349   **"I felt very bad"**: *Lakeland Ledger*, April 4, 1972, 1B.

349   **"nothing like a celebrity death"**: John Drof interview, April 2006.

349   **"It was more"**: *The Sporting News*, April 29, 1972, 12.

350   **"It's a personal loss to me"**: *New York Times*, April 3, 1972, 52.

350   **"Gil . . . never gave anyone"**: *New York Times*, April 3, 1972, 52.

350   **"I'm sick"**: *Courier*, April 3, 1972.

350   **"It's a saddening experience"**: *Courier*, April 3, 1972.

350   **"He was a wonderful man"**: *Courier*, April 3, 1972.

350   **"He was more than just a baseball manager"**: *New York Times*, April 5, 1972, 53.

351   **"he was the leader"**: *New York Times*, April 5, 1972, 53, 57.

351   **"He was reverent, friendly, strong, and silent"**: *New York Times*, April 3, 1972, 52.

351   **"was real [but] only"**: *New York Times*, April 5, 1972, 53. Seaver said, "He's only spoken with me directly about pitching three or four times in four years": *New York Times*, February 19, 1971, 44.

351   **"a tremendous baseball guy"**: Phone interview with Ron Swoboda, May 24, 2006.

351   **"I felt stranded"**: McGraw, *Screwball*, 144.

351   **"He's a gentle father"**: *New York Times*, December 17, 1967, 189.

352   **"We have a parade"**: *New York Times*, April 5, 1972, 53.

352   **"Hodges was so big"**: Phone interview with Karl Ehrhardt, August 21, 2007.

352   **funeral service**: *New York Times*, April 7, 1972, 17, 33.

352   **"big-splash"**: *New York Times*, April 5, 1972, 59.

353   **But not Roy Campanella**: *Newsweek*, April 17, 1972, 107, and *New York Times*, April 4, 1972, 50.

354   **Howard Cosell stuck a microphone**: Interview with Carl Erskine, Anderson IN, April 2006.

354   **eclectic mix buried**: Pamphlet found in the cemetery office.

354   **"our only concern"**: *New York Times*, April 4, 1972, 49, and *New York Times*, April 6, 1972, 58.

355   "I've never forgiven": Herzog, *White Rat*, 86.

355   "Gil has long been a good friend": *New York Times*, April 5, 1972, 53.

355   "the grace they valued in Hodges": *New York Times*, April 15, 1972, 24.

355   Even staid Arthur Daley punched out: *New York Times*, April 9, 1972, S2.

356   "I hope I can fill": *New York Times*, April 7, 1972, 1.

356   Before the Mets' home opener: *New York Times*, April 16, 1972, S1.

356   "We didn't want to make it": *The Sporting News*, April 29, 1972, 23.

EPILOGUE

357   A life is not important: Words engraved on Jackie Robinson's tombstone.

357   the dedication ceremony: Letters and articles in Father Vieck's scrapbook.

357   Chuck Harmon: Phone interview with Chuck Harmon, April 27, 2006.

358   For many years, Bob Hodges: Genealogical records, Petersburg Public Library.

358   Irene Hodges lived in Petersburg: Obituary, *Press-Dispatch*, March 10, 1988.

358   As a Dodgers coach, Jake Pitler: Obituary, *New York Times*, February 4, 1968.

358   Branch Rickey Jr.: Lowenfish, *Branch Rickey*, 578.

359   Hodges's favorite umpire, Larry Goetz: Smith, *To Absent Friends*, 277.

359   "competent man": Phone interview with Virginia Merchant, January 26, 2007.

359   In the 1960s, Chuck Askey: Email from Chuck Askey, December 2, 2006.

359   "Having the Dodgers in Los Angeles": *New York Times*, July 3, 1958, 28.

360   "had a huge impact": Phone interview with Tod Parrott, February 13, 2007.

360   "Gil Hodges was the greatest": Hirshey, "Old-Timers in Tribute," *Daily News*, June 9, 1973.

360   "I'm embarrassed to say it": *LA Times*, April 8, 2012.

360   "Gil might be in the Hall": February 2, 2007, phone interview with Ralph Kiner, who was referring to the fact that when a player is considered for election to the HOF, one of the factors often considered is if he ever led the league in a major statistical category.

361   "There is something symbolic": Amoruso, *Quiet Man*, 236.

361   Charlie DiGiovanna died: *Los Angeles Examiner*, December 29, 1958, 4.

361   $5,000 for his family: interview with Carl Erskine, April 21, 2006.

361   "Alan, you have something": phone interview with Alan Koch, June 21, 2010.

362   "thinking every time": *Washington Post*, August 25, 1964, D3.

362   "Chavez Ravine and Claude Osteen": *Washington Post*, October 9, 1965, D1.

362   fired Salerno: *New York Times*, December 3, 1971, 51, and phone interview with Al Salerno, June 7, 2007. Salerno died two months later on August 8, 2007.

362   "I liked the way": Phone interview with Marvin Miller, September 10, 2009.

362   "the greatest influence" and "how to get respect": Joe Torre's responses to questions at the Lisner Auditorium in Washington DC, February 15, 2012.

363   **Jon Matlack**: Phone interview with Jon Matlack, November 10, 2011. Matlack played for nine different managers in a thirteen-year career. He told me that Hodges had a better feel for how a game would play out in the late innings than any other manager he ever saw.

363   **Amos Otis**: *New York Times*, August 28, 1970, 47. Joe Foy, the player Otis was traded for, was out of baseball within a year and died of heart attack at forty-six: Obituary, *New York Times*, October 14, 1989.

363   **"I read that Gil"**: Ryan, *Throwing Heat*, 70. In his autobiography Nolan Ryan wrote, "I was really frustrated with the Mets, and Ruth [his wife] and I were frustrated living in New York." In the AL, Ryan benefited from the fact that umpires called a higher strike than they did in the NL because AL umpires, who then wore their chest protectors outside their jackets, stood taller when calling balls and strikes than the NL umpires, who wore their protectors inside their jackets. The AL umpires would be centered directly behind the catcher; the NL umpires would set up on the inside part of the plate: Phone interview with Jim Fregosi, January 7, 2012.

363   **"Background is not the primary concern"**: *New York Times*, October 28, 1969, 53.

363   **"and the rest is history"**: Phone interview with Ed Charles, January 17 and 18, 2007.

363   **"Too many players"**: *New York Times*, September 15, 1972, 27.

364   **At those moments, Karl Ehrhardt**: *New York Times*, June 18, 2006, S10, and obituary, *New York Times*, February 9, 2008.

364   **"If it wasn't for"**: I attended the fortieth anniversary celebration and heard Jones speak.

364   **"If I had just kept"**: Phone interview with Ron Swoboda, May 24, 2006.

364   **"Not figuring out how"**: Email from Ron Swoboda, January 6, 2010.

364   **"made me realize"**: *New York Times*, June 11, 1972, S3.

365   **"It goes back to the late 1960s"**: *New York Times*, October 11, 1981, section 5, 1.

365   **"I loved him"**: Allen, *After the Miracle*, 36.

365   **"And it was Gil who straightened me out"**: *New York Times*, April 5, 1972, 53.

365   **Bud Harrelson**: Phone interview with Bud Harrelson, September 15, 2010.

365   **"Gil Hodges was the most"**: Madden, *My 25 Years*, 49.

365   **"I've often wondered"**: *New York Times*, March 6, 1970.

366   **"My brother"**: Phone interview with Bob Mandt, July 20 and August 10, 2007.

366   **John Lindsay**: Cannato, *Ungovernable City*, 555 and 579.

366   **"Hodges died before"**: Phone interview with Rusty Staub, March 8, 2012.

366   **"was my idol"**: Clendenon, *Miracle in New York*, 97.

366   **"There must be very few of us"**: Angell, *New York Times*, June 29, 1972, 46 (*New Yorker* reprint).

366   **"a legacy for generations"**: Howie Rose, Citi Field, August 22, 2009.

366   **Hodges's headstone**: As seen on my visit to Holy Cross Cemetery, May 21, 2008.

367   **When little Nicky Lipariti**: Phone interview with Nick Lipariti, August 30, 2008.

367   **the sign overlooking the ballpark**: Hodges, *Game of Baseball*, 146. I've visited the field twice, and the most prominent sign at the ballpark now reads, "GRACE/ PEPSI."

AFTERWORD

369   **Voting shall be based**: Rule 5 of the BBWAA election rules for the Hall of Fame.

369   **Those whose careers**: Rule (B) of the rules for election for golden era candidates to the Hall of Fame.

370   **After the 1962 season**: *The Sporting News*, December 15, 1962, 19.

371   **The first time Hodges was on the ballot**: Thorn, *Total Baseball*, 8th ed., 741.

372   **"There has been an aggressive"**: Red Smith, *New York Times*, January 11, 1978, A15. As part of that lobbying effort, an op-ed piece, "One Vote for Gil Hodges: A Man of Integrity," appeared in the "Views of Sport" column in the *New York Times* on December 25, 1977, under the byline of Francis J. Mugavero, Bishop of the Roman Catholic Diocese of Brooklyn. The piece was ghostwritten by sportswriter Rob Edelman as a favor to Hodges's good friend Sid Loberfeld: Phone interview with Rob Edelman, June 28, 2011.

372   **"Translated, this means that all"**: *New York Times*, December 28, 1979, A24.

372   **"He always looked"**: Phone interview with Marty Noble, March 12, 2010.

372   **higher than any other player**: Craig Muder, Director of Communications, HOF, January 2, 2013, email. Jack Morris received 66.7 percent of the vote of the BBWAA on his thirteenth time on the ballot: Tyler Kepner, *New York Times*, January 7, 2013, D2.

373   **"Oh, you National League guys"**: Phone interview with Monte Irvin, December 21, 2009.

373   **"the insider's view"** and **"subliminal melding"**: Phone interview with Ernie Harwell, August 6, 2009. But when I spoke to Earl Weaver (phone interview, July 30, 2009), he was convinced that Hodges should only be evaluated based upon his playing record. Weaver's biases (losing the 1969 World Series to Hodges) limited his objectivity.

373   **all told me they never heard Williams mention**: Phone interview with Joe Camacho, August 7, 2010. Dom DiMaggio told Williams, "If you get me in this way, I don't want it."

373   **"I feel I'm a little bit"**: Red Smith, *New York Times*, February 2, 1972, 23.

375   **"That's a trick question"**: Interview with Reggie Jackson, New York City, prior to the 2008 All-Star Game held on July 15, 2008. Jackson's interview with the *New*

York Post can be seen on nysportspace.com/forum/topics/873694: Topic 14807. Hodges's career batting average (.273) is higher than Jackson's (.262), as is his on base percentage (.361 vs. .358).

375 **"He was a great human being"**: Letter from Roy Sievers, postmarked December 19, 2011.

ACKNOWLEDGMENTS

377 **It is always wise**: Barber, *Rhubarb in the Catbird Seat*, 39.

377 **I came across the following dialogue**: Zimmerman, *Year the Mets Lost*, 63.

BIBLIOGRAPHY

ARCHIVAL AND UNPUBLISHED SOURCES

Branch Rickey to Gilbert Carpenter, October 22, 1937. Private collection.

Gil Hodges scrapbook: Various clippings. Private collection.

Gil Hodges to Father Vieck, 1968–71. Private collection.

Gil Hodges to his parents and sister, 1941–45, 1956. Private collection.

Gil Hodges to Ty Cobb, spring 1953. Private collection.

Library of Congress, Washington DC: Branch Rickey Papers.

Museum of Television and Radio: Tape of the 1952 World Series; Gil Hodges's appearance on the *Steve Allen Show* in 1959; and various commercials.

Museum of the City of New York: Exhibit, "The Glory Days, New York Baseball, 1947–1957," on display June 27–December 31, 2007.

National Archives, College Park MD: After-action reports, memos, daily journals, and correspondence of the Sixteenth Anti-Aircraft Artillery Unit, U.S. Marine Corps, during World War II.

National Baseball Hall of Fame Library, Cooperstown NY: Gil Hodges clipping files.

New York Public Library, Grand Army Plaza Branch, Brooklyn: Gil Hodges clipping files.

United States Marine Library, Quantico VA: Papers of Robert Merchant.

PUBLISHED SOURCES

Adell, Ross, and Ken Samelson. *Amazing Mets Trivia*. New York: Taylor Trade Publishing, 2004.

Allen, Maury. *After the Miracle: The Amazin' Mets Twenty Years Later*. New York: Franklin Watts, 1989.

——. *Brooklyn Remembered*. Champaign IL: Sports Publishing, 2005.

——. *The Incredible Mets*. New York: Paperback Library, 1969.

Alston, Walter, with Jack Tobin. *A Year at a Time*. Waco TX: Word Books, 1976.

Amoruso, Marino. *Gil Hodges, the Quiet Man*. Middlebury VT: Paul S. Eriksson, 1991.

Anderson, Sparky, and Dan Ewald. *Sparky!* New York: Prentice Hall, 1990.

Angell, Roger. *The Summer Game*. New York: Viking Press, 1972.

Armour, Mark. *Joe Cronin: A Life in Baseball*. Lincoln: University of Nebraska Press, 2010.

Attiyeh, Mike. *Who Was Traded for Lefty Grove*. Baltimore MD: Johns Hopkins University Press, 2002.

Baldwin, Dave. *Snake Jazz*. Bloomington IN: Xlibris, 2007.

Barber, Red, and Robert Creamer. *Rhubarb in the Catbird Seat*. Lincoln: University of Nebraska Press, 1997.

Barney, Rex, and Norman Macht. *Rex Barney's Thank Youuuu*. Centreville MD: Tidewater Publishers, 1993

Bavasi, Buzzie. *Off the Record*. Chicago: Contemporary Books, 1987.

Belote, James, and William Belote. *Typhoon of Steel: The Battle for Okinawa*. New York: Harper & Row, 1970.

Berra, Yogi, with Tom Horton. *Yogi, It Ain't Over . . .* New York: Harper & Row, 1989.

Blauner, Andrew, ed. *Coach: 25 Writers Reflect on People Who Made a Difference*. New York: Warner Books, 2005.

Bragan, Bobby. *You Can't Hit the Ball with the Bat on Your Shoulder*. Fort Worth TX: Summit Group, 1992.

Campanella, Roy. *It's Good to Be Alive*. Boston: Little Brown, 1959.

Cannato, Vincent. *The Ungovernable City: John Lindsay and His Struggle to Save New York*. New York: Basic Books, 2001.

Chafets, Zev. *Cooperstown Confidential: Heroes, Rogues, and the Inside Story of the Baseball Hall of Fame*. New York: Bloomsbury, 2009.

Clendenon, Donn. *Miracle in New York*. Sioux Falls SD: Penmarch Publishing, 1999.

Cohen, Stanley. *A Magic Summer: The Amazin' Story of the 1969 New York Mets*. New York: Skyhorse Publishing, 2009.

Conlan, Jocko, and Robert Creamer. *Jocko*. Lincoln: University of Nebraska Press, 1997.

Creamer, Robert. *Stengel: His Life and Times*. New York: Simon & Schuster, 1984.

D'Agostino, Dennis, and Bonnie Crosby. *Through a Blue Lens*. Chicago: Triumph Books, 2007.

Daley, Arthur. *Kings of the Home Run*. New York: G. P. Putnam's Sons, 1962.

Davis, Tommy. *Tommy Davis's Tales from the Dodgers Dugout*. Champaign IL: Sports Publishing, 2005.

Day, Laraine. *Day with the Giants*. Garden City NY: Curtis Publishing, 1952.

DeBusschere, Dave. *The Open Man*. New York: Random House, 1970.

Deindorfer, Bob. *The Fireside Book of Baseball*. Edited by Charles Einstein. New York: Simon & Schuster, 1956.

DeLillo, Don. *Pafko at the Wall*. New York: Scribner, 1997.

Dellinger, Susan. *Red Legs and Black Sox: Edd Roush and the Untold Story of the 1919 World Series*. Cincinnati OH: Emmis Books, 2006.

Devaney, John. *Gil Hodges, Baseball Miracle Man*. New York: Putnam, 1973.

Devine, Bing. *The Memoirs of Bing Devine*. United States: Sports Publishing, 2004.

Dickson, Paul. *The New Dickson Baseball Dictionary*. New York: Harcourt Brace, 1989.

Drysdale, Don, with Bob Verdi. *Once a Bum, Always a Dodger*. New York: St. Martin's Press, 1990.

Duren, Ryne, and Tom Sabellico. *I Can See Clearly Now*. Chula Vista CA: Aventine Press, 2003.

Durocher, Leo, with Ed Linn. *Nice Guys Finish Last*. New York: Simon & Schuster, 1975.

Eig, Jonathan. *Opening Day*. New York: Simon & Schuster, 2007.

Erskine, Carl. *Tales from the Dodger Dugout*. Champaign IL: Sports Publishing, 2001.

———. *Tales from the Dodger Dugout: Extra Innings*. Champaign IL: Sports Publishing, 2004.

Falkner, David. *Nine Sides of the Diamond*. New York: Random House, 1990.

Farrell, James. *My Baseball Diary*. Carbondale and Edwardsville: Southern Illinois University Press, 1998.

Feifer, George. *Tennozan: The Battle of Okinawa and the Atomic Bomb*. New York: Ticknor & Fields, 1992.

Feldman, Doug. *Miracle Collapse: The 1969 Chicago Cubs*. Lincoln: University of Nebraska Press, 2006.

Fleder, Rob, ed. *Great Baseball Writing*. New York: Time, Inc., 2005.

Garagiola, Joe. *Baseball Is a Funny Game*. New York: Lippincott, 1960.

Garvey, Steve. *My Bat Boy Days*. New York: Scribner, 2008.

Gietschier, Steve. *Complete Baseball Record Book*. St. Louis: The Sporting News, 2005.

Gittleman, Sol. *Reynolds, Raschi and Lopat: New York's Big Three and the Great Yankee Dynasty of 1949–1953*. Jefferson NC: McFarland, 2007.

Golenbock, Peter. *Amazin'*. New York: St. Martin's Press, 2002.

———. *Bums*. New York: Putnam, 1984.

———. *Dynasty*. Chicago: Contemporary Books, 2000.

Goodwin, Doris Kearns. *Wait Till Next Year: A Memoir*. New York: Touchstone, 1998.

Gorman, Tom. *Three and Two! An Autobiography of Tom Gorman*. New York: Charles Scribner's Sons, 1979.

Graham, Frank, Jr. *A Farewell to Heroes*. Carbondale: Southern Illinois University Press, 1981.

Halberstam, David. *Summer of '49*. New York: William Morrow, 1989.

Harrelson, Ken, with Al Hirshberg. *Hawk*. New York: Viking, 1969.

Hartford, James. *Merton & Friends*. New York: Continuum, 2006.

Hartley, James. *Washington's Expansion Senators (1961-1971)*. Germantown MD: Corduroy Press, 1998.

Helyar, John. *Lords of the Realm*. New York: Ballantine Books, 1994.

Hernandez, Keith, and Mike Bryan. *Pure Baseball*. New York: Harper Collins, 1994.

Herzog, Whitey, and Kevin Horrigan. *White Rat: A Life in Baseball*. New York: Perennial Library, 1987.

Higbe, Kirby. *The High Hard One*. Lincoln: University of Nebraska Press, 1998.

Hirsch, James. *Willie Mays: The Life, the Legend*. New York: Scribner, 2010.

Hodges, Gil, with Frank Slocum. *The Game of Baseball*. New York: Crown, 1969.

Honig, Donald. *Baseball When the Grass Was Real*. New York: Coward, McCann & Geoghegan, 1975.

Huhn, Rick. *The Sizzler: George Sisler, Baseball's Forgotten Great*. Columbia: University of Missouri Press, 2004.

Isaacs, Neil. *Innocence & Wonder: Baseball through the Eyes of Batboys*. Indianapolis IN: Masters Press, 1994.

Jacobson, Steve. *Carrying Jackie's Torch: The Players Who Integrated Baseball . . . and America*. Chicago: Lawrence Hill Books, 2007.

James, Bill. *The Bill James Guide to Baseball Managers from 1870 to Today*. New York: Scribner, 1997.

———. *What Ever Happened to the Hall of Fame?* New York: Simon & Schuster, 1994.

———, and Rob Neyer. *Guide to Pitchers*. New York: Fireside, 2004.

Jensen, Don. *The Timeline History of Baseball*. San Diego: Thunder Bay Press, 2009.

Kahn, Roger. *The Boys of Summer*. New York: Harper & Row, 1972.

Keegan, Tom. *The First Baseman*. Cincinnati OH: Emmis Books, 2006.

Koppett, Leonard. *The Man in the Dugout*. New York: Crown, 1993.

Lanctot, Neil. *Campy*. New York: Simon & Schuster, 2011

Lang, Jack, and Peter Simon. *The New York Mets: Twenty-Five Years of Baseball Magic*. New York: Henry Holt, 1986.

Leavy, Jane. *Sandy Koufax, a Lefty's Legacy*. New York: Perennial, 2003.

Lipsyte, Robert. *Sports World: An American Dreamland*. New York: Quadrangle/The New York Times Book Co., 1975.

Lowenfish, Lee. *Branch Rickey: Baseball's Ferocious Gentleman*. Lincoln: University of Nebraska Press, 2007.

Lowry, Philip. *Green Cathedrals: The Ultimate Celebration of Major League and Negro League Ballparks*. New York: Walker, 2006.

Madden, Bill. *My 25 Years Covering Baseball's Heroes, Scoundrels, Triumphs and Tragedies*. Champaign IL: Sports Publishing, LLC, 2004.

Mantle, Mickey, and Phil Pepe. *Mickey Mantle: My Favorite Summer 1956*. New York: Dell, 1991.

Maraniss, David. *Clemente: The Passion and Grace of Baseball's Last Hero*. New York: Simon & Schuster, 2006.

Mathews, Eddie, and Bob Buege. *Eddie Mathews and the National Pastime*. Milwaukee WI: Douglas American Sports, 1994.

McCarver, Tim. *Diamond Gems*. New York: McGraw Hill, 2008.

McConn, Lucia Andrews. *A Nurse Recalls: The 1926 Frisco II Mine Explosion*. (Booklet in the Princeton IL Public Library.)

McGee, Bob. *The Greatest Ball Park Ever*. New Brunswick NJ: Rivergate Books, 2005.

McGraw, Tug, and Joseph Durso. *Screwball*. Boston: Houghton Mifflin Company, 1974.

Meany, Tom, ed. *The Artful Dodgers*. New York: Grosset & Dunlap, 1963.

Miley, Ruth. *Pike County History*. Petersburg IN: Pike County Historical Society, 1976.

Montville, Leigh. *Ted Williams: The Biography of an American Hero*. New York: Doubleday, 2004.

Musial, Stan, as told to Bob Broeg. *"The Man's" Own Story*. Garden City NY: Doubleday, 1964.

O'Donnell, Patrick. *Into the Rising Sun*. New York: Free Press, 2002.

The Official Major League Baseball Fact Book, 2001 Edition. St. Louis MO: The Sporting News, 2001.

Oliphant, Thomas. *Praying for Gil Hodges: A Memoir of the 1955 World Series and One Family's Love of the Brooklyn Dodgers*. New York: St. Martin's Press, 2005.

Parker, Gary. *Win or Go Home*. Jefferson NC: McFarland, 2002.

Parrott, Harold. *The Lords of Baseball*. New York: Praeger, 1976.

Peary, Danny. *We Played the Game*. New York: Black Dog & Leventhal, 1994.

———, and Tom Clavin. *Gil Hodges: The Brooklyn Bums, the Miracle Mets and the Extraordinary Life of a Baseball Legend*. New York: New American Press, 2012.

Peterson, Robert. *Only the Ball Was White: A History of Legendary Black Players and All-Black Professional Teams*. New York: Oxford University Press, 1992.

Polner, Murray. *Branch Rickey*. New York: Atheneum, 1982.

Prager, Joshua. *The Echoing Green*. New York: Pantheon, 2006.

Prince, Carl. *Brooklyn's Dodgers: The Bums, the Borough, and the Best of Baseball*. New York: Oxford, 1996.

Purdy, Dennis. *The Team by Team Encyclopedia of Major League Baseball*. New York: Workman Publishing, 2006.

Pyle, Ernie. *The Best of Ernie Pyle's WWII Dispatches*. New York: Random House, 1986.

Rampersad, Arnold. *Jackie Robinson, a Biography*. New York: Ballantine Books, 1997.

Reston, James. *Collision at Home Plate*. New York: Harper Collins, 1991.

Rickey, Branch. *The American Diamond*. New York: Simon & Schuster, 1965.

Ritter, Lawrence. *The Glory of Their Times*. New York: Harper Perennial, 2010.

Robinson, Jackie. *I Never Had It Made: Jackie Robinson, an Autobiography*. New York: Ecco, 1995.

Robinson, Rachel. *Jackie Robinson: An Intimate Portrait*. New York: Abrams, 2009.

Rudd, Irving, and Stan Fischler. *The Sporting Life*. New York: St. Martin's Press, 1990.

Ryan, Nolan, and Harvey Frommer. *Throwing Heat: The Autobiography of Nolan Ryan*. New York: Avon Books, 1990.

Seaver, Tom, with Dick Schaap. *Tom Seaver and the Mets*. New York: Dutton Books, 1970.

Shamsky, Art, with Barry Zeman. *The Magnificent Seasons*. New York: Thomas Dunne Books, 2004.

Shannon, Mike. *Tales from the Ballpark*. Chicago: Contemporary Books, 1999.

Shapiro, Michael. *The Last Good Season*. New York: Doubleday, 2003.

Shapiro, Milton. *The Gil Hodges Story*. New York: Julian Messner, 1960.

Shecter, Leonard. *Once upon a Time: The Early Years of the New York Mets*. New York: Dial Press, 1969.

Silverman, Matthew, and Ken Samelson. *The Miracle Has Landed*. Hanover MA: Maple Street Press and SABR, 2009.

Sledge, E. B. *With the Old Breed at Peleliu and Okinawa*. Novato CA: Presidio Press, 1981.

Smith, Ira. *Baseball's Famous First Basemen*. New York: A. S. Barnes, 1956.

Smith, Red. *Red Smith on Baseball*. Chicago: Ivan R. Dee, 2000.

———. *To Absent Friends*. New York: Signet, 1986.

Smith, Ron. *The Ballpark Book*. St. Louis: The Sporting News, 2003.

Snider, Duke, with Bill Gilbert. *The Duke of Flatbush*. New York: Kensington Publishing, 1988.

Staub, Rusty, with Phil Pepe. *Few and Chosen*. Chicago: Triumph Press, 2009.

Steinberg, Michael. *Still Pitching: A Memoir*. East Lansing: Michigan State University Press, 2003.

Stout, Glenn. *The Cubs*. New York: Houghton Mifflin, 2007.

———. *The Dodgers, 120 Years of Dodgers Baseball*. New York: Houghton Mifflin, 2004.

Szalontai, James. *Close Shave: The Life and Times of Baseball's Sal Maglie*. Jefferson NC: McFarland, 2002.

Talley, Rick. *The Cubs of '69*. Chicago: Contemporary Books, 1989.

Taubman, Howard. *The Pleasure of Their Company: A Reminiscence*. Portland OR: Amadeus Press, 1994.

Thomson, Bobby, with Lee Heiman and Bill Gutman. *The Giants Win the Pennant*. New York: Kensington Publishing, 1991.

Thorn, John, ed. *The Glory Days: New York Baseball 1947-1957*. New York: Collins, 2007.

———, et al. *Total Baseball: The Ultimate Baseball Encyclopedia, 8th Edition*. Toronto: Sports Media Publishing, 2004.

Turbo, Jason. *The Baseball Codes*. New York: Pantheon Books, 2010.

Tygiel, Jules. *Baseball's Great Experiment: Jackie Robinson and His Legacy*. New York: Oxford University Press, 1983.

Underwood, John. *It's Only Me: The Ted Williams We Hardly Knew*. Chicago: Triumph, 2005.

Vecsey, George. *Joy in Mudville*. New York: McCall, 1970.

———. *Stan Musial: An American Life*. New York: Ballantine Books and ESPN Books, 2011.

Williams, Dick, and Bill Plaschke. *No More Mr. Nice Guy*. New York: Harcourt Brace Jovanovich, 1990.

Zimmer, Don, with Bill Madden. *Zim: A Baseball Life*. New York: McGraw-Hill, 2001.

Zimmerman, Paul, and Dick Schaap. *The Year the Mets Lost Last Place*. New York: Signet Books, 1969.

INDEX

Page numbers in italic indicate illustrations.

Hodges, Gil (*continued*)

141-42, *142, 143,* 208, 398; college and, 21-23, 67; death of, 348-56; driving of, 49-50, 141; dugout rule of, 306, 444; early childhood of, 13, 14-15; family-comes-first view of, 2, 143, 177, 216, 251; family photos of, *91, 106, 140, 158*; and fielding, 51-54, *56,* 68, 77, 159, 185-88, *188,* 220-21, 244, 371, 415; footwork of, 187, 371; *The Game of Baseball,* 293, 302, 322, 338; Hall of Fame votes for, 371-72, 374; in Hawaii, 41-43; heart attacks of, 290-93, 296, 349, 439-40; high school years of, 16-21, *17, 18*; homes of, 96, 418-19; injuries and illnesses of, 130, *131, 132,* 136-37, 200-201, 202, 219, 222, 225-26, 422; and Little League, 157-58, 229; and marines, 37-48, *48,* 387; as marksman, 40; marriage of, 73; memorials to, 357, 361, 366-67; as most popular player, 1, 55, 224; name of, 383-84; office of, 297; as peacekeeper, 80-81, 147-48, 178-79; personality of, 2, 13, 33, 53, 95, 175-76; and pitching, 233-35, 261-63, 284-85, 337, 437-38; press and, 216, 302, 315-16, 326, 338-39, 372; public speaking and, 142, 429; respect for authority and, 223; as rifleman, 40; slumps of, 118-24, 127-36, 192-95; smoking and, 46, 120, 220, 273, 292, 335, 339; speaking appearances and, 142-43; team player philosophy of, 103-4, 130-31, 263-65, 396; temper of, 272-73, 287-88, 434, 438

Hodges, Gil, as catcher, 51-54, *56,* 68, 159, 371

Hodges, Gil, as first baseman: in 1948, 68-70, 71-72; in 1949, 75-76, 77-78; in 1951, 110; in 1952, 110, 124, 128; in 1953, 138; in 1956, 161; in 1957, 172, 185; in 1958, 196; advice and, 124, 190; career of, 186-87, 371, 399

Hodges, Gil, as hitter, *64*; in 1946, 54-55; in 1947, 65-66, 67; in 1948, 68, 70, 71, 75; in 1949, 76-78, 84, 392-93; in 1950, 94-99, 102; in 1951, 105-7, 397, 398, 400; in 1952, 113-14, 117-18, 127, 128, 401; in 1953, 134-39, 404-5; in 1954, 141; in 1955, 148-49, 150, 151-52, 153, 155, 407; in 1956, 159-61, 162-63, 164; in 1957, 171-73; in 1958, 191-95, 415; in 1959, 200-201, 205-6, 208, 417; in 1960, 418; in 1961, 171-73; in 1962, 219, 221-22; advice of, 244; career of, 370

Hodges, Gil, as manager of Mets: in 1968, 286-91, 437-38; in 1969, 295-96, 298-302, 303-15, 318-19, 321-26, 443, 444, 445-46; in 1970, 332-35, 338, 343-44, 449-50; in 1971, 339-42; in 1972, 346-47; building the team and, 279-85, 331; press and, 252; signing on of, 278-79

Hodges, Gil, as manager of Senators, *234*; in 1963, 231-36, 239, 241; in 1964, 239-40, 243-46, 252-53, 423, 424; in 1965, 255-56; in 1966, 260-61, 263-67; in 1967, 267-73; coaching staff of, 248, *250*; friends of, 248-51; pitchers and, 261-63; press and, 252; renewal of contract of, 246-47, 427; signing on of, 230-31; style of, 238; trades and, 247-48, 428

Hodges, Gil, Jr., 90, *91, 106, 140,* 156, *158,* 345, 351, 357, 358

Hodges, Irene (daughter), 105, *106, 140, 158,* 351-52

Hodges, Irene Horstmeyer (mother), 13, 15, 22, *158,* 174, 353, 358

Hodges, Joan, *327*; birth of children of, 87-88, 90, 104-5, 165, 216; death of